Irish Society, Anglo-Norman Settlers, Angevin Kingship

*Interactions in Ireland
in the Late Twelfth Century*

MARIE THERESE FLANAGAN

CLARENDON PRESS · OXFORD

Oxford University Press, Great Clarendon Street, Oxford OX2 6DP

Oxford New York

Athens Auckland Bangkok Bogota Buenos Aires Calcutta
Cape Town Chennai Dar es Salaam Delhi Florence Hong Kong Istanbul
Karachi Kuala Lumpur Madrid Melbourne Mexico City Mumbai
Nairobi Paris São Paolo Singapore Taipei Tokyo Toronto Warsaw

and associated companies in
Berlin Ibadan

Oxford is a registered trade mark of Oxford University Press

Published in the United States by
Oxford University Press Inc., New York

© Marie Therese Flanagan 1989
Special edition for Sandpiper Books Ltd., 1998

British Library Cataloguing in Publication Data
Data available

ISBN 0-19-822154-1

1 3 5 7 9 10 8 6 4 2

Printed in Great Britain
on acid-free paper by
Bookcraft (Bath) Ltd.,
Midsomer Norton

CONTENTS

Abbreviations and conventions   vii

Introduction   1

PART I: RELATIONS BETWEEN BRITAIN AND
IRELAND PRIOR TO ANGLO-NORMAN INTERVEN-
TION IN IRELAND

1. The see of Canterbury and the Irish Church   7

2. Diarmait Mac Murchada's request to Henry II for
   military aid   56

PART II: ANGLO-NORMAN ADVENTURERS IN
IRELAND

3. Diarmait Mac Murchada's offer of the kingdom of
   Leinster to Strongbow   79

4. Strongbow's succession to the lordship of Leinster   112

5. Adventurers from South Wales in Ireland   137

PART III: ANGEVIN KINGSHIP AND IRELAND

6. Henry II's relations with the Irish kings, 1171–1172   167

7. The treaty of Windsor, 1175   229

8. The lordship of Ireland within the Angevin
   dominions   273

Appendices:

1. Charter of John, count of Eu, in favour of Ralph
   Picot, dated 'at Winchester in the year in which a
   conquest of Ireland was discussed'   305

2. Irish kings who submitted to Henry II, 1171–1172   308

3. Text of the treaty of Windsor, 1175   312

Genealogical Tables:

1. Succession to the kingships of Uí Chennselaig and of Leinster   314

2. Diarmait Mac Murchada's immediate family   315

3. Strongbow's family   316

Bibliography   317

Index   338

ABBREVIATIONS AND CONVENTIONS

In addition to the abbreviations and short titles in *Rules for contributors to Irish historical studies*, supplement 1 (Jan. 1968) and *A new history of Ireland*, ii, ed. A. Cosgrove (1987), pp. xxxi–xlviii, the following abbreviations have been adopted:

Brut Hergest	*Brut y Tywysogyon or the chronicle of the princes; Peniarth MS. 20 version*, ed. T. Jones (Board of Celtic Studies, University of Wales History and Law series, 11; Cardiff, 1952)
Brut Peniarth	*Brut y Tywysogyon or the chronicle of the princes: Red Book of Hergest version*, ed. T. Jones (Board of Celtic Studies, University of Wales History and Law series, 16; Cardiff, 1955)
Episc. acts	*Episcopal acts relating to Welsh dioceses: 1066–1272*, ed. J. C. Davies (2 vols., Historical Society of the Church in Wales, Cardiff; 1, 1946, 3–4, 1948)
Eyton, *Itinerary*	Eyton, R. W., *Court, household, and itinerary of King Henry II* (London, 1878)
Gervase of Canterbury	Gervase of Canterbury, *Historical works*, ed. W. Stubbs (2 vols., Rolls series, London, 1879–80)
Lloyd, *Wales*	Lloyd, J. E., *A history of Wales from the earliest times to the conquest* (2 vols., London, 1911)
Ralph of Diss	*Radulphi de Diceto opera historica*, ed. W. Stubbs (2 vols., Rolls series, London, 1876)
Robert of Torigny	*Chronicles, Stephen, Henry II and Richard I*, ed. R. Howlett, iv (Rolls series, London, 1890)

Roger of Howden, *Gesta*	*Gesta regis Henrici secundi Benedicti abbatis*, ed. W. Stubbs (Rolls series, London, 1867)
Roger of Howden, *Chronica*	*Chronica Rogeri de Houedone*, ed. W. Stubbs (4 vols., Rolls series, London, 1868–71)
William of Newburgh	*Chronicles, Stephen, Henry II and Richard I*, ed. R. Howlett, i–ii (Rolls series, London, 1885)

Other references are given in full at their first appearance, and in the bibliography, but reduced elsewhere to author and short title.

An Irish surname without a forename indicates the ruling member of that particular family, in accordance with contemporary twelfth-century practice. Lower-case 'mac' indicates 'son of', while upper-case 'Mac' indicates an element of a surname.

ACKNOWLEDGEMENTS

I wish to thank the National University of Ireland which awarded me a travelling studentship in history that enabled me to pursue postgraduate studies at the University of Oxford, from which this book derives, and Somerville College for an hospitable and stimulating atmosphere during my time in Oxford. The late Professor R. Dudley Edwards read drafts of the thesis before its submission and, as always, made many thought-provoking comments. I am grateful to colleagues, including a former colleague, Dr Mark Ormrod, in the Department of Modern History, the Queen's University of Belfast, who carried my workload during a sabbatical year which provided the opportunity to revise the dissertation for publication, and particularly to my head of department, Professor Lewis Warren for his abiding humanity, encouragement, and understanding. But my greatest debt of gratitude by far is to my thesis-supervisor, John Prestwich, who was so unfailingly generous of his time and of his extensive knowledge of the period, and who afforded me such a valuable perspective on twelfth-century Ireland by enabling me to place it in the wider context of the British Isles and of the Angevin dominions.

Introduction

THIS study is not based on any new primary sources bearing on the Anglo-Normans in Ireland, but on a re-examination of the existing body of evidence within broader contexts, which have as yet not been fully explored. These include the twelfth-century Irish context into which the Anglo-Normans intruded, the wider context of relations between Ireland and Britain both before and after Anglo-Norman intervention, and the yet wider context of the Angevin dominions of which England after 1154 was but a province.

The arrival of Anglo-Normans in Ireland has traditionally been viewed as a turning-point in Irish history. It has also served as a demarcation between two distinct groups of historians. Irish history prior to Anglo-Norman intervention in Ireland has been the almost exclusive preserve of 'early Irish' historians, who have rarely concerned themselves with the period thereafter. Conversely, historians of Anglo-Norman Ireland have seldom dealt with the pre-Norman period. It is desirable that historians of the Anglo-Normans in Ireland should have some knowledge of the political, social, and economic structures which the Anglo-Normans encountered in twelfth-century pre-Norman Ireland. Many books on Anglo-Norman Ireland are prefaced with descriptions of Ireland on the eve of Anglo-Norman intervention, G. H. Orpen in his *Ireland under the Normans* set the trend with a first chapter entitled 'Anarchic Ireland: ninth to eleventh centuries'. The very title carried the implication that Anglo-Norman intervention represented a marked improvement on what had gone before. Orpen approached the pre-Norman period in Ireland from the standpoint of a late Victorian with a staunch belief in the institutions of British government in Ireland, and was predisposed to find in pre-Norman Ireland a tribal, anarchic society, incapable of governing itself, to which the Anglo-Normans introduced what Orpen termed the 'pax

Normannica'. A half-century later so intractable did pre-Norman Ireland still appear to A. J. Otway-Ruthven that she commissioned the early Irish historian, Kathleen Hughes, to write an introductory chapter for her *History of medieval Ireland* (1968). It might as well have formed part of another book, for there are no points of contact between the narratives of the two scholars. The major limitation of introductory chapters on pre-Norman Ireland, which preface accounts of Anglo-Norman intervention, is that they give a synchronic, generalized description of pre-Norman Ireland drawn indiscriminately from sources of various kinds, differing dates, and unequal reliability. Descriptions of Irish social organization, for example, are culled almost exclusively from the law tracts, which were compiled at the latest by the eighth century. Despite the oft-repeated cliché that twelfth-century Ireland was a highly conservative, archaic, and isolated society, twelfth-century Ireland was not like eighth-century Ireland.

Early Irish historians have concentrated on the pre-Viking period, and more detailed and rigorous research remains to be done on Ireland during the eleventh and twelfth centuries. Although this may be considered to be primarily a task requiring the specialized skills of the so-called early Irish historian, historians of Anglo-Norman Ireland also have a role to play in prompting investigation of those aspects of Irish society about which more knowledge is required in order to understand and assess the Anglo-Norman impact on Ireland. There is much still to be harvested from fruitful dialogue and exchange of information between the historians of pre-Norman and post-Norman Ireland, particularly for the twelfth century. The forms of discussion and debate about continuity and discontinuity which have engaged historians of Anglo-Saxon and Norman England in relation to the Norman conquest of 1066 have as yet scarcely been attempted for Anglo-Norman intervention in twelfth-century Ireland.

This study seeks to bridge the division between the pre-Norman and post-Norman periods in twelfth-century Ireland, which has been created artificially by scholars who have concentrated upon either the sources for early Irish history, or those for Anglo-Norman Ireland and England. It attempts to combine the evidence of both Irish and Anglo-Norman twelfth-century sources to examine aspects of the arrival of the Anglo-Normans in Ireland.

PART I

Relations between Britain and Ireland prior to Anglo-Norman Intervention in Ireland

The See of Canterbury and the Irish Church

A TRADITIONAL starting-point for accounts of Anglo-Norman intervention in Ireland is the accession of Henry II as king of England and the royal council held at Winchester in September 1155, which discussed a conquest of Ireland, upon which followed the granting of the bull *Laudabiliter* by Pope Adrian IV authorizing the English king's intervention in Ireland. A natural assumption from this train of events was that Henry II was intent on a conquest of Ireland from the beginning of his reign, even though he did not actually intervene in Ireland until after he had been approached by the exiled king of Leinster, Diarmait Mac Murchada, who in 1166–7 sought military aid from Henry. Such was the interpretation of G. H. Orpen, who argued that Diarmait had merely provided Henry with a convenient pretext to pursue an ambition which he had held since 1155.[1]

In 1933 J. F. O'Doherty cautiously questioned this assumption, querying why Henry took so long to implement a plan he had conceived allegedly in 1155, and pointing out that Henry's response to Diarmait Mac Murchada's appeal for help in 1166–7 was not very enthusiastic.[2] O'Doherty postulated that the moving force behind the council of Winchester in 1155 and the procural of *Laudabiliter* was not Henry II but the see of Canterbury, and that Canterbury's involvement arose from its links with the Irish Church. Canterbury had consecrated bishops for a number of Irish sees from the eleventh century,

---

[1] Orpen, *Normans*, i. 80–4, followed by F. X. Martin in Moody and Martin, *Ir. hist.* 125–6; Otway-Ruthven, *Med. Ire.* 47; Dolley, *Anglo-Norman Ire.* 44–5; Lydon, *Lordship*, 11–12, 29, 39.

[2] J. F. O'Doherty, *Laurentius von Dublin und das irische Normannentum*, Doct. diss. (Munich, 1933); 'The Anglo-Norman invasion, 1167–71', *IHS* 1 (1938–9), 154–7; 'Rome and the Anglo-Norman invasion of Ireland', *IER* 42 (1933), 131–45; 'St Laurence O'Toole and the Anglo-Norman invasion', ibid. 50 (1937), 449–77, 600–25; 51 (1938), 131–46.

but this practice was ended by the establishment of an independent diocesan structure for the Irish Church, which received papal recognition at the synod of Kells in 1152. The obtainment of the bull *Laudabiliter*, suggested O'Doherty, represented Canterbury's reaction to the synod of Kells; and he argued further that when Henry II did intervene in Ireland in 1171 it was not to realize an ambition to conquer Ireland which he had entertained since 1155, but because he felt obliged to exercise restraint over those of his subjects who had already gone there in response to Diarmait Mac Murchada's request for military aid.

O'Doherty's argument made few inroads on the widely held view that Henry II was the moving force behind the proposed conquest of Ireland in 1155, chiefly because nationalist Irish historians had little incentive to question the motivation for English royal intervention in Ireland, which was inevitably conceived of as colonial and malevolent in intent towards the Irish. The first serious consideration of O'Doherty's suggestion regarding the role of Canterbury was made by Denis Bethell in 1971, who provided convincing supporting evidence in its favour by highlighting the hostile reaction in contemporary English chronicle sources to the papal legation of Cardinal John Paparo to Ireland in 1152, which ratified an independent diocesan structure for the Irish Church, thus terminating Canterbury's links with a number of Irish episcopal sees.[3] Bethell also investigated possible justifications for Canterbury's claims to primacy over the Irish Church and argued that it stemmed in part from the *imperium*, or overlordship of Britain, which had been asserted by Anglo-Saxon kings in the tenth century. O'Doherty's and Bethell's arguments concerning Canterbury and *Laudabiliter* merit elaboration, since they have not won unanimous acceptance.[4]

The origins of Canterbury's involvement with the Irish Church are obscure. The first certain evidence dates from 1074, when Gilla Pátraic (Patricius), a bishop elect of the see of Dublin,

[3] D. Bethell, 'English monks and Irish reform in the eleventh and twelfth centuries', *Hist. Studies*, 8 (1971), 111–35.
[4] O'Doherty's thesis was rejected by Watt, *Ch. and two nations*, 36; *Ch. in medieval Ire.* 30. It has been accepted by Warren, *Henry II*, 194–9, and by Frame, *Colonial Ire.* 11–13.

presented himself for consecration to Lanfranc, archbishop of Canterbury. Lanfranc duly consecrated Gilla Pátraic, receiving from him a profession of obedience.[5] According to later tradition, as preserved both in the Book of Obits and a late fourteenth-century account of the foundation of the church of Holy Trinity, Dublin, in the Black Book of Christ Church, Gilla Pátraic was the second bishop of the see of Dublin, in which he succeeded one Dunán.[6] Had Dunán also been consecrated at Canterbury? The question is inextricably linked with the origins of the see of Dublin.

The fourteenth-century account of the foundation of the church of Holy Trinity, Dublin, credited Sitric, who was king of Dublin from 989 until 1036, as donor of the site.[7] In 1028 Sitric undertook a pilgrimage to Rome, and Aubrey Gwynn suggested that the most likely date both for the foundation of the church of Holy Trinity, and for the inauguration of the episcopate of Dunán, was some time after Sitric's manifestation of piety in travelling to Rome. He further posited that because of the political circumstances prevailing in Dublin in the early eleventh century Dunán had recourse to the archbishop of Canterbury for consecration.

A Scandinavian settlement at Dublin had been established in AD 841, abandoned in 902, and refounded about 917; by the mid tenth century its role as an important trading centre in the Irish Sea province was secured. By the early eleventh century Dublin had been accommodated within the Irish polity, being accorded a status similar to that of a petty Irish kingdom. Dublin, however, was also an important trading centre with external contacts within a wider Anglo-Scandinavian sphere. Knowledge of its trading relations is based largely on archaeological and numismatic evidence, which suggests that contacts with England were preponderant.[8] There is no documentary

[5] *Canterbury professions*, ed. M. Richter (Canterbury and York Society, 67, 1973), no. 36.

[6] 'Primus episcopus Dublin et fundator ecclesie nostre': *The Book of Obits and martyrology of the cathedral church of the Holy Trinity*, ed. J. H. Todd (Dublin, 1844), 23; A. Gwynn, 'Some unpublished texts from the Black Book of Christ Church, Dublin', *Anal. Hib.* 16 (1946), 281–337 (at 310–11); 'The origins of the see of Dublin', *IER* 57 (1941), 40–55, 97–112; 'The first bishops of Dublin', *Reportorium Novum*, 1 (1955), 1–26.

[7] Gwynn, 'Some unpublished texts', 309.

[8] P. F. Wallace, 'The origins of Dublin', in *Studies on early Ireland: essays in honour of M. V. Duignan*, ed. B. G. Scott [Belfast, 1982], 129–43; 'The archaeology of Viking

evidence to determine the personal or political relations of the Hiberno-Norse kings of Dublin with other rulers of the British Isles or of Scandinavia. It would be relevant to know how far the city of Dublin may have been affected by the accession in 1016 of the Dane, Cnut, as king of England. To what extent might the Hiberno-Norse settlements in Ireland have felt themselves to be, or were considered by King Cnut to be, part of his Anglo-Danish empire? Gwynn's argument that King Cnut may have attempted to exercise some form of political overlordship over the city of Dublin is plausible. The aftermath of the battle of Clontarf would have provided him with an opportunity to do so. One of the effects of the battle of Clontarf, fought in 1014 by Brian Bóruma, king of Munster, and contender for the high-kingship of Ireland, against an alliance of the men of north Leinster and the Hiberno-Norse of Dublin, was to weaken temporarily the control over the city of Dublin which Irish kings had attempted to assert. Although the family of Brian Bóruma won the day at Clontarf the victory proved a Pyrrhic one, because it depleted its resources to such an extent that it forfeited the overlordship of the city which Brian Bóruma had attained in 1000. Likewise, the defeated Uí Dúnlainge dynasty, which was centred in north Leinster and contiguous to Dublin, found itself in straitened circumstances as a result of the battle of Clontarf, from which indeed it never recovered. Not only was its assertion of lordship over the Hiberno-Norse of Dublin precluded, but it was ousted from the provincial kingship of Leinster, which it had monopolized since AD 738, by the south Leinster dynasty of Uí Chennselaig in 1042.[9] The Uí Chennselaig dynasty devoted considerable effort to establishing control over the city of Dublin. In 1052 the Uí Chennselaig king of Leinster, Diarmait mac Máel na mBó, installed his own son, Murchad, as king in Dublin and retained overlordship of the city until his own death in 1072. From the battle of Clontarf in 1014, therefore, until the assertion of overlordship over Dublin by Diarmait mac Máel na mBó in 1052,

Dublin', in *The comparative history of urban origins in non-Roman Europe*, ed. H. B. Clarke and A. Simms (Oxford, 1985), i. 103–46; A. P. Smyth, *Scandinavian York and Dublin* (Dublin, 1975–9); *Scandinavian kings in the British isles, 850–880* (Oxford, 1977).

[9] D. Ó Corráin, 'The career of Diarmait mac Máel na mBó, king of Leinster', *Old Wexford Soc. Jn.* 3 (1971), 27–35; 4 (1972–3), 17–24.

political circumstances in Ireland would have been favourable for King Cnut to try to draw the Hiberno-Norse settlement of Dublin into his sphere of political influence.

Gwynn inferred from the pilgrimage which Sitric, king of Dublin, made to Rome in 1028 that there may have been some relationship between Sitric and Cnut, suggesting that Sitric's journey may have been inspired by the example of Cnut, who had made a much publicized journey to Rome in 1027. Cnut had written a letter to the people of England describing his visit to Rome, in which he had stated that he had gone there 'to pray for the redemption of my sins and for the safety of the kingdoms and of the peoples subject to my rule'.[10] It is possible that Sitric, the Hiberno-Norse king of Dublin, received a copy, which motivated him to emulate Cnut's journey to Rome. Gwynn argued that Cnut's journey to Rome inaugurated a series of Irish royal pilgrimages there in the early eleventh century. However, the apparent chronological coincidence between Cnut's and Sitric's respective visits to Rome in 1027 and 1028 is weakened by annalistic entries recording Irish pilgrimages to Rome before 1028, which Gwynn overlooked. Céle Dabhaill, abbot of Bangor, and Fergil, abbot of Terryglass, died in Rome in 929.[11] Fachtna, lector of Clonmacnoise, died while on pilgrimage to Rome in 1024.[12] More importantly, Máel Ruanaid Ua Máel Doraid, king of Cenél Conaill, is recorded as having gone to Rome and died there in 1027.[13] And in 1028 King Sitric was accompanied to Rome by Flannacán Ua Cellaig, king of Brega, 'et multi alii'.[14] These entries, particularly that relating to Ua Máel Doraid, king of Cenél Conaill, undermine Gwynn's argument that Sitric was emulating Cnut's example in going to Rome in 1028.

---

[10] Text in F. Liebermann, *Die Gesetze der Angelsachsen*, i (Halle, 1903), 273–5; translation in *The laws of the kings of England from Edmund to Henry I*, ed. A. J. Robertson (Cambridge, 1925), 146–53.

[11] *Chron. Scot.* 928; *AU* 928, 929; *AFM* 926, 927 = 928, 929.

[12] *AFM*.

[13] *Ann. Inisf.* 1026. 4. Cf. *Ann. Tig.*, which recorded that he went on pilgrimage overseas; *Chron. Scot.* 1025, *AU* 1026, which recorded only that he went on pilgrimage. *Ann. Tig.*, *AFM* 1027 recorded his death on pilgrimage without naming the place. It is possible that other entries in the annals recording pilgrimages omitted to name Rome as the destination.

[14] *Ann. Tig.* 1026; *Chron. Scot.* 1026 (*recte* 1028); *Ann. Inisf.* 1028. 5; *Ann. Tig.*, *AU*, *AFM* 1028. *AFM* named Flannacán Ua Cellaig, king of Brega, before Sitric.

Gwynn assumed that the foundation of the church of Holy Trinity, Dublin, by Sitric postdated his pilgrimage to Rome, and that it had in some way influenced him in his decision. The primary purpose of a visit to Rome in the early eleventh century was devotional, to visit the shrine of St Peter, not consultation on matters of Church organization. The early eleventh-century popes were not notable Church leaders. The occupant of the chair of Peter when Sitric was in Rome in 1028 was the Tusculan Pope John XIX, who had succeeded his brother, Benedict VIII, and was succeeded, in turn, by his nephew, Benedict IX, in 1032. The counts of Tusculum were set fair to establishing a monopoly of the papacy when the German emperor, Henry III, intervened in 1046 'to lift the papacy out of the field of Roman party politics' and inaugurate a reform movement in Rome.[15]

Gwynn suggested that the city of Dublin might have looked to the see of Canterbury to consecrate its first bishop, Dunán, because of the structure of the Irish Church in the eleventh century: it lacked a regular diocesan organization, and the consecration of bishops was performed in what could have been considered an uncanonical manner.[16] It is difficult, however, to gauge how concerned the Hiberno-Norse king of Dublin may have been about the peculiarities of the Irish Church, since little is known of the circumstances of the conversion of the Hiberno-Norse to Christianity, nor of the probable part played in their conversion by Irish ecclesiastics.[17] Although it could be argued that the Hiberno-Norse city of Dublin might have had recourse to the English Church to consecrate its first bishop in order to ensure canonical procedure, this does not necessarily explain why the see of Canterbury would have been chosen. One might equally well have expected the archbishop of York to have been approached, in view of the dynastic and trading links between the cities of Dublin and York.[18] It was not neces-

[15] G. Barraclough, *The medieval papacy* (London, 1968), 63–72.

[16] About 1074 Lanfranc wrote to Toirdelbach Ua Briain that 'bishops are consecrated by a single bishop; many are ordained to villages or small towns': *The letters of Lanfranc, archbishop of Canterbury*, ed. H. Clover and M. Gibson (Oxford, 1979), 64–7.

[17] Olaf Cuaran, king of Dublin, died at Iona 'after the victory of repentance' in 980: *AU* 979; *Ann. Tig.* 979. The death of Ivar, king of all the Norsemen of Ireland and Britain, is recorded in 873 in terms which may suggest that he died as a Christian: according to *Chron. Scot.* 'quievit', and *AU* 'vitam finivit'.

[18] Cf. Smyth, *Scandinavian York and Dublin*.

sary to go as far as Canterbury to ensure canonical consecration. It therefore remains very much an open question whether Dunán was consecrated at Canterbury.

Between the possible consecration at Canterbury of Dunán, the first bishop of Dublin, and the certain consecration of Gilla Pátraic in 1074 a major political change occurred in England as a result of the Norman Conquest. In 1066 William the Conqueror took England out of the Scandinavian and into the Norman sphere of influence. This introduced the English Church to a new personnel and to the contemporary currents of ecclesiastical reform traditionally associated with the pontificate of Pope Gregory VII. An important aspect of this reform movement was the definition and elaboration of a legalistic conception of ecclesiastical jurisdiction. In 1070 the see of Canterbury received its first appointee under the Norman regime, the Italian schoolman, Lanfranc, who initiated an investigation into and clarification of the jurisdictional prerogatives of his new see.[19]

The necessity for such an investigation was made apparent to Lanfranc by the ill-defined nature of the relationship between the see of Canterbury and the see of York, the only other English archbishopric. Here, Lanfranc encountered a number of ambiguities, which ultimately reached back over 500 years to the obscurities of the instructions which Pope Gregory I had issued to the missionary, Augustine, ambiguities which Lanfranc determined to resolve in Canterbury's favour. In the very year in which Lanfranc became archbishop he was presented with an opportunity: he refused to consecrate William the Conqueror's nominee for the see of York, Thomas of Bayeux, unless Thomas made a written profession of obedience to the see of Canterbury. The archbishop elect of York was persuaded in 1072 to make a personal profession of obedience to Lanfranc, reserving, however, to a papal investigation the question of the submission of the see of York to the see of Canterbury.

In preparation for the papal inquiry Lanfranc compiled a dossier of documents in support of the primacy of Canterbury.

---

[19] See M. Gibson, *Lanfranc of Bec* (Oxford, 1978), of which chs. 6 and 7 are particularly relevant. Her treatment of Canterbury's relations with Ireland, however, contains some inaccuracies.

Among the sources which he scrutinized was Bede's *Ecclesiastical History*, from which, as he wrote to Pope Alexander II in 1072, it was evident to him that his 'predecessors exercised primacy over the Church of York and the whole island which men called Britain and over Ireland as well'.[20] Lanfranc's main concern was his struggle with the archbishop of York, but his reference in this context to a primacy over Britain (by which he almost certainly meant to include Wales and Scotland) and to a primacy over Ireland is portentous; it presages a strategy which Lanfranc and subsequent archbishops of Canterbury were to pursue, namely that of advancing wider hegemonic claims over the British Isles as a means of bolstering the claim to primacy over York.

Lanfranc's arguments in favour of a primacy over the British Isles including Ireland were formulated in the first instance to assert an *a fortiori* claim over York. Once the claim to assert authority in the wider context of the British Isles and Ireland had been formulated, however, there was every likelihood that attempts would be made to put it into practice if suitable opportunities were to arise. And in the case of Ireland an opportune occasion presented itself to Lanfranc in 1074 when Gilla Pátraic, bishop elect of Dublin, arrived voluntarily at Canterbury seeking consecration.

In Lanfranc's statement in a letter to Gofraid, king of Dublin, written about the time of Gilla Pátraic's consecration, that he had consecrated Gilla Pátraic 'in due form to his appointed duties and after his consecration we sent him back to his own see with our letter of commendation as was the custom of our predecessors',[21] Gwynn found further circumstantial evidence that the link between the see of Dublin and Canterbury had been established in the early eleventh century. He construed the phrase 'more antecessorum nostrorum' as implying a previous consecration or consecrations.[22] It is argu-

---

[20] Lanfranc, *Letters*, 50–1.

[21] Ibid. 66–9.

[22] Gwynn, 'Origins of the see of Dublin', 33; 'First bishops of Dublin', 4; Gwynn and Gleeson, *Killaloe*, 99; Gwynn, *The twelfth-century reform* (Dublin, 1968), 3. Gwynn may have been influenced by the interpretation of the early thirteenth-century compiler of the Annals of Saint Mary's Abbey, Dublin, who had access to copies of the letters sent by archbishops of Canterbury to Irish bishops and kings, and who wrote that in 1074 Lanfranc 'Patricium sacravit antistitem accepta prius ab ipso examinato professione de sua obediencia more antecessorum suorum sibi suisque successoribus exhibenda':

able, however, that Lanfranc meant no more than that he was
writing a letter of exhortation to the king as his predecessors
had been wont to do, a belief he certainly could have derived
from a careful reading of Bede's *Ecclesiastical History.*
Bede recounted that Laurence (604–19), Augustine's successor at
Canterbury, had written a 'letter of exhortation in conjunction
with his fellow bishops to the Irish'.[23] If Lanfranc's phrase
'more antecessorum nostrorum' casts little light on Canterbury's
possible consecration of a bishop of Dublin before 1074,
the fact that the bishop elect, Gilla Pátraic, had been trained as
a Benedictine monk in the Worcester community[24] is suggestive
of links between the see of Dublin and Worcester which predated
1074. It is possible that the request for the consecration of
Gilla Pátraic in 1074 was the first that had been made to
Canterbury by the people of Dublin and that it was prompted
by circumstances other than the consecration of Gilla Pátraic's
predecessor, Dunán, at Canterbury. It might have been Gilla
Pátraic himself who, because of his sojourn in the Worcester
community, advocated recourse to Canterbury. Gilla Pátraic
was personally acquainted with Wulfstan, prior of the Worcester
community, who became bishop of Worcester in 1062,
deliberately avoiding consecration by Stigand, the then archbishop
of Canterbury, because he was considered to have

Chartul. St Mary's, Dublin, ii. 249. Watt, *Ch. and two nations,* 6, likewise interpreted
'more antecessorum nostrorum' as referring to Lanfranc's consecration of Gilla
Pátraic. Lanfranc's phrase so interpreted would strictly speaking imply more than one
previous consecration, which creates a difficulty, since Gilla Pátraic had only one
known predecessor, Dunán, in the see of Dublin. Gwynn, *The twelfth-century reform,* 3,
wrote 'in the letter which the clergy and people of Dublin sent to Lanfranc in 1074, asking
him to consecrate Gilla Pátraic as their new bishop they claim that "we have always
gladly submitted to the government of your predecessors from whom we remember
that we received ecclesiastical dignity"'. This would be telling evidence for a link
between Canterbury and Dublin prior to 1074. But Gwynn inadvertently quoted from
the letter sent by the people of Dublin to Ralph, archbishop of Canterbury, in 1121; in
his 'Origins of the see of Dublin', 108, Gwynn correctly quoted the same passage as
referring to 1121. Watt, *Ch. and two nations,* 18, quoted this letter as referring to 1121,
but in *Ch. in med. Ire.* 2 he seems to have followed Gwynn in antedating the 1121 letter
to 1074.

[23] Cf. Bede, *Ecclesiastical history,* ii. 4, ed. B. Colgrave and R. A. B. Mynors (Oxford,
1969), 146–7; Lanfranc's letter to Pope Alexander II about May 1072 in which he stated
that he had consulted Bede: Lanfranc, *Letters,* 48–57.

[24] See *The writings of Bishop Patrick,* ed. A. Gwynn (Scriptores Latini Hiberniae, 1;
Dublin, 1955). On relations between Irish churchmen and English monasteries in the
10th and 11th centuries see further Bethell, 'English monks and Irish reform';
A. Gwynn, 'Ireland and Rome in the eleventh century', *IER* 57 (1941), 213–32.

succeeded to the see of Canterbury uncanonically. Lanfranc's elevation to the see of Canterbury in 1070 was occasioned by the deposition of Stigand on charges of uncanonical intrusion into the see. In 1062 Wulfstan had sought consecration from Ealdred, archbishop of York, without, however, making a profession of obedience to him in prejudice to the obedience which he considered was owed by the see of Worcester to Canterbury; in August 1070 Wulfstan made a profession of obedience to Lanfranc as canonically consecrated archbishop of Canterbury following the deposition of Stigand.[25] These circumstances would have been known to Gilla Pátraic via his contacts with Worcester. If Dunán had indeed been consecrated at Canterbury it seems incredible that Lanfranc, who made such detailed investigations into the rights and claims of the see of Canterbury, would not have ascertained that information from Gilla Pátraic in 1074 and made more explicit use of it.

When the chronology of contemporary developments in the field of canon law is taken into account, recourse to Canterbury is more readily explicable in the case of Gilla Pátraic in 1074 than it is in the case of his predecessor, Dunán. Canonical episcopal consecration did not require recourse to Canterbury in the period when Gwynn presumed that Dunán is most likely to have been consecrated as bishop of Dublin, that is about 1028–36: although participation of the metropolitan was seen as desirable, it was not insisted upon. Canon law required only that a bishop elect be consecrated by a plurality of bishops. By 1074, however, circumstances were different. At the council of Rheims, 1049, Pope Leo had inaugurated his reform of ecclesiastical offices with an attack on simony which had the effect of drawing attention to the procedure for the election of bishops. In 1057 the reforming Cardinal Humbert, in his *Adversus simoniacos libri tres*, insisted on three stages: election by the clergy, request by the people, and consecration by the bishops of the province on the authority of the metropolitan. Only concern for the involvement of a canonically consecrated metropolitan can explain satisfactorily a request to Canterbury for consecration from either Dunán or Gilla Pátraic. Consecration by a plurality of bishops was possible, though not apparently usual, in Ireland in the early eleventh century.

[25] F. Barlow, *The English Church, 1000–1066* (London, 1963), 302–8.

Bearing in mind developments in canon law it is unlikely that consecration with the participation or approval of a metropolitan was an issue at the time of the consecration of Dunán. On the other hand, it was more likely to have become a factor by 1074. Added to this was Gilla Pátraic's association with Worcester prior to his consecration, and the circumstances of Stigand's deposition and his replacement by Lanfranc in 1070. A major difficulty for Irish ecclesiastics anxious to adhere to contemporary standards of canonical procedure in 1074 regarding the involvement of a metropolitan was that the Irish Church lacked a canonically consecrated metropolitan. The *comarba* of Armagh, who, as the successor of Patrick, enjoyed a traditional pre-eminence in the Irish Church, was throughout the eleventh century a layman, who had succeeded hereditarily.[26] It is therefore possible that the consecration of Gilla Pátraic by Lanfranc in 1074 was the first such of an Irish bishop.

Recourse to the archbishop of Canterbury by Gilla Pátraic for consecration in 1074 would appear to have been approved by Toirdelbach Ua Briain, king of Munster and claimant to the high-kingship of Ireland, who had made a bid for overlordship of the city of Dublin after the death of Diarmait mac Máel na mBó, king of Leinster, in 1072. According to the *Vita Wulfstani* Irish kings had written letters to Wulfstan.[27] Toirdelbach Ua Briain is known to have been a supporter of Church reform. Following the consecration of Gilla Pátraic, Lanfranc addressed a letter to Gofraid, king of Dublin, styled 'glorioso Hiberniae regi', and to Toirdelbach Ua Briain, 'magnifico Hiberniae regi', which suggests that Lanfranc had knowledge of Toirdelbach Ua Briain's overlordship of the city.[28]

There is an undated letter from Pope Gregory VII addressed to Lanfranc, which appears from its introduction to have been written shortly after Gregory's consecration as pope on 30 June 1073, the purpose of which, apart from announcing Gregory's elevation, was to urge Lanfranc to

strive by every means open to you to ban the wicked practice which we have heard rumoured of the *Scotti*: namely that many of them not

---

[26] T. Ó Fiaich, 'The church of Armagh under lay control', *Seanchas Ardmhacha*, 5 (1969), 75–127.

[27] *Vita Wulfstani*, ed. R. R. Darlington (Camden Society, 40; London, 1928), 59, 102.

[28] Lanfranc, *Letters*, 71–3.

only desert their lawful wives but even sell them. In these matters we wish you to be sustained with apostolic authority, so that you may punish this crime with stern chastisement not only among the *Scotti* but among others too, if you know of any such men in the island of the English.[29]

If the modern editors of Lanfranc's letters are correct in translating *Scotti* as Irish,[30] this would suggest that Pope Gregory believed that Lanfranc could play a useful reforming role in Ireland and, if the editors are also correct in dating this letter to about July 1073, it would predate the request from Dublin in 1074 for the consecration of Gilla Pátraic. There also survives an undated letter from Pope Gregory VII addressed to Toirdelbach Ua Briain and the archbishops, bishops, and abbots of Ireland (the form *Hibernia* is used) urging that 'if any matters have arisen among you that seem to need our help, be prompt and ready to inform us of them and with God's help, you shall obtain what you have justly asked'.[31] It is conceivable that in response to this letter Toirdelbach Ua Briain may have consulted Pope Gregory on a number of issues, including possibly the question of canonical episcopal consecration involving a metropolitan, and that it was Pope Gregory who had inspired, if not actually suggested, the Irish request to Canterbury for the consecration of Gilla Pátraic.[32]

[29] Lanfranc, *Letters*, 64–7.

[30] They did so because of similarity with the charges which Lanfranc made in his letters to Gofraid, king of Dublin, and Toirdelbach Ua Briain. In 1072 the council at Windsor held in the presence of Hubert, papal legate, had declared that Thomas, archbishop of York, should have jurisdiction over all that lay north of the Humber, thus including Scotland in his ecclesiastical province: *Councils and synods with other documents relating to the English Church*, ed. D. Whitelock, M. Brett, and C. N. L. Brooke (Oxford, 1981), i. 591–604.

[31] Sheehy, *Pontificia Hib.*, no. 2. The text which survives in a late twelfth-century collection of papal letters concerning England was 'given at Sutri' (which has, however, been corrected to 'Marino') 'on the sixth day before the calends of March'. The (normal) absence of the year of pontificate and the correction in the *datum* make the dating of this letter very difficult. Gregory was elected pope on 23 April and consecrated on 29 or 30 June 1073. Bishop Dunán of Dublin died on 6 May 1074. It is conceivable that the letter could have been sent to Toirdelbach Ua Briain in February 1074. Its very general character might be said to support such an inference. A. Gwynn, 'Pope Gregory VII and the Irish Church', *IER* 58 (1941), 97–109, suggested 1076, 1078, or 1080 as years in which this letter may have been issued.

[32] Gregory VII's letter to Lanfranc and its possible reference to the Irish, and possibly also Gregory's letter to Toirdelbach Ua Briain, could of course have been prompted by a prior communication to the pope from Lanfranc suggesting a positive role for Canterbury in Ireland, a possibility which Lanfranc may have entertained from

Whatever the background to Gilla Pátraic's arrival at Canterbury for consecration in 1074, Lanfranc's reaction, typically, had been to make the most of the opportunity by exacting a profession of obedience from the new bishop of Dublin, in the text of which Lanfranc was styled 'Britanniarum primas'.[33] The undefined plural 'primate of the Britains' may have been intended to include Ireland. The exaction of a profession of obedience was a strategy which Lanfranc had used in the case of the archbishop of York in the first instance, which he then applied to suffragans within his own province, and which in 1074 he extended to the see of Dublin. After the death of Gilla Pátraic, Lanfranc received a request to consecrate Gilla Pátraic's successor, Donngus (Donatus), a former monk of Christ Church, Canterbury, which he did in 1085, again exacting a profession of obedience, in which, however, Lanfranc was this time simply styled archbishop of Canterbury.[34]

The link between Canterbury and the see of Dublin was maintained during the episcopate of Lanfranc's successor, Anselm (1093–1109). Anselm was consecrated archbishop on 4 December 1093. Shortly thereafter he addressed a letter, in which he styled himself 'Cantuariensis ecclesiae metropolitanus antistes', to Bishop Domnall Ua hÉnna (styled *senior*, in effect house bishop of Muirchertach Ua Briain, king of Munster and high-king of Ireland), to Donngus, bishop of Dublin, and to the other bishops of Ireland, announcing the circumstances of his consecration, requesting their prayers, and exorting that if any matters arose which the Irish bishops were unable to resolve according to canon law, they should bring them to his notice 'so that you may receive from us counsel and consolation rather than fall under God's judgement as transgressors of his commandments'.[35] It is difficult to

1072, when he first made explicit reference to Ireland in his submission to Pope Alexander II in the context of the dispute with the see of York. It is noteworthy, however, that Gregory VII's letter to Toirdelbach Ua Briain contained no reference to Canterbury.

[33] *Canterbury professions*, no. 36.

[34] Ibid., no. 51. According to the *Acta Lanfranci* Donngus was consecrated 'petente rege, clero et populo Hyberniae': *Two Saxon chronicles parallel*, ed. C. Plummer (Oxford, 1892), i. 290. The early thirteenth-century Cistercian annalist of St Mary's Abbey, Dublin, wrote that he was consecrated by Lanfranc 'petentibus atque eligentibus eum Terdyluaco Hibernie rege et episcopis Hibernie regionis atque clero et populo prefate civitatis': *Chartul. St Mary's, Dublin*, ii. 250.

[*See p. 20 for n. 35*]

judge from this letter how Anselm conceived his relationship with the Irish bishops. From Lanfranc's letter collection and from the *Acta Lanfranci* he would have been aware that Lanfranc had consecrated two bishops for the see of Dublin, had addressed letters of exhortation to two Irish kings,[36] and had replied to a query on canon law submitted by Bishop Domnall Ua hÉnna. Anselm only suggested, but did not order, the Irish bishops to have recourse to Canterbury. In 1096 following the death of Donngus, bishop of Dublin, Anselm received a request from Muirchertach Ua Briain and the clergy and people of Dublin for the consecration of Samuel Ua hAingliu, who, we learn from Eadmer, was a former monk of St Alban's.[37] Anselm duly consecrated Samuel, and obtained from him a profession of obedience, in which Anselm was styled 'totius Britanniae primas'.[38] About the same time Anselm addressed a letter to Muirchertach Ua Briain, urging the need for the observance of canon law in regard to marriage and the consecration of bishops, which is reminiscent of that sent by Lanfranc about 1074 to Toirdelbach Ua Briain.[39] In 1096 a new connection between Canterbury and Ireland was forged when Anselm consecrated Máel Ísu Ua hAinmere (who had been a monk of Walchelin, bishop of Winchester) as first bishop of the Hiberno-Norse city of Waterford.[40] It is certain from the text of the letter of request to Canterbury from the people of Waterford, which was transcribed by Eadmer into his *Historia novorum*, that they also had the permission of their overlord Muirchertach Ua Briain, and of his brother, Diarmait, who governed Waterford under his authority.[41] Muirchertach Ua Briain had also been associated with the request for con-

---

[35] *The whole works of the most Reverend James Ussher*, ed. C. R. Elrington (Dublin, 1847–69), iv. 515–17; A. Gwynn, 'St Anselm and the Irish Church', *IER* 59 (1942), 1–14.

[36] Anselm's letter to Muirchertach Ua Briain drew on Lanfranc's letter to Toirdelbach Ua Briain: see below, n. 39.

[37] Eadmer, *Historia novorum*, ed. M. Rule (Rolls series, London, 1884), 73. From a subsequent letter sent by Anselm to Samuel it emerges that he was a nephew of Donngus: see below.

[38] *Canterbury professions*, no. 51.   [39] Ussher, *Works*, iv. 520–3.

[40] *Canterbury professions*, no. 54; A. Gwynn, 'The origins of the diocese of Waterford', *IER* 59 (1942), 289–96.

[41] Eadmer, *Historia novorum*, 76–7; Ussher, *Works*, iv. 518–19; Kenney, *Sources*, no. 640. For Diarmait Ua Briain as governor of Waterford see below, p. 63.

secration to the see of Dublin of Donngus in 1085 and of Samuel in 1096, and Toirdelbach Ua Briain had received a letter from Lanfranc following the consecration of Gilla Pátraic in 1074. It may be inferred, therefore, that between 1074 and 1096 both Toirdelbach Ua Briain and Muirchertach Ua Briain, as claimants to the high-kingship and overlords of Dublin and Waterford, approved of the consecration by the archbishops of Canterbury of bishops for the sees of Dublin and Waterford. Recourse to Canterbury may also be interpreted as an implicit rejection on their part of the spiritual authority of the *comarba* of Armagh.

Resort to Canterbury for consecration of the first bishop of Waterford in 1096 was not imitated, however, by the Hiberno-Norse city of Limerick, or its overlord Muirchertach Ua Briain, when its first known bishop, Gilla Espaic (Gilbertus), was consecrated about 1106. From a letter which Gilla Espaic wrote to Anselm subsequently, it may be inferred that he had been consecrated in Ireland.[42] In the interval between the consecration by Anselm in 1096 of Samuel to the see of Dublin and of Máel Ísu to the see of Waterford, and the consecration of Gilla Espaic as bishop of Limerick, there had been two significant developments within the Irish Church. In 1101 a reforming synod had been held at Cashel under the auspices of Muirchertach Ua Briain.[43] Although both Lanfranc and Anselm had written letters of exhortation to Toirdelbach and Muirchertach Ua Briain urging them to support the cause of Church reform, there is no evidence for Canterbury's interest in or involvement with the synod of Cashel in 1101. In 1105 Domnall son of Amalgaid, *comarba* of Armagh, died, and his successor, Cellach son of Áed, took holy orders on assumption of the office. Furthermore, in 1106 he 'received the orders of a noble bishop (*uasalespoic*) by direction of the men of Ireland'.[44] It is significant that this event occurred while he was on a visitation of Munster; it implies the approval of Muirchertach Ua Briain. Aubrey Gwynn inferred that shortly thereafter Cellach canonically consecrated the first bishop of Limerick. This suggests a

---

[42] Ussher, *Works*, iv. 511–14; A. Gwynn, 'The diocese of Limerick in the twelfth century', *N. Munster Antiq. Jn.* 5 (1946–7), 35–48.
[43] A. Gwynn, 'The first synod of Cashel', *IER* 66 (1945), 81–92; 67 (1946), 109–22.
[44] *AU AFM* 1105, 1106.

shift by Muirchertach Ua Briain away from Canterbury and a recognition of the canonical orders of the *comarba* of Armagh. In 1102 Muirchertach Ua Briain had incurred the wrath of King Henry I because of his relations with the English king's rebellious subject, Arnulf de Montgomery.[45] This may in part have caused Muirchertach to reassess the wisdom of reliance upon the archbishop of Canterbury for the canonical consecration of bishops of the Hiberno-Norse settlements. It may also be significant that Anselm was in exile from England from December 1103 until August 1106, an exile arising out of his dispute with Henry I over investiture.[46] Anselm had already endured a period of exile from England from October 1097 until September 1100.[47] Possibly it was Anselm's manifold difficulties with his royal master which had spurred on the advocates of reform within the Irish Church to organize the reforming synod at Cashel in 1101 and the conferment of canonical episcopal orders on the *comarba* of Armagh in 1106. On his return from exile in August 1106 Anselm, who replied to Gilla Espaic's letter, and mentioned in passing that they had met in Rouen, appears to have raised no objection to Gilla Espaic's consecration in Ireland, nor to have protested that Canterbury's prerogatives had thereby been diminished.[48] There is likewise no suggestion in Anselm's letter to Gilla Espaic that he regarded himself as Gilla Espaic's metropolitan.

One other incident in Anselm's relations with Irish ecclesiastics remains for consideration. At some unknown date Anselm addressed a letter of rebuke to Samuel, bishop of Dublin, whom he had consecrated in 1096, in which he stated that he had heard that Samuel was causing his 'cross to be carried before you on your journeys. If this is true I order you to

---

[45] Below, pp. 67–8.

[46] Eadmer, *Historia novorum*, 149, 183; R. W. Southern, *St Anselm and his biographer* (Cambridge, 1963), 163–80.

[47] Ibid. 91–2, 124.

[48] Ussher, *Works*, 511–14; Kenney, *Sources*, nos. 645, 646. Gilbert and Anselm might have met at the provincial synod held at Rouen in 1096. The Rouen synod of 1096 promulgated some of the decisions of Pope Urban II's council of Clermont, 1095, relating to the Truce and Peace of God, to simoniacal practices, and to the intrusion of laymen into benefices: R. Foreville, 'The synod of the province of Rouen in the eleventh and twelfth centuries', in C. N. L. Brooke (ed.), *Church and government in the middle ages: essays presented to C. R. Cheney* (London, 1976), 19–39 (at 31). The intrusion of laymen into ecclesiastical offices was legislated against at the synod of Cashel.

do so no longer. For this right is reserved to archbishops who had been confirmed with the pall from the Roman pontiff.'[49] Although Anselm ordered Samuel to desist, he did not object to this practice, at any rate explicitly, on the grounds that it diminished the dignity of the church of Canterbury, but rather that it was contrary to canon law. Anselm's letter to Samuel, and a covering letter to Máel Ísu, bishop of Waterford, asking him to transmit in person Samuel's letter to him,[50] may date from Anselm's return to England from exile (since October 1097) in September 1100 or his return from his second exile (since December 1103) in August 1106. Bearing in mind developments in the Irish Church, the second date is perhaps preferable. It might be thought that Samuel was attempting to reject the authority of Anselm, except that this was not apparently very tangible apart from Samuel's consecration at Canterbury. It may be rather that Samuel's actions were directed not against Canterbury but against Cellach, *comarba* of Armagh, who may have been attempting to assert authority over the church of Dublin.

Anselm had maintained the link which he had inherited from Lanfranc with the see of Dublin, and a connection with the see of Waterford had been established in 1096. This marked an apparent advance in Canterbury's influence in Ireland, but against this achievement has to be offset the canonical episcopal consecration of the *comarba* of Armagh in 1106, and the establishment of an episcopal see at Limerick, whose bishop did not make a profession of obedience to Canterbury. During Anselm's period of office Canterbury's claims to a British patriarchate were invested with concrete substance in Wales: in 1107 Anselm consecrated a Norman bishop, Urban, for the see of Llandaff and secured a profession of obedience from him.[51] This, however, was more the result of political circumstances than any initiatives taken by Anselm personally. Anselm became archbishop at a time when the Norman colonists were beginning to penetrate successfully into Wales. In the wake of the Norman advance the episcopal sees began to be staffed either with Norman appointees or Welshmen who were compelled to recognize the authority of Canterbury. Anselm, traditionally, has been regarded as less successful than Lanfranc in

---

[49] Ussher, *Works*, iv. 528–31.   [50] Ibid.   [51] *Canterbury professions*, no. 59.

his assertion of Canterbury's primacy over York. On this issue his contemporaries, and notably the monks of Christ Church, Canterbury, compared Anselm unfavourably with Lanfranc. Their criticism was unfair, however, in so far as it ignored the unresolved difficulties which Anselm had inherited from Lanfranc. Lanfranc had failed to exact an oath of obedience from Thomas, archbishop of York, which would be binding on Thomas's successors; he had also failed to secure a papal confirmation of the compromise worked out in the English royal court between Canterbury and York in 1072.[52] The consequences of these failures were to surface during Anselm's term of office. The acid test came in 1108 with the nomination of a new archbishop of York, Thomas II. Anselm used all his powers to try to bring Thomas to submission, but died in 1109 before York's obedience to Canterbury had been secured. During the vacancy following Anselm's death, Thomas's submission to a future archbishop of Canterbury was obtained, but only because of the intervention of the king in support of the vacant see of Canterbury.[53]

Royal support for Canterbury's claims was an important factor in determining their advance. Whatever Lanfranc had achieved in relation to the see of York he had owed to William the Conqueror's support. King William had endorsed the concept of the unity of the English Church under the primacy of Canterbury because he saw it as a means of strengthening political unity and, in particular, as a means of discouraging northern English separatist tendencies. William was also prepared to countenance Lanfranc's pretensions to a British patriarchate, since this notion went hand in hand with the Conqueror's own political conception of a secular overlordship of the British Isles. In so far as the claims of Canterbury were urged successfully during Lanfranc's episcopate it was because they had the support of the king. It was the close co-operation between William and Lanfranc against the see of York which had led to the personal profession of obedience by York to Canterbury in 1072. An alliance of the king and the see of Canterbury proved its value again in 1109 after Anselm's death, when another personal oath of obedience was extracted from York.

---

[52] Gibson, *Lanfranc*, 117–22; Southern, *St Anselm*, 135–40.   [53] Ibid. 139.

During Anselm's episcopate such an alliance had been jeopardized by Anselm's continuous quarrels with the king. A valid criticism which the monks of Canterbury could level against Anselm, by comparison with Lanfranc, was that he had compromised the very valuable working relationship between the see of Canterbury and the king: because of his difficulties with Anselm, King Henry I had supported the archbishop of York against Canterbury. It was only after Anselm's death that Henry was prepared to revert to the previous royal policy of support for Canterbury.

During Anselm's episcopate the tide, in fact, had begun to turn against the conception of Canterbury's primacy formulated by Lanfranc, although this was not in any way conceded by the Canterbury camp; quite the contrary. Lanfranc had set out almost single-handedly to formulate the concept of a British patriarchate. In 1072 the archbishops of Canterbury and York had faced each other in single combat, well nigh bereft of supporters from their own cathedrals. By the time of Anselm's death in 1109, however, the monastery of Christ Church, Canterbury, numbered some 130 monks, who had been tutored in the rights of their see by both Lanfranc and Anselm, and were now emotionally identified with their archbishops in their claims to primacy. These monks formed a group of vigilantes who could be relied upon to uphold and transmit Canterbury's claims from one episcopate to another, regardless of how practicable those claims might be or become.[54] This channel of preservation and transmission of claims is worth keeping in mind, because Anselm's death in 1109 was followed by a vacancy until Henry I's appointment of Ralph d'Escures in 1114, during which the see of Canterbury's rights and claims were guarded jealously and fostered zealously by the monks of Christ Church, Canterbury, and notably by their leading publicist, Anselm's biographer, Eadmer.[55]

During this vacancy a synod met at Ráith Bressail in 1111 under the auspices of Muirchertach Ua Briain as high-king, which proposed a national diocesan hierarchy for the Irish Church. No allowance was made at Ráith Bressail for possible

[54] A point well made by D. Nicholl, *Thurstan, archbishop of York* (London, 1964), 37.
[55] See Southern, *St Anselm.*

claims to jurisdiction by Canterbury in relation to the pre-existing sees of Dublin and Waterford, whose bishops had previously been consecrated at Canterbury. The intention appears to have been that the sees of Dublin and Waterford would be incorporated into the newly created adjacent dioceses of Glendalough and Lismore when their incumbents died.[56] The timing of the synod of Ráith Bressail during a vacancy at Canterbury may be more than fortuitous. At any rate, plans for an independent national diocesan structure for the Irish Church were launched at a time when a potential source of opposition, the see of Canterbury, was vacant and in no position to protest about the synod's decision in relation to the pre-existing bishoprics of Dublin and Waterford.

Within weeks of Ralph d'Escures's election to the see of Canterbury in 1114 the see of York fell vacant, and this brought the dispute between Canterbury and York to the fore again. Thurstan, the archbishop elect of York, successfully held out for five years against consecration by the archbishop of Canterbury, which would also have necessitated his submission. The king and the archbishop of Canterbury each tried to bully York into submission, but the effectiveness of a resumption of the former alliance between king and Canterbury was now undermined by a new factor, namely the increasing intervention of the papacy in the affairs of the English Church. In 1119 the archbishop of York won a decisive victory by securing consecration from the pope himself.[57] In 1120 Callistus II also gave a definitive verdict on the relationship between the two archbishoprics: he forbade the archbishops of Canterbury to demand a profession of obedience from the archbishops of York, and he forbade the archbishops of York to make any such profession to Canterbury.[58] The papal privilege

---

[56] The boundaries of the diocese of Glendalough were defined as running from Greenoge near Ratoath, Co. Meath, to Begerin Island in the harbour of Wexford, and from Naas to Lambay: J. MacErlean, 'The synod of Ráith Bresail: boundaries of the dioceses of Ireland', *Archiv. Hib.* 3 (1914), 1–33 (at 11, 16). This encompassed the city of Dublin. The problem of the pre-existing see of Waterford was apparently resolved by translating its bishop, Máel Ísu Ua hAinmere, who had been consecrated at Canterbury in 1096, to the see of Cashel, for his *signum* to the decrees of Ráith Bressail is given as archbishop of Cashel: ibid. 12, 16. The best account of the synod of Ráith Bressail is contained in Gwynn and Gleeson, *Killaloe*, 116–27.   [57] Nicholl, *Thurstan*, 3.

[58] M. Cheney, 'Some observations on a papal privilege of 1120 for the archbishops of York', in *Jn. Ecc. Hist.* 31 (1980), 429–39.

of 1120 to York was a decisive turning-point in the struggle over status and authority which had been waged by the two English archbishoprics for more than fifty years. Before the privilege of 1120 three successive archbishops of York had been forced to make personal professions of obedience to Canterbury. After 1120 none was to do so.

The attitude of Henry I during the final phase of the struggle between 1114 and 1120 had been to support the see of Canterbury against York, partly in line with traditional royal policy that subjection of York to Canterbury was politically desirable, and partly because of a new factor, namely that the king was anxious to discourage appeals to Rome and increasing papal intervention in the English Church.[59] The papacy between 1114 and 1119 had tried to force the two archbishops to present their respective cases at the Curia and to accept a papal judgement on the dispute. The king, however, had refused to grant permission to the two archbishops to go to Rome. The archbishop of Canterbury had been glad in this instance to shelter behind the royal refusal. The papal privilege of 1120 to York was accompanied by letters to the archbishop of Canterbury and to King Henry I, threatening suspension of the archbishop and an interdict on England if the verdict was not accepted. The pope intended the letters as an ultimatum to settle the issue finally. They were accepted as such by the king: Henry permitted Thurstan to take possession of the see of York, thus ending five years of dispute and periods of exile, or semi-exile, for the archbishop.

Archbishop Ralph and the monks of Canterbury, however, did not so readily accept the papal verdict and continued with desperate efforts to retrieve lost ground, efforts which ultimately only served to weaken their position further. A series of documents known as the 'primatial forgeries' were presented at Rome in 1123, where, however, they were easily exposed as fraudulent and laughed out of the papal court.[60] The exposure

---

[59] See C. H. Lawrence (ed.), *The English Church and the papacy in the Middle Ages* (London, 1965), 65–84; F. Barlow, *The English Church, 1066–1154* (London, 1979), 105–15.

[60] R. W. Southern suggested that the forgeries were concocted about 1120: 'The Canterbury forgeries', *EHR* 53 (1958), 193–226; *St Anselm*, 304–9. Gibson, *Lanfranc*, 231–7, however, argues that the monks of Christ Church, Canterbury, began to forge them as early as 1070 and gradually assembled a dossier which was not directed solely against York. Her view has been accepted by Barlow, *The English Church, 1066–1154*, 41 n. 60.

of the forgeries represented a further humiliation and weakening of Canterbury's position *vis-à-vis* York.

If the pursuit of Canterbury's claims against York appeared increasingly unrealistic after 1120, there still remained the possibility of pursuing its primatial claims in the wider context of a patriarchate over Britain and Ireland. Yet in this context too the period around 1120 marked a weakening of Canterbury's position. Between 1114 and 1119 Archbishop Ralph d'Escures's main preoccupation had been the exaction of a profession of obedience from Thurstan of York. But, as successor of Lanfranc and Anselm, Archbishop Ralph was also aware that the possibility of claiming and demonstrating a wider jurisdiction over the British Isles, and even Ireland, was useful supporting evidence for Canterbury's claims over York: in 1119 in the course of a letter to Pope Callistus II, outlining the rights and dignities of the see of Canterbury, Archbishop Ralph asserted that the see of Canterbury had pastoral responsibility 'for the inhabitants of Britain as well as for the Irish who inhabited the island next to Britain'.[61] Ralph, however, was to have little opportunity to advance Canterbury's claims to a wider patriarchate after 1120. It was not just that Canterbury's prestige had been diminished by the settlement of the dispute with York; significant also was that the alliance between the king and the see of Canterbury weakened considerably thereafter. Once King Henry had accepted the papal ruling of 1120, and reached a settlement with Thurstan, archbishop of York, he lost sympathy with Canterbury's wider hegemonic claims.

Canterbury's claims to a British patriarchate had drawn validity from the secular concept of a quasi-imperial authority over Britain, which both William the Conqueror and William Rufus appear to have believed they had inherited from their English royal predecessors.[62] As long as the Norman kings were themselves prepared to indulge pretensions to a British overlordship, and even a possible overlordship of Ireland, the see of Canterbury could derive strength and support for the advancement of a British ecclesiastical patriarchate from the

---

[61] *Historians of the church of York*, ed. J. Raine (Rolls series, London, 1866), ii. 236.
[62] F. Barlow, *Edward the Confessor* (London, 1970), 135–8; J. Le Patourel, *The Norman empire* (Oxford, 1976), 319–35; below, ch. 2.

concept of a secular *imperium*. During Henry I's reign, however, there was a change in royal policy in regard to hegemonic pretensions.[63] Shortly after his accession in 1100 Henry
married Matilda, sister of Edgar, king of the Scots, which
inaugurated a policy of maintaining peaceful and friendly
relations with the Scottish king. This was further advanced in
1124 with the accession as king of Scotland of David, who had
married Matilda, daughter of Waltheof, earl of Northampton
and Huntingdon, in right of whom he held estates in England
from about 1114 and was in consequence a vassal of Henry I.
In Wales also, partly because of difficulties in Normandy,
Henry I began to rely increasingly on encouraging political
quiescence rather than aggressive Norman expansion. This
shift in royal policy was a blow to the advancement of
Canterbury's assertion of primacy in both Scotland and
Wales, which in turn must have served to weaken Canterbury's claims in Ireland.

Given the establishment of an Irish diocesan structure at the
synod of Ráith Bressail in 1111, which planned for the incorporation of the pre-existing sees of Dublin and Waterford
into its scheme, given the defeat of Canterbury's primatial
claims in relation to York in 1119–20, and the king's disengage-
ment from Canterbury's wider aspirations, it is conceivable
that Canterbury's links with the Irish Church might have
lapsed entirely after 1120. That this did not happen was due
not to any positive efforts made by the archbishops of Canterbury, whose enthusiasm to fight on was at a low ebb, but to the
fact that overtures to Canterbury continued to come from Ireland.

In 1121, at a time when Canterbury's prestige was particularly low after the humiliating defeat of its case against York,
and after the recent unsuccessful attempt by the Canterbury
monk, Eadmer, to be consecrated as bishop of St Andrews
giving obedience to Canterbury,[64] at a time when Ralph, archbishop of Canterbury, was still suffering from the effects of a
stroke which he had had in 1119, from which indeed he never

---

[63] See C. W. Hollister and T. K. Keefe, 'The making of the Angevin empire', *Journal of British Studies*, 12 (1973), 1–25 (at 5–6).

[64] Southern, *St Anselm*, 135, 236. For Canterbury's relations with the Scottish Church see M. Brett, *The English Church under Henry I* (Oxford, 1975), 14–28.

recovered,[65] one Gréne (Gregorius) presented himself as bishop elect of Dublin for consecration at Canterbury. This must have been a very gratifying, possibly even surprising, event for the monks of Christ Church, Canterbury.

That a bishop elect of Dublin was anxious to seek consecration at Canterbury in 1121 was occasioned by rival factions within the city of Dublin. The synod of Ráith Bressail had intended that, on the death of the incumbent of the pre-existing see of Dublin, that see should be incorporated into the adjacent diocese of Glendalough, which had been created at Ráith Bressail. The Ráith Bressail scheme foundered, however, because of the apparent unwillingness of a party within the city of Dublin to forgo its own bishop and the expeditious dispatch to the archbishop of Canterbury of an episcopal candidate for consecration. From the Annals of Ulster it would appear that Cellach as archbishop of Armagh assumed administration of the diocese himself.[66] Muirchertach Ua Briain, the secular guarantor of the synod of Ráith Bressail and overlord of the city of Dublin, had died in 1119. His son, Domnall, who had ruled Dublin on his behalf, had been expelled in 1118 following a military expedition to Dublin by Toirdelbach Ua Conchobair, king of Connacht and contender for the high-kingship, who installed Énna mac Donnchada, king of Leinster, in the kingship of Dublin.[67] The dispute over succession to the see of

---

[65] Orderic Vitalis, *Historia ecclesiastica*, ed. M. Chibnall, vi (Oxford, 1978), 170–1, 318–19.

[66] *AU* 1121. 7; cf. Eadmer, *Historia novorum*, 297–8; *Chartul. St Mary's, Dublin*, ii. 254–5. Cellach's intervention in Dublin is reflected in a charter of Gilla in Choimded Ua Caráin, archbishop of Armagh, 1175–80, whereby he granted to St Mary's Abbey, Dublin, 'terram sancti Patricii que dicitur Balibachel' to have and to hold 'sicut predecessor meus pie memorie Kellach, archiepiscopus et primas tocius Hybernie eas melius et liberius tenuit et habuit unquam': ibid. i. 141–2; cf. 143, 146–7. C. Ó Conbhuí, 'The lands of St Mary's Abbey, Dublin', *RIA Proc.* 62 (1962), 21–84 (at 36), has shown that Ballyboghill did not belong to St Mary's Abbey before 1175.

[67] *Misc. Ir. annals*, 1119. 2; *Ann. Tig.*, *AU*, *Ann. Inisf.*, *AFM* 1118. Ussher printed the following prima facie genuine text from BL Cotton Claudius E. V, fo. 255d, of a writ addressed by Henry I to Archbishop Ralph: 'Henricus rex Angliae [*sic*], Radulpho Cantuariensis archiepiscopo salutem. Mandavit mihi rex Hiberniae [*sic*] per breve suum et burgenses Dublinae quod elegerunt hunc Gregorium in episcopum et eum tibi mittunt consecrandum. Unde tibi mando, ut petitioni eorum satisfaciens ejus consecrationem sine dilatione expleas. Teste Ranulpho cancellario apud Windelsor': Ussher, *Works*, iv. 534. The Irish king is not named, but the most likely candidates are Toirdelbach Ua Conchobair, king of Connacht, or Énna mac Donnchada Mac Murchada, king of Leinster. This writ is not included in *Regesta regum Anglo-Normannorum*. Ranulph was chancellor to Henry I from 1107 to 1123: *Regesta* ii,

Dublin in 1121 may reflect rivalry between different political factions struggling for control of the city of Dublin, possibly even a struggle between the archbishops of Armagh and Cashel about primacy and jurisdiction over the see of Dublin. Whatever the background, Ralph, archbishop of Canterbury, caused Gréne to be consecrated when he presented himself in 1121, exacting the traditional profession of obedience from him, and after some initial difficulty Gréne succeeded in gaining possession of the see of Dublin.[68]

Recourse to Canterbury for consecration of Gréne as bishop of Dublin in 1121 gratuitously maintained a link between Canterbury and an Irish episcopal see at a time when Canterbury's fortunes were at a particularly low ebb, when, if the see of Dublin had been suppressed and absorbed into the diocese of Glendalough, the archbishop of Canterbury, if he had wished to do so, would not have been in a strong position to object. The request to Canterbury for the consecration of Gréne in 1121 is also important in an Irish context, in that it highlighted the fact that resort could be made to Canterbury as an alternative source for episcopal consecration by rival factions within the Irish Church.

As far as extant evidence goes, after the consecration of Gréne as bishop for Dublin in 1121 Canterbury had no further contact with, nor took any active interest in, the Irish Church for a period of twenty years, until in 1140 one Patricius was consecrated for the see of Limerick by Theobald, archbishop of Canterbury.[69] This consecration appears to have been occasioned by circumstances similar to those in 1121, namely a disputed election to the see of Limerick, with one of the candidates having recourse to Canterbury for consecration. Unlike Gréne, Bishop Patricius, however, seems never to have gained possession of the see of Limerick. In fact, the Irish sources, perhaps deliberately, reveal no knowledge of his existence. In 1145 Patricius, bishop of Limerick, witnessed an agreement at St Paul's, London;[70] in 1148 he assisted the archbishop of

p. ix and *passim*. Eadmer quoted the text of a letter from 'omnes burgenses Dublinae civitatis' requesting Gréne's consecration, in which, however, there is no mention of an Irish king: Eadmer, *Historia novorum*, 297–8.

[68] *Canterbury professions*, no. 69; Eadmer, *Historia novorum*, 298.
[69] *Canterbury professions*, no. 81; Gwynn, 'Diocese of Limerick'.

[*See p. 32 for n. 70*]

Canterbury at the consecration of Robert de Chesney, bishop of Lincoln, and even more significantly, perhaps, at the consecration of David fitz Gerald as bishop of St Davids, which took place on the same day.[71] Nothing more is known of him. From Canterbury's viewpoint the request for consecration in 1140 from a prospective bishop of Limerick must have appeared timely, for it coincided with important ecclesiastical developments both in an Irish and an English context. Late in 1139, or early in 1140, St Malachy of Armagh travelled to Rome to attend the second Lateran council as the representative of the Irish Church and with a commission to seek palls for the two archiepiscopal sees of Armagh and Cashel which had been agreed at the synod of Ráith Bressail in 1111.[72] Pope Innocent II declined to accede to Malachy's request. He instructed Malachy to return to Ireland and to convene a general council of the Irish Church: if the prelates of that council made a united demand (united is probably of some significance here) and sent messengers of good repute to Rome the pope promised to reconsider the matter.[73] It is possible that Innocent's hesitation in 1140 was occasioned by a desire to observe certain canonical procedures which the Irish delegation had not met; but it may also be that the pope was made aware of disagreements within the Irish Church, such as that in relation to the see of Limerick about this very time, where one candidate was seeking consecration from the see of Canterbury.

Theobald, archbishop of Canterbury, had also travelled to Rome in 1139 to attend the second Lateran council.[74] It is possible that Theobald had received the request for consecration of Patricius to the see of Limerick before his departure, and that it was he who raised arguments at Rome which induced the pope to delay recognition of the Irish diocesan structure at this juncture. Innocent II may have been presented with

---

[70] W. Dugdale, *Monasticon Anglicanum*, ed. J. Caley, H. Ellis, and B. Bandinel, iii (London, 1846), 372, = BL Cotton XI. 8, an original charter of Alexander, bishop of Lincoln.

[71] *Canterbury professions*, no. 92; Gervase of Canterbury, i. 138; see below.

[72] See *St Bernard of Clairvaux's life of St Malachy of Armagh*, ed. H. J. Lawlor (London, 1920); A. Gwynn, 'St Malachy of Armagh', *IER* 70 (1948), 961–78; 71 (1949), 134–48, 317–31.

[73] *Sancti Bernardi opera*, ed. J. Leclercq and H. M. Rochais, iii (Rome, 1963), 344.

[74] A. Saltman, *Theobald, archbishop of Canterbury* (London, 1956), 13–15.

grounds for thinking that the Irish Church was not unanimous in its desire for an independent diocesan structure and that there was a possible conflict of jurisdiction with Canterbury.

By 1140 the Irish diocesan structure had had a *de facto* existence of almost thirty years without any serious attempts having been made by Canterbury to challenge it. It may be questioned whether Archbishop Theobald seriously thought, or even desired, that this development within the Irish Church could be reversed. It would certainly have been in Theobald's interest in 1140, however, at least to delay formal papal recognition of the Irish diocesan hierarchy. To appreciate why this was so it is necessary to consider Canterbury's relations with the Welsh Church at that time: the see of St Davids was mounting a formidable challenge against Canterbury to win metropolitan status for St Davids and recognition of the independence of the entire Welsh Church from Canterbury, a challenge which was taken sufficiently seriously at Canterbury to stimulate fabrication of evidence to suggest that the bishops of St Davids and Llandaff had been consecrated at Canterbury since the early tenth century.[75] If the Irish Church were to gain papal recognition of its independent diocesan structure in 1140 by the granting of palls to the sees of Armagh and Cashel, this would provide a dangerous precedent from Canterbury's standpoint for the setting up of an independent diocesan structure for the Welsh Church. In 1140 it would, therefore, have been advantageous to Archbishop Theobald if papal recognition of an independent Irish diocesan structure could be deferred at least until such time as the attack mounted against Canterbury's interest in Wales had been met and the status of the Welsh Church had been decided upon conclusively by the papacy. The request for consecration from a prospective candidate for the see of Limerick in 1140 may, therefore, have provided Canterbury with a timely argument in favour of postponing papal recognition of the Irish diocesan structure.

Theobald may even have been faced with active collusion

---

[75] *Episc. acts*, i. 190–208; M. Richter, 'Professions of obedience and the metropolitan claims of St David's', *National Library of Wales Journal*, 15 (1967–8), 197–214; 'Canterbury's primacy in Wales and the first stage of Bishop Bernard's opposition', *Jn. Ecc. Hist.* 22 (1971), 177–89; C. Brooke, 'The archbishops of St David's, Llandaff and Caerleon-on-Usk', in *Studies in the early British Church*, ed. N. K. Chadwick (Cambridge, 1958), 201–42.

between Irish and Welsh ecclesiastics against the interests of
Canterbury around this time. The potential for such collaboration had been apparent as early as 1120. In that year, Gruffydd
ap Cynan, king of Gwynedd, had written to Ralph, archbishop
of Canterbury, requesting consecration of his nominee, David
the Irishman, for the bishopric of Bangor, and threatening that,
if the archbishop did not comply, Gruffydd would procure a
bishop from the Irish Church.[76] Archbishop Theobald was
placed in a very similar situation in 1140. In that year he consecrated Meurig (Mauritius) to the see of Bangor. Meurig,
however, was prevented from taking possession of the see
because of opposition from Owain, king of Gwynedd,[77] who
was by this stage actively supporting the claims to metropolitan
status being advanced by the see of St Davids.[78] Meurig excom-
municated a number of the clergy and laity of North Wales
who had opposed him, but as we learn from a letter written by
the archbishop of Canterbury to the pope around 1140 these
excommunicates were 'wandering here and there, flying for
refuge to the neighbouring bishops of Wales, England, Ireland
and Scotland, from whom they fraudulently were receiving
orders, unction and the sacraments'.[79] In 1140 Archbishop
Theobald requested the pope to send letters to the bishops of
Ireland, among others, urging them to observe whatever he
would decree canonically against the enemies of the newly consecrated bishop of Bangor. As this episode suggests, Theobald
would have been well aware of the possibility of Welsh
ecclesiastics seeking the aid of the Irish Church in their bid to
establish the independence of the Welsh Church. The first
letter which the chapter of St Davids wrote to launch its claim
to metropolitan status, which was addressed to Pope Honorius
II some time between 1124 and 1130, sought to use Irish
evidence in support of its case. It claimed that the consecration
of Bernard to the bishopric of St Davids by Ralph, archbishop
of Canterbury, in 1115 could not be taken as a precedent, since
its own histories 'and those of other nations' proved that a

---

[76] Eadmer, *Historia novorum*, 259–60; Lloyd, *Wales*, ii. 455. Gruffydd had been born
and spent the greater part of his youth in Ireland: see below, ch. 2.
[77] Lloyd, *Wales*, ii. 483–4.
[78] *Episc. acts*, i. 259–60, no. 122.
[79] John of Salisbury, *Letters*, ed. W. J. Millor and H. E. Butler (London, 1955),
135–6.

single incident, such as the consecration of Bernard, could not make the church of St Davids permanently subject to Canterbury. The 'other nations' are not named, but Ireland may well have been intended. Certainly, the letter immediately went on to assert that the church of St Davids had consecrated archbishops and bishops to preach the faith in Ireland, notably St Patrick, but also other disciples sent to that country by St David.[80]

Coincidentally, by 1140 the Scottish Church under the leadership of the see of St Andrews, and with the active support of King David, was also seeking papal recognition of its independent status from the see of York. In 1139–40 Malachy had travelled to the Continent via Scotland, where he had spent some time at the court of the Scottish king. King David and Malachy shared a common interest in securing papal recognition of the independent status of the Churches in their respective countries. King David can be shown to have had contacts also with Welsh ecclesiastics who sought the independence of the Welsh Church from Canterbury, and especially with Bernard, bishop of St Davids, who pioneered the case for metropolitan status for the see of St Davids.[81] The most convincing evidence of co-operation between Welsh and Scottish ecclesiastics in Rome in 1140 comes from two papal bulls issued on 14 May of that year, one in favour of Bernard, bishop of St Davids, the other in favour of the prior of St Andrew's, Glasgow, and both granted 'at the request of the bishop of St Davids'.[82] Against this background of co-operation between Welsh and Scottish ecclesiastics, King David's association with St Malachy, especially in the period 1139–40, assumes an added significance. It may be that Archbishop Theobald of Canterbury feared a concerted campaign by Welsh, Scottish, and Irish ecclesiastics to gain papal recognition of the independent status of their respective Churches. It is thus possible

---

[80] *Episc. acts*, i. 249–50.

[81] Bishop Bernard's acquaintance with King David may have stemmed initially from the fact that Bernard had been chaplain to David's sister, Queen Matilda, wife of Henry I, before his elevation to the see of St Davids in 1115. King David's acquisition of the honour of Lancaster about 1141 also created opportunities for the co-operation of the king and the bishop which is attested from 1141 onwards: G. W. S. Barrow, 'King David I and the honour of Lancaster', *EHR* 70 (1955), 85–9.

[82] A. C. Lawrie, *Early Scottish charters* (Glasgow, 1905), no. 165; *Episc. acts*, i. 260, no. 123; *Scotia pontificia*, ed. R. Somerville (Oxford, 1982), no. 25.

that Malachy's request for palls for the sees of Armagh and
Cashel foundered in 1140 because of the intervention of Canterbury at Rome.

That this may have been the case is suggested by the
sequence of events which followed a renewed request from the
Irish Church for papal ratification of its diocesan structure in
1147–8. In 1147 Malachy embarked on another journey to the
Continent to attend the council of Rheims, at the same time
intending to re-petition for palls for the Irish archbishoprics.
Malachy, however, died at Clairvaux before he had an opportunity to consult with Pope Innocent II. It is not known how, or
by whom, the Irish petition was presented subsequently, but in
1151 Pope Eugenius III decided to act on the request and a
papal legate, Cardinal John Paparo, was dispatched to Ireland.

King Stephen prevented Malachy from journeying to the
Continent via England in 1147, and Cardinal Paparo faced a
similar restriction on his travelling through England in 1151. In
1139–40 Malachy had travelled via Scotland and England to
Rome, and in 1147 he had intended to do so again. King
Stephen, however, barred him from journeying through
England and he was compelled to board ship for the Continent
from Scotland.[83] Why did King Stephen oppose Malachy's
passage through England in 1147? Was this a reflection of the
domestic quarrel in England between the Crown and the
papacy over the jurisdiction of papal legates? Malachy had
been appointed native papal legate for Ireland in 1140. The
legate Cardinal Paparo was also refused access to England in
1151 by King Stephen, who demanded a sworn undertaking
that Paparo would do nothing to the injury of England while he
was in Ireland.

In what way did King Stephen think that English interests
might be harmed by Paparo's mission to Ireland? As Denis
Bethell has pointed out, it is noteworthy how much attention
Paparo's legation to Ireland received from English chroniclers:
John of Hexham, John of Salisbury, Robert of Torigny, Roger
of Howden, and Ralph of Diss mentioned it, and, with the
exception of John of Hexham, their attitude was hostile.[84]

---

[83] Bernard of Clairvaux, *Life of St Malachy*, 120–2. Cf. Symeon of Durham, *Historical
works*, ed. T. Arnold, ii (Rolls series, London, 1885), 321.

[84] Robert of Torigny, 166; John of Salisbury, *Historia pontificalis*, ed. M. Chibnall

Robert of Torigny stated that Paparo's mission to Ireland was at the expense of Canterbury, that it injured 'the ancient customs and dignity of that church, where it was customary for the bishops of Ireland to seek and obtain the blessing of consecration'. John of Salisbury recorded that he had met Paparo at the papal court and had formed no favourable impression of him; he accused Paparo of cunning and duplicity and of scheming with the king of Scotland to attain metropolitan status for St Andrews at the expense of both the sees of York and Canterbury. This is a very interesting accusation, bearing in mind Malachy's links with King David of Scotland. John of Salisbury did not level a like charge against Paparo in relation to the Irish Church, but he did reveal his interest in Paparo's legation in Ireland by commenting on decisions of the synod of Kells, over which Paparo presided in 1152. A copy of its decrees, John reported, was preserved in the papal archives, where he had consulted them, and from which he quoted a decision concerning the status of the abbess of Kildare. That English churchmen resented Paparo is evidenced also from the very unfavourable obituary notice accorded him in 1156 by the annalist of Winchester, who wrote 'This year Cardinal John died; when he was dead sailors heard a voice under Mount Etna saying "stoke up the fire".'[85] The annals of Winchester would hardly have included such an obit for a member of the Roman Curia unless it had some topical relevance in English ecclesiastical circles. Almost certainly, it should be linked to resentment of Paparo's contacts with King David of Scotland and support for metropolitan status for the see of St Andrews, and his mission to Ireland, the outcome of which at the synod of Kells was formal papal approval of the independent diocesan structure of the Irish Church in 1152.

Fear of concerted action by Welsh, Scottish, and Irish ecclesiastics against the interests of Canterbury provides a plausible context for the difficulties which both Malachy and Paparo encountered in trying to travel through England in 1147–8 and 1151–2. It is questionable whether the primary

(London, 1956), 6, 12, 71–2; Roger of Howden, *Chronica*, i. 212; Ralph of Diss, i. 295; Symeon of Durham, *Historical works*, ii. 326–7.

[85] *Annales monastici*, ed. H. R. Luard (Rolls series, London, 1864–9), ii. 55, iv. 380, as cited by Bethell, 'English monks', 135.

concern of either Theobald or King Stephen during the period 1140–52 was to prevent the ultimate recognition of the Irish diocesan structure. More likely it was the implications which recognition of the independent status of the Irish Church might have for the Welsh and Scottish Churches which archbishop and king had most reason to fear. An additional concern for King Stephen may have been the fact that the individuals who were most actively seeking the independence of the Welsh and Scottish Churches were also supporters of the Angevin cause.[86]

THE COUNCIL OF WINCHESTER, 1155

What course of action remained to the see of Canterbury and the king of England after formal papal ratification of the independent status of the Irish Church at the synod of Kells in 1152? Protest by Canterbury to Pope Eugenius III, who had countenanced the decision, was futile. Eugenius, however, died on 8 July 1153 and, after the brief pontificate of Anastasius IV, was succeeded by the Englishman, Adrian IV, on 4 December 1154. Adrian's accession coincided with the coronation of King Henry II in England on 19 December 1154.

The question of metropolitan status for the see of St Davids was still a vital issue for Theobald, archbishop of Canterbury. A preliminary hearing had taken place in 1147, at which the pope had commanded that Bishop Bernard should remain subject to the archbishop of Canterbury pending a full hearing at the papal court.[87] Bishop Bernard died in 1148 before the second hearing at which the pope was to have given a definitive judgement. The timing of Bishop Bernard's death was very much in Canterbury's favour. Archbishop Theobald acted swiftly to secure an unusually detailed profession of obedience from Bernard's successor, David fitz Gerald, and, furthermore, extorted from him an additional oath that he personally would not raise the question of the dignity of St Davids. This did not, of course, preclude the cathedral chapter of St Davids from doing so, but it gave Canterbury a distinct advantage in any appeals that might be made to Rome.

---

[86] Below, pp. 70–2.   [87] Richter, 'Professions of obedience'.

Among Henry II's first actions as king was the convening of a number of great councils attended by prominent lay and ecclesiastical magnates. The first was held at London in March 1155, at which a large number of bishops sought renewal of their royal charters; at a second in April at Wallingford the barons recognized the succession rights of Henry's sons; at a third at Bridgnorth in July the king made peace with Hugh de Mortimer.[88] The next recorded council met on 29 September 1155 at Winchester, and its purpose, according to its sole chronicler, Robert of Torigny, was to discuss plans for an invasion of Ireland, which the king proposed to bestow on his youngest brother, William.[89]

Since Robert was the only chronicler to record details of this council, doubt has been raised about the accuracy of his account of a discussion of a projected invasion of Ireland. W. L. Warren called it 'fragile evidence', suggesting that Robert was not the most reliable witness of events outside northern France and that his account of a planned conquest of Ireland in 1155 was a retrospective insertion made subsequent to King Henry's expedition to Ireland in 1171–2.[90] That the council of Winchester is not mentioned by any English chroniclers is less surprising when it is borne in mind just how few contemporary historians were writing in the decade of the 1150s.[91] Furthermore, there is independent evidence which can be brought to bear on Robert of Torigny's account of the council of Winchester in 1155. That such a council did take place is borne out by two charters issued by Henry II which are dated 'apud Wintoniam in concilio'.[92] William, the brother to whom, according to Robert of Torigny, Henry proposed to make a grant of Ireland, was present at the council, since he was a

[88] Eyton, *Itinerary*, 1–13.

[89] Robert of Torigny, 186.

[90] Warren, *Henry II*, 195. It is noteworthy that Robert gave precise and correct dates in this section of his work; e.g. he dated Henry's coronation (19 December 1154), the birth of young Henry (28 February 1155), the oath to Henry's son (10 April), the settlement between Henry and Mortimer (7 July), and then the Winchester council (Michaelmas). This suggests that he had good information on activities in Henry II's court during this period. Henry visited the abbey of Mont Saint Michel on at least two occasions, in 1158 and 1166: Eyton, *Itinerary*, 41, 97.

[91] Cf. A. Gransden, *Historical writing in England*, c.550–1307 (London, 1974), 526.

[92] *Recueil des actes de Henri II*, ed. L. Delisle and E. Berger, i (Paris, 1916), nos. 6, 7.

witness to one of the charters.[93] That the question of Ireland was debated by the council of Winchester is confirmed by another charter, an extant original, issued by John, count of Eu, which is dated 'apud Wintoniam eo anno quo verbum factum est de Hibernia conquirenda'.[94] The count of Eu's charter is in close agreement with Robert of Torigny's statement that 'Henricus rex Anglorum, habito concilio apud Wincestre, de conquirendo regno Hiberniae . . . cum optimatibus suis tractavit'. There was, then, a discussion about a conquest of Ireland at a council held at Winchester in 1155.

Why and by whom was a conquest of Ireland contemplated in 1155? There is some additional evidence from the anonymous continuator of the chronicle of Sigebert of Gembloux, writing in the monastery of Afflighem in Flanders and incorporating the chronicle of Robert of Torigny, who elaborated on the latter's entry for 1155 that it was 'bishops and certain religious men' who wished the king to go to Ireland.[95] The witness lists of Henry II's two charters dated at Winchester reveal that the archbishops of Canterbury and York and the bishops of London, Lincoln, Hereford, Chichester, and Norwich were present at the council.[96] It is not difficult to suggest a reason why some English ecclesiastics might have favoured a conquest of Ireland by Henry II, given the background of Canterbury's claims to primacy over a number of Irish episcopal sees, the fact that these had been set aside at the synod of Kells, the hostile English reaction to the legation of Cardinal John Paparo in Ireland in 1152, and the implications which papal recognition of the independent status of the Irish Church had for the arch-

---

[93] Among the arguments which Warren put forward against Robert of Torigny's account of the council of Winchester was that Henry II never did much for his younger brother William: Warren, *Henry II*, 195. But Henry presumably backed the proposed marriage between William and the countess of Warenne, which would have given him considerable estates, but which fell through because of opposition from Thomas Becket: William fitz Stephen, 'Vita S. Thomae', in *Materials for the history of Thomas Becket, archbishop of Canterbury*, ed. J. C. Robertson, iii (Rolls series, London, 1877), 142.

[94] Such a precise date is unusual in twelfth-century private charters, but detailed dating clauses were a feature of the charters of the counts of Eu: see Appendix 1, n. 5.

[95] *Monumenta Germaniae Historica, scriptores*, ed. G. H. Pertz, vi (Hanover, 1844), 403, as cited by Bethell, 'English monks', 135.

[96] Eyton, *Itinerary*, 12. See also Henry II's charters in favour of Archbishop Theobald and Shrewsbury abbey, dated at Winchester, which may almost certainly be assigned to 1155: *Cartae antiquae rolls, 1–10* (Pipe Roll Society, NS 17; London, 1939), 101.

bishop of Canterbury's dispute with the see of St Davids. Intervention by Henry II in Ireland may have been viewed by some English ecclesiastics as desirable in that it might provide an opportunity of overturning the papally approved decisions of the synod of Kells. Canterbury had advanced its claims to primacy over the Welsh Church in the wake of Norman conquest and colonization.[97] Might a similar strategy not be employed in Ireland?

What sort of arguments might ecclesiastics have used to encourage Henry II to undertake a conquest of Ireland? The archbishops of Canterbury had grounds to claim primacy over certain Irish sees by the indisputable fact that certainly since 1074, and possibly earlier, individual bishops from Ireland had presented themselves for consecration at Canterbury. But they had also to consider the question of a theoretical justification for this claim, if at no other time, then at least when the professions of obedience from Irish bishops were being drafted. The first such extant profession of obedience is that sworn by Gilla Pátraic, bishop elect of Dublin, in 1074. In it Lanfranc was styled 'Britanniarum primas'.[98] This was certainly an assertion of primatial authority within Britain, but the indefined plural 'primate of the Britains' may also have been intended to embrace Ireland. In 1072, when writing to Pope Alexander II in support of the primacy of Canterbury over York, Lanfranc had explicitly claimed primacy over Ireland as well as Britain on the basis, he said, of what he had read in Bede's *Ecclesiastical history*.[99] Lanfranc paraphrased rather than quoted the passage(s) of Bede which he had in mind. One possibility is the section of Bede which contained the reply of Pope Gregory I to a query from Augustine, the first bishop of Canterbury, as to how he should act towards the bishops of the provinces of Gaul and of Britain ('Britanniarum').[100] An inference could be drawn from this that Britain was made up of a number of different

---

[97] Contemporaries were aware that ecclesiastical subordination and secular conquest were linked. As Gerald of Wales wrote of Henry I, 'conquering Wales with a strong hand, he ordained that the Welsh Church, which he found free, should be placed under the Church of his own realm, just as he subdued the country to his kingdom': R. Bartlett, *Gerald of Wales* (Oxford, 1982), 53.

[98] *Canterbury professions*, no. 36.

[99] Lanfranc, *Letters*, 50–1.

[100] Bede, *Ecclesiastical history*, i. 27 (Colgrave and Mynors, 86–9).

provinces, among which Lanfranc may have thought Ireland was included.

What could have lent support to such an interpretation was a belief, which is attested in some quarters already by the early eleventh century, that the English kings of the tenth century had exercised some form of overlordship over Ireland. This eleventh-century belief was based on the tenth-century hegemonic titles accorded kings Athelstan (925–39), Edwy (955–9), and Edgar (959–75) in their charters, which claimed for them an *imperium* over the peoples living in Britain and the islands around Britain.[101] The hegemonic titles accorded tenth-century English kings were not very specific (none in an indubitably authentic charter mentioned Ireland), probably because they went far beyond the actuality of lordship exercised by them.[102] Doubts about the authenticity of individual charters with hegemonic titles have been raised, but a tenth-century document of un-questionable authenticity, the *Regularis concordia*, the rule by which all pre-Conquest English monks lived, described King Edgar as 'egregious king by Christ's grace of the English and all other peoples living in the ambit of the British island'.[103] The very lack of definition of the 'British ambit' in this instance, and of the hegemonic titles used in tenth-century English royal charters, provided scope for a variety of interpretations in the post-Conquest period.[104]

The accuracy, or reality, of the grandiloquent titles accorded English kings in the tenth century is not relevant here, only the effect which such titles might have had on a post-Conquest ecclesiastic researching into the origins of the primacy of Canterbury. In addition to the *Regularis concordia*, the library at Canterbury contained some notable instances. Two Canter-

---

[101] The tenth-century hegemonic titles may themselves have been based on an earlier classical notion of an *orbis Britanniae* beyond the *orbis Romanae*: E. John, *Orbis Britanniae* (Leicester, 1966), 1–64.

[102] H. R. Loyn, 'The imperial style of the tenth-century Anglo-Saxon kings', *History*, 40 (1955), 111–15; on Athelstan's overlordship of Wales see H. R. Loyn, 'Wales and England in the tenth century: the context of the Athelstan charters', *Welsh History Review*, 10 (1981), 283–301.

[103] *Regularis concordia*, ed. T. Symons (London, 1953), 1.

[104] The chronicler, Aethelweard, writing between 975 and 1002, appears to have thought that Julius Caesar was referring to Ireland when he used the term Britain: *The Chronicle of Aethelweard*, ed. A. Campbell (London, 1962), 62, as cited by Bethell, 'English monks', 130.

bury manuscripts, which can be dated palaeographically to the tenth century, contain the text of a charter purported to have been granted by King Edred to Oda, archbishop of Canterbury, asserting that the archbishop of Canterbury had the power of St Peter over the whole region of Britain and the 'arva Britannica'. The authenticity of the text of this charter may be doubted, but if it is a forgery, in whole or in part, it dates from the tenth century.[105] Two tenth-century gospel-books owned by the monks of Canterbury could also have provided inspiration for Lanfranc and his successors in their pursuit of the primatial claims of Canterbury. King Athelstan's dedication in a gospel-book, which he had received from the emperor Otto I, and which he, in turn, bestowed on Canterbury, read 'Athelstan, *basileus* of the English, and *curagulus* of all Britain, gives this book to the primatial see of Canterbury'.[106] Even more striking with Ireland in mind was the inscription in the gospel-book which Máel Brigte mac Tornáin, *comarba* of Armagh (883–927) and of Iona (891–927), gave to Athelstan and which the king subsequently bestowed on Canterbury: 'Máel Brigte, son of Tornán, *comarba* of Armagh, taught this gospel worthily for God's sake through the *triquadrum*; the Anglo-Saxon king and ruler, Athelstan, gives it for ever to the metropolitan church of Canterbury.'[107] A post-Conquest ecclesiastic at Canterbury, encountering such material in the library, and faced also with the arrival of bishops from Ireland seeking consecration from the archbishop of Canterbury, could be forgiven for concluding that Ireland fell within the British ambit.

It is uncertain to what extent Lanfranc and his successor, Anselm, believed that Ireland had fallen within the *imperium* of the pre-Conquest English kings, and how far this may have contributed to their conception of a theoretical claim to primacy over the Irish church, or whether it sufficed in their view to base claims to primacy in Ireland on the indisputable fact that Irish bishops voluntarily presented themselves for consecration at Canterbury. The attitude of Anselm's biographer, Eadmer, writing the *Historia novorum* about 1115, is, however,

---

[105] Bethell, 'English monks', 130–1.

[106] J. A. Robinson, *The times of St Dunstan* (Oxford, 1923), 60, as cited in Bethell, 'English monks', 132.

[107] Robinson, *St Dunstan*, 57–9, as cited by Bethell, 'English monks', 132.

more certain: on the death of Anselm, William Rufus is said to have confiscated 'the mother church of the whole of England, Scotland, Ireland, and the neighbouring isles'; at Rockingham in 1095 the bishops say to the king 'Anselm is primate not only of this kingdom but also of Scotland, Ireland, and the neighbouring isles'.[108] Eadmer's phrase 'neighbouring isles' is redolent of the prologues of the tenth-century royal charters, and it is scarcely necessary to emphasize how much Eadmer and his contemporaries drew inspiration from the golden age of King Edgar.[109] In 1098, according to Eadmer, Pope Urban II called Anselm 'almost our equal, since he is pope and patriarch of the "second world" (*alterius orbis*)'.[110] In 1119 Anselm's successor, Archbishop Ralph d'Escures, in the course of a long letter outlining the rights and dignities of Canterbury to Pope Callistus II on his accession, argued that the see of Canterbury had responsibility 'for the Irish who inhabited the island of Ireland next door to Britain' because it had been given to Augustine's successor, Laurence, as he had read in Bede, and that from that time the church of Canterbury had never ceased in its pastoral care and primacy of Britain and Ireland.[111] The belief then that the archbishops of Canterbury could claim primacy over the Irish Church on the basis of inherited rights from the pre-Conquest period was certainly current at Canterbury by the early twelfth century.

Apart from Canterbury, this belief is most clearly attested at Worcester. In the so-called *Altitonantis* charter alleged to have been granted to Worcester abbey by King Edgar (959–73) the king is made to state: 'To me God has conceded together with the Empire of the English all the islands of the ocean with their most fierce kings as far as Norway, and has subjected the greater part of Ireland with its most noble city of Dublin to the kingdom of the English.'[112] The earliest authority for this charter is an early twelfth-century manuscript of Worcester

---

[108] Eadmer, *Historia novorum*, 26; cf. also 63, 189.

[109] Cf. Southern, *St Anselm*.

[110] Eadmer, *The life of St Anselm, archbishop of Canterbury*, ed. R. W. Southern (Oxford, 1962), 105.

[111] *Historians of the church of York*, ed. Raine, ii. 236.

[112] Printed most recently in *The Worcester cartulary*, ed. R. R. Darlington (Pipe Roll Society, NS 38; London, 1962–3), 4–7, which gives details of earlier editions; cf. P. H. Sawyer, *Anglo-Saxon charters: an annotated list and bibliography* (London, 1968), no. 731.

provenance. Not surprisingly, doubts have been raised about the authenticity of the text. Although no scholar has been prepared to accept the charter as genuine in its entirety, some would argue for a core text which is authentic.[113] If the reference to King Edgar's overlordship over the greater part of Ireland, and Dublin in particular, did not form part of a possible tenth-century original charter, it can at least be said to throw light on beliefs in early twelfth-century Worcester. If it is not genuine, it must have been inspired by notions of an *imperium* exercised by Edgar in the tenth century which was believed to have included Ireland.

That King Edgar did indeed have maritime interests in the Irish Sea province is attested by the submission of a number of petty kings who rowed him on the river Dee in 973 (including possibly an Hiberno-Norse king), a fact which was certainly known at Worcester in the early twelfth century.[114] Eric John has suggested that the origins of shipsoke may go back to Edgar's reign; he did not rule out the possibility that Edgar may have taken his shipfyrd to Dublin on an expedition before 964.[115] The links between the Vikings of Dublin and York would certainly have provided a motive for such an expedition.[116] Janet Nelson gathered convincing evidence for hegemonic pretensions during Edgar's reign, and contends that the ceremony which Edgar underwent in Bath in 973 was not a delayed royal coronation but an imperial coronation.[117] And

---

[113] E. John, *Land tenure in early England* (Leicester, 1960), 80–139, 162–7. See also the comments of P. H. Sawyer, 'Charters of the reform movement: the Worcester archive', in *Tenth-century studies*, ed. D. Parsons (London, 1975), 84–93. It is surely significant, as Darlington pointed out in *The Worcester cartulary*, p. xv, that the text, or a similar one, is not to be found in the late eleventh-century Hemming's cartulary. Darlington suggested that the text was fabricated about 1136–9.

[114] Aelfric, *Life of Swithun*, trans. D. Whitelock (London, 1955), 853; *Anglo-Saxon Chronicle*, A version, s.a. 973, E version, s.a. 972; Florence of Worcester, *Chronicon ex chronicis*, ed. B. Thorpe (English Historical Society, London, 1848–9), ii. 142–3. The 'Maccus plurimarum rex insularum' of Florence of Worcester has been identified as Magnus mac Arailt, who is mentioned in *AFM* as taking part in an action at Inis Cathaig in 974, that is Magnus, son of Harold, son of Sitric, lord of Limerick, died 896, son of Ivar who ruled in Dublin about 853–73; G. Broderick, 'Irish and Welsh strands in the genealogy of Godred Crovan', *Journal of the Manx Museum*, 8 (1980), 32–8 (at 32). See also D. Hill, *Atlas of Anglo-Saxon England* (Oxford, 1981), 61–2.

[115] Eric John in J. Campbell (ed.), *The Anglo-Saxons* (London, 1982), 172–3, 255.

[116] See Smyth, *Scandinavian York and Dublin*.

[117] 'Inauguration rituals', in P. H. Sawyer and I. N. Wood (edd.), *Early medieval kingship* (Leeds, 1977), 50–71 (at 63–70).

James Campbell has pointed out how the saints reputedly assembled at Edgar's favoured monastery of Glastonbury, where he was buried, namely Patrick, David, Gildas, and Aidan, may also be said to reflect British imperial ambitions.[118] Possible links between the Hiberno-Norse settlements and Cnut's Anglo-Danish empire may have helped to crystallize the notion that the *imperium* of the tenth-century English kings had extended to Ireland, or at least to the Hiberno-Norse cities.[119]

The *Altitonantis* charter has to be viewed against the background of the close relations between Worcester and the see of Dublin on the one hand, and between Worcester and Canterbury on the other, in the eleventh and twelfth centuries. Gilla Pátraic, bishop of Dublin (1074–84), was a former pupil of the school of Worcester.[120] That Worcester's interest in Dublin was sustained beyond his lifetime is indicated by the fact that the chronicler, John of Worcester, recorded details of the consecration of Gréne as bishop of Dublin by Ralph, archbishop of Canterbury, in 1121, taking the information from Eadmer's *Historia novorum*.[121] Eadmer's contacts with Worcester at about the very time that the *Altitonantis* charter was being copied, if not actually formulated, deserve notice. Eadmer wrote a life of St Oswald for the Worcester community.[122] In his life of St Dunstan of Canterbury, among the reasons which Eadmer adduced to justify his new version were two mistakes about Worcester made by Dunstan's previous biographer, mistakes which, Eadmer said, had been pointed out to him by friends from the Worcester community.[123] At least one of Eadmer's friends at Worcester can be named: Nicholas, a monk of Worcester, was sent to Canterbury by St Wulfstan, bishop of Worcester, to train under Lanfranc. He returned about 1113 to become prior of Worcester, and until his death in 1124

---

[118] 'Some twelfth-century views of the Anglo-Saxon past', *Peritia*, 3 (1984), 131–50 (at 139).

[119] Above, pp. 10–11.

[120] See *The writings of Bishop Patrick*, ed. Gwynn.

[121] *The chronicle of John of Worcester*, ed. J. R. H. Weaver (Anecdota Oxoniensia, Oxford, 1908), s.a. 1121; *Annales monastici*, ed. Luard, iv. 380. The survival of Pope Gregory VII's letter to Toirdelbach Ua Briain in BL MS Cotton Claudius A 1 and Lanfranc's letter to Bishop Domnall Ua hÉnna in BL Cotton Vespasian E. iv, ff. 204–6, two Worcester manuscripts, may also be noted.

[122] Southern, *St Anselm*, 283–6.

[123] *Memorials of St Dunstan*, ed. W. Stubbs (Rolls series, London, 1874), lxvii, 162–4.

remained in correspondence with Eadmer, whom he had known at Canterbury. A letter written by Nicholas to Eadmer actually asserted that King Edgar had subjugated Dublin.[124]

In view of the close contacts between Canterbury and Worcester in the early twelfth century it is hardly surprising to find an interpretation of the 'orbis Britanniae' as including Ireland in both Eadmer and the *Altitonantis* charter. Whatever the origins and contributory factors to the belief that the *imperium* of the Anglo-Saxon kings had included Ireland, there seems little doubt that this view was held in certain ecclesiastical circles in England by the early twelfth century and that it went hand in hand with the notion that Canterbury could claim primacy over the Irish Church.

The *imperium* attributed to the tenth-century English kings could be and was exploited not merely in the ecclesiastical sphere but also for secular political purposes to enhance the prestige of the kings of England in the eleventh and early twelfth centuries. An early eleventh-century illustration comes from the duchy of Normandy. Dudo of St Quentin, the historian of the Norman duchy, wrote a panegyric about 1015–16 of Duke Richard II (995–1026). As an oblique form of compliment to the duke, Dudo put the following speech into the mouth of one of the followers of the French king in order to try and incite him to attack the duke:

It is unworthy of your authority that the duke has authority over the Burgundians, that he reproves and threatens the Aquitanians, rules and governs the Bretons and Normans, threatens and devastates the Flemish, wins over and allies with the Danes and Lotharingians and even the Saxons. The English also are obediently subject to him and the Scots and Irish are ruled under his protection (*patrocinio reguntur*).[125]

---

[124] 'Super omnem Angliam et Scottiam et universas insulas circumque positas et usque ad Dublinam Hiberniae civitatem cujus etiam regem sibi subjugaverat imperium potentissime protendit': ibid. 422–3. The letter was written in reply to a question of Eadmer, and since Eadmer included its information in his 'Life of Dunstan' it probably belongs to the time when he was writing that life, that is around 1105–9: Southern, *St Anselm*, 279–84, 369; cf. *Vita Wulfstani*, ed. Darlington, p. xxxviii; D. Knowles, *The monastic order in England* (London, 1940), 159–71. On the links between Canterbury and Worcester in the twelfth century see M. Brett, 'John of Worcester and his contemporaries', in R. H. C. Davis *et al.* (edd.), *The writing of history in the Middle Ages* (Oxford, 1981), 101–26 (at 111–13).

[125] R. H. C. Davis, *The Normans and their myth* (London, 1976), 62. Cf. E. Searle, 'Fact and pattern in heroic history: Dudo of St Quentin', *Viator*, 15 (1984), 119–37.

One of Dudo's objectives was to stake a Norman claim to the crown of England. The duke did not, of course, exercise authority over the English, but Dudo clearly thought that if he had done so it would have given him *patrocinium* over the Scots and Irish as well.

After the Norman Conquest of England in 1066 the Norman kings exploited the concept of an old English overlordship of Britain and the surrounding islands for their own ends.[126] William of Poitiers eulogized William the Conqueror as an *imperator*, arguing that he had conquered Britain where Caesar himself had failed.[127] That Norman propaganda in the reign of William the Conqueror asserted that Ireland was part of the *imperium* inherited by William is suggested by the remark of the Anglo-Saxon Chronicler at William's death in 1087 that, had he lived a year or two longer, he would have subjugated Ireland.[128] There were sound practical reasons why William might have contemplated a conquest of Ireland,[129] but he may have exploited the *imperium* attributed to the English kings in order to justify his intention.

Gerald of Wales related that William Rufus (1087–1100) also considered a conquest of Ireland. Gerald depicted the king standing at St Davids Head, looking across to Ireland and boasting that he would conquer it.[130] There is no corroborative

---

[126] Le Patourel, *Norman empire*, 319–35.   [127] Ibid. 323 n. 1.

[128] *Anglo-Saxon Chronicle*, E version, s.a. 1086.   [129] Below, ch. 2 n. 49.

[130] *Gir. Camb. op.* vi. 108–9, viii. 290. Gerald depicted *Murchardus*, ruler of Leinster, being informed of William Rufus's plans and piously asking whether William had added 'God willing', and on being told that William had not mentioned God at all replying that he had no reason to fear a conquest by William. The name *Murchardus* creates a difficulty. There was no king of Leinster with the forename of Murchad or Muirchertach during the reign of William Rufus (1087–1100). In the 12th century, however, when Gerald was writing, the surname of the kings of Leinster was Mac Murchada, and Gerald may have chosen this name for the king of Leinster to give a semblance of authority to his anecdote, to introduce what folklorists term a 'verification factor', a technique which Gerald certainly used in his *Topography of Ireland*. On the other hand it is possible that there is confusion here with Muirchertach Ua Briain, who was high-king of Ireland during the reign of William Rufus. Eadmer reported that William Rufus refused to invoke saints: E. A. Freeman, *The reign of William Rufus* (Oxford, 1882), i. 166. There is a curious entry in Hanmer's chronicle, repeated by Geoffrey Keating, that in 1098 William Rufus sent to Ireland for timber with which to roof Westminster Hall, which may indicate some contact with Ireland: *Ancient Irish histories of Spencer, Campion, Hanmer and Marleburgh*, ed. J. Ware (Dublin, 1809), ii. 194–5; Keating, *Foras feasa*, iii. 294–5. A request for timber appears in at least one twelfth-century Irish source as a form of tribute, demanded by an overking from a subordinate; the king of Leinster is depicted carrying timber to Brian Bóruma's court; see

evidence that William Rufus visited St Davids Head as king, though he may have accompanied his father on his journey to St Davids in 1081.[131] Gerald's ability to invent such a story cannot be underestimated; yet the tale is characteristic of William Rufus, who was prepared to boast of grandiose schemes, even if he never executed them. Suger, the biographer of Louis VI, recorded that it was commonly said that William Rufus aspired to the kingdom of the French; he was also prepared to consider a scheme for the annexation of Poitou, if not Aquitaine.[132] Gerald's story may reflect that the idea of a conquest of Ireland, which may have been mooted in the time of the Conqueror, was still in the air in the reign of William Rufus. There would also have been practical grounds for William Rufus to contemplate intervention in Ireland as a means of checking Irish support for the Welsh princes, which was causing difficulties for the Norman advance into Wales at that time.[133]

Last but not least, claims to overlordship of Ireland for the kings of England were to be vested with even greater antiquity when Geoffrey of Monmouth attributed to King Arthur a conquest of Ireland, in his *Historia regum Britanniae* completed some time before 1138.[134]

It is possible that claims to quasi-imperial authority on behalf of the Norman kings were actively fostered at Canterbury as a correlative to Canterbury's own claims to primacy, which were thought to derive support from the *imperium* of the old English kings. Both William the Conqueror and William Rufus apparently were prepared to indulge such pretensions. Canterbury's wider aspirations to a British patriarchate suffered

---

Cog. Gaedhel, clxi, 142–3. According to the Chronicle of Man, Magnus, king of Norway, compelled the men of Galloway in 1098 to cut timber for the construction of fortresses: *Chronica regum Mannie et insularum*, ed. G. Broderick (Belfast, 1979), 34. In 1103 Magnus called at Anglesey and collected timber: *Brut Hergest*, 44–5; *Brut Peniarth*, 24.

[131] F. Barlow, *William Rufus* (London, 1983), 37; see below, ch. 2.

[132] Suger, *Vie de Louis VI le Gros*, ed. H. Waquet (Paris, 1964), 10–11; Freeman, *Reign of William Rufus*, ii. 313–14; Barlow, *William Rufus*, 416–19. Cf. J. O. Prestwich, 'The military household of the Norman kings', *EHR* 96 (1981), 1–35 (at 26).

[133] Below, pp. 63–6.

[134] Geoffrey of Monmouth, *Historia regum Britanniae*, iii. 12, ix. 10, 12, ed. A. Griscom (London, 1929), 292, 445, 451–2. Gerald of Wales, *Expugnatio*, 148–9, cited the *Historia Britannica* as providing one of the fivefold rights of the English king over Ireland. Cf. also William of Newburgh, i. 166, writing on Anglo-Norman intervention in Ireland: 'for what the Britons assert as to Ireland having been under the subjugation of their Arthur is merely fabulous'.

a setback, however, after Henry I reached a reconciliation with Thurstan, archbishop of York, in 1120.[135] Thereafter, the king lost sympathy with Canterbury's more extravagant claims. Coincidentally, in the secular context, Henry began to rely increasingly on peaceful relations with King David of Scotland and political quiescence in Wales.[136] Coupled with the emergence of stronger rulers in Scotland, Wales, and Ireland in the first half of the twelfth century, and papal willingness to acknowledge those rulers and their aspirations for independent Churches within their dominions, this represented a serious blow to Canterbury's assertions of primacy over a widely defined British patriarchate.

From his accession in 1135 King Stephen faced the prospect of a war of succession resulting from the rival claim of Matilda, daughter of Henry I, and her husband, Geoffrey of Anjou. The weakness of King Stephen's political position, especially after his humiliating capture by his Angevin rivals at Lincoln in 1141, only gave further stimulus to Welsh and Scottish ecclesiastics to loosen their ties with Canterbury at a time when the archbishop of Canterbury could not draw on royal support to defend his claims. This broadly remained the position until Stephen's death in 1154. The synod of Kells in 1152 was held at an opportune time, when, if they had wished to do so, neither the archbishop of Canterbury nor the English king was in a particularly strong position to voice Canterbury's claims in relation to the Irish Church. At that time, furthermore, relations between Archbishop Theobald and the king were strained by the fact that Theobald was refusing to crown Stephen's heir, Eustace, as king.[137] It is probably no coincidence that, although the scheme for a national diocesan structure for the Irish Church had been formulated as early as 1111 at the synod of Ráith Bressail, although there had been a native papal legate resident in Ireland almost continuously for half a century,[138] although St Malachy had requested *pallia* for the Irish archbishops from the pope in person in 1140,[139] the

---

[135] Above, p. 27.
[136] See Hollister and Keefe, 'The making of the Angevin empire', 5–6.
[137] Saltman, *Theobald*, 37–8. From about 1150 Archbishop Theobald was distancing himself from King Stephen, and by 1153 he had joined the Angevin faction.
[138] A. Gwynn, 'Papal legates in Ireland during the twelfth century', *IER* 58 (1944), 361–70.   [139] Above, p. 32.

Irish diocesan structure was not ratified by the papacy until 1152, that is at a time when little effective opposition could be mounted either by Canterbury or the English king.

The accession of Henry II in 1154 may have seemed to Archbishop Theobald an opportune time to enlist royal support for Canterbury's primatial pretensions. Previous experience had shown that little could be achieved without royal support. The church of Canterbury may have appealed to Henry II on the basis of a primacy it claimed over the Irish Church, but that primacy was grounded at least in part on the overlordship believed to have been exercised by English kings in the tenth century, which in some circles was deemed to have included Ireland. Consequently, it is possible that arguments in favour of Henry's intervention in Ireland were presented not only in terms of the interests of Canterbury, but that an appeal to existing rights of the king of England to overlordship of Ireland was also made.[140]

Evidence is slight, but John of Salisbury's account of his procural of authorization from Pope Adrian IV for intervention in Ireland by Henry II is suggestive. John of Salisbury, whose comments on the synod of Kells and Cardinal Paparo's mission to Ireland in 1152 have already been noted,[141] had joined the household of Archbishop Theobald of Canterbury in 1147.[142] It was at his request shortly after the council of Winchester that Adrian IV made a grant to Henry II and his successors of the island of Ireland.[143] Ullmann has argued that

---

[140] That ecclesiastics might employ secular political arguments to further their cause is instanced by Lanfranc's arguments to William the Conqueror that the archbishop of York should make a profession of obedience to Canterbury, not merely because custom demanded it, but also because 'it was expedient for the union and solidarity of the kingdom that all Britain should be subject to one primate': Hugh the Chantor, *The history of the church of York, 1066–1127*, ed. C. Johnson (London, 1961), 3.

[141] Above, pp. 36–7.   [142] Saltman, *Theobald*, 169–73.

[143] Text in Sheehy, *Pontificia Hib.* i, no. 4. John of Salisbury may have helped to draft *Laudabiliter*. Cf. Peter of Celle's letter in which he referred to a papal privilege which John procured from him 'quod tu ipse vidisti et partim fabricasti': John of Salisbury, *Letters*, 255; M. Richter, 'The first century of Anglo-Irish relations', *History*, 59 (1974), 195–210 (at 206–9), made the point that John of Salisbury could have read the letters of Lanfranc and Anselm, relating to Ireland and the need for reform, in the library at Canterbury. The importance of the libraries of Christ Church and St Augustine's at Canterbury for John of Salisbury's classical scholarship has been emphasized by J. Martin: 'John of Salisbury as a classical scholar', in M. Wilks (ed.), *The world of John of Salisbury* (Studies in Church History: subsidia, 3; Oxford 1984), 179–201; D. Luscombe, 'John of Salisbury in recent scholarship', ibid. 21–37 (at 28–9).

John of Salisbury interpreted *Laudabiliter* not as a papal grant but as a papal confirmation. In John's *Metalogicon*, where he recounted his own part in procuring the papal letter, he stated that the pope 'Henrico secundo concessit et dedit Hiberniam jure hereditario possidendam sicut litterae ipsius testantur in hodiernam diem'.[144] According to Ullmann this passage implies that Henry II already possessed a *jus hereditarium* in Ireland even before the granting of *Laudabiliter*, which merely confirmed that right.[145] In John of Salisbury's account of *Laudabiliter* may be embedded echoes of arguments for pre-existing rights of English kings in Ireland, which may have been rehearsed by ecclesiastics at the council of Winchester in support of a projected conquest of Ireland.

Another justification which the archbishop of Canterbury must have offered, if not at the council of Winchester, then obviously to the pope, was concern for reform of the Irish Church. This may be inferred from the text of *Laudabiliter* authorizing English intervention to promote reform in the Irish Church. Certainly from the time of Lanfranc, Canterbury could cite its interest in the welfare of the Irish Church by quoting the texts of letters urging reform addressed to Irish ecclesiastics and kings. Just as it would be unfair to stress the juridical nature of Lanfranc's claims to primacy of England without acknowledging the undoubted advantages for the progress of reform that ecclesiastical centralization within England could offer,[146] so in regard to the Irish Church Lanfranc and his successors genuinely believed that links with Canterbury would foster reform. Both Lanfranc and Anselm had addressed letters to a number of Irish ecclesiastics and kings, condemning specific abuses, and urging their espousal of reform. The significance of this correspondence in relation to the council of Winchester was that it was preserved in Canterbury manuscripts, where it could be consulted, and cited as evidence both of links between Canterbury and the Irish Church, and of the concern of Canterbury for the Irish Church.

That English ecclesiastics rather than King Henry II were

---

[144] John of Salisbury, *Metalogicon*, ed. C. C. J. Webb (Oxford, 1929), 217.

[145] W. Ullmann, 'On the influence of Geoffrey of Monmouth in English history', in C. Bauer, L. Boehm, and M. Müller (edd.), *Speculum historiale* (Freiburg, 1965), 257–76.

[146] Z. N. Brooke, *The English Church and the papacy* (London, 1931), 119–20.

more likely advocates of a conquest of Ireland in 1155 is suggested by consideration of the circumstances which Henry faced after his accession.[147] He had inherited a kingdom in England in which civil war was brought to an end, but the priority remained the reconciliation of rivals and the settlement of the conflicting claims of the Angevin party and the supporters of the former King Stephen. The country was still armed and strife might readily break out again. The time was hardly propitious for a large-scale military operation to Ireland. Henry, furthermore, began his reign heavily burdened with debt from his Continental campaign of 1153: he would have found it difficult to raise or pay for an army. In his Continental dominions Henry was menaced by the refusal of King Louis of France to recognize him as duke of Aquitaine and by the resentment of his brother Geoffrey at the paucity of his inheritance. King Louis and Geoffrey in alliance could prove troublesome; Henry's estimation of the gravity of the situation is demonstrated by his efforts to raise considerable sums of money in England for the hire of mercenaries on the Continent by levies upon his barons, and by the extraction of what were euphemistically termed 'gifts'. It is conceivable that Henry was momentarily tempted by the notion of enhancing his own prestige and uniting former opponents with his own followers in a conquest of Ireland, and that he may have been prepared to give the project serious consideration, but if so his mother was surely right to dissuade him, as Robert of Torigny says that she did.

Some time between November 1155 and July 1156, John of Salisbury spent three months with Pope Adrian IV, whom he had known when the latter was abbot of St Albans. John returned to England with the bull *Laudabiliter*. Whether he presented it to Henry II, and what the king's reaction was, are not known. Certainly from the standpoint of Canterbury *Laudabiliter* was a failure in that it did not revoke the independence of the Irish Church, which had been ratified by the papacy at the synod of Kells. If it was Canterbury that had proposed a conquest of Ireland in order to associate the king of England with its attempts to re-establish its links with the Irish Church, which had been terminated by the synod of Kells, then the plan

[147] See Warren, *Henry II*, 54–64.

had backfired. *Laudabiliter* permitted a conquest of the island of Ireland by Henry II, but Pope Adrian IV upheld the independence of the Irish Church. The council of Winchester in 1155 and its outcome, *Laudabiliter*, foreshadow Henry II's intervention in Ireland in 1171 only in so far as reform of the Irish Church was raised as justification for a conquest. In 1155 the argument for reform was advanced by the see of Canterbury, whereas after 1171 it was to be promoted by Irish bishops and Henry II, ironically under threat of excommunication for the murder of Thomas Becket, archbishop of Canterbury, and not surprisingly it was to evoke no response from the see of Canterbury.

Canterbury's relations with the Irish Church have been subject to differing interpretations from Irish and English historians. Irish historians have tended to view Canterbury's intentions in regard to the Irish Church as 'distinctly predatory'. Nationalist opinion has been prone to indignation at the 'ecclesiastical imperialism' of Canterbury, which has been seen as but an aspect of English colonialism in Ireland.[148] By contrast, English historians have interpreted Canterbury's interest in Ireland as incidental to the main issue of Canterbury's assertion of primatial authority over the see of York.[149] It was largely in reaction to what he perceived as an unduly nationalist interpretation of Canterbury's involvement with the Irish Church that J. A. Watt was disinclined to allow that Canterbury could have been involved in the promotion of plans for a conquest of Ireland in 1155, and the procural of the papal bull *Laudabiliter*. When, however, Canterbury's relations with the Welsh Church, and more particularly the issue of the metropolitan claims being advanced by Bishop Bernard for the see of St

---

[148] Kenney, *Sources*, 757, 758, wrote of the 'Anglo-Norman ecclesiastical intrusion into Ireland', and of the 'spirit of aggression' and 'imperialism of Canterbury'; cf. also 'Archbishop Lanfranc of Canterbury lost no time in opening what may be fairly described as a wellplanned campaign of ecclesiastical imperialism', Gwynn, 'The first bishops of Dublin', 8; 'that Norman desire to extend its power into Ireland which manifested itself in the efforts of Archbishop Lanfranc to establish ecclesiastical jurisdiction over Ireland', F. X. Martin, 'The first Normans in Munster', *Cork Hist. Soc. Jn.* 76 (1971), 48–71 (at 49); 'After 1066 this interest in the ecclesiastical affairs of Ireland became distinctly predatory', M. P. Sheehy, *When the Normans came to Ireland* (Dublin, 1975), 7.

[149] Barlow, *The English Church, 1066–1154*, 32.

Davids, are taken into account it is possible to reconcile the views of English historians, such as Watt or Barlow, that Canterbury was only peripherally interested in asserting primacy over the Irish Church, with the thesis originally put forward by O'Doherty, and elaborated upon by Bethell, that the procural of *Laudabiliter* in 1155 represented Canterbury's reaction to papal ratification at the synod of Kells in 1152 of the independent diocesan structure of the Irish Church.

The fact that an independent Irish diocesan structure was ratified by the papacy before Anglo-Norman intervention in Ireland meant that it was not subsequently compromised by that intervention.[150] It was unfortunate for the Welsh Church that its leading champion, Bishop Bernard, should have died in 1148 at such a crucial point in the struggle. If the Irish Church had secured papal sanction for its independent diocesan structure in 1140, when first requested by Malachy, it would have made it more likely that Bernard, bishop of St Davids, might have achieved papal recognition of the independent status of the Welsh Church before his death in 1148. Welsh ecclesiastics, and notably Gerald of Wales, were to keep the cause of St Davids alive into the early thirteenth century, but the turning-point which determined its ultimate failure had occurred in 1148. In the case of the Scottish Church the papacy eventually compromised by personally nominating and consecrating the Scottish bishops from 1192.[151] The main beneficiary, therefore, of the concerted attack mounted by Scottish, Welsh, and Irish ecclesiastics against Canterbury's claims to a British patriarchate was the Irish Church.

---

[150] M. T. Flanagan, 'Hiberno-papal relations in the late twelfth century', *Archiv. Hib.* 20 (1976–7), 55–70.

[151] *Scotia pontificia*, no. 156; R. K. Hannay, 'The date of the *filia specialis* bull', *Scot. Hist. Rev.* 23 (1926), 171–7.

Diarmait Mac Murchada's Request to Henry II for Military Aid

HENRY II eventually intervened personally in Ireland in 1171, but the background was very different from that of the proposed conquest of 1155: it has to be sought in Ireland and in the field of secular rather than ecclesiastical politics. In the winter of 1166–7 Henry's attention was redirected to Ireland when Diarmait Mac Murchada, exiled king of Leinster, arrived at his court seeking military aid to regain his kingdom. Diarmait Mac Murchada was not the first Irish king, indeed not even the first king of Leinster, to lose his kingdom and be forced into exile abroad. Bran mac Máel Mórda, former king of Leinster, had died in exile in Cologne in 1052.[1] Donnchad, son of Briain Bóruma, former king of Munster, died in exile in Rome in 1064.[2] The novelty of Diarmait Mac Murchada's exile lay in his seeking a remedy from the king of England. In the autumn of 1166 Diarmait set sail for England, and finding that Henry II was in Aquitaine he travelled on to that region to seek a personal meeting with the English king.

Why did Diarmait Mac Murchada turn to Henry II in 1166? Interpretation of Diarmait's action has been influenced by what one might call, to borrow a phrase from Frank O'Connor, 'the backward look'.[3] T. F. O'Rahilly suggested that in seeking military aid abroad Diarmait Mac Murchada may have been inspired by one of the origin legends of the men of Leinster, namely the story of Labraid Loingsech,[4] a surmise which has been endorsed by F. J. Byrne.[5] Labraid Loingsech reputedly was a member of the royal dynasty of the Laigin in the prehistoric period, who was exiled by Cobtach, king of Ireland,

---

[1] AU 1052. 3; AFM.
[2] AU 1064. 4; Ann. Inisf. 1064. 5; Ann. Tig.; AFM.
[3] F. O'Connor, The backward look: a survey of Irish literature (London, 1967).
[4] O'Rahilly, Early Ir. hist. 116–17.
[5] Byrne, Ir. kings, 9–11, 272–3.

but returned after a twenty-year absence to recover his patrimony with the aid of foreign troops raised in Gaul.[6] The story of Labraid Loingsech would have been known to Diarmait Mac Murchada, and no doubt he would have been prepared to use it for propaganda purposes if it proved apposite to do so.[7] It is possible, however, and indeed more realistic, to seek an explanation of Mac Murchada's action in a less remote past than the prehistoric period. It can be placed plausibly within the context of an aspect of relations between Ireland and Britain in the medieval period which has received less attention than it deserves, namely that of political refugees from Britain seeking asylum in Ireland.

The eighth-century Irish law tracts, in so far as they dealt with exiles from abroad in Irish society, assumed that the typical alien, or *cú glas*, from overseas living in Ireland was an *Albanach*, or Briton, whence derives the medieval Latin *albanus*, or *albanicus*, for an alien.[8] A prominent English exile of the early medieval period was Aldfrith, a member of the Bernician royal dynasty, who enjoyed the hospitality of the southern Uí Néill dynasty, and became king of Northumbria in 685 with Irish support. Aldfrith is unique among English kings in having a distinct Irish personal name, Flann Fína, acquired during his sojourn in Ireland.[9]

From the eleventh century onwards political refugees from Britain gravitated towards Leinster. This was determined by the foundation of the Hiberno-Norse towns of Dublin, Waterford, and Wexford, ports which had a particular attraction for political exiles intent on attempting a restoration of their former position in Britain, since ships to transport mercenaries could be hired there. The most important English political refugees to seek aid in eleventh-century Ireland were members of the powerful family of Godwin, earl of Wessex, formidable

[6] Cf. M. Dillon, *The cycles of the kings* (London, 1946), 4–10.

[7] The Book of Leinster, which contained so much of the official lore of Leinster, was compiled, if not under the actual patronage of Diarmait Mac Murchada, by men who supported him.

[8] T. M. Charles-Edwards, 'The social background to Irish *peregrinatio*', *Celtica*, 11 (1976), 43–59 (at 47).

[9] The name derived from his Irish mother, Fín, a member of the southern Uí Neill dynasty, whom Aldfrith's father, Oswiu, had married, which in part explains Aldfrith's taking refuge in Ireland: H. Moisl, 'The Bernician royal dynasty and the Irish in the seventh century', *Peritia*, 2 (1983), 103–26.

rivals of King Edward the Confessor. In 1051, when Godwin and his sons were banished by Edward the Confessor from England, two of his sons, Harold and Leofwine, fled via Bristol to Ireland, where they raised a fleet, and returned to England in 1052 to launch attacks on the Devonshire, Somersetshire, and Kentish coasts.[10] The life of Edward the Confessor reveals that they received hospitality at the court of Diarmait mac Máel na mBó, king of Uí Chennselaig and of Leinster (1042–72), and great-grandfather of Diarmait Mac Murchada.[11] The approval of Diarmait mac Máel na mBó would have been desirable for the hiring of a fleet in Dublin in 1051; by 1052 it would have become essential, for in that year Diarmait expelled Echmarcach, son of Ragnall, the Hiberno-Norse king of Dublin, and established his own son, Murchad, as king in the city.[12] It was undoubtedly because Diarmait mac Máel na mBó had access to the Hiberno-Norse fleets, not just of Dublin, but also Wexford and possibly Waterford, that the sons of Earl Godwin made their way to his court in 1051.

After the battle of Hastings in 1066, the sons of the slain King Harold, son of Earl Godwin, likewise sought aid from Diarmait mac Máel na mBó. 'He and the princes of his kingdom gave them support', according to Orderic Vitalis, and with Irish ships they mounted an expedition to England in 1068 and another in 1069.[13] Indirect corroboration of the presence at Diarmait's court of these English refugees comes from the Annals of Inisfallen, which recorded that the battle standard of the king of the Saxons was bestowed by Diarmait, king of Leinster, on Toirdelbach Ua Briain, king of Munster, in 1068.[14]

---

[10] *Anglo-Saxon Chronicle*, 1051, 1052, C, D, E versions (the D version recorded that Ealdred, bishop of Worcester, was instrumental in allowing Harold to escape to Ireland); Florence of Worcester, *Chronicon ex chronicis*, i. 207–8. For links between Worcester and Dublin in the eleventh century see above, pp. 15–17, 44–7.

[11] *Vita Edwardi*, ed. F. Barlow (London, 1962), 25.

[12] Ó Corráin, 'Career of Diarmait', 31.

[13] Orderic Vitalis, *Historia ecclesiastica*, ii. 224; *Anglo-Saxon Chronicle*, 1067, 1068, 1069; Florence of Worcester, *Chronicon ex chronicis*, ii. 2–3; Symeon of Durham, *Historical works*, ii. 186; *Annales monastici*, ed. Luard, ii. 28; E. A. Freeman, *The history of the Norman conquest of England*, iv (Oxford, 1879), 224–7, 791–3; B. Hudson, 'The family of Harold Godwinson and the Irish sea province', *RSAI Jn.* (1979), 92–100.

[14] *Ann. Inisf.* 1068. 5. Cf. Diarmait mac Máel na mBó's obit in *Ann. Tig.* 1071, where he is described as 'rí Breatan ocus Indsi Gall ocus Atha Cliath ocus Leithi Mogha Nuadhad'. The possibility that when Diarmait gained control of Dublin he also took

Diarmait must himself have received this object as a gift from the sons of Harold, and in turn bestowed it on the king of Munster as *tuarastal*, a ceremonial gift, designed to emphasize his superior status and, in this instance, his contacts abroad.[15] The fact that in 1066 Harold's sons chose Ireland as a refuge, and specifically the court of Diarmait, must have been conditioned by the previous aid which the Godwinson family had received there in 1051–2. Gytha, wife of Godwin, earl of Wessex, and mother of King Harold, would have known that her husband and sons had received valuable assistance from Ireland in 1051–2. It may have been she who encouraged her grandsons to explore that source again in 1066.[16]

There is some evidence to suggest that Gytha was the main inspiration behind the refusal of the Godwinson family to accept the defeat at Hastings as final, and their mounting of a counter-offensive against the Conqueror. While Harold's sons went to Ireland directly after the battle of Hastings, Gytha sought to organize a base around Exeter and in the West Country, where the Godwinson family had extensive estates.[17] She may also have explored the possibility of seeking military aid from her nephew, Swein Estrithson, king of Denmark.[18] William of Poitiers said that after Hastings overtures were made to the Danes and others, and that from the winter of 1067 a Danish invasion of England was feared.[19] It is possible that Gytha planned a concerted attack on England from Denmark

over a sphere of political influence which included North Wales has been raised by W. Davies, *Wales in the early Middle Ages* (Leicester, 1982), 196.

[15] On *tuarastal* see below, pp. 180–2.

[16] King Harold had taken as his second wife Ealgyth, daughter of Earl Aelfgar of Mercia, who also took refuge and raised military aid in Ireland in 1055 and 1058; see below, p. 61. Ealgyth was the widow of Gruffydd ap Llewelyn, Earl Aelfgar's former political ally: Orderic Vitalis, *Historia ecclesiastica*, ii. 138, 217; William of Jumièges, *Gesta Normannorum ducum*, ed. J. Marx (Rouen, 1914), 192. Ealgyth via her father's and her first husband's careers would have been aware that Ireland afforded a potential recruiting-ground for mercenaries.

[17] Freeman, *History*, iv. 140–59, 750–3; A. Williams, 'Land and power in the eleventh century: the estates of Harold Godwinson', *Proceedings of the Battle Conference on Anglo-Norman studies*, ed. R. A. Brown, 3 (1980), 171–87.

[18] Gytha's brother, Ulf, had married Estrith, sister of King Cnut, and their son Swein Estrithson became king of Denmark in 1047. See the genealogy in Barlow, *Edward the Confessor*, table after p. 376.

[19] William of Poitiers, *Gesta Guillelmi ducis Normannorum et regis Anglorum*, ed. R. Foreville (Paris, 1952), 264.

and Ireland. If so, King William forestalled her by returning from Normandy to England in the last days of 1067 and making immediately for the Godwinson base at Exeter.[20] After a siege lasting eighteen days the city was taken, and Gytha was obliged to flee to an island in the Bristol Channel. Consequently, when the first Irish expedition arrived in 1068, the secure base in the south-west of England, which Harold's sons would otherwise have expected at Exeter, had been destroyed by the Conqueror's swift reaction to the threat of external intervention on behalf of the Godwinsons. The Irish expedition of 1068 concentrated on the Bristol Channel area, probably because it was in this locality that Gytha had taken refuge after the loss of Exeter. Another expedition from Ireland in 1069, which went to Exeter and the surrounding area, may have hoped to retake this region for the Godwinson family, but it was halted by Brian, son of Count Eudo of Brittany. Yet the threat which the Irish landings posed should not be underestimated: in 1082 the Exeter Domesday recorded nine manors, distributed over a wide area of Devon, which still lay waste as a result of the Irish expeditions.[21]

In 1069 Swein Estrithson launched his long-anticipated attack on England, choosing Yorkshire as his point of entry. It was planned on a vast scale but it came too late. That the original intention may have been to co-ordinate a joint Irish and Danish attack on behalf of Harold is suggested by a speech which Orderic Vitalis put into the mouth of William the Conqueror in 1082 after he had fallen out with his half-brother, Odo of Bayeux; William berated Odo that he had spent time despoiling English churches when he should have been protecting England 'from the Danes and the Irish'.[22] This may be a

---

[20] D. C. Douglas, *William the Conqueror* (London, 1964), 213, depicted William returning to England at the end of 1067 because of a threatened Danish invasion, but on arrival having to divert his attention to the siege of Exeter. His move against Exeter should probably be interpreted as part of William's strategy to forestall a Danish invasion, for William may have calculated that Swein would most likely seek to land at his aunt's stronghold.

[21] Freeman, *History*, iv. 793.

[22] Orderic Vitalis, *Historia ecclesiastica*, iv. 42. Given the close relations between Dublin and York (see above, ch. 1 n. 8) it is possible that Swein Estrithson anticipated further aid from Ireland in 1069. Cf. the remarks which Hugh the Chantor put into Lanfranc's mouth in 1079 about the danger of attacks by the Danes, Norwegians, and *Scotti* on the city of York: Hugh the Chantor, *History*, 3. It is not impossible that *Scotti* may stand for Irish here.

reference back to a potentially dangerous situation which William had faced when he returned to Normandy after the battle of Hastings and left Odo in charge of England. The speech suggests that the Conqueror was only too well aware of the danger which Ireland posed as a haven for English dissidents, and as a place where fleets could be hired readily, and lends credence to the obituary comment of the Anglo-Saxon Chronicle that William had contemplated a conquest of Ireland.[23]

Another subject of Edward the Confessor who took refuge in Ireland was Aelfgar, earl of East Anglia, son of Leofric, earl of Mercia. In 1055 when Aelfgar was banished for treason from England he too went to Ireland, where he raised a fleet of eighteen ships, formed an alliance with Gruffydd ap Llewelyn, king of Gwynedd, and led their combined forces in an attack on the city of Hereford, as a result of which King Edward was obliged to make peace and restore the earldom of East Anglia to him.[24] In 1057, after Aelfgar had succeeded his father as earl of Mercia and was again outlawed for treason, he took refuge once more with his former ally, Gruffydd ap Llewelyn, and in 1058 a major Norwegian attack on England was co-ordinated by Magnus, son of Harold Hardráda, king of Norway, in alliance with Aelfgar and Gruffydd, in which the fleet of Dublin participated.[25]

Even more numerous than the English who took refuge in Ireland in the eleventh century were Welsh political exiles who had been dispossessed either by fellow Welshmen or by incoming Normans.[26] In 1039 King Iago of Gwynedd was deprived of his kingdom and killed by the intruder Gruffydd ap Llewelyn. Iago's family took refuge in Dublin, from where his son Cynan was to mount two unsuccessful campaigns to regain the kingdom of Gwynedd. Cynan had a son, Gruffydd, born in Dublin

---

[23] Cf. above, p. 48.

[24] *Anglo-Saxon Chronicle*, 1055 (C, D versions to Ireland and then Wales, E version to Wales); Florence of Worcester, *Chronicon ex chronicis*, i. 212–14; *Brut Peniarth*, 14; *Brut Hergest*, 25; *Brenhinedd y Saesson*, ed. T. Jones (Cardiff, 1971), 70–1.

[25] *Ann. Tig.* 1058; *Brut Hergest*, 26–7; *Brut Peniarth*, 14; *Brenhinedd y Saesson*, 70–1; *Annales Cambriae*, 25; *Anglo-Saxon Chronicle*, 1058 (D version); cf. S. Körner, *The battle of Hastings, England, and Europe, 1035–1066* (Lund, 1964), 151–4.

[26] See C. O'Rahilly, *Ireland and Wales: their historical and literary relations* (London, 1924); B. G. Charles, *Old Norse relations with Wales* (Cardiff, 1934).

about 1054, whose mother, on the testimony of *Hanes Gruffydd ap Cynan* written about 1170–80, was Ragnailt, daughter of Amlaib, son of Sitric, king of Dublin.[27] The marriage was not mentioned in contemporary Irish sources, but it is indirectly corroborated by an incidental detail in *Hanes Gruffydd ap Cynan*, that Gruffydd was reared on the estate of the monastery of Swords.[28] Although originally in the kingdom of Mide, Swords was by the eleventh century attached to the Hiberno-Norse city-state of Dublin. Descendants of Gruffydd are subsequently recorded holding land in the vicinity of Swords.[29]

Gruffydd made his first attempt to recover his Welsh patrimony in 1075, with an Irish fleet which he had raised with the permission of King 'Murchath'.[30] Almost certainly 'Murchath' may be identified as Muirchertach Ua Briain, who ruled the city of Dublin from 1075 to 1086 under his father, Toirdelbach, king of Munster and high-king of Ireland.[31] The attempt failed and Gruffydd was obliged to retreat back to Ireland, where he put in at Wexford. This may have brought him into contact with Donnchad mac Domnaill Remair, king of Uí Chennselaig (1075–89) and provincial king of Leinster, for the Uí Chennselaig dynasty controlled the Hiberno-Norse town of Wexford. A second expedition to Wales shortly afterwards,[32] possibly with aid provided by Donnchad, failed. A third attempt was made in 1081 with the help of 'King Diarmait', at

[27] *The history of Gruffydd ap Cynan*, ed. A. Jones (Manchester, 1910), 103–5; *Historia Gruffud vab Kenan*, ed. D. Simon Evans (Cardiff, 1977), 1–2.

[28] Ibid.; *AFM* 1035; *Chron. Scot.* 1146.

[29] See E. Curtis, 'The Fitz Rerys. Welsh lords of Cloghran, Co. Dublin', *Louth Arch. Soc. Jn.* 5 (1921), 13–17.

[30] *The history of Gruffydd ap Cynan*, 112–13; *Historia Gruffud vab Kenan*, 6; *Brut Hergest*, 27–8; *Brut Peniarth*, 16; *Brenhinedd y Saesson*, 78–9.

[31] *Ann. Inisf.*, *Chron. Scot.*, *Ann. Clon.*, *AFM* 1075 (O'Donovan inadvertently omitted this entry from the English translation in *AFM*; J. Ryan, 'The O'Briens in Munster after Clontarf', *N Munster Antiq. Jn.* 2 (1941), 141–52 (at 147–52). A. Jones and D. Simon Evans identified 'Murchath' as Murchad, son of Diarmait mac Máel na mBó, king of Leinster, who ruled the city of Dublin under his father from 1052 until his own death in 1070; *The history of Gruffydd ap Cynan*, 163; *Historia Gruffud vab Kenan*, 59. Gruffydd's expedition, however, took place in 1075, when Muirchertach Ua Briain had been installed as king of Dublin under his father Toirdelbach. The form 'Murchath' might be thought to equate more readily with Murchad rather than Muirchertach, but it is used elsewhere in *Hanes Gruffydd ap Cynan* of Muirchertach Ua Briain, high-king of Ireland, where the identification is beyond doubt.

[32] *The history of Gruffydd ap Cynan*, 122–5; *Historia Gruffud vab Kenan*, 12–13.

whose court according to *Hanes Gruffydd ap Cynan* Gruffydd had spent a year, and who provided him with a fleet from Waterford. 'King Diarmait' may almost certainly be identified as Diarmait Ua Briain, another son of Toirdelbach Ua Briain, who appears to have governed Waterford on behalf of his father.[33] In 1081 Gruffydd sailed from Waterford to South Wales, where he allied with Rhys ap Tewdwr, king of Deheubarth, and as a result of a victory over the princes of Gwent, Powys, and Arwystli at Mynydd Carn, north of St Davids, in which Irish mercenaries played a prominent part, he succeeded in restoring the title of king of Gwynedd to his family.[34] His succession in 1081 was to be short-lived; not long afterwards he was captured by the Normans advancing into North Wales. Little is known of Gruffydd's subsequent escape and activities in Gwynedd until 1094, when he fled once again to Ireland, where he raised another fleet. This time his host in Ireland was Gofraid Meránach, king of Man, who about 1091 had

[33] Jones, in *The history of Gruffydd ap Cynan*, 169, identified King 'Diermit' as Diarmait mac Énna, king of Leinster. There were two kings of Leinster with the name Diarmait mac Énna during this period; the first reigned from 1092 to 1098, the second from 1115 to 1117; D. Ó Corráin, 'Irish regnal succession: a reappraisal', *Studia Hib.* 11 (1971), 7–39 (at 23–5). Neither was reigning in 1081 when Gruffydd raised the fleet at Waterford. Waterford was not, as stated by Jones, in Leinster, but in Munster. We should, therefore, expect Gruffydd ap Cynan to seek permission for the hiring of the Waterford fleet from the king of Munster. In 1081 Toirdelbach Ua Briain was not only king of Munster but also high-king of Ireland and, moreover, one who exercised considerable control over the Hiberno-Norse towns. In 1074 he had placed his son Muirchertach in the kingship of Dublin. *Ann. Inisf.* 1080. 4 recorded that 'Diarmait Ua Briain brought a fleet to Wales and took great spoil therefrom'. Almost certainly Diarmait governed Waterford on behalf of his father. After Toirdelbach Ua Briain's death in 1086 Muirchertach, who succeeded him as king of Munster and high-king, faced opposition from his brother Diarmait. In 1092 Muirchertach banished Diarmait to Ulaid, but the following year the two brothers were reconciled as a result of the mediation of prominent ecclesiastics: *Ann. Inisf.* 1086. 4, 5, 7, 1092. 3, 1093. 11. In 1096, when Muirchertach Ua Briain as *rex Hiberniae* wrote to Anselm, archbishop of Canterbury, requesting the consecration of Malchus as bishop of Waterford, his subscription was followed by that of 'Diarmait dux frater regis': Kenney, *Sources*, no. 640. Although Diarmait is not explicitly styled *dux* of Waterford, it may be inferred that he was acting as governor of Waterford in 1096. His death is recorded in 1118 in Cork, another Hiberno-Norse city: *Ann. Inisf.* 1118. 2. In 1119 his sons led a fleet on behalf of the men of Thomond into Ciarraige Luachra, which suggests that they followed in the footsteps of their father as leader of Ua Briain naval expeditions: *Ann. Inisf.* 1119. 4. Cf. *Ann. Inisf.* 1088. 2, which records Diarmait Ua Briain leading a naval force on expedition off the Co. Cork coast.

[34] *The history of Gruffydd ap Cynan*, 124–31; *Historia Gruffud vab Kenan*, 13–16; *Brut Hergest*, 30–1; *Brut Peniarth*, 16–17; *Brenhinedd y Saesson*, 80–1.

succeeded temporarily in taking control of the city of Dublin from Muirchertach Ua Briain, high-king of Ireland.[35] Gruffydd returned to Gwynedd in 1094, but in 1097, when the Normans overran Anglesey, and following the Norman victory of Mon, he was back in Ireland seeking aid, almost certainly this time from Muirchertach Ua Briain.[36] Gruffydd returned from Ireland to recover the kingdom of Gwynedd in 1099, and retained it until his death in 1137.

Gruffydd's achievements as king of Gwynedd after 1099 were considerable but he had spent twenty-five years from his first attempt to retake Gwynedd in 1075 essentially as an adventurer pursuing legitimist claims, principally with the aid of Irish mercenaries, enjoying periods of success, punctuated by spells of defeat and exile. He had been born and reared in Ireland and spent no less than five subsequent periods of exile in that country. His contacts in Ireland had been wide-ranging: he received mercenary aid from Toirdelbach Ua Briain, king of Munster (1068–86) and high-king of Ireland, from Muirchertach and Diarmait, two sons of Toirdelbach, while they were governors of Dublin and Waterford on behalf of their father, from Muirchertach as high-king of Ireland, from Gofraid Meránach, king of Dublin (1090–4), and possibly also from the Uí Chennselaig kings of Leinster. Before his death he is reputed to have sent twenty shillings to Christ Church in Dublin and a similar amount to all the chief churches in Ireland.[37] Gruffydd had also been prepared to have recourse to Ireland in ecclesiastical matters: in 1120 he had threatened the archbishop of Canterbury that if he refused to consecrate Gruffydd's appointee, David the Irishman, for the see of Bangor, Gruffydd would seek a bishop in Ireland.[38]

Gruffydd ap Cynan was succeeded by his son Owain as king of Gwynedd (1137–70); in 1143–4 Owain was to find mercenaries from Ireland, who had played such a prominent role in the restoration of his father, used against him by his own

---

[35] For a possible relationship by marriage between Gofraid Meránach and Gruffydd ap Cynan see Broderick, 'Irish and Welsh strands'.

[36] *The history of Gruffydd ap Cynan*, 131–50; *Historia Gruffud vab Kenan*, 17–27; *Brut Hergest*, 37–9; *Brut Peniarth*, 21; *Brenhinedd y Saesson*, 90–3.

[37] *The history of Gruffydd ap Cynan*, 154–5. Cf. 156–7: 'Welshmen and Irishmen and Danes lamented the decease of King Gruffydd.'

[38] Eadmer, *Historia novorum*, 259–60; *Episc. acts*, i. 97–101.

brother, Cadwaladr, who thereby forced Owain to reinstate him in an apanage.[39] Owain Gwynedd was also prepared to have recourse to Irish bishops in his struggle to resist the intrusion of a Norman nominee into the see of Bangor by either the king of England or the archbishop of Canterbury. In 1139–40 he had opposed the promotion of Meurig to the see of Bangor, who had been consecrated by Theobald, archbishop of Canterbury,[40] and on the death of Meurig in 1161 Owain determined to secure the election of his nominee, Arthur of Bardsey, whom he eventually sent to Ireland for consecration in 1165 after failing to secure the co-operation of Archbishop Thomas Becket.[41] Following the death of Owain Gwynedd in 1170 a disputed succession ensued between his sons. The first victim was Owain's son by an Irish mother,[42] Hywel, who was killed in 1170 by Owain's widow, Christina, and her sons, Dafydd and Rhodri. In 1173 when Maelgwn ap Owain Gwynedd, his son by Gwladus daughter of Llywarch ap Trahaearn of Arwystli, who had received Anglesey as his portion, was expelled by his half-brother Dafydd, he took refuge in Ireland, whence he returned in the following year to challenge Dafydd, albeit unsuccessfully, for the kingship of Gwynedd.[43]

The kings of Powys also used Ireland as a haven during the late eleventh and twelfth centuries. Cadwgan ap Bleddyn, prince of Powys, and his son Owain were among the party which fled with Gruffydd ap Cynan to Ireland after the Norman victory of Mon in 1097.[44] Cadwgan returned from

[39] *Brut Hergest*, 118–19; *Brut Peniarth*, 53; *Brenhinedd y Saesson*, 148–9. Otir son of Otir, a Mac Turcaill, and a Mac 'Cherulf' are mentioned as leaders of the fleet from Ireland. The names Otir son of Otir and Mac Turcaill are both associated with the city of Dublin. The death of Ragnall Mac Turcaill, king of Dublin, is recorded in 1146: *Chron. Scot.*, *Ann. Tig.*, *AU*, *AFM*; see references below, ch. 7 n. 12. For Mac Ottar see *Ann. Clon.* 1134; *AFM* 1142; *Ann. Tig.*, *Chron. Scot.* 1148. [40] Above, p. 34.

[41] *Materials for the history of Thomas Becket*, ed. Robertson, v. 225–38; *Councils and ecclesiastical documents relating to Great Britain and Ireland*, ed. A. W. Haddan and W. Stubbs, i (Oxford, 1869), 364–74; *Episc. acts*, i. 415–33.

[42] Named as Pyfog by Lloyd, *Wales*, ii. 549; O'Rahilly, *Ireland and Wales*, 130; R. R. Davies, *Conquest, coexistence and change; Wales, 1063–1415* (Oxford, 1987), 11; as Fynnod in *Early Welsh genealogical tracts*, ed. C. C. Bartrum (Cardiff, 1966), 97 (1); *Welsh genealogies, A.D. 300–1400*, ed. C. C. Bartrum, iii (Cardiff, 1974), 445. The form Seinioes also occurs: *Historia Gruffud vab Kenan*, p. cxv, n. 323.

[43] *Brut Hergest*, 162–3; *Brut Peniarth*, 69–70; *Brenhinedd y Saesson*, 178–9; Lloyd, *Wales*, ii. 549, 766.

[44] *Brut Hergest*, 37–9; *Brut Peniarth*, 20–1; *Annales Cambriae*, 31; *Brenhinedd y Saesson*, 90–1.

Ireland in 1099 to reach an accommodation with the Normans, but the uneasy compromise was subsequently threatened by the behaviour of his son Owain. In 1109 Owain violated Nesta, daughter of Rhys ap Tewdwr, king of Deheubarth, and wife of Gerald, castellan of Pembroke. Owain first took refuge in an Irish merchant ship anchored in the Teifi estuary and subsequently fled to Ireland, where he was kindly received by Muirchertach Ua Briain, king of Ireland, 'for he had formerly been with him and by him he was reared during the war in which Mona was devastated by the two earls'.[45] On his return from Ireland Owain mounted a number of plundering expeditions into Dyfed and seized Norman captives, whom he shipped as slaves to Ireland. Another period in exile in Ireland followed, but Owain eventually returned to make peace with the Normans and with Henry I, and ruled Powys from the death of his father in 1111 until his own death in 1116.[46]

In 1044 Hywel ap Edwin, king of Deheubarth, was expelled by Gruffydd ap Llewelyn, who sought to make himself master not only of Gwynedd and Powys but also Deheubarth. Hywel ap Edwin sought refuge in Ireland, raised a fleet there, and attempted to retake Deheubarth, but he and a large number of his Irish mercenaries were slain in battle by Gruffydd ap Llewelyn.[47] The sinking of an Irish fleet on its way to Deheubarth is recorded in 1050, but the purpose, or possible employer, of the fleet is not known.[48] In 1088 when Rhys ap Tewdwr, king of Deheubarth, was expelled by Cadwgan, Madog, and Rhiryd, sons of Bleddyn, king of Powys, he fled to Ireland, where he raised a fleet in Dublin and returned to defeat them and retake his kingdom.[49] In 1093, when Rhys ap Tewdwr was killed by the Normans, one Turcaill mac Eola died alongside him; he may have been one of the Dublin Norse

---

[45] *Brut Hergest*, 58–63, 69–75; *Brut Peniarth*, 28–35; *Annales Cambriae*, 34; *Brenhinedd y Saesson*, 108–9.

[46] Lloyd, *Wales*, ii. 417–22.

[47] *Brut Hergest*, 24–5; *Brut Peniarth*, 14; *Brenhinedd y Saesson*, 58–61.

[48] *Brut Hergest*, 24–5; *Brut Peniarth*, 14; *Brenhinedd y Saesson*, 68–9.

[49] *Brut Hergest*, 30–1; *Brut Peniarth*, 18; *Brenhinedd y Saesson*, 82–3. In the year of the battle of Mynydd Carn, William the Conqueror visited St Davids (possibly accompanied by his son William Rufus) and on that occasion almost certainly concluded negotiations with one of the participants, Rhys ap Tewdwr: Lloyd, *Wales*, ii. 393–4; L. Nelson, *The Normans in South Wales, 1070–1171* (Austin, 1966), 35–41. This visit may have focused William's attention on Irish mercenary participation in Wales.

whose fleet had accompanied Rhys on his return from Ireland to Wales in 1088 and who had remained in his employ.[50] Gruffydd, son of Rhys ap Tewdwr, was fostered in Ireland. He may have gone there with his father in 1088, or have been taken there for safety on the latter's death in 1093, but at any rate it was from Ireland that he returned to Wales about 1113 in a bid to regain the kingdom of Deheubarth. He managed to obtain a portion of Cantref Mawr with the permission of Henry I, but in 1127, as a result of charges made against him by his Norman neighbours, he was obliged to seek temporary asylum in Ireland.[51]

Given Irish involvement in native Welsh political struggles during this period,[52] it is not surprising to find contact with Ireland extended to the Norman settlers in Wales. In 1102 Arnulf de Montgomery, who had been granted the lordship of Pembroke by King William Rufus about 1093, revolted along with his brother, Robert, earl of Shrewsbury, against Henry I and in consequence sought a marriage alliance with Muirchertach Ua Briain, king of Munster (1086–1119) and high-king of Ireland.[53] The advantage which Arnulf's Irish bride afforded him was that her father controlled Dublin and Waterford and the fleets of those towns; even more importantly, perhaps, Muirchertach concluded an alliance with Magnus, king of Norway, thereby neutralizing the activities of Norwegian fleets in the Irish sea.[54] Magnus's landing in North Wales in 1098, and his slaying of Arnulf's brother, Hugh, earl of Shrewsbury, must have been still fresh in Arnulf's memory. In 1102 Arnulf's aim was to secure the sea-coast of Pembroke from Irish and Scandinavian attack, thus leaving him an unfettered hand on land against Henry I, and to raise mercenaries in Ireland.[55] Despite

[50] *Ann. Inisf.* 1093. 5; cf. *Brut Peniarth*, 19; Florence of Worcester, *Chronicon ex chronicis*, ii. 31.

[51] *Brut Hergest*, 82–3; *Brut Peniarth*, 39; *Brenhinedd y Saesson*, 124–5; Lloyd, *Wales*, ii. 435.

[52] There are many other references to pirate fleets from Ireland operating off the Welsh coast in the 11th and 12th centuries.

[53] E. Curtis, 'Murchertach O'Brien, high-king of Ireland, and his Norman son-in-law, Arnulf de Montgomery, *circa* 1100; *RSAI Jn.* 51 (1921), 116–34; J. F. A. Mason, 'Roger de Montgomery and his sons (1067–1102)', *R. Hist. Soc. Trans.*, 5th ser., 13 (1963), 1–28.

[54] R. Power, 'Magnus Barelegs' expeditions to the West', *Scot. Hist. Rev.* 65 (1986), 107–32.

[55] Orderic Vitalis stated that Arnulf de Montgomery aspired to a kingdom in

his Irish alliance Arnulf forfeited the lordship of Pembroke, and sought a temporary haven in Ireland before eventually settling in Normandy. Arnulf's relations with his Irish wife's family appear to have deteriorated after he went to stay with them in Ireland.[56] Muirchertach Ua Briain may well have regretted the alliance when he discovered that it led to friction with the king of England: in a letter to Anselm, archbishop of Canterbury, Muirchertach thanked him for interceding with Henry I on behalf of his son-in-law.[57] William of Malmesbury, moreover, wrote that when Muirchertach acted superciliously towards the English for a time, Henry I retaliated with an embargo on shipping between the two countries, which soon caused the Irish king to modify his attitude.[58] The impact of Henry's action would not have been negligible, bearing in mind that Muirchertach, as overlord of Dublin and Waterford, derived considerable wealth from the Hiberno-Norse towns. The degree to which Henry I may have been able to deplete the revenue of the Irish king would depend on the volume of trade between Ireland and Britain at this period. This is difficult to assess, but archaeological evidence from excavations in Dublin suggests that England was the principal source of imported goods.[59] Documentary evidence yields incidental references to Irish trade with Bristol,[60] Chester,[61]

Ireland: *Historia ecclesiastica*, vi. 32–3. This has been accepted unquestioningly and a parallel drawn with Strongbow's acquisition of the lordship of Leinster in succession to Diarmait Mac Murchada in 1171: Mason, 'Robert de Montgomery', 23; cf. Le Patourel, *Norman empire*, 293. In 1166–7, when Diarmait concluded an alliance with Strongbow, the Irish partner was in straitened circumstances; in 1102, when Arnulf de Montgomery entered into a marriage alliance with Muirchertach Ua Briain, the Norman party was not in a position to dictate the terms of the agreement. Muirchertach Ua Briain's relations with Arnulf de Montgomery were a minor chapter in his foreign policy which had little relevance to or influence on domestic politics in Ireland, in marked contrast with the aims and consequences of Diarmait Mac Murchada's alliance with Strongbow.

[56] Orderic Vitalis, *Historia ecclesiastica*, vi. 50–1.

[57] Kenney, *Sources*, no. 644. Cf. the ancedote in Eadmer's life of Anselm of how Arnulf de Montgomery and his men were saved from a hazardous sea crossing after invoking the aid of St Anselm, 'whom we have often seen, to whom we have clung, with whose sacred teaching we are imbued and whose holy blessing we have so often enjoyed': Eadmer, *St Anselm*, 146–7.

[58] William of Malmesbury, *Gesta regum*, ed. W. Stubbs, ii (Rolls series, London, 1889), 488.

[59] Wallace, 'The origins of Dublin'.

[60] Migne, *PL* xlvi. 985–6; A. Gwynn, 'Medieval Bristol and Dublin', *IHS* 5 (1947), 275–86.

[*See opposite page for n. 61*]

York,[62] Exeter,[63] Gloucester,[64] and Cambridge.[65] William of Malmesbury's assertion that Henry I could exercise a measure of control over trade between the two countries is supported by an entry some years later on the pipe roll of 1130, which records that the burgesses of Gloucester apparently had sufficient confidence in Henry I's ability to retrieve money stolen from them while trading in Ireland to offer him a payment of 30 marks to do so.[66]

THE ANGEVIN PARTY AND IRELAND

When King Henry I died in 1135 there ensued a disputed succession between his nephew Stephen of Blois and his daughter Matilda and her husband, Geoffrey, count of Anjou. Stephen secured the crown, but throughout his reign, from 1135 until his death and the eventual succession of Henry II in 1154, England was split into rival political factions. The general pattern of individuals seeking, or deprived of, power in Britain looking to Ireland as a recruiting-ground for mercenaries would lead one to expect that the Angevin faction might do so during the reign of Stephen. Add to this the more specific factor that the major Angevin stronghold in England during Stephen's reign was Bristol, which is known both from archaeological and documentary evidence to have had strong trading links with Dublin during the eleventh and twelfth centuries.[67]

There is indeed indirect evidence to suggest that the Angevin party had contacts in Ireland during Stephen's reign. William of Malmesbury, in his account in the *Historia novella* of the capture by King Stephen's party of the Angevin supporter Robert, earl of Gloucester, at a time when the king himself was

[61] *Liber Luciani de laude Cestrie*, ed. M. V. Taylor (Lancashire and Cheshire Record Society, 54; Manchester, 1912), 44–6 and *passim*; J. H. Round, *Feudal England* (new edn., London, 1964), 465–7.

[62] William of Malmesbury, *Gesta pontificum*, ed. N. E. S. A. Hamilton (Rolls series, London, 1870), 208.

[63] Orderic Vitalis, *Historia ecclesiastica*, ii. 210.

[64] *Pipe roll 31 Henry I*, ed. J. Hunter (London, 1833; facsimile reprint, 1929), 77.

[65] *Liber Eliensis*, ed. E. O. Blake (Camden Society, 92; London, 1962), 107.

[66] J. O. Prestwich, 'War and finance in the Anglo-Norman state', *R. Hist. Soc. Trans.*, 5th ser., 6 (1964), 19–43 (at 31).

[67] Above, n. 60.

being held prisoner by the Angevin party, described how Stephen's supporters threatened to hold the earl of Gloucester a prisoner for life in the stronghold of Boulogne, but Earl Robert 'making light of their threats with a calm countenance asserted that he feared nothing less—a true and resolute response, for he had confidence in the high spirit of his wife, the countess, and the determination of his men, who would send the king to Ireland at once if they heard of any wrong done to the earl'.[68] The implication is that just as Stephen's supporters had a stronghold across the channel in Boulogne, so Earl Robert and his men were confident of finding support in Ireland, if indeed William of Malmesbury is not asserting that they already had a haven there. Such a base would most likely have been situated along the east coast of Ireland and, in view of the strong trading links between the earl of Gloucester's city of Bristol and Dublin, possibly in Dublin itself. Considerable weight may be given to William of Malmesbury's remark, for the patron for whom he wrote the *Historia novella* was none other than Robert, earl of Gloucester, who was also one of the most prominent supporters of the Angevin cause.[69]

Irish ecclesiastics can certainly be shown to have had contacts with Angevin supporters. The relations between St Malachy of Armagh and King David of Scotland, and the latter's contacts with Bernard, bishop of St Davids, have already been noted in the context of possible joint action by the Irish, Scottish, and Welsh Churches against the primatial pretensions of the archbishop of Canterbury about 1139–40.[70] There was an added dimension to these relations, for both King David and Bishop Bernard also supported the Angevin cause.[71] King David was Matilda's uncle; he espoused her cause about 1135, launched military campaigns into England in 1138–9, partly to support Matilda, partly to further his own ambitions, and, after a period of possibly doubtful allegiance, returned to her party in 1141, to which he remained committed for the rest of Stephen's reign. Bishop Bernard was a member of Matilda's entourage between 1141 and 1144.

[68] William of Malmesbury, *Historia novella*, ed. K. R. Potter (London, 1955), 67–8.

[69] R. B. Patterson, 'William of Malmesbury's Robert of Gloucester: a re-evaluation of the *Historia novella*', *AHR* 70 (July 1965), 983–97.

[70] Above, pp. 33–8.

[71] R. H. C. Davis, *King Stephen, 1135–1154* (London, 1967), 56–65.

The Angevin party was associated with both King David of Scotland and Bishop Bernard of St Davids, each of whom aspired to and co-operated for the independence of the Scottish and Welsh Churches from Canterbury. If the efforts of the Irish Church to break its links with Canterbury were co-ordinated with those of the Welsh and Scottish Churches, under the leadership of King David, about 1140,[72] this would have drawn a number of Irish ecclesiastics into contact with the Angevin party. St Malachy of Armagh, for example, must have been sympathetically informed about the Angevin cause during his stay at the court of King David, when travelling to and from the Continent in 1139–40. Matilda's claim to the English throne was discussed at the Lateran council of 1139. Malachy had reached the Continent too late to attend the council, but he must subsequently have received an account of its proceedings. Pope Innocent II did not commit himself to supporting the Angevin claim at the council in 1139, but from the accession of Eugenius III in 1145 the papacy declared openly in favour of Matilda, chiefly because of the influence which Bernard of Clairvaux exerted on Pope Eugenius. There may thus have been a secular political dimension to the opposition which King Stephen raised to St Malachy travelling via England to the Continent in 1147: the king's objections may have been occasioned, not merely by anxiety to safeguard the rights of the English Church, as he conceived them, but also by an awareness of collaboration between those who aspired to the independence of the Irish, Scottish, and Welsh Churches, and of their links with Angevin supporters.[73]

When Malachy had travelled via Scotland and England on his way to the Lateran council he had stopped at York, where the see was vacant following the resignation of Archbishop Thurstan on 25 January 1140, and the impending episcopal election a topical issue. Among the prospective candidates was Waldef, prior of Kirkham, a stepson of King David of Scotland, who was the first choice of the York chapter, and whose candidacy may have been supported by the Scottish king.[74] While

---

[72] Above, pp. 35–8.
[73] H. Gleber, *Papst Eugen III* (Jena, 1936), 68–72, 95–8, 163–6. Cf. 97, 'je mehr Eugen den Grafen von Anjou begünstete, um so schärfer wurden die Gewaltmassnahmen Stephans gegen die Anhänger des Papstes.'

[*See p. 72 for n. 74*]

Malachy was at York, Waldef came to visit him, possibly in the knowledge that Malachy would shortly have the ear of the pope and of St Bernard of Clairvaux.[75] King Stephen, however, was vehemently opposed to the promotion of Waldef because of his close associations with the Scottish court and therefore with the Angevin cause. King Stephen favoured the election of his nephew, Henry of Sully, abbot of Fécamp, who, however, withdrew when the pope refused to allow him to hold both offices concurrently. The canons were then urged to accept another royal nephew, William fitz Herbert, treasurer of York and archdeacon of the East Riding, who was elected in January 1141 under pressure from William of Aumale, earl of York, acting, apparently, on the king's behalf. William fitz Herbert had some support among the canons, but was bitterly opposed by the archdeacons of York, who levelled charges of intrusion against him. As the dispute developed the northern Cistercian and Augustinian abbots, and eventually St Bernard of Clairvaux, became involved and the charges were elaborated to include unchastity and simony. With the help of St Bernard, William fitz Herbert's deposition was eventually procured from the Cistercian pope, Eugenius III. He was replaced by the Cistercian abbot, Henry Murdac, whom Bernard had sent to England to be elected abbot of Fountains in 1144, and who was consecrated as archbishop by Pope Eugenius in person on 7 December 1147.[76] Smarting under this recent failure to secure his candidate for York, King Stephen may have found Malachy's presence in England unacceptable in 1147–8 because of the contacts which Malachy had made on his previous journey in 1139–40, not just at the Scottish court, but also in England with such individuals as Waldef, prior of Kirkham.

The history of the order of Savigny in England during Stephen's reign illustrates ecclesiastical entanglement in the war of succession between Stephen and the Angevins.[77] King

---

[74] D. Baker, 'Legend and reality: the case of Waldef of Melrose', *Studies in Church History*, 12 (1975), 59–82.

[75] Bernard of Clairvaux, *Opera*, 342, and *Life of St Malachy*, 120–2; Symeon of Durham, *Historical works*, ii. 321.

[76] D. Knowles, 'The case of Saint William of York', *Cambridge Hist. Jn.* 5 (1935), 162–77, 212–14; D. Baker, '*Viri religiosi* and the York election dispute', *Studies in Church History*, 7 (1971), 87–100. [77] Davis, *King Stephen*, 102–3.

Stephen had come into contact with the mother house at Savigny when he became count of Mortain in 1113, and proved a generous patron of the monastery and its order. He was responsible for the introduction of the Savignac observance into England, when he founded the monastery of Tulketh in 1124, which transferred to Furness in 1127. Savigny remained the religious order most favoured by King Stephen until 1142, when, as a result of the conquest of western Normandy by Count Geoffrey of Anjou, the mother house fell within the sphere of influence of the Angevin party. This resulted in a split along political lines within the order, the Norman and French houses supporting the Angevin cause after 1142, the majority of English houses remaining loyal to Stephen.

News of the schism within the Savignac filiation had reached the pope by December 1144 at the latest, when Lucius II issued a bull enjoining obedience to the mother house of Savigny on all its daughter houses, the English houses being named in detail. The bull did not prove very effective, for at the general chapter of 1147 only the abbots of Neath, Quarr, and Byland attended from England. It is significant that the lay patrons of Neath and Quarr were respectively Robert, earl of Gloucester, and Baldwin de Redvers, earl of Devon, two of the most prominent supporters of the Angevin party in England.[78] The presence of the abbot of the northern English house of Byland may probably be explained by the fact that this abbey was embroiled in a major dispute with its English mother house, Furness, which remained loyal to Stephen.

From 1142 onwards, as a direct consequence of the rivalry between supporters of King Stephen and the Angevin party, the abbot of Savigny experienced difficulty in exercising authority over the English houses of the filiation. In 1147 St Bernard of Clairvaux intervened to suggest a merger of the filiation of Savigny with that of Cîteaux, in the belief that the stronger Cistercian organization could more forcefully resolve the difficulties. The offer was accepted gratefully by the abbot of Savigny: in the same year the Savignac houses merged with Cîteaux through filiation to Clairvaux. However, the merger was resisted by the English houses for a time, the most vigorous

---

[78] Cf. F. Hockey, 'The house of Redvers and its monastic foundations', *Anglo-Norman Studies*, 5 (1982), 146–52.

opponent being Furness, whose abbot had to be deposed before the union with Clairvaux could be effected.

Two Savignac houses had been founded in Ireland before the schism of 1142, the first in 1127 at Erenagh, Co. Down, from Furness Abbey,[79] the second at Dublin in 1139, founded apparently directly from Savigny.[80] It is not known whether either of these houses took any part in the schism after 1142 or how they reacted to the union of 1147. Erenagh was situated in the diocese of Down, of which St Malachy became bishop in 1124. The foundation lapsed at some unknown date. Did the split in the Savignac order in England after 1142 contribute to Erenagh's difficulties? Would the monks of Erenagh have followed the loyalties of their mother house of Furness and its reaction to the merger of 1147? Did this lead to tensions with St Malachy of Armagh, the local bishop and associate of St Bernard? These are some of the problems which Erenagh could have faced and which might have contributed to its dissolution. There is likewise very little extant evidence about the circumstances of foundation of St Mary's Abbey, Dublin, in 1139. It is not known whether initial contact was made directly with the mother house in Normandy or via Erenagh or an existing English foundation, and whether the Dublin house became embroiled in the schism and perhaps followed the political affiliation of its mother house of Savigny in supporting the Angevin party.

None of this is hard and fast evidence, and it does not really take us beyond William of Malmesbury's remark that the Angevin party intended to send King Stephen as a prisoner to Ireland if Robert, earl of Gloucester, was dispatched by King Stephen's supporters to Boulogne, but it may serve to invest his statement with more authority. It would be rash to assume that contemporaries in Ireland were unaware of the conflict between Stephen and the Angevin party in England. The schism in the order of Savigny which it occasioned provides a possible instance of how that conflict might have spilled over into Ireland. Firm evidence for Irish associations with Angevin supporters emanates from the ecclesiastical rather than the secular sphere, but if the Angevin party did seek help in Ireland

[79] Gwynn and Hadcock, *Med. relig. houses*, 132.
[80] A. Gwynn, 'The origins of St Mary's abbey, Dublin', *RSAI Jn.* 79 (1949), 110–25.

during the reign of Stephen it would most likely have come into contact with Diarmait Mac Murchada, king of Leinster, who exercised overlordship over Wexford and Dublin, and intermittently over Waterford.

Control of the ports of Dublin, Waterford, and Wexford was the crucial factor in determining which Irish king might host political exiles from Britain. From the battle of Clontarf in 1014 until about 1050 the Hiberno-Norse kings were largely free of effective Irish lordship. In the first half of the eleventh century, therefore, the Hiberno-Norse would have been able to hire out their fleets without undue restrictions from an Irish overking. From 1052 until 1072 Diarmait mac Máel na mBó, king of Leinster, was overlord of Dublin,[81] and consequently political refugees who fled to Ireland during this period to hire fleets were to be found at his court. The death of Diarmait in 1072 enabled the Ua Briain dynasty to reassert control over Dublin, which it retained until the collapse of Muirchertach Ua Briain's high-kingship in 1114. Political refugees who fled to Ireland during the period 1072–1114 were therefore most likely to come into contact with the Ua Briain kings, who also had control over the city of Waterford during the same period. In 1118 Toirdelbach Ua Conchobair, king of Connacht and aspirant to the high-kingship, gained temporary control of Dublin. After 1118 Toirdelbach Ua Conchobair was not as successful as the Ua Briain kings had been in maintaining control over the eastern ports, and this facilitated the reassertion of lordship over Dublin by the kings of Leinster.[82]

The first evidence for Diarmait Mac Murchada's influence in Dublin dates from 1137, when he used a fleet of 200 ships from Dublin to attack Waterford.[83] Thereafter, until his exile in 1166 Diarmait was intermittently overlord of the city of Dublin.[84] Dublin's most important trading links during this period were with Bristol and Chester, the two main Angevin strongholds. Consequently, if the Angevin party did look for

[81] Above, ch. 1 n. 9.
[82] Cf. *AU* 1118, 1122, 1126, 1127, 1128; *Ann. Tig.* 1118, 1119, 1125, 1126.
[83] *AFM.*
[84] Cf. *Misc. Ir. annals*, 1139. 3, 1149. 1, 1157. 1; *Ann. Tig.* 1161, 1162; *AFM* 1149, 1156, 1161. In the charter granted by Diarmait to All Saints, Dublin, about 1162 he is styled 'rex Dubliniae': *Registrum prioratus omnium sanctorum iuxta Dublin*, ed. R. Butler (Dublin, 1845), 50.

allies and support in Ireland it would almost certainly have had contact with Diarmait Mac Murchada. Diarmait's request for aid to Henry II in 1166 may have been an appeal to a man whom he had once helped when it was Henry who was endeavouring to gain a kingdom.

It is significant that, when forced to leave Ireland in 1166, Diarmait Mac Murchada made for Bristol, where he appears to have had prior contacts. At Bristol he stayed with Robert fitz Harding, who had been one of the most prominent supporters of the Angevin cause throughout Stephen's reign.[85] It is also perhaps significant that when Mac Murchada did not find Henry in England he was prepared to travel on to the Continent to speak with him in person. It suggests that Diarmait felt he had good reason to believe that Henry would receive him favourably. The fact that Diarmait went to the length of travelling to Aquitaine[86] to seek out Henry II suggests that there may have been earlier contacts between the two men. Whether or not these dated back to Angevin contacts in Ireland during the reign of Stephen, it is certain that Henry II had hired a fleet from Dublin for his Welsh campaign of 1165.[87] That fleet can only have been made available to Henry with the consent of Diarmait Mac Murchada as overlord of Dublin. In 1166, whether because of help given to Henry II in the recent or in the more distant past, Diarmait obviously felt that he had grounds for presuming that Henry would respond favourably to his request for aid to regain his kingdom.

---

[85] *Song of Dermot*, ll. 230–40, 300–10.
[86] On Gerald of Wales's testimony Diarmait Mac Murchada found Henry II in Aquitaine: Giraldus, *Expugnatio*, 26–7. According to the *Song of Dermot*, ll. 241–59, Diarmait sought Henry in Normandy 'up and down and back and forth', and eventually found him in a city of which he was lord, the name of which is left blank in the text. Henry spent the autumn of 1166 in Normandy and moved in December to Poitiers, where he celebrated Christmas. He remained south of the Loire until May 1166, when he returned to Normandy: Eyton, *Itinerary*, 103–6.
[87] *AU*; *Brut Peniarth*, 64; *Brut Hergest*, 146–7; *Brenhinedd y Saesson*, 166–7.

PART II

Anglo-Norman Adventurers
in Ireland

Diarmait Mac Murchada's Offer of the Kingdom of Leinster to Strongbow

IN the autumn of 1166 Diarmait Mac Murchada, deprived of his patrimonial kingdom of Uí Chennselaig and of the provincial kingship of Leinster, sought aid from Henry II. The immediate circumstance leading to Mac Murchada's deposition was a struggle for the high-kingship of Ireland.[1] In 1166 Ruaidrí Ua Conchobair, king of Connacht, challenged the high-kingship of Muirchertach Mac Lochlainn, king of Cenél nEógain and high-king of Ireland (1156–66). Ruaidrí's father, Toirdelbach, had held the high-kingship (1120/1–1156) before the accession of Muirchertach Mac Lochlainn. Diarmait Mac Murchada refused to recognize Ruaidrí as high-king, an office to which he himself aspired. In the ensuing conflict Mac Murchada lost not only the prospect of succession to the high-kingship but also the kingship of Leinster and of Uí Chennselaig. He did not easily accept defeat; although he was fifty-nine years of age he determined to try and regain what he had lost with the help of foreign aid.

Diarmait Mac Murchada sought assistance from Henry II. Henry was not willing to intervene personally in Ireland on Mac Murchada's behalf. He had pressing political problems to contend with in his Continental dominions.[2] Henry did allow permission for Diarmait to hire troops within his dominions. Mac Murchada directed his recruiting campaign towards the Norman settlers and the native Welsh of South Wales. From the geographical standpoint of Leinster and of Uí Chennselaig in particular, that is of Mac Murchada's patrimonial kingdom,

[1] D. Ó Corráin, *Ireland before the Normans* (Dublin, 1972), 163–74; Byrne, *Ir. kings*, 269–74; Curtis, *Med. Ire.* 1–44; Orpen, *Normans*, i. 1–77; Otway-Ruthven, *Med. Ire.* 35–42.
[2] See Warren, *Henry II*, ch. 3.

which had been centred around Ferns (Co. Wexford) and had been his most secure power base in Leinster before his exile, South Wales was the most strategically situated location in which to recruit paid troops. In general, Diarmait Mac Murchada offered money and land by way of recompense for military service, but to one individual, Richard fitz Gilbert, lord of Strigoil, otherwise known as Strongbow,[3] he offered more, namely his daughter Aífe in marriage, together with succession to the kingdom of Leinster after his death.

The conventional interpretation of Diarmait Mac Murchada's offer of the kingdom of Leinster to Strongbow with the hand of his daughter in marriage has been that it was in contravention of Irish law on a number of fundamental points. Mac Murchada's agreement with Strongbow is so presented chiefly because historians of Anglo-Norman intervention in Ireland have assumed that Irish society was highly conservative and bound by immutable legal custom.[4] A more critical approach is needed to the evidence on which the conventional depiction of twelfth-century Irish society is based, before it is possible to assess the extent to which Diarmait Mac Murchada's offer of the kingdom of Leinster marked a radical departure from contemporary Irish practice.

SUCCESSION TO KINGSHIP IN PRE-NORMAN IRELAND

Diarmait Mac Murchada's offer to Strongbow of the kingdom of Leinster along with his daughter in marriage has been interpreted as contravening an Irish law of regnal succession and inheritance which was characterized by elective succession to

---

[3] Although the term has no contemporary authority it is used here for convenience, to avoid confusion with the other Richards of the period.

[4] An extreme instance of this view is A. L. Poole, *From Domesday Book to Magna Carta* (2nd edn., Oxford, 1955), 303: 'She [Ireland] had remained untouched by the advance of civilization which was in the eleventh and twelfth centuries affecting other European societies. While other countries were progressing, Ireland regressed.' More reasoned but misguided is W. L. Warren, 'The interpretation of twelfth-century Irish history', *Hist. Studies*, 7 (1969), 1–19; *Henry II*, 187–206. A qualified version is F. X. Martin's 'Ireland, living its civil [as distinct from ecclesiastical] life for so long in a splendid and warlike isolation': *NHI* ii, p. lix. For a critique of Warren's arguments and a more realistic assessment of twelfth-century Ireland see D. Ó Corráin, 'Nationality and kingship in pre-Norman Ireland', *Hist. Studies*, 11 (1978), 1–35.

kingship or lordship and partible inheritance of property among male descendants of a common great-grandfather. According to Edmund Curtis,

By this marriage Strongbow became heir-in-succession to Leinster at such time as Dermot should die. It was sound enough in feudal law; but in Irish law it was unknown that a man should acquire a kingdom by right of a woman, whether mother or wife. Dermot was setting aside the elective rights of his royal stock and depriving his sons and his brother of their right to succeed him.[5]

More recently, F. J. Byrne argued that 'Diarmait's readiness to overthrow Irish law in order to win Strongbow's support—thereby ignoring the claims of his sons and agnatic kinsmen—can only be explained on the hypothesis that he was aiming at total innovation'.[6] No detailed attempt has been made to explain why Diarmait Mac Murchada was prepared to take such extreme action.

Curtis in his estimation of Mac Murchada's contravention of Irish law was relying on a theory of succession to kingship in pre-Norman Ireland which was formulated by Eoin MacNeill in 1919.[7] MacNeill had proceeded from the premise that 'the law of succession to office would bear the closest possible analogy to the law of succession to property'.[8] According to the eighth-century law tracts the legal family in Irish society was a four-generation kin group, comprising the male descendants of a common great-grandfather, known as the *derbfine*. In theory, land was held in common by this group and, on the death of any one of its members, property was redistributed among the others. Mac-Neill postulated that succession to kingship was modelled on the

---

[5] Curtis, *Med. Ire.* 49; cf. Orpen, *Normans*, i. 91, 'Whatever might be said for the legality of this arrangement had Dermot been dealing with a Norman seignory it was of course inoperative under Irish law whereby the provincial kings were, in theory at any rate, selected by the tribesmen from one or more ruling families'; Otway-Ruthven, *Med. Ire.* 41–2, 'a grave breach in the fabric of native right and custom'; Dolley, *Anglo-Norman Ire.* 56–7, 'In Irish law such a succession would have been unthinkable'; *NHI* ii. 44, 'a startling innovation', 65, 'the kingship he promised Strongbow was not his to give'. The initiative for the marriage proposal is there attributed to Strongbow not Diarmait Mac Murchada.

[6] Byrne, *Ir. kings*, 273–4.

[7] E. MacNeill, 'The Irish law of dynastic succession', *Studies*, 8 (1919), 367–82, 640–53, reprinted in his *Celtic Ireland* (Dublin, 1921), 114–43.

[8] MacNeill, *Celtic Ireland*, 121.

law of private property inheritance which, according to the law tracts, operated within this four-generation kindred group; in other words that within a royal dynasty succession to kingship was confined to members of the *derbfine* of previous holders of the office. Since, however, the office of king, unlike property, was not divisible, MacNeill postulated an electoral procedure whereby one candidate was chosen from among those eligible for kingship in virtue of their membership of a kindred group of a previous king. It is noteworthy that, although MacNeill derived his knowledge of the operation of the *derbfine* within Irish society from the law tracts, these did not provide him with any direct information about the process of regnal succession: nowhere in their exposition of the *derbfine* was there any reference to its possible relevance to succession to kingship.

MacNeill was motivated to formulate a regulatory mechanism for regnal succession in pre-Norman Ireland partly as a reaction to a contemporary scholar, G. H. Orpen, who posited a view of Irish society prior to Anglo-Norman intervention as primitive and anarchic, which he contrasted with the apparent order and customary regulation of feudal society.[9] To counter an impression of pre-Norman Irish society as anarchic, Mac-Neill was anxious to demonstrate that there existed an orderly procedure for succession to kingship in pre-Norman Ireland which was comparable with the practice of primogeniture in feudal society.

MacNeill's postulation of an Irish law of regnal succession gained general acceptance, partly because it had the same attraction for successive early Irish historians as it had for Mac-Neill, namely that it suggested an organized society. Few attempts were made to investigate in detail whether the procedure postulated by MacNeill operated within petty kingships, overkingships, or provincial kingships, and whether it underwent modification or change over a period of time.[10] It is in reliance on MacNeill's construct that historians have categorized Diarmait Mac Murchada's offer of the kingship of Leinster to Strongbow after his death as invalid in Irish law.

---

[9] Cf. MacNeill's criticism of Orpen's views in his *Phases*, especially chs. 10 and 11.

[10] The only detailed study of regnal succession patterns undertaken with MacNeill's law in view was that of J. Hogan, 'The Irish law of kingship with special reference to Ailech and Cenél Eoghain', *RIA Proc.* 40 (1932), 186–254.

In 1971 Donnchadh Ó Corráin reopened for discussion the question of how succession to kingship was determined in pre-Norman Ireland.[11] Ó Corráin's reassessment proceeded from a different premise to that of MacNeill, who had held that succession to royal office would bear close analogy with the law of succession to private property inheritance, namely that kingship is a unique institution to which customary rules for the inheritance of private property do not universally apply. Ó Corráin derived his starting-point from anthropological studies of African societies, which showed that succession to high office was not usually determined by normal rules of inheritance. The regnal succession patterns in the early medieval period among the Frankish and Anglo-Saxon royal dynasties also form useful, if not preferable, comparisons for early Irish society. They suggest that the determination of regnal succession was generally the exclusive concern of the royal family and its supporters, who acted in their own interests and in reaction to pragmatic political circumstances without undue reference to precedent or custom.[12]

MacNeill was misled by historians of feudal society, whom he sought to refute, and particularly Orpen, into drawing an initial analogy between the laws governing inheritance to private property and succession to kingship, in that they assumed that the practice of primogeniture, which regulated inheritance of private property increasingly from the ninth century onwards, also applied to succession to kingship. In reality, the application of primogeniture to regnal succession was a relatively late development; in the majority of European royal dynasties it did not become invariable practice before the thirteenth century.

In order to test MacNeill's thesis, that within a hereditary royal dynasty eligibility for kingship was confined to members of the kindred groups of previous holders of the kingship,

---

[11] Ó Corráin, 'Irish regnal succession'.

[12] I. N. Wood, 'Kings, kingdoms and consent', in P. H. Sawyer and I. N. Wood (edd.), *Early medieval kingship* (Leeds, 1977), 6–29; cf. P. Grierson, 'Election and inheritance in early Germanic kingship', *Cambridge Hist. Jn.* 7 (1941), 1–22; A. Williams, 'Some notes and considerations on problems connected with the English royal succession, 860–1066', in *Proceedings of the Battle Conference on Anglo-Norman Studies, 1978*, ed. R. A. Brown (Ipswich, 1979), 144–67, 225–33; P. Stafford, 'The king's wife in Wessex', *Past and Present*, 91 (1981), 3–27.

Ó Corráin made a detailed investigation of the regnal succession pattern of the Uí Chennselaig royal dynasty from the earliest documentation to 1171. Diarmait Mac Murchada was of the Uí Chennselaig dynasty, which from 1042 also held the provincial kingship of Leinster. Ó Corráin's analysis of the blood relationship of succeeding kings of Uí Chennselaig to their predecessors showed that:

73 per cent could be defined as having belonged to the kindred group of a previous king.

20 per cent did not belong to the kindred group of a previous king, but were members of the Uí Chennselaig dynasty.

7 per cent were of unknown origin, that is, they may have been members of the Uí Chennselaig dynasty, or they may have been outsiders.

A figure of at least 20 per cent, and possibly as high as 27 per cent, non-membership of a *derbfine* of a previous king indicates that MacNeill's 'law of dynastic succession' was not invariably observed within the Uí Chennselaig dynasty.

Of the 73 per cent of kings who could be defined as members of the *derbfine* of a previous king, the relationship was

54 per cent were sons of previous kings.

16 per cent were grandsons of previous kings.

3 per cent were great-grandsons of previous kings.

As Ó Corráin pointed out, the low percentage of great-grandsons is significant, for if MacNeill's hypothesis was correct that succession was limited to members of kindred groups of previous holders of the office, one would expect great-grandsons to furnish a higher proportion of kings, since it would be the last occasion on which they would still be eligible for election in virtue of membership of a *derbfine* of a previous king and they might, therefore, be expected to make aggressive attempts to secure the kingship for themselves and ensure a claim for their successors.

A difficulty with MacNeill's thesis in regard to the role of the *derbfine* stems from the fact that knowledge of the operation of the *derbfine* in the realm of private property inheritance derives exclusively from the law tracts compiled in the eighth century and, indeed, even in the law tracts there is little enough detailed evidence about the working of the *derbfine* in the period up to the eighth century. But next to nothing is known about its operation in society after the eighth century. Obviously, the history of the institution of the *derbfine* in the sphere of private inheritance has an important bearing on assessing its possible relevance to the determination of regnal succession. Ó Corráin took a four-generation kindred group as the *derbfine* throughout his analysis; he did not take into account possible changes in the composition of the kindred group during the extensive period which he covered from the earliest historical evidence down to 1171. D. A. Binchy, the modern editor of the early Irish law tracts, has argued that a narrowing of the kindred from a four- to a three-generation group was taking place during the time when the law tracts were receiving their final written form around the eighth century. The typical family unit depicted in the oldest stratum of the law tracts was the *derbfine* or four-generation group of agnatic descendants of a common great-grandfather. But even before all the law tracts had been written down, a narrower group had emerged known as the *gelfine*, confined to three generations, that is the agnatic descendants of a common grandfather. The more archaic texts refer to the *derbfine* in legal situations where the main strata of texts substitute the *gelfine*. Later scholiasts tried to resolve the inconsistency by glossing *derbfine .i. an gelfine* ('*derbfine* used here for *gelfine*').[13] It is reasonable to postulate, on the analogy of the fate of the kindred group in Anglo-Saxon society, a further narrowing to a two-generation or nuclear family group as the basic social unit.[14] If the *derbfine* was already obsolescent in the eighth century, as Binchy suggested, it is unlikely that an archaic kindred structure would have been preserved within royal dynasties for the sole purpose of selecting a king.

On the evidence of his analysis of regnal succession in the Uí Chennselaig dynasty, Ó Corráin argued that it would be more meaningful to think in terms of lineages rather than kindred groups within an Irish royal dynasty. According to Ó Corráin, Irish royal dynasties 'consisted of polysegmental agnatic lineage

[13] D. A. Binchy, 'The linguistic and historical value of the Irish law tracts', *Brit. Acad. Proc.* 29 (1943), 195–228 (at 221–2); 'Irish history and Irish law II', *Studia Hib.* 16 (1976), 7–45 (at 31–45).
[14] T. M. Charles-Edwards, 'Kinship, status and the origins of the hide', *Past and Present*, 65 (1972), 3–33; H. R. Loyn, 'Kinship in Anglo-Saxon England', *Anglo-Saxon England*, 3 (1974), 197–209.

groups which were constantly being created by polygamic royal marriage and an inclusive rule of legitimacy'.[15] Every male member of a royal dynasty had the potential to form a lineage or segment within the dynasty, and the number of prospective lineages was quite high, since the Church had not succeeded in establishing the concept of the legitimacy of the issue of only one recognized Christian union.

Ó Corráin identified seven main segments of lineages within the royal dynasty of Uí Chennselaig and demonstrated how all but one were gradually eliminated from the kingship, leading to the exclusive monopoly by the Síl nOnchon segment from the mid eleventh century onwards, and within the Síl nOnchon segment to a further restriction to descendants of Murchad (d. 1070) son of Diarmait mac Máel na mBó, from whom the surname Mac Murchada derived, who successfully limited the proliferation of further lineages within the Síl nOnchon lineage.

Ó Corráin concluded that firm evidence for insistence on membership of the *derbfine* of a previous king as a prerequisite for succession to royal office was lacking within the Uí Chennselaig dynasty. The regnal succession pattern suggested rather that every male member of the hereditary royal dynasty was eligible to succeed to the kingship, and that within the hereditary dynasty the determining factors in succession to kingship were not membership of a particular kindred group but of a particular lineage, and within that lineage the degree of proximity of the candidate to the power base of the previous king.

Another feature of MacNeill's law of regnal succession was the postulation of a formal electoral procedure, whereby a candidate was chosen from among the restricted group within the dynasty whom MacNeill held were eligible for the kingship. His belief in a formal procedure for election to kingship in pre-Norman Ireland might be said to be supported by the existence of the terms *rídomna* and *tánaise*, which broadly translate as 'presumptive successor' and 'successor designate'.[16] Ó Corráin queried whether the terms *tánaise* and *rídomna* can be used as

---

[15] Ó Corráin, 'Irish regnal succession', 8.

[16] G. Mac Niocaill, 'The "heir-designate" in early medieval Ireland', *Ir. Jurist*, NS 3 (1968), 326–9.

evidence for the existence of an electoral procedure which operated in every instance when a new king succeeded. He postulated that successor designates may have been named only in exceptional circumstances after a particularly severe power struggle between rival factions within the royal dynasty had occurred, and that acquiescence in the succession of a particular candidate could be assured only by a promise of the succeeding kingship to a member of the rival faction.[17] If this interpretation is correct, it follows that the selection of a successor designate need not have been made on each occasion when a new king was chosen, but only when a severe power struggle took place within a royal dynasty. A strong dynasty, or lineage within a dynasty, which had achieved a monopoly of the kingship would have had no need to make concessions to its rivals. From the mid eleventh century, as Ó Corráin demonstrated, the Síl nOnchon lineage within the Uí Chennselaig dynasty gained an exclusive monopoly of the kingship.

No detailed diachronic analysis of the use of the terms *rídomna* and *tánaise* has yet been made, but they were apparently applied in different senses to individuals of different dynasties at different periods. In Munster the term *rídomna* would appear to have been used of individuals of the Eóganachta royal dynasty who belonged to segments long deprived of office which had no realistic expectation of succession to kingship; it seems to have been used as an honorary designation. Elsewhere, there are instances of the term *rídomna* being applied to individuals who belonged to the lineage of the reigning king and were often also members of his nuclear family and had a realistic expectation of succession.[18] Since the existence of terms connoting 'presumptive successor' or 'successor designate' do not provide firm evidence for the operation of a formal electoral procedure for determining regnal succession in pre-Norman Ireland, there would appear to be no secure basis for the view that Diarmait Mac Murchada ignored the 'elective rights of his royal stock' when he offered the succession of the kingdom of Leinster to Strongbow.

If MacNeill's 'Irish law of dynastic succession' is not appropriate to twelfth-century regnal succession practices within the

---

[17] Ó Corráin, 'Irish regnal succession', 34–9.

[18] As in the case of two of Diarmait Mac Murchada's sons, Énna and Conchobar: see below, p. 96 and nn. 50, 52, 83.

Uí Chennselaig dynasty and, therefore, to Diarmait Mac Murchada's offer to Strongbow of succession to the kingship of Leinster, Diarmait's offer may nevertheless be considered in the light of other factors which can be identified as influencing regnal succession certainly from the eleventh century onwards. From at least the second half of the eleventh century, when annalistic evidence becomes increasingly detailed, there is a discernible tendency for the more powerful king to try to predetermine the regnal succession in favour of a candidate of his choice, usually his son, by associating the chosen individual with him in the kingship during his lifetime in the expectation that he would succeed him after his death. An example of such anticipatory association is provided by Diarmait mac Máel na mBó, great-grandfather of Diarmait Mac Murchada, who ruled the province of Leinster in collaboration with his son Murchad, to whom he delegated responsibility for the defence of the northern frontier of Leinster and control of the Hiberno-Norse city of Dublin. The regnal list of the kings of Leinster in the Book of Leinster described Murchad's position as *rí rí láim a athar*, 'king under the hand of his father'.[19]

Typically, royal office was the monopoly of a hereditary royal dynasty. But the power of individual dynasties did not remain constant. If a dynasty declined, a new and totally unrelated one might forcibly seize the kingship. The seizure of kingship by military force was recognized as one of the possible routes to power in the Irish *Fürstenspiegel*. The seventh-century *Audacht Morainn* referred disparagingly to the 'ruler of occupation with hosts from outside' by contrast with the true ruler.[20]

---

[19] *Bk Leinster*, i. 183; *Ann. Tig.* 1070; *AU, Ann. Clon.* 1069. Cf. Toirdelbach Ua Briain, king of Munster and high-king of Ireland, who installed his son Muirchertach as ruler in Dublin under him in 1075, and was succeeded as king on his death in 1086 by Muirchertach, despite opposition from his brothers, Tadc and Diarmait: see above, pp. 62–3. Muirchertach Ua Briain in turn 'left his own son, Domnall Ua Briain, in the kingship of Dublin': *Misc. Ir. annals*, 1114. 3. Donnchad Ua Cerbaill, king of Airgialla (d. 1168), installed his son Murchad, his eventual successor, as king of Uí Meith under him, as evidenced in the charter granted in 1156 by Muirchertach Mac Lochlainn, king of Cenél nEógain, to Newry Abbey: Dugdale, *Monasticon Anglicanum*, vi. 2. 1133. In 1113 Niall, son of Domnall Mac Lochlainn, king of Cenél nEógain, 'took the kingship of Cenél Conaill': *Ann. Inisf.* 1113. 7. Cf. also below, p. 196.

[20] *Audacht Morainn*, ed. F. Kelly (Dublin, 1976), 19, §§58, 61. Cf. the Middle Irish *Tecosca Cormaic*, which details one of the avenues to the acquisition of rulership as 'the strength of fighting and an army': *The instructions of King Cormac mac Airt*, ed. K. Meyer (RIA Todd Lecture series, 15; Dublin, 1909), 12–13.

A notable instance of a change of dynasty was the displacement of the Eóganachta dynasty from the kingship of Cashel by the Dál Cais dynasty in AD 964.[21] The genealogists frequently went to considerable lengths to conceal such political change by fabricating fictitious relationships between the ousted and the ouster, as they did in the case of the Eóganachta and Dál Cais dynasties. Such adjustment of Irish genealogies to reflect changed political circumstances may have obscured just how common was the displacement of one dynasty by another.

A change of dynasty represented a dramatic form of external intervention in the process of succession to a particular kingship. There was another form of external intervention or deflection of the process by which a successor usually emerged within the hereditary royal dynasty: powerful overkings might intervene to determine regnal succession in subordinate kingships under their influence. Their intervention might take the form of support for one member or faction of the hereditary royal dynasty at the expense of a rival.[22] In the twelfth century there was a notable increase in the imposition by overkings of external candidates who had no hereditary claims to kingship. The continuator of the Annals of Tigernach referred to one such individual, Conchobar, son of Toirdelbach Ua Conchobair, king of Connacht and contender for the high-kingship of Ireland, who was intruded by his father into the kingship of Mide in 1144, as a 'stranger in sovereignty'.[23] When the compiler of the twelfth-century pseudo-historical tract *Cogadh Gaedhel re Gallaibh* detailed the imposition by the Viking leader, Imar, of a *rí*, or king, on every *tír*, and a *toisech* on every *tuath*, as an indication of the Viking oppression of Ireland, it was a contemporary reflex of a relatively common practice.[24] The instances of strangers in sovereignty in the twelfth century are sufficiently common to raise the question of the degree to which membership of a hereditary royal dynasty was an essential qualification for succession to kingship on the eve of

[21] Ó Corráin, *Ireland before the Normans*, 111–17; J. Ryan, 'The Dalcassians', *N Munster Antiq. Jn.* 3 (1943), 189–202; J. Kelleher, 'The rise of the Dál Cais', in E. Rynne (ed.), *North Munster studies* (Limerick, 1967), 230–41.

[22] *Ann. Tig.* 1122, 1125, 1127, 1132, 1152.

[23] *Ann. Tig.* 1144. Cf. *Chron. Scot.*, *AFM*, *Ann. Clon.* 1140 (= 1144); *Misc. Ir. annals*, 1143. 2 (= 1144); D. Ó Corráin, 'Onomata', *Ériu*, 30 (1979), 165–80 (at 167).

[24] *Cog. Gaedhel*, 48–9.

Anglo-Norman intervention.[25] It is a notable feature of twelfth-century royal obituary notices in the annals that in addition to a king's hereditary title he might also be accorded royal titles of kingdoms in which he had managed to assert strong political influence, or into which he had intruded himself, even if only temporarily.[26] In short, there is a discernible development in twelfth-century Ireland towards what might be termed 'occupative kingships' which exhibited scant regard for traditional hereditary claims.

Diarmait Mac Murchada's offer of the kingship of Leinster to Strongbow was not as radical a departure from twelfth-century Irish practices in regard to succession to kingship as some historians have suggested. There is at best insufficient evidence that succession to the kingship of Uí Chennselaig was confined by law to certain individuals within the royal dynasty, and regulated by an invariably observed electoral procedure which Diarmait Mac Murchada had no right to pre-empt. Nor was Diarmait's action of determining the succession to the kingship of Leinster by offering it to Strongbow during his lifetime an instance for which there was no precedent. If Diarmait's choice had not been Strongbow, he would certainly have tried to select another individual within his own lifetime. Typically, his choice would have fallen on a close male relative, and ideally a son. Diarmait's offer to Strongbow may be placed in a context where direct male descent within a hereditary royal dynasty was not invariable by the twelfth century. Strongbow

[25] Cf. the intrusion of Conchobar and Cennétig Ua Briain of the Dál Cais dynasty into the northern Uí Néill kingship of Tulach Óc in 1078, and the intrusion of the same Cennétig into the kingship of Gailenga under the auspices of Donnchad Ua Ruairc, king of Bréifne, later in the same year: J. Hogan, 'The Ua Briain kingship in Tulach Óc', in *Féil-sgríbhinn Eóin Mhic Néill*, 406–44. In a charter dating from 1073–87 relating to the church of Kells, which was situated in Gailenga, Donnchad Ua Ruairc, king of Bréifne, was also styled king of Gailenga: G. Mac Niocaill, *Notitiae as Leabhar Cheanannais, 1033–1161* (Dublin, 1961), 14. By 1133 Gofraid Ua Ragallaig, a collateral descendant of the royal dynasty of Bréifne, had been installed as king of Gailenga under the overlordship of Tigernán Ua Ruairc, king of Bréifne: ibid.

[26] Cf. the obit of Toirdelbach Ua Conchobair in 1156 as 'king of Connacht, Mide, Bréifne, and Munster, and of all Ireland with opposition': *AFM* 1156. Donnchad Ua Cerbaill's obit in 1168 described him as 'overking of Airgialla, who obtained the kingship of Mide as far as Clochán na hImrime and the kingship of Ulaid and to whom was offered many times the kingship of Cenél nEógain': *Misc. Ir. annals*, 1167. 5 (*recte* 1168). Tigernán Ua Ruairc, king of Bréifne, was styled 'king of Bréifne and Conmaicne and the greater part of the land of Mide, one capable of control of one of the districts of Airgialla': *Ann. Tig.* 1172. Cf. also below, p. 242.

could be viewed as a 'stranger in sovereignty' and not indeed the first in the kingship of Leinster. In 1126 Toirdelbach Ua Conchobair, king of Connacht and high-king of Ireland, had attempted to instal his son Conchobar as provincial king of Leinster.[27] It is a moot point whether Strongbow, as Diarmait Mac Murchada's nominee, would have been viewed as more of an outsider than a prince of the royal dynasty of Connacht externally intruded into the kingship of Leinster. Strongbow at least was marrying into the family of Diarmait Mac Murchada.

ARISTOCRATIC MARRIAGE IN PRE-NORMAN IRELAND

The marriage between Aífe, daughter of Diarmait Mac Murchada, and Strongbow, which took place in 1170, has been viewed as irrelevant to the question of Strongbow's succession to the kingship of Leinster, since Irish customary law did not recognize inheritance in the female line. There is little evidence, however, to suggest that Irish customary law played a determining role in regnal succession in twelfth-century Ireland. Diarmait Mac Murchada's proposal to Strongbow of marriage to his daughter Aífe should more realistically be seen in the contemporary political context rather than in the context of Irish customary law in regard to female inheritance, knowledge of which in any event derives from the eighth-century law tracts, with no detailed studies having been made of developments after the eighth century.[28] The law tracts are a misleading source for the legal status of women in Ireland by the twelfth century, if not before. Descent through the female line may have been more important in Irish society than either the law tracts or the genealogies, with their emphasis on agnatic descent, might suggest. Hagiographers from the earliest period certainly strove to record the descent of the mother of their saint. The *Banshenchas*, or 'Lore of women', which was compiled in 1147, and was devoted to recording the parentage of well-born women and their marriages, suggests that cognatic

[27] *Ann. Tig.*

[28] A brief survey is provided by D. Ó Corráin, 'Women in early Irish society', in M. Mac Curtain and D. Ó Corráin (edd.), *Women in Irish society: the historical dimension* (Dublin, 1978), 1–13; cf. also his 'Marriage in early Ireland', in A. Cosgrove (ed.), *Marriage in Ireland* (Dublin, 1985), 5–24.

relationships were important in the aristocratic sphere as a means of forming and consolidating political alliances.[29] The choice of personal names within certain royal dynasties, where sons can be seen to have been named after their mothers' kinsmen, also suggests the importance of female relatives.[30]

Marriage played a prominent role in twelfth-century Irish politics. It was usual for an Irish king to marry several times.[31] Diarmait Mac Murchada was married at least three times.[32] Royal remarriage was invariably occasioned by political realignments, by a necessity to seek new political allies. The marriage alliance between Aífe and Strongbow should be viewed in the context of the very important role which aristocratic women could play as agents for the formation of political alliances. It was presumably to prevent Eochaid Mac Duinn Sléibe, king of Ulaid, from using his daughter as a means of acquiring a political ally that in 1165 Muirchertach Mac Lochlainn, king of Cenél nEógain and high-king of Ireland, required the king of Ulaid to hand over not only a son of every lord under him in Ulaid as hostages but also his own daughter.[33]

By the twelfth century an aristocratic woman might have considerable resources at her disposal both in terms of land and movable wealth. To give just two examples, in 1077 the annals recorded how Gormflaith, daughter of Ua Focarta, king of Éle, and wife of Toirdelbach Ua Briain, king of Munster and high-king of Ireland, bequeathed an immense amount of goods to the Church just before her death.[34] In 1157, on the occasion of the consecration of the church of the Cistercian abbey of Mellifont, Derbforgaill, daughter of Murchad Ua Máel Sechlainn, king of Mide (d. 1153), and wife of Tigernán Ua Ruairc, king of Bréifne, gave more than 60 ounces of gold, as well as a

---

[29] M. C. Dobbs, 'The Ban-Shenchus', *Rev. Celt.* 47 (1930), 282–339; 48 (1931), 163–234; 49 (1932), 437–89; M. Ní Bhrolcháin, 'The manuscript tradition of the Banshenchas', *Ériu*, 33 (1981), 109–35.

[30] Toirdelbach Mór Ua Conchobair, king of Connacht (d. 1156), owed his first name to the fact that his mother was Mór, daughter of Toirdelbach Ua Briain, king of Munster (d. 1086): Ó Corráin, 'Onomata', 166–7.

[31] Although it is often stated that polygamy was practised in early Irish society, serial monogamy, or divorce and remarriage, would be more appropriate terms, since the evidence suggests that in the majority of cases an Irish king generally set one wife aside before taking another.

[32] See below, p. 96.   [33] *AU* 1165.   [34] *Ann. Tig.*, *Ann. Clon.*

gold chalice for the altar of Mary, and cloth for each of the other nine altars in the church.[35] Her generosity matched the donations made by those kings who were present. Derbforgaill was also responsible for the building of the nun's church at Clonmacnoise, completed in 1167.[36] Not only may aristocratic ladies have had their own considerable personal movable wealth at their disposal, but a queen was also assigned mensal lands by her husband from his demesne. The twelfth-century life of Colmán mac Luacháin, the patron saint of the royal dynasty of Mide, contains an interesting account of the seizure by Conchobar Ua Máel Sechlainn, king of Mide (about 1039–49), of a fortress of one of his subkings, Ua Dublaích of Fir Tulach, which Conchobar then bestowed on his wife, Mór:

Dún Carraic had always been the residence of the kings of Fir Tulach until there came the daughter of the son of Conchobar, that is the wife of Conchobar Ua Máel Sechlainn, king of Mide, when the latter and his queen took it by force from the king of Fir Tulach, that is Cú Caille, son of Dublaích, so that it was violated by being deprived of its king and forfeited to the king of Mide, so that she is the first woman that took it and every queen of Mide after her has held it since then, and it is their property free from the king of Fir Tulach.[37]

The hagiographer here incidentally revealed how the king of Mide alienated a residence of one of his subkings and set it aside permanently for the use of the queens of Mide.

Control of movable and landed wealth usually brought power and political influence in medieval society. The annals reflect the increasing importance of women in the political arena. From the tenth century onwards there is a noticeable change of nomenclature: queens were no longer referred to simply as the consort of a particular king but specifically associated with his kingdom. For example, Gormflaith, the ex-wife of Brian Bóruma, who died in 1030, and Gormflaith, wife of Toirdelbach Ua Briain, were each described as 'queen of Munster'.[38] There can be little doubt that royal wives could exercise considerable influence on politics, especially since

---

[35] *AU, AFM.*   [36] *AFM.*

[37] *Betha Colmáin maic Luacháin,* ed. K. Meyer (Dublin, 1911), 52–3. For Cú Caille son of Dublaích see the genealogy of the Uí Dublaích in *The O Clery book of genealogies,* ed. S. Pender, 18 (1951), 132, §1772.

[38] *Ann. Inisf.* 1030. 4, 1076. 7.

their marriages were frequently contracted for political pur-
poses. The Annals of the Four Masters recorded that in 1053
Diarmait mac Máel na mBó, king of Leinster, and Mac Gilla
Pátraic, king of Osraige, 'went into Mide, whence they carried
off captives and very great spoils in revenge of the going of Mór,
daughter of Congalach Ua Conchobair, king of Uí Failge, to
Conchobar Ua Máel Sechlainn, in violation of [her husband]
Mac Gilla Pátraic and in revenge also of the cattle spoils which
Ua Máel Sechlainn had carried off from Mide'.[39] The twelfth-
century pseudo-historical propaganda tract *Cogadh Gaedhel re
Gallaibh* depicted Gormflaith, wife of Brian Bóruma, as responsible for the falling out between Brian and the king of
Leinster which eventually led to the battle of Clontarf.[40] The
twelfth-century Book of Rights depicted the queen of Airgialla
as entitled to a stipend from the queen of Tara on the occasion
when the king of Airgialla received one from the king of Tara.[41]
Perhaps the best indication of the importance of women in the
political sphere in twelfth-century Ireland was the abduction of
Derbforgaill, wife of Tigernán Ua Ruairc, king of Bréifne, by
Diarmait Mac Murchada in 1152, which has cast her in the role
of an Irish Helen of Troy, and an indirect cause of Anglo-
Norman intervention in Ireland. The Anglo-Norman sources
imply that she went willingly and had invited Diarmait Mac
Murchada to fetch her.[42] The 'Song of Dermot' actually says
that she asked Mac Murchada to 'take all the land along with
her'. According to the seventeenth-century translation of the
Annals of Clonmacnoise, her brother, Máel Sechlainn, had
induced her action 'for some abuses of her husband Tyernan
done before'.[43] The Annals of Tigernach recorded the abduction
of Derbforgaill in the context of a joint raid and defeat inflicted
by Toirdelbach Ua Conchobair, king of Connacht, and Diarmait Mac Murchada on Tigernán Ua Ruairc, as a result of
which he was deposed and replaced by a collateral, Áed son
of Gilla Braite Ua Ruairc. The Annals of the Four Masters

[39] *AFM* 1053.   [40] *Cog. Gaedhel*, 142–6.
[41] *Bk Rights*, ed. Dillon, ll. 1030, 1115.
[42] Cf. *Ann. Clon.*, *AFM* 1152; *Song of Dermot*, ll. 26–99; Giraldus, *Expugnatio*, 24–5.
[43] Máel Sechlainn is also mentioned in *AFM* as urging his sister's abduction. Both
were by the same mother, Mór, daughter of Muirchertach Ua Briain, wife of Murchad
Ua Máel Sechlainn, king of Mide: Dobbs, 'The Ban-Shenchus', *Rev. Celt.* 48 (1931),
191, 232.

recorded the participation of Muirchertach Mac Lochlainn, king of Cenél nEógain, and provide the additional information that on the same occasion Mide was divided between Murchad Ua Máel Sechlainn, king of Mide, and his son, Máel Sechlainn, who was granted the eastern portion. It is not impossible that Máel Sechlainn did, in fact, offer the kingship of East Mide to Diarmait Mac Murchada along with his sister Derbforgaill, as a means of preventing Tigernán Ua Ruairc's further encroachment into east Mide.[44] An instance of the political role of marriage in twelfth-century Ireland is provided by Gerald of Wales, who recorded that in 1170, when Diarmait Mac Murchada and Ruaidrí Ua Conchobair negotiated the terms of a peace settlement, Diarmait gave Ruaidrí his son Conchobar as a hostage, and Ruaidrí, for his part, promised to give his daughter to Conchobar 'in wedlock when in due course of time the peace had gained stability by its terms having been translated into deeds'.[45]

Although there is no known instance of a woman inheriting political office or governing as an independent ruler in pre-Norman Ireland, Diarmait Mac Murchada's offer to Strongbow makes more sense if the daughter of an Irish king is regarded as an important individual within the royal family, whose marriage was invariably exploited by her father for political purposes, rather than as a woman of no independent legal status, a totally anachronistic view, which derives from the eighth-century law tracts and makes no allowance for subsequent developments.

DIARMAIT MAC MURCHADA'S OFFER TO STRONGBOW

Did Diarmait Mac Murchada seriously intend in 1166–7, when, on the evidence of Gerald of Wales and the 'Song of Dermot',[46] he first made the offer to Strongbow of marriage to his daughter Aífe and succession to the kingship of Leinster, that Strongbow should succeed him as lord of Leinster after his death? Or was his primary concern at that time to gain military

[44] Cf. above, n. 26 and below, pp. 224–5.
[45] Giraldus, *Expugnatio*, 50–1.
[46] Giraldus, *Expugnatio*, 28–9; *Song of Dermot*, ll. 240–5.

aid, and in order to do so was he prepared to make an oppor-
tunistic proposal which he did not necessarily intend to implement? It is necessary to consider the prospects of Diarmait
Mac Murchada in exile in 1166–7 being succeeded by a
member of his immediate family. Diarmait had at least four
sons and three daughters. By his marriage to Mór, daughter of
Muirchertach Ua Tuathail, king of Uí Muiredaig, he had a son
Conchobar, and Aífe, whom he offered to Strongbow in
marriage.[47] By Sadb, daughter of Cerball Mac Fáeláin, king of
Uí Fáeláin, he had a son, Donnchad, and a daughter, Órlaith,
who married Domnall Mór Ua Briain, king of Thomond.[48] He
had, in addition, two sons, Domnall Caemánach and Énna,
and a daughter, Derbforgaill, the mother or mothers of these
last three being unknown.

It is not clear whether Diarmait Mac Murchada had designated a successor before his exile in 1166, although the likelihood is that he had. His son Énna witnessed a charter of
Diarmait Mac Murchada relating to a grant of land in the city
of Dublin about 1162.[49] This might be interpreted as an indication that Énna had some governmental function in Dublin
under his father and that he may have been regarded as a likely
successor; this is also suggested by the fact that Énna was taken
prisoner by the king of Osraige in 1166, and blinded in 1168
after Diarmait Mac Murchada's return, presumably in order to
render him unsuitable for succession to the kingship.[50] On the
other hand, Domnall Caemánach was the only one of Diarmait's sons who figured in the annals in a military capacity
before Diarmait's exile in 1166: in 1161 Domnall Caemánach
led a victorious expedition of the men of Uí Chennselaig
against the men of Wexford.[51] Conchobar, who was given as
hostage to Ruaidrí Ua Conchobair in the autumn of 1169, is
described in 1170 in the Annals of the Four Masters as *rídomna*

---

[47] O'Brien, *Corpus geneal. Hib.* i. 13; Dobbs, 'The Ban-Shenchus', *Rev. Celt.* 48
(1931), 231–3.
[48] Ibid.   [49] *Registrum prioratus omnium sanctorum*, 50.
[50] *Ann. Tig.* 1166, 1168; *Ann. Inisf.* 1168. 2; *AFM* 1168. Énna is styled *rídomna Laigin*,
that is a possible successor in the kingship of Leinster, in *Ann. Tig.* 1168.
[51] *AFM* 1161. There are lacunae in the major annalistic compilations for this period.
Ann. Inisf. lacks the years 1130–58; *Chron. Scot.* lacks 1132–40 and ceases in 1150; *AU*
lacks 1132–54; *ALC* lacks 1139–70. For a brief guide to the Irish annals see G. Mac
Niocaill, *The medieval Irish annals* (Dublin, 1975).

Laigin when he was put to death by Ruaidrí, along with the son of Domnall Caemánach, after Strongbow's arrival in Ireland, his marriage to Aífe, and the successful siege of Dublin on behalf of Mac Murchada. If the term *rídomna* was not inserted by the seventeenth-century compilers of the Annals of the Four Masters this certainly implies that in 1170 Conchobar was considered by Ruaidrí Ua Conchobair to be a possible, and perhaps the most likely, successor to Diarmait Mac Murchada.[52]

The fate of Diarmait Mac Murchada's immediate family is unknown during his period of exile.[53] If Mac Murchada offered the succession to the kingship of Leinster to Strongbow in 1166–7, it may at that time have seemed to him that he might organize an attempt abroad to regain the kingdom of Leinster only to find that he had no immediate family left to succeed him. He instigated the maiming and killing of a large number of dynasts of the royal families of Leinster, no fewer than seventeen on a single occasion,[54] and there would have been many anxious to take revenge on his immediate family in his absence.

Apart from the enmity of rival royal dynasties in Leinster, Diarmait Mac Murchada's immediate family could have faced opposition from within the Uí Chennselaig dynasty. That opposition would most likely have come from Diarmait's brother, Murchad, and the latter's son, Muirchertach. It is significant that in the charter granted by Diarmait Mac Murchada to Kilkenny Abbey, about 1162–5, Murchad and his son Muirchertach headed the list of lay witnesses, taking precedence over Diarmait's own son Domnall Caemánach, who came third in the list.[55] The prospect of Murchad, rather than one of

---

[52] *AFM* 1170, but not in *Ann. Tig.* Conchobar was styled *rídomna* in the *Banshenchas*: Dobbs, 'The Ban-Shenchus', *Rev. Celt.* 48 (1931), 232.

[53] William of Newburgh stated that Diarmait Mac Murchada sent a son to England to raise mercenaries: William of Newburgh, i. 167. The Irish and other Norman sources are in agreement that Diarmait Mac Murchada went abroad himself in 1166. According to the *Song of Dermot*, ll. 236–7, Diarmait was accompanied by his wife. A series of memoranda on Adam de Hereford compiled in the early 13th century and copied into the cartulary of St Thomas's Abbey, Dublin, assert that Diarmait was accompanied into exile 'una cum uxore et unica filia quam pulcherrima': *Reg. St. Thomas, Dublin*, 104.   [54] *AFM, Ann. Tig.* 1141.

[55] C. M. Butler and J. H. Bernard, 'The charters of the Cistercian abbey of Duiske in the county of Kilkenny', *RIA Proc.* 35 C (1918), 1–188 (at 5–8). Murchad Mac Murchada is listed as holding the kingship of Osraige jointly with Conchobar mac Cerbaill Mac Gilla Pátraic, about 1123–6, that is about the time of the accession of Diarmait Mac Murchada to the kingship of Uí Chennselaig: *Bk Leinster*, i. 190.

Diarmait's own sons, succeeding him appears to have hung over Diarmait Mac Murchada throughout his reign.

It is no surprise that on Diarmait Mac Murchada's banishment in 1166, Ruaidrí Ua Conchobar, king of Connacht, in his capacity as high-king, divided the kingdom of Uí Chennselaig between Murchad Mac Murchada and Domnall Mac Gilla Pátraic, king of Osraige.[56] The 'Song of Dermot' asserted that a number of Diarmait's own kinsmen took part in the revolt against him.[57] His brother Murchad may almost certainly be identified as the chief instigator, since he gained most directly by it. Diarmait was faced in exile with the possibility that his brother and his heirs would preclude succession to the kingship of Leinster of one of Diarmait's own sons. The regnal succession within Leinster was a real and urgent issue in 1166–7 when Mac Murchada made his offer to Strongbow.

When Diarmait Mac Murchada returned to Ireland in the autumn of 1167 with a small group of paid troops recruited in South Wales, he regained his patrimonial kingdom of Uí Chennselaig with little apparent difficulty. Within a week of his return, Ruaidrí Ua Conchobair, king of Connacht and high-king of Ireland, who had acted as overlord of Leinster since Mac Murchada's departure in 1166, mounted an expedition into Leinster, and obliged Mac Murchada to acknowledge him as high-king, and to give hostages for the maintenance of his allegiance, but he did not oust him from the kingship of Uí Chennselaig.[58]

In 1168 the annals record the apparently unprovoked blinding of Énna, son of Diarmait Mac Murchada, by Donnchad Mac Gilla Pátraic, king of Osraige, who had held Énna prisoner from 1166.[59] Obviously, Mac Gilla Pátraic viewed the reinstallation of Mac Murchada in Uí Chennselaig as a threat to his own position. It may have been in 1168 that Mac Murchada concluded an alliance with Domnall Ua Briain, who succeeded to the kingship of Thomond in that year, an alliance which may be inferred from Ua Briain's support for Mac Murchada in the period 1168–71, and the fact that Órlaith,

---

[56] *Ann. Tig.* 1166.   [57] *Song of Dermot*, ll. 146–50.
[58] *Ann. Inisf.* 1167. 2; *Ann. Tig.*; *AU*; Giraldus, *Expugnatio*, 30–1. The Anglo-Norman chroniclers either ignore or telescope events between the autumn of 1167 and the arrival of Anglo-Norman mercenaries in 1169.
[59] *Ann. Inisf.* 1168. 2; *Ann. Tig.*, where he is styled *rídomna*.

daughter of Diarmait Mac Murchada, is known to have married Domnall Mór Ua Briain.[60] Mac Murchada's alliance with Ua Briain would have represented a potential threat to the king of Osraige on his western frontier.

In May 1169 a contingent of Cambro-Norman troops arrived in Ireland under the leadership of Robert fitz Stephen. Gerald of Wales, the principal source for events at this period, was a nephew of Robert fitz Stephen, to whom he assigned a prominent role. It is significant, however, that this expedition was accompanied, on Gerald's own admission, by Hervey de Montmorency, an uncle of Strongbow, whom Gerald depicted in the role of a spy on behalf of Strongbow.[61] With his new recruits Mac Murchada mounted an attack on the town of Wexford and an expedition into Osraige. The reaction of Ruaidrí Ua Conchobair was to host into Uí Chennselaig and demand a son from Diarmait Mac Murchada as hostage.[62]

In the autumn of 1169 additional Cambro-Norman troops arrived under the leadership of Maurice fitz Gerald, and the city of Dublin, which had been under the overlordship of Ruaidrí Ua Conchobair since Mac Murchada's departure in 1166, was successfully retaken on behalf of Mac Murchada. According to Gerald of Wales, Mac Murchada's ambitions grew apace: he now desired to obtain the submission of the province of Connacht and to take the high-kingship of Ireland. He consulted Robert fitz Stephen and Maurice fitz Gerald as to how this might be accomplished, and they advised the recruitment of more overseas troops. Accordingly, Mac Murchada decided to send messengers to Strongbow renewing the offer of the hand of his daughter in marriage. Gerald of Wales depicted Mac Murchada first suggesting marriage to Aífe in turn to Robert fitz Stephen and Maurice fitz Gerald, but since both men already had legal wives, they were obliged to decline.[63] It is likely that Gerald invented this sequence to

---

[60] M. C. Dobbs, 'The Ban-Shenchus', *Rev. Celt.* 48 (1931), 233. Domnall's accession in 1168 would have provided a suitable occasion for the marriage.

[61] Giraldus, *Expugnatio*, 31–51.

[62] *Ann. Tig.* 1169; named as Conchobar in Giraldus, *Expugnatio*, 50–1; cf. *Ann. Tig.*, *AU*, *AFM* 1170. Ruaidrí Ua Conchobair exacted hostages from Diarmait Mac Murchada after his return in 1167; it is not clear whether these were still in his custody, or had been released in the interim.

[63] Giraldus, *Expugnatio*, 51–5.

explain why, if his own relatives had achieved so much in Ireland on behalf of Mac Murchada, the latter was still anxious in 1169 to secure the personal intervention of Strongbow.

In the spring of 1170 a further group of Cambro-Normans arrived under the leadership of Raymond le Gros. Raymond was a relative of Gerald of Wales and, as such, another of his heroes; but he was also, on Gerald's own testimony, a member of Strongbow's *familia*.[64] The city of Waterford was taken by Raymond, and in the autumn of 1170 Strongbow arrived in person, and his marriage to Aífe was celebrated in Waterford. Mac Murchada's choice of son-in-law may be said to have been justified, in so far as there was a dramatic improvement in his position after the arrival of Strongbow. Despite the fact that Dublin apparently had been restored to Mac Murchada's control by Maurice fitz Gerald before the arrival of either Raymond le Gros or Strongbow, the first task which Strongbow undertook on behalf of Mac Murchada was the recapture of Dublin; Strongbow also withstood a subsequent siege mounted by the high-king. After the arrival of Strongbow, furthermore, it became possible for Mac Murchada to extend his activities beyond Leinster into Mide and Bréifne.[65] Strongbow's intervention thus far was successful from the point of view of Diarmait Mac Murchada.

It is difficult to judge how Diarmait Mac Murchada's relationship with Strongbow might have developed thereafter, since Diarmait died in May 1171 within a short time of Strongbow's arrival in Ireland. After Diarmait's death Strongbow asserted a claim to the lordship of Leinster. Curtis argued that this was 'sound enough' in feudal law.[66] This statement, however, requires qualification. Strongbow's succession in right of his wife could proceed according to feudal custom only in a case where there were no legitimate male heirs. When Diarmait Mac Murchada died in 1171 at least one of his sons, and

---

[64] Giraldus, *Expugnatio*, 57–65.
[65] Ibid. 64–9; *Ann. Tig.*, *AU* 1170. Strongbow's force was numerically greater than the preceding Norman contingents. According to Gerald, Strongbow was accompanied by 200 knights and 1000 others: Giraldus, *Expugnatio*, 64–5; cf. *Song of Dermot*, l. 1503. This compares with Robert fitz Stephen's 30 knights, 60 wearing mail, and 300 archers, with Maurice fitz Gerald's 10 knights and 100 archers, and Raymond le Gros's 10 knights and 70 archers: Giraldus, *Expugnatio*, 30, 50, 56; *Song of Dermot*, ll. 440–60.
[66] See above, p. 81.

possibly two, were still alive; although Énna had been blinded by the king of Osraige in 1168 he was probably still alive in 1171,[67] and Domnall Caemánach did not die until 1175.[68] The question is whether these sons would have been regarded as legitimate heirs in canon law or feudal custom.

Although it is usual to state that Irish society did not draw a distinction between legitimate and illegitimate offspring, this assertion is based primarily on the evidence of the eighth-century law tracts and makes no allowance for possible subsequent changes in this sphere, and in particular for the possible impact of the twelfth-century Irish Church reform movement. Gerald of Wales stated that Domnall Caemánach was illegitimate.[69] Domnall was probably among the first-born of Diarmait Mac Murchada's children. His soubriquet Caemánach is believed to derive from his place of fosterage in Kilcavan (Co. Wexford) in Uí Chennselaig,[70] which suggests that he was born in the early years of Mac Murchada's career when Mac Murchada did not have extensive political influence beyond his patrimonial kingdom of Uí Chennselaig. Mac Murchada's union with Sadb, daughter of Cerball Mac Fáeláin, king of Uí Fáeláin, almost certainly dates from the period of his first attempts to pursue an expansionist policy beyond Uí Chennselaig, when he was concentrating on extending his influence into north Leinster, as evidenced by his attempts to gain control of the church of Kildare.[71] Mac Murchada's marriage to Mór, daughter of Muirchertach Ua Tuathail, king of Uí Muiredaig, probably took place around or after 1153. Certainly, good relations between Diarmait Mac Murchada and the Ua Tuathail royal dynasty may be presumed by 1153, when Lorcán (Laurentius) Ua Tuathail, half-brother of Mór, became abbot of Glendalough. In 1162 Lorcán was appointed archbishop of Dublin, and for both ecclesiastical offices the acquiescence of Diarmait Mac Murchada as

---

[67] Cf. the charter issued by Derbforgaill, daughter of Diarmait Mac Murchada and wife of Domnall Mac Gilla Mo Cholmóc, king of Uí Dunchada, to St Mary's Abbey, Dublin, after 1168, where Henne Mac Murchada headed the list of witnesses: *Chartul. St Mary's, Dublin*, i. 31–2. It is possible that he should be identified as Énna, son of Diarmait Mac Murchada and brother of Derbforgaill.

[68] *Ann. Tig.* 1175. He was killed by the Uí Nualláin of Fotharta.

[69] Giraldus, *Expugnatio*, 32–3.

[70] E. Hogan, *Onomasticon Goedelicum* (Dublin, 1910), 179.

[71] *AU, ALC, Chron. Scot.* 1132; *Ann. Clon.* 1135 (= 1132).

the provincial king of Leinster may be assumed.[72] Such evidence as there is suggests that Mac Murchada's marriage to Mór was his last.[73]

This marriage may have been recognized as canonically valid by the Church. There is no doubt that the Church reform party was attempting to insist on the observance of the canon law of marriage in twelfth-century Ireland,[74] although it is difficult to gauge the extent of their success. From 1148 at the latest, Diarmait Mac Murchada was associated with the Church reform party.[75] In 1152 the papal legate, Cardinal John Paparo, convened a synod at Kells at which he enacted that 'kinswomen and concubines should be put away by men'.[76] Paparo spent three to four months in Ireland, during which time he may have met the principal kings. During this period he granted a confirmation of a charter issued by Diarmait Mac Murchada to the nunnery of Aghade.[77] It is likely that Paparo

[72] *AFM* 1153, 1162; C. Plummer, 'Vie et miracles de St Laurent, archevêque de Dublin', *Anal. Bolland.* 33 (1914), 121–85; J. Ryan, 'The ancestry of St Laurence O'Toole', *Reportorium Novum*, 1 (1955), 64–75.

[73] Aífe, Diarmait's daughter by Mór, may just have reached nubile age when she was married to Strongbow in 1170.

[74] Lanfranc had written to Gofraid, king of Dublin, and to Toirdelbach Ua Briain, king of Munster and high-king of Ireland, urging observance of the canon law regarding marriage: Lanfranc, *Letters*, 66–73. Archbishop Anselm wrote to Muirchertach Ua Briain in the same vein: Ussher, *Works*, iv. 520–5. The seventh decree of the synod of Cashel, 1101, dealt with marriage within the forbidden degrees of kinship: Gwynn, 'The first synod of Cashel', *IER* 67 (1946), 109–22. St Bernard attributed to St Malachy the reintroduction into Ireland of the sacrament of marriage: Bernard, *Opera*, iii. 316, 325–6. Cf. the obit of Donnchad Ua Cerbaill, king of Airgialla, 1168, a supporter of ecclesiastical reform, in the so-called antiphonary of Armagh, which states that in his time 'marriage was assented to': Kenney, *Sources*, 770. The first decree of the synod of Cashel, 1172, decreed lawful marriage unions and forbade marriage within forbidden degrees of kinship: Giraldus, *Expugnatio*, 98–9. Pope Alexander III in his letter to Henry II, 1172, also referred to the reprehensible marriage practices of the Irish: Sheehy, *Pontificia Hib.* i, no. 6.

[75] Diarmait founded the Cistercian monastery of Baltinglass, Co. Wicklow, the date of foundation of which is given as 1148 in the Cistercian *tabulae*: Gwynn and Hadcock, *Med. relig. houses*, 127. Mac Murchada's charter of foundation is referred to in a confirmation of John, lord of Ireland, given in 1185: *Cal. pat. rolls, 1334–8*, 402; Dugdale, *Monasticon Anglicanum*, vi, 2. 1136.

[76] *AFM* 1152; A. Gwynn, 'The centenary of the Synod of Kells', *IER* 77 (1952), 161–76; 78 (1952), 250–64.

[77] Archbishop Alen, the first Henrician bishop of Dublin (1529–34), an assiduous historian of the rights and privileges of his diocese and well acquainted with its archives, stated that he had inspected a papal confirmation of a grant of Diarmait Mac Murchada to the Augustinian nunnery of Aghade, Co. Carlow, issued by Cardinal

would have tried to persuade Irish kings, including possibly Mac Murchada, to regularize their marriages in accordance with canon law.[78] In 1177, before the papal legate, Cardinal Vivian, visited Ireland, he halted for a few days on the Isle of Man to regularize the marriage of Godred, king of Man, to Finnguala, daughter of Niall Mac Lochlainn, king of Cenél nEógain (1170–6).[79] Diarmait Mac Murchada's contacts with the Church reform movement deserve emphasis; he received a letter from St Bernard of Clairvaux, who rejoiced in the good reports he had heard of him.[80] In 1162, the year in which Lorcán Ua Tuathail became archbishop of Dublin (he was by this stage almost certainly Diarmait's brother-in-law), Diarmait Mac Murchada presided over a reforming synod at Clane.[81] Gerald of Wales's statement that the clergy welcomed Diarmait on his return to Ireland in 1167 may also be noted.[82] It is reasonable to assume that Lorcán, as Mór's brother, either as abbot of Glendalough or archbishop of Dublin, and as an associate of the reform party, would have tried to persuade Diarmait Mac Murchada to marry his sister in accordance with canon law, in which case the only legitimate issue in the eyes of reform-minded ecclesiastics were Mac Murchada's children by that marriage. These were, as far as is known, a son, Conchobar, and a daughter, Aífe. Conchobar was executed by Ruaidrí Ua Conchobair in 1170.[83] On Diarmait's death in 1171,

John Paparo, *legatus de latere*: *Calendar of Archbishop Alen's register*, ed. C. MacNeill (Dublin, 1950), 293.

[78] Nicholas Breakspear, during his legation to Norway in 1153 to set up an independent diocesan structure for that country, extracted concessions from the Norwegian kings in regard to their uncanonical marriage practices: A. O. Johnsen, 'Nicholaus Brekespear and the Norwegian church province, 1153', *The Norseman*, 11 (1953), 244–51 (at 246–8).

[79] William of Newburgh, i. 238–9; Roger of Howden, *Gesta*, i. 136–8, 161, 166–7; *Chronica*, i. 119–20, 135; Gervase of Canterbury, i. 259; *Gir. Camb. op.* v. 340–5; *Chronica regum Manniae et Insularum*, i (Manx Society, xxii; Douglas, 1874), 76–7; A. O. Anderson and M. O. Anderson, *The chronicle of Melrose* (London, 1936), 41–2.

[80] Bernard, *Opera*, viii. 513–14; G. G. Meersman, 'Two unknown confraternity letters of St Bernard', in *Cîteaux in de Nederlanden, Achel et Westmalle*, 6 (1955), 173–8; J. Leclercq, 'Deux épitres de St Bernard et de son secrétaire', in J. Leclercq (ed.), *Recueil d'études sur Saint Bernard et ses écrits*, ii (Rome, 1966), 313–18.

[81] *Ann. Tig.*   [82] Giraldus, *Expugnatio*, 30–1.

[83] *Ann. Tig.* 1170, entry 13, details the killing of the hostages of Diarmait Mac Murchada at the instigation of Tigernán Ua Ruairc, namely the son of Domnall Caemánach, and the son of Murchad Ua Cáellaide, foster-brother of Diarmait Mac Murchada, while entry 15 states that Conchobar son of Diarmait Mac Murchada

therefore, it is possible that ecclesiastics, such as Archbishop Lorcán Ua Tuathail, would have been prepared to endorse the view that Aífe was the sole surviving legitimate issue of Diarmait Mac Murchada.[84]

In the absence of evidence to the contrary one is obliged to assume that Diarmait Mac Murchada did seriously contemplate Strongbow as his successor in the provincial kingship of Leinster from 1167, and that the Anglo-Norman sources are substantially correct in their presentation of the agreement between Mac Murchada and Strongbow, and are not making an *ex post facto* justification of events after 1171. The manner in which Diarmait's son Domnall Caemánach subsequently co-operated with Strongbow suggests that he acceded to his father's agreement with Strongbow. If the concept of the nuclear family was current in Ireland by the twelfth century, the succession of his daughter's husband may have been seen by Diarmait in 1166–7 as preferable to the succession of another member of the royal dynasty who did not belong to his immediate family, and certainly preferable to that of his brother Murchad, or his heirs, who had profited so materially from his exile. It may have been an innovation on Mac Murchada's part to suggest a succession in right of his daughter, but it was one which can be paralleled in similar circumstances in other societies in which male normally took precedence over female descent.

The offer of succession to the kingship of Leinster made by Diarmait Mac Murchada to Strongbow cannot be justified according to feudal custom in 1166–7, in that Mac Murchada still had sons living at that time, at least one of whom, Concho-

mortuus est. AU and *AFM* 1170 record Conchobar's death as taking place at the same time as that of the son of Domnall Caemánach and the son of Murchad Ua Cáellaide. *AFM*, but not *AU* or *Ann. Tig.*, styles Conchobar *rídomna Laigin*.

[84] One means by which ecclesiastics may have sought to promote the canonical observance of matrimony among the aristocracy was by attempting to deny rights of inheritance to the offspring of non-canonical unions. This may be inferred from the sixth decree of the synod of Cashel, 1172, concerning the making of wills and the disposition of property among legitimate heirs. Giraldus, *Expugnatio*, 100–1. The provincial synod of Dublin, 1186, decreed that no individual born of concubinage was to be considered for ecclesiastical orders, or as heir of his father or mother, unless his parents were subsequently united in legitimate wedlock: Sheehy, *Pontificia Hib.* i, no. 16, and *When the Normans came*, 43. For the development of the canonical theory of the testament and the canonical will at this period see M. Sheehan, *The will in medieval England* (Toronto, 1963).

bar, could have been recognized as legitimate by the Church. In an Irish context, however, it could be argued that Diarmait was doing no more than naming a successor designate. If the sequence of events in the annals is in correct order, Conchobar was still alive in 1170 when the marriage between Strongbow and Aífe was celebrated, but was killed later in the same year by Ruaidrí Ua Conchobair. Conchobar's death created the possibility of justifying Strongbow's acquisition in 1171 according to feudal custom. Strongbow's succession to the lordship of Leinster, therefore, cannot be understood solely in terms of Irish or of Anglo-Norman society; it incorporated aspects of both Irish and Anglo-Norman practices.

THE DISTINCTION BETWEEN THE KINGSHIP OF UÍ CHENNSELAIG AND THE PROVINCIAL KINGSHIP OF LEINSTER

It is necessary to draw a distinction between Mac Murchada's patrimonial kingship of Uí Chennselaig and the provincial kingship of Leinster. The Uí Chennselaig dynasty only attained the provincial kingship of Leinster in the mid eleventh century. From the early eighth century until 1037 it had been held by the Uí Dúnlainge dynasty of north Leinster.

Geographically, the province of Leinster can be divided into two distinct areas lying to the north and south of the watershed between the Liffey and Slaney rivers. This geographical division was also reflected in two distinct spheres of political influence in the pre-Norman period. From the early historic period the northern half of Leinster was dominated by the Uí Dúnlainge dynasty, while the southern half was dominated by the Uí Chennselaig dynasty.[85]

According to 'official' historical tradition, the Uí Chennselaig dynasty had held the provincial kingship of Leinster twice in the prehistoric period, and once in the historic period, when in the early seventh century it had provided a very successful provincial king, Brandub mac Echach (d. 605/608). But from 738 until 1037 the provincial kingship of Leinster was

[85] See A. P. Smyth, *Celtic Leinster* (Dublin, 1982); Byrne, *Ir. kings*, ch. 8; P. Walsh, 'Leinster states and kings in Christian times', *IER* 53 (1939), 47–61.

held exclusively by the Uí Dúnlainge dynasty. In 1037 the removal of the Uí Dúnlainge dynasty from the provincial kingship of Leinster was effected by Donnchad mac Gilla Pátraic, king of Osraige. Osraige had originally been a subkingdom within the province of Munster, situated along its eastern frontier with Leinster. The overlordship of the kings of Munster over Osraige, however, was fitful and ineffectual, and by the eleventh century its status had become more that of a semi-independent buffer kingdom gravitating towards the political orbit of Leinster.[86] The seizure of the provincial kingship of Leinster by a king of Osraige, a kingdom which had no traditional association with Leinster, was a remarkable accomplishment,[87] but the Osraige dynasty failed to consolidate its hold on the provincial kingship, and the Uí Chennselaig dynasty was to be the real beneficiary of the Osraige achievement.

In 1042 Diarmait mac Máel na mBó, who had been king of Uí Chennselaig since 1032, seized the provincial kingship of Leinster, which he retained until his death in 1072.[88] He was sufficiently powerful for the admittedly partisan Book of Leinster to accord him the title 'high-king of Ireland with opposition'. Diarmait mac Máel na mBó tackled the problem of extending his control into the north Leinster area by associating his son Murchad with him in government, assigning him responsibility for the city of Dublin and the northern half of Leinster.[89] Diarmait must have intended that Murchad should succeed him as king of Uí Chennselaig and as provincial king of Leinster, but Murchad died in 1070, predeceasing his father by two years.

After Diarmait mac Máel na mBó died in 1072, succession to the kingship of Uí Chennselaig and to the provincial kingship of Leinster diverged recurrently until 1115 between rival contestants within the Uí Chennselaig dynasty.[90] In addition,

---

[86] In 859 the king of Cashel was forced by the king of Tara to renounce overlordship over Osraige: D. A. Binchy, 'The passing of the old order', in B. Ó Cuív (ed.), *The impact of the Scandinavian invasions on the Celtic-speaking peoples* (Dublin, 1975), 119–32 (at 128–30); D. Ó Corráin, 'High-kings, Vikings and other kings', *IHS* 21 (1979), 283–323 (at 309–11).

[87] This political reorientation is reflected in the revision of the Osraige genealogies: O'Brien, *Corpus geneal. Hib.* i. 101.

[88] Ó Corráin, 'The career of Diarmait'; 'Irish regnal succession', 18–27.

[89] Ibid. 18–19.

[90] See Genealogical Table 1.

Conchobar Ua Conchobair, king of Uí Failge, which was situated in north-west Leinster, made a bid for the provincial kingship of Leinster. According to the regnal list in the Book of Leinster, he shared the provincial kingship of Leinster with Donnchad, son of Murchad son of Diarmait mac Maél na mBó, between 1114 and 1115.[91]

On the death of Donnchad, son of Murchad son of Diarmait mac Máel na mBó, and Conchobar Ua Conchobair in battle in 1115, the kingship of Uí Chennselaig and the provincial kingship of Leinster were reunited in the person of Diarmait, son of Énna son of Murchad son of Diarmait mac Máel na mBó. Diarmait died as king of Uí Chennselaig, Dublin, and Leinster after a short but apparently successful reign in 1117. On his death in 1117 Énna, son of Donnchad son of Murchad son of Diarmait mac Máel na mBó, succeeded to the kingship of Uí Chennselaig and of Leinster without any recorded opposition. The apparent absence of any powerful rival within the Uí Chennselaig dynasty and the fact that Énna gained the support of Toirdelbach Ua Conchobair, king of Connacht, who became high-king in 1118, enabled Énna to play a prominent role in interprovincial politics. In 1118 Toirdelbach Ua Conchobair is recorded to have 'left Énna son of Donnchad under his own hand in the kingship of Leinster and of Dublin'.[92] On Énna's death in 1126 Toirdelbach Ua Conchobair adopted a more aggressive interventionist policy towards Leinster: he hosted into Uí Chennselaig 'to constitute a king', deposed 'the son of Mac Murchada', and installed his own son, Conchobar, in the provincial kingship of Leinster.[93] In 1127, however, there was a revolt in Leinster which resulted in the expulsion of Conchobar Ua Conchobair. Toirdelbach Ua Conchobair reacted by installing another candidate as provincial king of Leinster, Domnall Mac Fáeláin, king of Uí Fáeláin.[94]

The regnal succession in the kingdom of Uí Chennselaig after Énna's death in 1126 is obscure. The identity of the 'son of

[91] For regnal lists of the kings of Uí Chennselaig and Leinster see *Bk Leinster*, i. 181–6. For discussion of the successions see D. Ó Corráin, 'Irish regnal succession', 18–27; 'The Uí Chennselaig kingship of Leinster, 1072–1126', *Old Wexford Soc. Jn.* 5 (1974–5), 26–31; 6 (1976–7), 45–53; 7 (1978–9), 46–9.

[92] *Misc. Ir. annals*, 1119. 2.

[93] *Ann. Tig.*, *Ann. Inisf.*, *AU*, *AFM* 1126; *Chron. Scot.* 1122 (*recte* 1126).

[94] *AU* 1127.

Mac Murchada' whom Toirdelbach Ua Conchobair deposed in 1126 is unknown, as is the individual whom he then installed as king in Uí Chennselaig. According to the regnal list in the Book of Leinster, Diarmait Mac Murchada ruled Uí Chennselaig and Leinster for forty-six years, which implies that he became king in 1126 in succession to his brother, Énna. The regnal list in the Book of Ballymote, however, states that Diarmait ruled Leinster for forty years, which would suggest that he became king of Leinster in 1131 or 1132. The annalistic evidence tends to corroborate the Book of Ballymote, in so far as Diarmait is not mentioned either as king of Uí Chennselaig or of Leinster before 1132. There is some evidence that Diarmait faced opposition from within the Uí Chennselaig dynasty, for the death is recorded in 1133 of Máel Sechlainn, son of Diarmait, son of Murchad, styled *tigerna* of Uí Chennselaig.[95] Certainly from 1133 onwards Diarmait Mac Murchada was king both of Uí Chennselaig and of Leinster, until his expulsion from Ireland in the autumn of 1166.

The acquisition by the kings of Uí Chennselaig of the provincial kingship of Leinster was, therefore, of relatively recent origin. Apart from the early seventh-century Uí Chennselaig king, Brandub mac Echach, before the accession of Diarmait Mac Murchada the provincial kingship of Leinster had been exercised effectively, and for a sustained period, by only two previous kings of Uí Chennselaig: Diarmait mac Máel na mBó, his great-grandfather, and Énna son of Donnchad, his brother.

When Diarmait Mac Murchada negotiated a marriage alliance with Strongbow in 1166–7 there were two succession issues at stake: succession to the kingship of Uí Chennselaig and succession to the provincial kingship of Leinster. The problem which exercised Diarmait in 1166–7 was not recovery of the kingdom of Uí Chennselaig, but recovery of the provincial kingship of Leinster. As events after his return to Ireland in 1167 suggest, the retaking of Uí Chennselaig was a relatively easy operation. The regnal lists in the Book of Leinster draw a distinction between succession to the kingdom of Uí Chennselaig and succession to the provincial kingship of Leinster after the death of Diarmait Mac Murchada in 1171. While the

[95] See Ó Corráin, 'Irish regnal succession', 26–7; 'The education of Diarmait Mac Murchada', *Ériu*, 28 (1977), 71–81.

continued succession of the Mac Murchada family in the kingship of Uí Chennselaig is recorded, it is stated of the provincial
kingship of Leinster: 'Saxons thereafter *miserabiliter regnant.*'
Domnall Caemánach is given as immediate successor to Diarmait, his father, in Uí Chennselaig, followed by Diarmait's
brother Murchad, and the latter's son Muirchertach.[96] It is
difficult to reconcile the sequence in the regnal list with events
as recorded in the annals. Domnall Caemánach may have been
recognized as king of Uí Chennselaig for a short period,[97] but
was obliged to give way to Murchad Mac Murchada, as the
regnal list asserts. If this was the case, neither Domnall
Caemánach nor Murchad can have been in possession for any
length of time, for Murchad was killed by Anglo-Normans in
1172.[98]

Domnall Caemánach did not succeed to the kingship of Uí
Chennselaig after Murchad's death in 1172. This is attested not
merely by the regnal list in the Book of Leinster but also by
the 'Song of Dermot', which stated that Strongbow granted
Uí Chennselaig to Muirchertach, son of Murchad Mac
Murchada.[99] It is a measure of the threat to Diarmait Mac
Murchada presented by his brother Murchad and the latter's
son Muirchertach, that Strongbow was obliged to recognize
Muirchertach rather than Domnall Caemánach as king of Uí
Chennselaig. The death of Muirchertach Mac Murchada,
styled king of Uí Chennselaig, is recorded in the annals in
1193.[100]

Domnall Caemánach appears to have co-operated with
Strongbow until his own death in 1175.[101] He brought news of

---

[96] *Bk Leinster*, i. 181–6. The compiler of this list was favourable to Diarmait Mac
Murchada. According to the Annals of the Four Masters, Murchad Mac Murchada
reigned as king of Uí Chennselaig under the authority of Ruaidrí Ua Conchobair
during the absence of Diarmait Mac Murchada, 1166–7: *AFM* 1166. The compiler of
the regnal list has chosen to ignore the period in exile of Diarmait Mac Murchada.

[97] In support thereof might be cited the entry in *Misc. Ir. annals*, 1172. 2 (*recte* 1171),
which lists Domnall Caemánach Mac Murchada as king of Leinster when Henry II
arrived in Ireland in October 1171.

[98] *Ann. Tig.* 1172. He is not, however, styled 'king'.

[99] *Song of Dermot*, ll. 2180–6.

[100] *AU* 1193. His death almost coincided with William Marshal's seisin of Leinster
and renewed subinfeudation: see below, pp. 131–3.

[101] His son, however, revolted against Strongbow in 1173: *Ann. Tig.* 1173. His revolt
may have been occasioned by the grant of the kingship of Uí Chennselaig to Muirchertach Mac Murchada.

Robert fitz Stephen's beleaguerment in Wexford to Strongbow in Dublin in 1171; and he took part in the Anglo-Norman rout of Ruaidrí Ua Conchobair's forces at Dublin.[102] According to the 'Song of Dermot', Strongbow 'gave the pleas of Leinster' to Domnall Caemánach.[103] Whatever the precise significance of this grant,[104] it should probably be interpreted as an acknowledgement of Domnall Caemánach's part in aiding Strongbow to establish his authority over the Irish of Leinster beyond Uí Chennselaig.

There is little extant evidence about the Mac Murchada family in the thirteenth century.[105] Sources dealing with the Irish of Leinster after Anglo-Norman intervention are practically non-existent. When information becomes available about the Mac Murchada family in the later thirteenth century it is because their activities had begun to impinge on the royal administration in Dublin. About 1274 Muirchertach Mac Murchada, grandson of Domnall Caemánach, styled king of Leinster, and his brother Art, appear as disturbers of the peace in the Carlow area. Although Muirchertach and Art figured as rebels in the records of the royal administration in Dublin, nevertheless they appear to have been on amicable terms with Roger Bigod, earl of Norfolk, and lord of the liberty of Carlow; they must in fact have been under his protection when they were killed, apparently with the connivance of the justiciar, in 1282, since Roger protested about their murder to the king.[106]

Diarmait Mac Murchada may be deemed to have achieved his aim of ensuring that the kingship of Uí Chennselaig and the provincial kingship of Leinster were restored to, and remained

---

[102] *Song of Dermot*, ll. 1605–10, 1784–7.

[103] Ibid. 2186–90, 3211. Dr Evelyn Mullally, Dept. of French, Queen's University, Belfast, is preparing a new edition and translation of the so-called 'Song of Dermot and the Earl', which she kindly allowed me to consult.

[104] An overking would appear to have been entitled to a portion of the legal fines paid in compensation to his subordinates: see below, pp. 238–41. It is possible that it was the legal fees accruing from the provincial kingship of Leinster which Strongbow assigned to Domnall Caemánach for his support. It is conceivable that Domnall already held these in the time of Diarmait Mac Murchada.

[105] Mauricius Mac Murchat witnessed a charter of Stephen Archdeacon in favour of Inistioge priory in Osraige about 1218–28, and a Luke Mac Morecud witnessed a charter of Claricia, daughter of Gilbert fitz Griffin, about 1240–54: *Ormond deeds, 1172–1350*, nos. 45, 57.

[106] *Ann. Inisf.* 1282. 3; *Ann. Conn.* 1282. 2; R. Frame, 'The justiciar and the murder of the MacMurroughs in 1282', *IHS* 18 (1972), 223–30.

with, his descendants. Strongbow established himself as lord of Leinster after Diarmait's death in 1171 and successfully defended his possession thereof against Irish opponents in Leinster, as well as against the high-king Ruaidrí Ua Conchobair, and King Henry II. When Strongbow died in 1176 he was succeeded by his son Gilbert, and when the latter died about 1185, by his daughter Isabella, grandchildren of Diarmait Mac Murchada.[107] This was succession in the female line in right of Aífe, but the evidence suggests that for Diarmait this would have been preferable to the succession of his brother, or his brother's heirs, or of any other Irish royal dynast. When the Anglo-Norman colony in Leinster began to decline in the thirteenth century the Gaelic hegemony of Leinster was reclaimed by direct descendants of Diarmait, via his son Domnall Caemánach, who are recorded as using the title of king of Leinster until 1603.[108]

---

[107] See below, pp. 124–6 and ch. 4 n. 73.

[108] *NHI* ix. 149; K. W. Nicholls, 'The Kavanaghs, 1400–1700', *Ir. Geneal.* 5, no. 4 (1977), 435–47; no. 5 (1978), 573–80; no. 6 (1979), 730–4; 6, no. 2 (1981), 189–203.

4

Strongbow's Succession to the Lordship of Leinster

THE marriage proposal made to Strongbow by Diarmait Mac Murchada also has to be considered from the standpoint of Strongbow. Why was he prepared to entertain Mac Murchada's offer of marriage to Aífe and succession to the kingship of Leinster after his death when it was made in 1166–7, and to go to Ireland and marry Aífe in 1170, and what effect did it have on his career and fortunes?

It is necessary to consider Strongbow's family origins and determine the extent of the estates which he held in England, Wales, and Normandy prior to his involvement in Ireland. Strongbow was a descendant of Richard fitz Gilbert, lord of Orbec and Bienfaite, who had crossed with William the Conqueror to England in 1066 and was rewarded with the lordships of Clare in Suffolk and Tonbridge in Kent. When Richard died in 1090 his Norman lands were inherited by his eldest son, Roger, while the English estates went to his younger son, Gilbert, founder of the Clare line of the family in England.[1] The family enjoyed the favour of King Henry I.[2] Walter, a younger brother of Gilbert, lord of Clare, was granted the lordship of Strigoil by Henry I some time before 1119. Henry also granted to Walter a number of additional English estates which had been held by the previous lord of Strigoil,

An earlier version of this chapter appeared as M. T. Flanagan, 'Strongbow, Henry II and Anglo-Norman intervention in Ireland', in J. Gillingham and J. C. Holt (edd.), *War and government in the Middle Ages: essays in honour of J. O. Prestwich* (Woodbridge, 1984), 62–77.

[1] I. J. Sanders, *English baronies: a study of their origins and descent, 1086–1327* (London, 1960), 34–5; M. Altschul, *A baronial family in medieval England: the Clares, 1217–1314* (Baltimore, 1965), 17–28; G. E. C., *Peerage*, iii. 242–4, vi. 498–501, x. 348–57.

[2] Gilbert fitz Richard and his brothers, Walter, Robert, and Richard, abbot of Ely, were frequent witnesses to Henry I's charters: *Regesta regum Anglo-Normannorum*, ii. 420–1, s.n. Clare. Robert was granted the lordship of Little Dunmow in Essex by Henry I: Sanders, *English baronies*, 129.

William of Eu, notably the manors of Weston in Hertfordshire and Badgeworth in Gloucestershire.[3] In 1130, when Roger, lord of Orbec and Bienfaite, died without heirs, his lands passed to Gilbert, a younger son of Gilbert, lord of Clare. About 1138 Walter, who had been granted the lordship of Strigoil by Henry I, died without heirs and his estates also passed to Gilbert. Gilbert now held the lands of the senior branch of the family in Normandy, which had been held by his paternal uncle Roger, and the lordship of Strigoil, which his paternal uncle Walter, a younger son like himself, had received from Henry I. In addition, in 1138 King Stephen created Gilbert earl of Pembroke.[4] Such was the inheritance to which

---

[3] Walter fitz Richard was in possession by October 1119, when he was named in a bull of Pope Callistus relating to the church of Llandaff: *Episc. acts*, i. 616. The lordship of Strigoil included at this period the later lordship of Usk: A. J. Taylor, 'Usk castle and the pipe roll of 1185', *Archaeologia Cambrensis*, 99 (1947), 249–55. The nucleus of the lordship of Strigoil had been granted by William the Conqueror to William fitz Osbern, earl of Hereford, who built the first castle at Chepstow, whence he subdued most of the land west of the Wye, the present county of Gwent. Earl William added several villages in Wales to the customary payment of King 'Griffin'. He also enfeoffed Ralph de Limesi of fifty carucates of land in Wales, and he himself held in demesne at least seven villages in Wales: *Domesday Book*, i. 162a; cf. W. E. Wightman, 'The palatine earldom of William fitz Osbern in Gloucestershire and Worcestershire', *EHR* 77 (1962), 6–17. In 1075, Roger, earl of Hereford, who had succeeded his father in 1071, forfeited the lordship of Strigoil and other lands on account of rebellion against the Conqueror. His vassal, Ralph de Limesi, also forfeited his holdings. By 1086, when Domesday Book was compiled, the lordship of Strigoil and the other holdings of Ralph de Limesi were held of the king by William of Eu: *Domesday Book*, i. 162a; A. S. Ellis, 'On the landholders of Gloucestershire named in Domesday Book', *Trans. Bristol and Glos. Arch. Soc.* 4 (1879–80), 86–198 (at 125–9). William of Eu in turn forfeited the lordship of Strigoil and the former holdings of Ralph de Limesi, but not apparently his patrimonial lands, by rebelling against William Rufus in 1096: Freeman, *William Rufus*, ii. 64–5, 68. The lands which were additional to the original lordship of Strigoil may be identified by isolating in Domesday Book those holdings of William of Eu which had been held previously by Ralph de Limesi and/or Alestan of Buscombe, whose estates Ralph de Limesi acquired after the Conquest. In 1130 Walter fitz Richard paid danegeld on land in Herts., Beds., Glos., Berks., and Wilts.: *Pipe Roll 31 Henry II*, 23, 62, 80, 104 (the counties of Somerset, Worcestershire, and Herefordshire are missing from the 1130 pipe roll). For William of Eu's holdings in these counties see *Domesday Book*, i. 61a, xii. 71b, xxxii. 162a, xxxi. 211b, xviii. In addition, Walter fitz Richard acquired the manor of Chesterford in Essex, which almost certainly came from the royal demesne: see below, n. 58. Walter's nephew, Baldwin, son of Gilbert fitz Richard, lord of Clare, another frequent witness of Henry I's charters, was given the heiress and honour of Bourne, Lincs., by Henry I: *Facsimiles of early charters from Northamptonshire collections*, ed. F. M. Stenton (Northamptonshire Record Society, 4; [Northampton] 1929), 18–20; Sanders, *English baronies*, 107–8.

[4] Orderic Vitalis, *Ecclesiastical history*, vi. 520. For Gilbert's subsequent relations with Stephen see G. E. C., *Peerage*, x. 348–51; Davis, *King Stephen*, 95–6, 136, 145.

Gilbert's son, Richard, known as Richard fitz Gilbert, or Strongbow, succeeded on the death of his father in 1148. In 1153 Strongbow witnessed the treaty between King Stephen and Henry, duke of Normandy, as 'comes de Pembroc'.[5] This is the last occasion in any royal document in which Strongbow was so named: after Henry II's accession he was not accorded a comital title in official sources, being termed merely Richard fitz Gilbert, or at best Richard, son of Earl Gilbert.[6] This suggests that Henry II refused to acknowledge Strongbow as earl of Pembroke.[7]

The reason why Henry did so is obscure. It may have been because Strongbow supported King Stephen against Henry fitz Empress, and this despite the fact that the lordship of Strigoil was menacingly close to the Angevin stronghold of Bristol: Chepstow, the *caput* of the lordship of Strigoil, overlooked a harbour through which the castle could be supplied at all times of the year from Bristol. That Strongbow's adherence to Stephen was the reason why Henry refused to acknowledge Strongbow as earl of Pembroke is suggested by his loss of the lordship of Orbec and Bienfaite when the Angevin party gained control of Normandy: from 1153 onwards Orbec and Bienfaite was in the possession of Robert de Montfort, who must have been granted it by Henry as duke of Normandy.[8] Henry, after

---

[5] *Regesta regum Anglo-Normannorum*, iii, no. 272; *Recueil des actes de Henri II*, ed. Delisle and Berger, i. 64.

[6] In January 1156 Richard fitz Gilbert without comital title was a witness to a charter of Henry II in favour of Aubrey de Vere: *Sir Christopher Hatton's book of seals*, ed. L. C. Loyd and D. M. Stenton (Oxford, 1950), no. 40; Eyton, *Itinerary*, 16. Strongbow is not found again in the company of Henry II until late 1167 or early 1168, when he accompanied Henry's daughter Matilda to Germany: see below, n. 24. See also *Recueil des actes de Henri II*, i. 310, 467; ii. 376, 398.

[7] Strongbow was not the only one denied a comital title by Henry II after his accession. At least ten of the earldoms created by Stephen or Matilda were either not recognized by Henry or were allowed to lapse when their holder died: Warren, *Henry II*, 365. That Strongbow was earl of Pembroke only between 1148 and 1154 has been overlooked by G. E. C., *Peerage*, x. 352–60, and many others. G. H. Orpen's interpretation of Strongbow's circumstances in his *Normans*, i. 85–91, was substantially correct, but his remarks have been largely ignored by subsequent writers on the Normans in Ireland, and Strongbow is titled earl of Pembroke without qualification in numerous works.

[8] In 1153 Orbec was in the hands of Robert de Montfort of Montfort-sur-Risle, son of Hugh de Montfort by Adeline, daughter of Robert de Beaumont, count of Meulan and earl of Leicester, and sister of Isabella, mother of Strongbow: Robert of Torigny, 177–8. Orbec was still held by Robert de Montfort in 1172: *Magni rotuli scaccarii Normanniae*, ed. T. Stapleton, ii (London, 1844), p. cxxxvii. After Robert's death in 1178

his accession as king, must have had some negotiations with Strongbow, as he had with the majority of Stephen's supporters, but the details are not known. He recognized Strongbow's inheritance of the lordship of Strigoil and other estates in England and Normandy, but he was not prepared to restore to him the lordship of Orbec and Bienfaite, nor to allow him the use of a comital title, nor possession of the earldom of Pembroke.[9] Pembroke appears to have been retained as a royal county throughout Henry's reign.[10]

From 1164 onwards Strongbow could claim that he was further deprived by Henry II of lands to which he had an inherited claim. In that year, Walter, Earl Giffard, died without male heirs. Strongbow and his cousin, Roger fitz Richard, lord of Clare, each had an entitlement to the estate as descendants of Rohesia Giffard, daughter of Walter Giffard, who had been married to Richard fitz Gilbert, the companion of the Conqueror.[11]

it was in the possession of his widow Clemence: *Cartulaires de Saint Ymer-en-Auge et de Bricquebec*, ed. C. Bréard (Société de l'Histoire de Normandie, 71; Rouen, 1908), no. xii. This charter, which has been dated by Bréard to 1194, should probably be assigned to a period after 1181–2, as Clemence's gift is not mentioned in the papal bull of 1182 (as pointed out in G. E. C., *Peerage*, x. 353), but before 1194. By 1194 Orbec was held by Clemence's son, Hugh de Montfort: *Cartulaires*, no. xiii. It was recovered by William Marshal in right of his wife Isabella, daughter of Strongbow, at some point between 1194 and 1204; in 1204, in the division of estates resultant upon John's forfeiture of Normandy to the French king, Orbec was retained by William Marshal: F. M. Powicke, *The loss of Normandy* (2nd edn., London, 1961), 350.

[9] Strongbow issued at least three charters in which he styled himself 'comes de Pembroc': in favour of Bertram son of Thierry, relating to Barrow in Suffolk, *Cal. chart. rolls, 1300–1326*, 64; in favour of Biddlesden Abbey, see below, ch. 5 n. 93; and confirming the church of Everton in Bedfordshire to the priory of St Neots (without witness list), BL Cott. Faust. A. iv, fo. 73a. *Cal. chart. rolls, 1257–1300*, 72, contains an English summary of a charter granted by Strongbow styled 'earl of Pembroke' to Tintern Abbey, but, as I have not checked the enrolment, I do not know whether the title actually occurs on it. The charters cannot be dated precisely. They may have been issued during the period 1148–54.

[10] A positive indication that Strongbow did not enjoy the earldom of Pembroke after Henry II's accession is the fact that William Marshal did not succeed to the earldom of Pembroke in 1189 when he married Strongbow's daughter Isabella, but had to wait until 1199, when it was conferred on him by King John: see below, n. 91. Returns from Pembroke are not recorded on the pipe rolls, but Gerald of Wales mentioned one William Carquit, about 1174–6, as sheriff of Pembroke: *Gir. Camb. op.* i. 25–6. In 1171 before Henry II crossed to Ireland he assigned royal custodians to the castles of Pembroke: Giraldus, *Expugnatio*, 91, and below, ch. 5. Cf. his general confirmation of the rights of the see of St Davids issued about the same time: *Cal. chart. rolls, 1226–57*, 258.

[11] Altschul, *A baronial family*, 24–5; S. Painter, *William Marshal* (Baltimore, 1933), 74.

Henry II, however, was to retain the Giffard honour in his own hands until his death in 1189.[12]

According to Gerald of Wales, when Strongbow entered into an agreement with Diarmait Mac Murchada about 1166–7 'he had a great name, rather than great prospects, ancestral prestige rather than ability; he had succeeded to a name rather than possessions'.[13] Gerald's statement is apt, in so far as Strongbow had lost Orbec and Bienfaite and the earldom of Pembroke and had been withheld from his entitlement to part of the honour of Giffard. William of Newburgh gave a similar assessment of Strongbow's circumstances: the reason why Strongbow was anxious to go to Ireland was that he had wasted most of his inheritance and wanted to get away from his creditors.[14] During the winter of 1166–7, when Diarmait Mac Murchada was actively recruiting troops for military service in Ireland, he was the guest of the Bristol merchant Robert fitz Harding.[15] It may have been fitz Harding who first put Diarmait in touch with Strongbow. Fitz Harding had been an astute money-lender during Stephen's reign, with a keen eye for impoverished landowners.[16] There is circumstantial evid-

---

[12] Pipe Rolls 14–34 Henry II under Bucks. = Pipe Roll Society, vols. 12–28; *Magni rotuli scaccarii Normanniae*, i. 59.

[13] Giraldus, *Expugnatio*, 54–5.

[14] William of Newburgh, 167–8. It may be inferred that Strongbow was in debt to Aaron the Jew of Lincoln: Pipe Roll 3 Richard I, 1191, reveals the 'comes de Strigoil' owing 80 marks to Aaron mortgaged on Weston: *Pipe rolls 3 and 4 Richard I*, 290. This was the first year in which the exchequer recorded the debt. Aaron died early in 1186 and his estate escheated to the Crown. Debts formerly owing to him were then collected on behalf of the king: H. G. Richardson, *The English Jewry under the Angevin kings* (London, 1960), 247. The debt must have been incurred before Aaron's death in 1186; Strongbow was therefore the only 'comes de Strigoil' who could have borrowed from Aaron. The debt is listed under Glos., a county under which Strigoil was occasionally entered on the pipe rolls, but Weston must refer to Strongbow's demesne manor in Herts. From Pipe Rolls 3 Richard I, 1191, to Pipe Rolls 3 John, 1202, the debt is re-entered each year under Glos. until in 1202 William Marshal, who had married Isabella, Strongbow's daughter and heir, in 1189, finally secured a pardon for it from King John: *Pipe roll 3 John*, 41. An entry on *Pipe roll 16 Henry II*, 78, records that Josce, a Jew of Gloucester, owed 100 shillings as an amercement for the money which he lent to those who went against the king's prohibition to Ireland. Strongbow may also have borrowed from Josce of Gloucester. Walter fitz Richard had two burgess tenants in the town of Gloucester in the reign of Henry I: Ellis, 'Landholders of Gloucestershire', 91.

[15] *Song of Dermot*, ll. 230–5, 300–11.

[16] A suggestion which I owe to John Prestwich. Robert fitz Harding purchased estates in Somerset from Robert, earl of Gloucester, Richard de Morevill, and Julian de Banton, in Gloucestershire from Richard Foliot, and in Devon from William de Braose: John Smyth of Nibley, *The lives of the Berkeleys*, ed. J. Maclean (Gloucester, 1883),

ence to suggest that Strongbow had financial dealings with Robert fitz Harding. Nicholas, second son of Robert fitz Harding, and his heirs held the manor and advowson of Tickenham in Somerset, which was attached to the honour of Strigoil.[17] In Domesday Book Tickenham was held in demesne by William of Eu,[18] whose lordship of Strigoil was subsequently granted to Walter fitz Richard, Strongbow's granduncle.[19] It is likely that Tickenham was a portion of the lordship of Strigoil which had been mortgaged or sold by Strongbow to Robert fitz Harding, whence it passed to Nicholas fitz Harding.[20] It may have been Robert fitz Harding who considered Strongbow just the man to take a gamble on recovering his fortunes in Ireland. If the venture succeeded, it might create more favourable conditions for an increase in the existent trade between Bristol and Dublin,[21] in which fitz Harding would have had a vested interest.

According to Gerald of Wales and the 'Song of Dermot', Strongbow sought permission from Henry II to go to the aid of Diarmait Mac Murchada in Ireland. Gerald stated that Henry gave it, although more in jest than in earnest.[22] Gervase of Canterbury agrees with Gerald that Strongbow secured the king's permission to go to Ireland, but adds that nevertheless Strongbow's relations with Henry remained strained.[23] Gervase dated Henry's displeasure with Strongbow to three years before the king's own expedition to Ireland. Since Henry went to Ireland in October 1171, this would assign the incident which Gervase had in mind to about 1168. In that year Strongbow was a member of the escort of Henry's daughter Matilda to Germany, on the occasion of her marriage to Henry, duke of Saxony.[24] There is little evidence that Strongbow had enjoyed the favour of the king at any point between 1154 and 1168:

---

i. 34–5. Fitz Harding also leased land from the Benedictine abbey of Gloucester for a term of 5 years in return for a loan of £80: *VCH Glos.* ii. 54 and n. 32.

[17] John Smyth of Nibley, i. 45–6.

[18] *Domesday Book*, i. 96b.

[19] See above, n. 3.

[20] It continued to be held of the honour of Strigoil for the service of 40 days guard duty at the castle of Strigoil in time of war: Ellis, 'Landholders of Gloucestershire', 125–9.

[21] Gwynn, 'Medieval Bristol and Dublin'.

[22] Giraldus, *Expugnatio*, 54–7; *Song of Dermot*, ll. 356–62.

[23] Gervase of Canterbury, i. 234

[24] Ralph of Diss, i. 330.

he was not a regular member of Henry's household, nor frequently seen at court. Possibly Strongbow had gone to the king to request permission to go to Ireland and to marry Aífe, and Henry had delayed his departure deliberately by dispatching him on the embassy to Germany. Henry may then have agreed, albeit reluctantly, to let Strongbow go to Ireland. According to William of Newburgh, Strongbow was about to sail for Ireland when persons acting on behalf of Henry tried to prevent his departure, threatening him with sequestration of his estates.[25] Despite these threats Strongbow set sail about August 1170.

That Strongbow's lands in Wales and England were sequestrated subsequently is evidenced from the pipe rolls: pipe roll 16 Henry II (19 December 1169–18 December 1170) records a payment of ten pounds by the king's writ for the fortification of the castle of Strigoil, indicating that it had been taken into the king's hand.[26] Strongbow's demesne manor of Weston in Hertfordshire is listed on pipe rolls 16 and 17 Henry II as in the king's hand.[27]

Strongbow's arrival in Ireland in August 1170 was not his first positive response to Diarmait Mac Murchada's proposal of military service and reward in Ireland. The group of mercenaries led by Robert fitz Stephen who went to Ireland in the autumn of 1169 had been accompanied by Strongbow's uncle, Hervey de Montmorency. Raymond le Gros, whom Gerald termed a member of Strongbow's household, was acting on Strongbow's behalf when he captured the city of Waterford in the spring of 1170.[28] Despite Gerald of Wales's unfavourable portrayal of Strongbow and his poor opinion of him as a military leader, compared with the greater achievements of Gerald's relatives as he depicted them, it was not until after the arrival of Strongbow that Diarmait Mac Murchada was able to extend his activities beyond Leinster. Even Gerald of Wales had to admit grudgingly that within a short time of his arrival 'Strongbow had overrun not only Leinster but many other places which did not belong to himself or his wife by any legal right'.[29]

---

[25] William of Newburgh, i. 167–8.   [26] *Pipe roll 16 Henry II*, 75.
[27] *Pipe roll 16 Henry II*, 105; *17 Henry II*, 119.
[28] Giraldus, *Expugnatio*, 56–7.   [29] Ibid. 70–1.

Gerald recounted that news of these events spread rapidly and that, in reaction, Henry II closed the ports to Ireland and ordered that all persons from his dominions who had gone there without permission should either return before Easter 1171, or face seizure of their estates.[30] The closing of the ports is corroborated by William of Newburgh and the pipe rolls, which furnish evidence of a number of fines paid by individuals who went to Ireland without the king's permission.[31]

Already in 1170, therefore, Henry II was disquieted by Strongbow's activities in Ireland. William of Newburgh related that Henry obliged Strongbow, 'now nearly a king', to make peace with him.[32] Gerald of Wales described Strongbow sending Raymond le Gros to speak on his behalf to Henry, and still awaiting a reply from a procrastinating king when news of the murder of Thomas Becket (29 December 1170) reached the court.[33] Raymond apparently had to return to Ireland without a favourable response from Henry.

When Diarmait Mac Murchada died in May 1171, having regained the kingship of Leinster, and with his overseas troops in control of the Hiberno-Norse towns of Dublin and Waterford, Ruaidrí Ua Conchobair, king of Connacht and high-king of Ireland, immediately challenged Strongbow for control of the city of Dublin. Strongbow resisted successfully, but nevertheless failed to win formal recognition of his Irish acquisitions from Ruaidrí Ua Conchobair. In these circumstances Strongbow had little option but to continue to negotiate with Henry II. His estates in England, Wales, and Normandy had been sequestrated, and it was by no means clear in 1171 that his gains in Ireland would be sufficiently great or permanent to enable him to abandon his lands in Henry's dominions.

Accordingly, Strongbow dispatched his uncle, Hervey de Montmorency, to continue negotiations with Henry. Robert of

---

[30] Ibid.

[31] William of Newburgh, i. 167–8; Wido Wallensis entered under Somerset, Geoffrey Cophin under Devon, Roger de Ulhela under War. and Leics.: *Pipe roll 17 Henry II*, 17, 29, 92; Peter Morell under Bucks. and Beds.: *Pipe roll 18 Henry II*, 49.

[31] The death of Robert fitz Harding in February 1170 may have been a contributory factor to Henry's disquiet, news of which may have caused Henry to try and prevent Strongbow's departure for Ireland. It is possible that fitz Harding had indicated to Henry that he would act as guarantor for Strongbow's conduct in Ireland.

[33] Giraldus, *Expugnatio*, 72–3.

Torigny, writing in Normandy, detailed de Montmorency's arrival at the court of Argentan in July 1171. On behalf of Strongbow, Hervey offered the surrender of his nephew's Irish acquisitions to the king. Henry's response, according to Robert, was to persist in the sequestration of Strongbow's lands in England and Normandy, and to order Strongbow to surrender to Henry the land which he had acquired in Ireland in right of his wife, although he conceded to Strongbow that he might be constable or seneschal of Ireland.[34] On de Montmorency's return to Ireland Strongbow was persuaded, both by his uncle's personal entreaty and by letters brought to him from the king, that it would be politic to go to Henry in person.

Strongbow travelled to meet Henry at Newnham in Gloucestershire and, after lengthy argument ('post multas et varias altercaciones, tandem Herveii circumventu pariter et interventu regia erga ipsum sic resedit indignacio'), agreed to surrender the city of Dublin and its adjacent territory, the coastal towns, and all castles to the king and to hold from Henry the remainder of the land which he had acquired in Ireland.[35] Strongbow might promise to do so; it was another matter to effect his compliance. Henry still felt it was necessary to go to Ireland to enforce the agreement and to demonstrate publicly

---

[34] 'Mense Julio rex congregavit barones suos apud Argentonium et cum ibi tractaretur de profectione sua in Hiberniam, legati comitis Ricardi venerunt ad eum, dicentes ex parte comitis quod traderet ei civitatem Duvelinae, et Waterford, et alias firmitates suas, quas habebat causa uxoris suae, quae fuerat filia regis Duvelinensis, qui jam obierat. Rex, itaque, audito hoc nuncio, mandavit comiti quod redderet ei terram suam in Anglia et in Normanniae et plenam terram in Hibernia, quam acceperat cum uxore sua, et concessit ei ut esset stabuli vel senescallus totius Hiberniae': Robert of Torigny, 252. Robert may have attributed Henry's appointment of Strongbow as his agent in 1173 back to 1171. F. X. Martin in Giraldus, *Expugnatio*, 309, incorrectly construing this passage, apparently following Orpen, *Normans*, i. 248, stated that to Strongbow's offer 'the king responded in equally generous fashion, confirming Strongbow in his lands in England, Wales, and Normandy, granting him (with obvious reservations) the territories he had acquired in Leinster, and even honouring him with the post of royal constable in Ireland'; repeated verbatim in *NHI* ix. 87, where it is argued that 'historians have misunderstood what took place between Henry and Strongbow'. On the basis of his interpretation of this passage of Robert of Torigny, Martin argued that Henry knew that 'Strongbow had no intention of setting up an independent kingdom in Ireland. He saw the Irish scene as an opportunity to solve several of his other pressing problems, notably Wales, and more immediately, the papal legates who were on his trail.' But from Giraldus, *Expugnatio*, 88–9, and *Song of Dermot*, ll. 2239–47, it is clear that Strongbow was not reconciled with Henry II as early as July 1171. Cf. J. E. A. Jolliffe, *Angevin kingship* (2nd edn., London, 1963), 128.

[35] Giraldus, *Expugnatio*, 88–9.

lordship of those areas which Strongbow had ceded to him and to take the towns into his own hands. It is a tribute to Strongbow's military successes in Ireland during 1170–1 that Henry felt obliged to intervene there personally.

It was not merely Strongbow's uncontrolled activities within Ireland which may have worried Henry II but, even more importantly perhaps, the potential resources which Strongbow's Irish acquisitions placed at his disposal for creating trouble within Henry's dominions, and particularly in Pembroke. From 1153 onwards Strongbow harboured a claim to the lordships of Orbec and Bienfaite, from 1154 to the lordship of Pembroke, and from 1164 to a share of the Giffard honour, all of which Henry had refused to concede. The fact that Strongbow was still unmarried in 1170 indicates that Henry had also denied Strongbow advancement by way of marriage to an heiress, which, as a tenant-in-chief of the Crown, he would normally have expected. Strongbow had most recently raised with the king the issue of the 'lands which fell to him by right of inheritance' when he sought his permission to go to Ireland about 1168.[36] In 1171 Henry was faced with the possibility that Strongbow's geographically strategic acquisitions in Leinster would provide him with the means of forcibly taking Pembroke from the king. As Gerald of Wales remarked, on a clear day Ireland was visible from St Davids Head, and the sea crossing between Pembroke and the Irish coast was but a short day's journey.[37] The majority of the troops who had gone to fight in Ireland were drawn from the district of Pembroke.[38] If Strongbow had not managed to gain *de jure* recognition as their lord in Pembroke from Henry II between 1154 and 1171, he was now *de facto* their lord in Ireland. The security of their newly-won possessions in Ireland depended on him. Were Strongbow to stage a revolt in Pembroke it was possible that he might be able to raise a significant measure of support.

The negotiations that took place between Henry and Strongbow at Newnham in 1171, and subsequently in Ireland, must indeed have been argued long and hard, and not just about what lands Strongbow might hold in Ireland, but also in relation to the lands which he held or claimed in England, Wales, and Normandy. The first concession which Strongbow appears

[36] Ibid. 54–5.   [37] *Gir. Camb. op.* vi. 109.   [38] See below, ch. 5.

to have wrung from Henry was acknowledgement of comital status. In the charter granted by Henry to Hugh de Lacy before his departure from Waterford in 1172, Strongbow, who acted as a witness, was styled 'comes Ricardus' for the first time in a royal document since Henry's accession in 1154.[39] Contemporary chroniclers, thereafter, referred to Strongbow as 'comes de Strigoil'.

Henry put Strongbow's loyalty and obedience to the test at the earliest opportunity: in 1173, when the king was faced with the rebellion in Normandy of his son, the young King Henry, he summoned Strongbow to fight on his behalf. As Kate Norgate so perceptively remarked, Henry II was guarding 'against all danger of the rebels finding support in Ireland by recalling the garrisons which he had left in the Irish coast-towns and summoning the chief men of the new vassal state, particularly Richard of Striguil and Hugh de Lacy, to join him personally in Normandy'.[40] As Strongbow had shown in Ireland, so he proved again to be a competent military commander, successfully defending Gisors for the king.[41] Strongbow had thereby managed to convince Henry of his loyalty and won further concessions from him: he returned to Ireland in the autumn of 1173 as 'vices regis Anglie in Hibernia agens', a position which he held until his premature death in 1176.[42] In 1173 Henry also ceded to Strongbow the town of Wexford and the castle of Wicklow, which he had retained in his own hand in 1171.[43]

Strongbow's gamble to try to repair his fortunes by accepting Diarmait Mac Murchada's invitation to Ireland may be said to have yielded results. A man who had been unable to find favour with Henry II throughout the period 1154–71 died as

---

[39] Orpen, *Normans*, i. 285–6.

[40] K. Norgate, *England under the Angevin kings* (London, 1887), ii. 181–2. Contrast 'for Henry to encourage such of his subjects as were bellicose and restless to take service with Mac Murchada could siphon off dissident groups within his scattered territories', *NHI* ii. 65.

[41] Roger of Howden, *Gesta*, i. 51; *Song of Dermot*, ll. 2864–945; Ralph of Diss, i. 375.

[42] Strongbow styled himself thus in a charter issued on behalf of Henry II to Thomas, abbot of Glendalough, about 1173–6; *Crede mihi*, ed. J. T. Gilbert (Dublin, 1897), 46–7.

[43] Giraldus, *Expugnatio*, 120–1; *Song of Dermot*, ll. 2902–5; M. T. Flanagan, 'Henry II and the kingdom of Uí Fáeláin', in J. Bradley (ed.), *Settlement and society in medieval Ireland: studies presented to F. X. Martin, O.S.A.* (Kilkenny, 1988), 312–24.

Henry's agent in Ireland in 1176.[44] If Strongbow had not succeeded in getting possession of the earldom of Pembroke, he had managed to persuade the king to recognize him as 'comes de Strigoil'. William of Newburgh recounted, furthermore, that as a result of his acquisitions in Ireland Strongbow, who had had little fortune previously, became celebrated for his wealth and great prosperity in England and Wales.[45]

The extent to which Strongbow's reconciliation with Henry II was effective may also be demonstrated by the fate of his estates in England, Wales, Normandy, and Ireland after his death. In 1171 Henry had ordered Strongbow to surrender his Irish acquisitions to the king. Theoretically, Henry had taken them into his own hands and regranted them to Strongbow, who then held them neither in virtue of his marriage to Aífe, daughter of Diarmait Mac Murchada, nor by right of conquest, but as a grant from Henry II. Although Gerald of Wales and the 'Song of Dermot' agree that Henry's grant to Strongbow of his Irish lands was made in fee 'to him and his heirs',[46] Henry nevertheless might have taken the opportunity afforded by Strongbow's death in 1176 to grant the lordship of Leinster to another feudatory. Henry was quite capable of ignoring the rights of inheritance of his subjects even where there was no ambiguity in their title,[47] as it might be argued there was in the case of the lands which Strongbow had acquired in Ireland.[48] There was little compulsion on Henry to honour the succession to the lordship of Leinster of Strongbow's heirs; yet he chose to recognize Strongbow's wife Aífe, and her two children, Gilbert and Isabella, as the beneficiaries and heirs of Strongbow in respect of his lands in Leinster, Wales, England, and Normandy.

[44] 'Comes Ricardus de Strigoil' was also at court about the time when the treaty of Windsor was being negotiated with Ruaidrí Ua Conchobair: Eyton, *Itinerary*, 196; *Chartul. St Mary's, Dublin*, i. 79–80.

[45] William of Newburgh, i. 169.

[46] Giraldus, *Expugnatio*, 88–9; *Song of Dermot*, ll. 2616–22.

[47] In 1175 Henry denied inheritance of the estates of Reginald, earl of Cornwall, to his daughters and to his brother William: Jolliffe, *Angevin kingship*, 128. Cf. Henry's treatment of the earldom of Gloucester: *Earldom of Gloucester charters*, ed. R. B. Patterson (London, 1973), 5 and n. 7.

[48] On the distinction between inheritance and acquisition and the king's possible intervention see J. C. Holt, 'Politics and property in early medieval England', *Past and Present*, 57 (1972), 1–52.

When Strongbow died in 1176 his only son, Gilbert, was a minor, and the responsibility of administering Strongbow's estates fell to the Crown. Gilbert died some time after 1185 before coming of age, whereupon Isabella became Strongbow's sole remaining heir.[49] The Crown retained responsibility for the wardship of Strongbow's children, and for the administration of his estates from 1176 until they passed to William Marshal in 1189 in virtue of his marriage to Isabella.

Strongbow's widow Aífe is mentioned in royal records on a number of occasions between 1176 and Isabella's marriage in 1189. Aífe, countess of Strigoil, received a payment of 60 shillings in 1176–7, and a payment of 4 pounds in 1180–1, levied on Strongbow's demesne manor of Weston.[50] In 1183–4 the 'comitissa Hiberniae' was granted an advance of 20 pounds from the king to support herself in the Welsh March.[51] In 1184–5 the 'comitissa Hiberniae' was granted 26 shillings out of the honour of Strigoil and 20 marks out of Strongbow's estates in Cambridgeshire.[52] In 1186–7, when the honour of Strigoil was assessed for the scutage of Galloway at sixty-five and a half knights' fees, 10 pounds of the sum due to the king was remitted to Aífe.[53]

The *Rotuli de dominabus* of 1185 (which recorded details of heirs and heiresses in the wardship of the Crown from some but not all counties) shows Aífe in enjoyment of the manors of Weston in Hertfordshire and Chesterford in Essex in dower.[54] She may have been assigned other lands in dower of which no record has survived. That Aífe enjoyed the use of estates in England is evidenced also by a charter which she granted to the Benedictine nunnery at Ickleton in Cambridgeshire. In 1309 the prioress of Ickleton claimed an annual rent of 13 shillings from a mill which had been granted to her convent by Aífe,

---

[49] Gilbert's existence has been generally overlooked by Irish historians. To the references concerning him in G. E. C., *Peerage*, x. 357–8, may be added the charter granted by his mother Aífe which names him: see below, p. 125.

[50] *Pipe roll 23 Henry II*, 149; *Pipe roll 27 Henry II*, 106.

[51] *Pipe roll 30 Henry II*, 154.

[52] *Pipe roll 31 Henry II*, 8, 55.

[53] *Pipe roll 33 Henry II*, 142; *Red Book of the Exchequer*, ed. H. Hall (Rolls series, London, 1897), i. 67.

[54] *Rotuli de dominabus*, 66, 76. The manors were estimated to yield a potential annual income of £40 and in 1185 yielded an actual income of £27.

countess of Ireland, and cited the following charter in support of her claim:[55]

Eva comitissa Hibernensis uxor Ricardi comitis omnibus hominibus et amicis suis presentibus et futuris salutem. Notum sit vobis quod ego pro salute anime mee et anime Ricardi comitis domini mei et anime Gilberti filii mei dedi et concessi et hac presenti carta mea confirmavi Deo et ecclesie Sancte Marie Magdalene de Ikelington et eiusdem ecclesie monialibus unam marcam redditus in molendino meo de Sproteford in liberam et puram et perpetuam elemosinam scilicet unam dimidiam marcam argenti ad coquinam earum et aliam dimidiam marcam ad luminare ecclesie. Et predicte moniales recipient supradictam redditus ad duos anni terminos scilicet unam dimidiam marcam ad pascham et aliam dimidiam marcam ad festum sancti Michaelis. Hiis testibus Willelmo capellano, Silvestro persona de ville de Sancto Leg., Willelmo de la More, Waltero le Balde, Petro le Botiler, Waltero Maltravers, Godefrido Butiler, Willelmo Venator, Radulpho de Bedeford, Henrico filio Willemi de Dukesworth, Ricardo scriptore.

It is impossible to date this charter precisely because of the obscurity of the witnesses. It probably dates from the period between Aífe's marriage to Strongbow in 1170 and his death in 1176.[56] Thereafter, since Aífe merely had a life interest in her dower lands, she should not have granted away any portion without the consent of her husband's heir and the confirmation of the king. It has not proved possible to identify the mill of

---

[55] London, PRO, E 159/82/m. 62. I wish to thank Dr J. R. S. Phillips, Dept. of medieval History, University College, Dublin, for bringing this text to my notice.

[56] Cf. the small grant of a yearly payment of a half mark from her mill in Carbrooke given by Matilda of St Hilary, wife of Roger, earl of Hertford (d. 1173), of the senior branch of the Clare family and of a messuage in Sudbury, Suffolk, given by Amicia, wife of Richard, earl of Hertford (d. 1217), to the priory of Stoke by Clare, both probably made from their *maritagia*: J. C. Ward, 'Fashions in monastic endowment: the foundations of the Clare family', *Jn. Ecc. Hist.* 32 (1981), 427–51. The Benedictine nunnery of Ickleton was founded by a member of the de Valoines family. Benedictine nunneries had not previously enjoyed Clare patronage. Strongbow founded a Benedictine nunnery at Usk about 1173 after the recapture of Usk from the Welsh: T. Wakeman, 'On the town, castle, and priory of Usk', *Journal of the British Archaeological Association*, 10 (1855), 257–65; below, ch. 5 n. 88. This may have been due to Aífe's influence. Diarmait Mac Murchada founded at least three nunneries in Leinster before 1152: St Mary de Hogges in Dublin, Aghade in Co. Carlow, and Kilculiheen in Co. Kilkenny: *Calendar of Archbishop Alen's register*, 293; Gwynn and Hadcock, *Med. relig. houses*, 312, 316–17, 319. The most important nunnery in Leinster was at Kildare, the abbacy of which was on several occasions in the 12th century occupied by members of the Mac Murchada family.

Sproteford from which the prioress of Ickleton claimed a mark originally granted to her convent by Aífe. It is noteworthy, however, that Ickleton priory held land in Chesterford,[57] and that a portion of the lands attached to Strongbow's manor of Chesterford was located in Cambridgeshire.[58] This provides a satisfactory explanation of how Aífe might have come into contact with the Cambridgeshire nunnery of Ickleton, and strongly supports the authenticity of the claim and the text of the charter recited by the prioress of Ickleton before the king's court in 1309. Although this is a fourteenth-century transcript of a twelfth-century charter, there is no reason to doubt the reliability of the text. The style 'comitissa Hibernensis', apparently used by Aífe in the charter, can be paralleled in contemporary references to Aífe on the pipe rolls and the *Rotuli de dominabus*.[59] Although Henry had refused to acknowledge Strongbow as earl of Pembroke, Strongbow did win royal recognition after 1171 for his enjoyment of a comital title. After his death Aífe was styled variously 'comitissa de Strigoil' and 'comitissa Hiberniae' in royal records. This charter suggests that the latter was the title which she herself preferred. It may be that she, or her advisers, were attempting to associate the comital title with the lordship of Leinster.

Aífe's proven enjoyment of Strongbow's estates in England and Wales raises an interesting question about the negotiations

---

[57] Dugdale, *Monasticon Anglicanum*, iv. 440; *VCH Cambs.* ii. 223–6.

[58] In the Domesday survey of Essex the manor of Chesterford appears as royal demesne consisting of 10 hides in the custody of Picot, the sheriff. One and a half hides, however, are stated to have been in Cambs. These may be located at Histon, for the Cambridgeshire Domesday Book recorded that Picot had 1½ hides of the manor of Chesterford, which were taxed in the hundred in which they were situated in Cambs., but which had been appraised in Essex: *Domesday Book*, i. 189b, ii. 3. The Cambridgeshire lands of Chesterford manor explain the payment of 20 marks to Aífe on the pipe roll of 1184–5 which were accounted for by the sheriff of Cambs. and Hunts.: above, n. 52. The manor of Chesterford did not, as Painter thought, come to Strongbow's predecessors out of escheated estates of William of Eu: Painter, *William Marshal*, 77. It was almost certainly granted to Walter fitz Richard out of royal demesne, possibly after 1130 and before Walter's death in 1138, since Walter does not appear to have paid danegeld on lands in Essex in 1130; see above, n. 3.

[59] *Pipe roll 27 Henry II*, 106; *Pipe roll 30 Henry II*, 154; *Pipe roll 31 Henry II*, 55 (note that she is also styled 'comitissa de Strigoil', on the same roll, 8); *Rotuli de dominabus*, 66, 76. Compare J. H. Round, 'The countess of Ireland', *The Genealogist*, NS 18 (1901), 166–7. A small point in favour of the authenticity of the charter is the witness William Dukesworth. William Marshal can be shown to have held £5 worth of land at Dukesworth: *Red Book of the Exchequer*, ii. 331, 575.

which may have taken place between Diarmait Mac Murchada and Strongbow either in 1166–7 or on the occasion of the marriage of Aífe and Strongbow in 1170. Irish historians have not been slow to suggest that Strongbow's inheritance of Leinster in right of his wife was invalid in Irish law,[60] but it has been overlooked that if Strongbow gained an inheritance in right of his wife in Ireland, so too did Aífe and her children gain an inheritance in right of Strongbow in England, Wales, and Normandy. Was Diarmait Mac Murchada aware of this possibility when he offered his daughter in marriage to Strongbow? On the evidence of contemporaries, neither Strongbow's wealth nor position was considered great in 1166–7. But they had potential. The lordship of Strigoil[61] was conveniently situated to the port of Bristol, which had important trading relations with the eastern ports of Dublin, Waterford, and Wexford, in which Diarmait Mac Murchada had strong connections and interests. In addition, Strongbow had a claim to the lordship of Pembroke, which, if obtained, would be appositely positioned across the Irish sea from Diarmait's patrimonial lands of Uí Chennselaig, the area over which he exercised the most effective lordship. It is possible that the recovery not merely of the kingdom of Leinster, but also of the lordship of Pembroke was discussed by Diarmait and Strongbow. As Diarmait would have been aware, Irish aid recruited in Leinster had restored a number of Welsh rulers to their kingdoms in the eleventh and twelfth centuries.[62] He may have calculated on another advantage from the alliance with Strongbow besides military aid to recover the lordship of Leinster. He may also have taken into account that, in accordance with feudal inheritance practices, Aífe might enjoy certain revenues from Strongbow's estates in England, Wales, and Normandy during her lifetime, and that any children from the marriage of Aífe and Strongbow would inherit the title to Stronghow's estates within the Angevin dominions. According to feudal custom a widow was entitled for the duration of her life to the

---

[60] See above, pp. 80–1.

[61] In addition to the lands situated in the Welsh March between the Wye and the Usk, the honour of Strigoil comprised the demesne manors of Weston in Herts., Chesterford in Essex, and Badgeworth in Glos., and 65½ knights' fees scattered through 9 different counties in England: *Red Book of the Exchequer*, i. 288.

[62] See above, pp. 61–7.

profits of one-third of her husband's demesne estates.[63] The designation of dower lands was often determined before or on the occasion of marriage. It is possible that Strongbow may have assigned dower lands to Aífe either in 1166–7 or when they married in 1170. That this is not improbable is suggested by the surviving text of a dower charter which John de Courcy, the Anglo-Norman conqueror of Ulaid, granted to Affreca, daughter of Godred, king of the Isle of Man, on the occasion of their marriage about 1180.[64] Indeed, de Courcy's marriage to the daughter of the king of the Isle of Man bears comparison with that of Strongbow and Aífe in its awareness of the potential for co-ordinated co-operation across the Irish Sea: a major advantage which de Courcy's marriage to Affreca afforded him was access to his father-in-law's fleet.

There is no extant dower charter from Strongbow to Aífe, which might have indicated that such matters as Aífe's enjoyment of Strongbow's estates in Henry's dominions had been raised before she married Strongbow in 1170. But even if dower was not determined in detail, Diarmait Mac Murchada may well have been content to gamble on the advantages of a marriage alliance which might provide him with grandchildren who would inherit the lordship of Strigoil and other estates in England and Normandy and a claim to the lordship of Pembroke.

Whether or not Strongbow made a formal settlement of dower on Aífe, she was still entitled in the event of her husband's death to the customary enjoyment of one-third of those estates which her husband possessed in demesne at the time of their marriage. The king, who took custody of the entire estates of a tenant-in-chief at death if he died without heirs, or if his heir was a minor, was in theory obliged to allow dower to his widow.[65] In practice, the king might, and often did, decide

---

[63] *The treatise on the laws and customs of the realm of England commonly called Glanvill*, ed. G. D. G. Hall (London, 1965), 58–69, 183–4. A demesne manor was one which the lord retained in his own hands as an economic unit and which remained directly accountable to his officials. Only such a manor could be given in dower. The manors known to have been held by Aífe in dower provide no indication of the extent of Strongbow's lands which were held by tenants in fee from him.

[64] E. Curtis, 'Two unpublished charters of John de Courcy, *princeps Ulidiae*', *Belfast Nat. Hist. Soc. Proc.*, session 1928–9 (1930), 2–9.

[65] See above, n. 63.

quite arbitrarily just how much or how little she would get. Henry did allow Aífe dower, though whether she received her full entitlement is impossible to say.

Aífe's first recorded allowance, levied on Strongbow's demesne manor of Weston, was paid by the king in 1176–7, that is within a short time of Strongbow's death.[66] In addition to other payments which she subsequently received, there is some evidence to suggest that she may also have enjoyed the Marcher lordship of Strigoil in person for a period.[67] How the lordship of Strigoil was administered between Strongbow's death in 1176 and 1183–4, when it is first mentioned on the pipe rolls, is obscure. The 1183–4 pipe roll records an advance of 20 pounds from the king to Aífe to support herself in the Welsh March.[68] The Welsh were attacking Glamorgan in 1184 and it is possible that Strigoil was considered to be endangered.[69] The sum of 20 pounds suggests that Aífe was, in fact, being assigned the responsibilities of a military commander in this region, for 20 pounds was precisely the figure paid to Ralph Bloet from 1184–5 onwards for his custody of the honour and castle of Strigoil on behalf of the king.[70] The expenditure on repairs to the castle and on restocking and seed, also recorded in 1184–5, suggests that the administration of Strigoil may have been taken over by the Crown for the first time in that year. There is also a separate entry on the pipe roll of 1184–5 for Strongbow's castle of Usk.[71] Thereafter, Strigoil (there is no further separate mention of Usk) appears as farmed by the Crown until the end of Henry's reign.[72] There is a blank entry for Strigoil on the pipe roll of 1 Richard I, presumably because the exchequer had prepared the headings for the roll in

[66] See above, n. 50.

[67] It is not impossible that she held the Marcher lordship in dower. Margaret, countess of Warwick, held the Marcher lordship of Gower in dower: D. Crouch, 'Oddities in the early history of the Marcher lordship of Gower, 1107–1166', *Bulletin of the Board of Celtic Studies*, 31 (1984), 133–42.

[68] See above, n. 51.

[69] The seriousness of the threat in South Wales in the last decade of Henry's reign is reflected in the increased expenditure upon castles in this area: R. A. Brown, 'Royal castle-building in England, 1154–1216', *EHR* 70 (1955), 353–98 (at 359–60).

[70] *Pipe roll 31 Henry II*, 8; *Pipe roll 32 Henry II*, 203; *Pipe roll 33 Henry II*, 16, 29, 141, 142; *Pipe roll 34 Henry II*, 203.

[71] *Pipe roll 31 Henry II*, 8, 10, 55. Cf. Taylor, 'Usk castle'.

[72] *The great roll of the pipe for the first year of the reign of King Richard the First, 1188–89*, ed. J. Hunter (London, 1844), 5.

advance and then ascertained that Strigoil had been taken over by William Marshal on the occasion of his marriage to Strongbow's daughter and heir, Isabella, in 1189.

There is, therefore, a possibility that Aífe retained control of the Marcher lordship of Strigoil from 1176 until 1184, when Henry took over responsibility for its administration in response to the Welsh military threat. If Aífe did, in fact, enjoy its use between 1176 and 1184 she was being treated very favourably by Henry II. Alternatively, it may be that Henry had taken over Strigoil in 1176 and had the revenues paid directly into the chamber, so that the details were not recorded on the pipe rolls of the exchequer, although this seems less likely in view of the fact that Aífe appears to have been responsible for the defence of her portion of the Welsh March in 1183–4.[73]

Little is known about the administration of the estates held or claimed by Strongbow in Normandy during his children's minority in 1176–89. Although Orbec and Bienfaite had been lost by Strongbow in 1153 and were still in the possession of his cousin Robert de Montfort in 1172.[74] Strongbow held other lands in Normandy, since Robert of Torigny mentioned that at the meeting between Hervey de Montmorency and Henry II at Argentan in July 1171 the king had refused to reverse the sequestration of Strongbow's estates in England and Normandy.[75] There are very few extant exchequer rolls from Normandy: complete rolls survive only for the years 1180, 1195, and 1198, and partial rolls from the years 1184 and 1203. The complete roll of 1180 reveals that the 'terra comitis Ricardi' situated in Saint-Saëns and the neighbouring Omonville was being farmed by ducal agents;[76] this may have been on behalf of Strongbow's heirs.

---

[73] The change in 1184 may be associated with an illness or the death of Strongbow's son Gilbert around this time.   [74] See above, n. 8.   [75] See above, n. 34.

[76] *Magni rotuli scaccarii Normanniae*, i. 59; ii, p. cxxxvii. Stapleton thought that these lands belonged to Richard fitz Roger, who had succeeded his father as lord of Clare and earl of Hertford in 1173. As Powicke pointed out, however, there is no reason why Richard fitz Roger's lands should have been in the hands of ducal agents in 1173. He suggested that the lands belonged to Strongbow and that they may have been confiscated during the civil war period: Powicke, *Loss of Normandy*, 336. Confirmation of his suggestion comes from the fact that Isabella, widow of Earl Gilbert, and Strongbow's mother, was a benefactor of the convent of Saint-Saëns: *Recueil des actes de Henri II*, ed. Delisle and Berger, ii. 161.

In the absence of early Angevin administrative documents from Ireland, it is difficult to determine in detail Henry's intentions towards and treatment of Strongbow's lordship of Leinster in the period 1176–89. In 1189, when William Marshal succeeded to the lordship of Leinster in virtue of his marriage to Isabella, daughter of Strongbow, Richard I, in consenting to the marriage, was, according to the *Histoire de Guillaume le Maréchal*, merely fulfilling the wishes of Henry II.[77] From the death of Strongbow in 1176 until the assumption of the lordship of Ireland by John in 1185, Leinster was administered by custodians appointed by Henry II.[78] There is no evidence of any new infeudations made by Henry in Leinster between 1176 and 1185. In 1177 at the council of Oxford Henry designated his son John as lord of Ireland, and in 1185, when John formally took over the Angevin lordship of Ireland from his father, the administration of Leinster became the responsibility of his household.

According to the *Histoire de Guillaume le Maréchal*, William Marshal had to invoke the aid of King Richard against John in order to obtain seisin of all his wife's lands in Leinster after their marriage in 1189. Upon Richard's intervention, John agreed to give seisin provided that the grants of land which he had made to his own men within Leinster should remain and be confirmed to them. King Richard is depicted as responding, 'What would then remain to the Marshal seeing that you have given all to your people?' John then requested that the lands which he had granted to Theobald Walter within Leinster should be left to him, and King Richard consented provided that Theobald held them of the Marshal and not John.[79]

Despite King Richard's assertion that nothing would remain to the Marshal if John's grants in Leinster were allowed to stand, the known instances of encroachment by John on the rights of the lord of Leinster are a series of relatively unimportant grants made to his chamberlain, Alard, son of William, during his visit to Ireland in 1185,[80] and his grants to Theobald

---

[77] *Histoire de Guillaume le Maréchal*, ed. P. Meyer, ii (Paris, 1894), 8303–5.
[78] Roger of Howden, *Gesta*, i. 164, and *Chronica*, ii. 134.
[79] *Histoire de Guillaume le Maréchal*, ii, ll. 9584–624.
[80] John's charter given at Wexford, 1185, granted to Alard 'the land of Carrec Kenard near Waterford; the land of Carrec Eghon with its appurtenances, and his

Walter of the castle and vill of Arklow for the service of one knight made between 1185 and 1189,[81] and of the manor of Tullach Ua Felmeda made some time between 1189 and 1192.[82] The charter recording the grant of Arklow stated that it was made 'de voluntate et assensu domini regis Henrici patris mei', and it was witnessed by Ranulf de Glanville, which suggests that John had Henry's approval for this grant. Since Arklow was a coastal town, it is possible that Henry had

entertainment at Waterford in the house of John *Episcopus*; and in the Island, his entertainment in the house of Henry Noth, and 20 acres of land; near Wexford, the land which belonged to Uccranathan and to Ubrenan, with all its appurtenances, and his entertainment in the house of Richard Janitor at Wexford; and near Dublin, the land of Lescher with its appurtenances as Gileholman held it, and his entertainment at Dublin in the house of John *Episcopus*; and beside Kildare, Balioculenan and at his hospice a place outside the castle of Kildare where hay used to stand; and his entertainment at Wicklow in the house of Ralph Palmerius; and the land of Maquini to be held by free service of six pairs of furred gloves of lambskin and a tunic rendered yearly at Michaelmas': *Ormond deeds, 1172–1350*, no. 7 = NLI D. 8. Waterford and Dublin formed part of the royal demesne. Wexford, retained by Henry II in 1172, was restored to Strongbow about 1173–4, as was also Wicklow; see above, n. 43. The grants at Wexford, Wicklow, and Kildare appear to impinge on the rights of the lord of Leinster. John's other charters relating to Leinster issued between 1185 and 1189 respected the rights of the lord of Leinster. In 1185 John confirmed to William, son of Maurice fitz Gerald, the lands 'quam comes Ricardus dedit Moricio patri ipsius Willelmi tenendam de heredibus comitis Ricardi per servicium v militum pro omni servicio': *Gormanston reg.* 145, 193. Between 1185 and 1189 John confirmed to Walter de Ridelsford 'totam terram quam comes Ricardus filius comitis Gilberti dedit . . . tenenda de heredibus comitis Ricardi per servicium quatuor militum pro omni servitio comitis': NLI MS 1, fo. 19r; E. St J. Brooks, 'The de Ridelesfords', *RSAI Jn.* 81 (1951), 115–38; 82 (1952), 45–61. A charter from John to Gerald fitz Maurice confirmed to him a half cantred in Uí Fáeláin in Leinster as well as lands in Cork 'salvis serviciis dominorum suorum': *Red Bk Kildare*, 14.

[81]   *Ormond deeds, 1172–1350*, no. 17 = NLI D. 19.

[82]   *Red Bk Ormond*, 9. The text of this 14th-century transcript, which states that John granted to Theobald 'manerium de tulauth in Ofelmyth in Ossoria', is corrupt. Tullach Ua Felmeda was not in Osraige. It is possible that in the original charter John granted Theobald the manor of Tullach in Uí Felmeda and the manor of Tullach in Osraige, and that the 14th-century scribe was guilty of homoeoteleuton. This is suggested by the charter granted to Theobald Walter by William Marshal some time between 1189 and 1199, which confirmed to Theobald Walter 'the vill of Arklow and the castle there by the service of one knight, Machtalewi by service of 4 knights and the vill of Tullach [= Tullaherin, Tullach Chiaráin] in Osraige by the service of 4 knights': *Ormond deeds, 1172–1350*, no. 31 = NLI D. 41. For the identification of Tullach in Osraige as Tullach Chiaráin see K. W. Nicholls, 'The land of the Leinstermen', *Peritia*, 3 (1984), 535–58 (at 553). The grant of Machtalewi in the Marshal's charter represents the manor of Tullach Ua Felmeda: M. T. Flanagan, 'Mac Dalbaig, a Leinster chieftain', *RSAI Jn.* 111 (1981), 5–13. Since William Marshal's charter confirmed to Theobald the grants of Arklow and Tullach Ua Felmeda, known to have been made to him by John, it is very likely that John was responsible for the grant to Theobald of Tullach Chiaráin in Osraige.

actually retained it in his own hand and that John's grant to Theobald Walter was not a diminution of the rights of the lord of Leinster.[83] However, John's grant of the lordship of Tullach Ua Felmeda to Theobald, made after Henry II's death, undoubtedly was. After the Marshal's seisin of Leinster Theobald was allowed to retain the lordships of Arklow and Tullach Ua Felmeda, but they were held thereafter from the lord of Leinster.[84]

From the death of Strongbow in 1176 until his own death in 1189, therefore, Henry II appears to have acknowledged the hereditary claims of Strongbow's heirs in Leinster, and, with the possible exception of the grant of Arklow to Theobald Walter, seems to have respected the rights of Strongbow's heir as lord of Leinster. Henry seems to have kept a vigilant eye on John's activities as lord of Ireland through the person of Ranulf de Glanville, to whose tutelage John had been entrusted.[85] With the accession of Richard I in 1189, who had little time for Glanville, and with Glanville's death in 1190, there was much less constraint on John's actions in Ireland.

The only evidence of Aífe's presence in Leinster after Strongbow's death is a copy of a charter which she issued as 'Eva comitissa heres regis Deremicii', in which she confirmed to John Cumin, archbishop of Dublin (1181–1212), and his successors, 'omnes possessiones et elemosinas tam in ecclesiasticis quam in mundanis tenementis quas eis comes Johannes et alii boni viri de Lagenia pia largitione contulerunt'.[86] The reference to 'comes Johannes' in this charter is curious and is almost certainly an error. If it refers to the Lord John, Aífe's charter ought to date from the period between 1185 and the accession of William Marshal to the lordship of Leinster in

---

[83] Gerald of Wales stated that Henry II obliged Strongbow to surrender to the king 'the city of Dublin, its adjacent cantreds, and also the coastal cities and castles': Giraldus, *Expugnatio*, 88–9. After Strongbow's service to the king in Normandy in 1173, Henry restored to him the city of Wexford and the castle of Wicklow: ibid. 120–1; *Song of Dermot*, ll. 2902–5. It is possible that the king still retained the castle and coastal vill of Arklow for his own use.

[84] They were confirmed to Theobald by William Marshal: see above, n. 82.

[85] Cf. W. L. Warren, 'John in Ireland', in J. Bossy and P. Jupp (edd.), *Essays presented to Michael Roberts* (Belfast, 1976), 11–23 (at 16–17). William Marshal collected Strongbow's daughter, Isabella, from Ranulf de Glanville's household on the occasion of his marriage in 1189: *Histoire de Guillaume le Maréchal*, ii, ll. 9513–14.

[86] *Crede mihi*, 50.

1189. John can have given neither grants nor confirmations to the archbishop of Dublin before 1185, when he took over the administration of the lordship of Ireland from Henry II. However, the reference to John as *comes* implies a date after 1189, for he did not become count of Mortain or earl of Gloucester until that year.[87] It is possible that the scribe who transcribed Aífe's charter into the episcopal register inadvertently substituted 'comes Johannes' for 'dominus Johannes', the latter being the style by which John was known between 1185 and 1189. The only alternative explanation is that Aífe issued a confirmation charter to the archbishop of Dublin after 1189, in spite of the fact that William Marshal became lord of Leinster in that year. Since the date of Aífe's death is unknown, it is conceivable that she could have issued this charter after 1189. The *Histoire de Guillaume le Maréchal* implied that William Marshal did not gain immediate possession of Leinster in 1189, because John had arrogated it to his own use. There may have been uncertainty in Ireland for a number of years after 1189 as to whether John or William Marshal was lord of Leinster. The issue was resolved in the Marshal's favour by 1194 at the latest, when John's lands in England and Normandy together with the lordship of Ireland were taken into Richard I's hands pending John's trial for rebellion against Richard. It may have been in the years of uncertainty between 1189 and 1194 that the archbishop of Dublin, who had received a number of charters of grant and confirmation from John as lord of Ireland,[88] took the precaution of securing a general confirmation of the lands which he held in Leinster from Aífe as the heir of Diarmait Mac Murchada. The tenor of Aífe's charter, which contains nothing other than a very general statement of confirmation, as well as the style 'Eva comitissa heres regis Deremicii', might be said to support such an interpretation.

As a result of his marriage to Isabella in 1189, William Marshal succeeded to Strongbow's estates in Wales, England, and Normandy and to the lordship of Leinster. William asserted himself vigorously and successfully against attempts by John to diminish his wife Isabella's inheritance in Leinster.

---

[87] John seldom used the latter title: *Earldom of Gloucester charters*, 23.

[88] G. Mac Niocaill, 'The charters of John, lord of Ireland, to the see of Dublin', *Reportorium Novum*, 3 (1963–4), 282–306.

Furthermore, William Marshal persuaded Richard I to allow him the half portion of the Giffard honour to which Strongbow, and through him William's wife, had a claim as a descendant of Rohesia Giffard, and which the Crown had withheld since 1164.[89] William Marshal also managed to recover the lordships of Orbec and Bienfaite.[90] But undoubtedly his greatest achievement was the recovery of the earldom of Pembroke from King John in 1199,[91] thereby effecting a full restoration of the estates which Strongbow had inherited from his father Gilbert in 1148.

Although it fell to William Marshal to complete the restoration of Strongbow's inheritance, it was Strongbow's intervention in Ireland in 1170 which had paved the way for the recovery of his fortunes and eventually led to the full restoration of his patrimonial inheritance to his heirs. King John's grant of the earldom of Pembroke to William Marshal in 1199 was the final dividend resulting from the alliance which Strongbow had entered into with Diarmait Mac Murchada in 1166–7.

A more far-reaching consequence of the successful alliance

---

[89] In 1189 William Marshal paid Richard I a fine of 2000 marks for a half portion of the Giffard honour, the other half going to the lord of Clare: *Pipe roll 2 Richard I*, 102, 144; *Cartae antiquae rolls, 11–20* (Pipe Roll Society, 71; London, 1957), 165–6.

[90] See above, n. 8.

[91] There is no evidence for William Marshal's recognition as earl of Pembroke before 1199, when he was girt by King John. S. Painter, *William Marshal*, 77, assumed that William Marshal became earl of Pembroke when he married Isabella, but in *The reign of King John* (Baltimore, 1949), 14, he altered his opinion, pointing out that Pembroke castle was in the custody of the king in 1199: *Pipe roll 1 John*, 182. According to *Gir. Camb. op.* i. 76, the lordship of Pembroke was granted by Henry II to his son John in 1185, at about the same time, therefore, as he was made lord of Ireland. It would certainly have made sense to do so, because of the proximity of Pembroke to Leinster and the fact that there were many landholders in Pembroke who also held land in Ireland. There is no evidence, apart from Gerald's statement, that John did exercise lordship in Pembroke. There are no extant charters issued by him relating to Pembroke in the period 1185–99. It is possible that it was Henry's intention to give Pembroke to John, but that he changed his mind after John's disastrous expedition to Ireland in 1185 and Pembroke continued to be administered by the Crown, although there is no evidence for this on the pipe rolls. There is an obscure statement in Giraldus, *Expugnatio*, 239, where Gerald, in detailing the reasons for the lack of success of John's expedition in 1185, described John's associates as men of the same type as William fitz Audelin, 'a man under whose administration Ireland and Wales together lamented their total destruction and ruin'. Gerald seems to be drawing an analogy here between the failures of William fitz Audelin's period of administration in Ireland and John's expedition in 1185. It may be that when fitz Audelin was appointed to administer Strongbow's estates in Leinster after his death in April 1176 he also became temporarily responsible for the lordship of Strigoil and perhaps even Pembroke, a possible foreshadowing of the proposal apparently made in 1185.

between Diarmait and Strongbow was the reaction which it provoked from Henry II and his determination to intervene personally in Ireland in 1171–2, thus inaugurating English royal lordship in Ireland.

5

Adventurers from South Wales
in Ireland

APART from Strongbow, Diarmait Mac Murchada recruited a significant number of Cambro-Normans from South Wales for service in Ireland. The causes and consequences of involvement in Ireland for these men, and their relations with both Strongbow and Henry II, merit separate consideration.

The background to Cambro-Norman involvement in Ireland from 1167 onwards was a Welsh revival, which had not only curtailed Norman expansion in South Wales but had encroached on and reclaimed territory which had been won from the Welsh by the Normans. The first major Norman incursions into South Wales, undertaken in 1093 by Roger de Montgomery, earl of Shrewsbury, and William fitz Baldwin, sheriff of Devon, almost certainly with royal consent, if not tangible support, had been swift and unopposed by the Welsh.[1] As a result of these campaigns the Dyfed peninsula was conferred by King William Rufus upon Arnulf, younger brother of Earl Roger, who fixed the *caput* of his new lordship at Pembroke. Arnulf was also accorded comital status, almost certainly in respect of Pembroke, by William Rufus.[2]

The process of permanent Norman occupation and settlement of Dyfed was to prove more difficult than the initial take-over. Having staked his claim in 1093, Arnulf apparently departed for England, leaving the defence of Pembroke Castle and the lordship in the hands of his castellan, Gerald of Windsor. Periodic Welsh offensives from 1094 onwards rendered the Norman hold on Dyfed precarious at times: in

---

[1] See Lloyd, *Wales*, ii, chs. 11–15; Nelson, *Normans in South Wales*; I. W. Rowlands, 'The making of the March: aspects of the Norman settlement in Dyfed', in R. A. Brown (ed.), *Proceedings of the Battle Conference on Anglo-Norman studies*, 3, 1980 (Woodbridge, 1981), 142–57, 221–5; W. Rees, *An historical atlas of Wales from early to modern times* (2nd edn., London, 1959), plates 29–36.

[2] Mason, 'Roger de Montgomery', 17–18.

1096 Gerald of Windsor saved Pembroke Castle from a serious Welsh attack, and with it the Norman foothold in western Dyfed.[3] The vulnerability of the early Norman settlers is graphically illustrated by the manner in which the early castles of Pembroke, Carew, and Manorbier were huddled along the coastline of the Castlemartin peninsula. Nevertheless, the rudiments of administration, a central castle, a castle church, an official, and enfeoffed tenants, and possibly even a nascent borough, date from Arnulf de Montgomery's period of tenure of Pembroke, 1093–1102.[4]

In 1099 King William Rufus campaigned in South Wales, which brought some weakening of Welsh resistance to Norman settlement, but it was not until the reign of Henry I that the English king himself acquired territories in South Wales. Henry's interest in Wales was occasioned at the very beginning of his reign by the revolt in 1102 of Robert de Montgomery, earl of Shrewsbury, who conspired with the Welsh dynasty of Powys, and of his brother, Arnulf, lord of Pembroke. Arnulf, like many a Welsh prince of Dyfed before him, sought a marriage alliance in Ireland.[5] As a result of this revolt Henry took Pembroke into his own hands, initially giving custody to a Norman knight, Saher, but in 1105 returning responsibility for the castle and lordship of Pembroke to Gerald of Windsor. From 1102 onwards the lordship of Pembroke was administered as a royal county. It would appear to have been divided into two component parts, the *comitatus* or shire, which was administered directly by the king's official, and the remainder, which was made up of smaller subordinate lordships. That Pembroke was subject to a full and vigorous exploitation of the king's fiscal and jurisdictional rights is evidenced by the 1130 pipe roll. The annual farm of the mint and borough was set at 60 pounds. The routine nature of the entries, visitation by royal justices, *oblata* for royal intervention in matters of inheritance and succession, suggests a long period of firm royal control.[6] About the year 1108 Henry had settled Flemish immigrants in the central part of Pembrokeshire in the cantreds of Rhos and

[3] *Gir. Camb. op.* i. 89–90.
[4] Mason, 'Roger de Montgomery', 18.
[5] See above, pp. 67–8.
[6] *Pipe roll 31 Henry I* (London, 1929), 136–7.

Daugleddau.[7] Royal control of these Flemish settlers is under-
lined by the pipe roll of 1130, from which it may be inferred
that they were under the supervision of the royal agent at Pembroke. It is probable that the king's direct lordship of Pembroke
extended essentially over the Castlemartin peninsula, and that
he exercised a feudal overlordship over the subordinate lordships of Cemais, Emlyn, and Narberth.[8] Another index of royal
influence in South Wales was the election to the see of Llandaff
in 1107 of Urban, Henry I's nominee, and to the see of St
Davids in 1115 of Bernard, Queen Matilda's chaplain. As
bishop, Bernard controlled the cantred of Pebidiog, almost all
the land of which belonged to the church of St David. Bishop
Bernard conferred the stewardship of St Davids on Henry,
illegitimate son of Henry I by Nesta, daughter of Rhys ap
Tewdwr, king of Deheubarth.[9]

In eastern Dyfed Henry I created virtually a new march, using
the area as an important source of royal patronage. About the
year 1109 he acquired the strategic site of Carmarthen, which
became the centre of a royal honour, from which vantage-point
the king was able to exercise considerable influence throughout
South Wales. Around the core of the old Welsh kingdom of
Deheubarth, the native dynasty of which had not been totally
dispossessed and still retained a territorial base in Cantref
Mawr, Henry established a ring of new Norman lordships:
Brecon (Miles of Gloucester), Abergavenny (Brian fitz Count),
Strigoil and Usk (Walter fitz Richard), Glamorgan (Robert of
Gloucester), Gower (Henry de Beaumont), Kidwelly (Roger of
Salisbury), Cantref Bychan (Richard fitz Pons), and Ceredigion
(Gilbert fitz Richard).[10] The beneficiaries were very much
Henry's men, drawn mostly from the inner governing circle.
No less impressively did Henry I deal with the Welsh princes,
employing a variety of strategies to draw them into a nexus of
obligation, patronage, and reward.[11]

[7] The chief sources for this plantation and Henry I's role in it are *Brut Peniarth*,
27–8; William of Malmesbury, *Gesta regum*, ii. 365, 477; Florence of Worcester,
Chronicon, ii. 64; *Worcester cartulary*, 134–5.

[8] Rowlands, 'Making of the March', 152.

[9] *Episc. acts*, i. 280–1.

[10] R. R. Davies, 'King Henry I and Wales', in H. Mayr-Harting and R. I. Moore
(edd.), *Studies in medieval history presented to R. H. C. Davis* (Oxford, 1985), 132–47;
Rowlands, 'Making of the March', 151.

[11] Davies, 'King Henry I', 138–41.

Thus, virtually the greater part of Deheubarth was lost to the Welsh during Henry's reign, but the momentum was not maintained after his death in December 1135. Stephen's accession coincided with a Welsh resurgence, while the succession dispute precluded any effective royal commitment to Welsh affairs.[12] In January 1136 the Welsh of Brycheiniog attacked the Norman settlers in Gower and wrought immense damage; less successful was an attack on the lordship of Kidwelly in the same year by Gwenlliann, wife of Gruffydd ap Rhys of the Deheubarth royal dynasty. But the real threat to Norman domination in South Wales came from Gwynedd, and it was in Ceredigion that the struggle was chiefly waged. The prelude was the killing in April 1136 in the Usk valley of Richard fitz Gilbert, lord of Ceredigion, by the men of Gwent. In 1136–7 Ceredigion was twice overrun by Welsh expeditions mounted from Gwynedd, during which all but Cardigan Castle was taken. It was defended successfully by Stephen, the constable, by Robert fitz Martin, lord of Cemais, and by William and Maurice, sons of Gerald, the castellan of Pembroke. At the same time Gruffydd ap Rhys of Deheubarth, taking advantage of the action of the men of Gwynedd in Ceredigion, invaded the Flemish settlement in Rhos in 1137, killing among others one Letard 'Little King'. A further expedition mounted from Gwynedd invaded Ceredigion again and destroyed in succession the castles of Ystrad Meurig, Lampeter, and Castell Hywel. Emboldened, the Welsh made for the royal stronghold of Carmarthen and captured it. King Stephen's response was to send Baldwin fitz Gilbert, brother of the murdered lord of Ceredigion, to Wales, but he could not even reach Ceredigion, for his passage was halted at Llandovery, the Clifford family having lost all control and authority in this region. It was to be 1158 before a member of the Clare family was able to return to Ceredigion. Even the valley of the lower Usk was subjected to Welsh attack, and in 1138 the castle of Usk was seized at the expense of another branch of the Clare family, Gilbert fitz Gilbert.[13] In 1138 Stephen created Gilbert earl of Pembroke, with the apparent intention that he should take responsibility for control of South Wales.[14] In fact, Gilbert

[12] For what follows see Lloyd, *Wales*, ii, ch. 13, especially 470–4.
[13] It was not recovered until 1173; see below, n. 88.   [14] Davis, *King Stephen*, 136.

does not appear to have visited Wales until 1145. Initially he met with some success, recapturing Carmarthen Castle for the king and building another castle at or in the vicinity of Pencader, probably with a view to undertaking campaigns against the Welsh in Ceredigion.[15] Both castles, however, were recaptured by the Welsh within the year. Llansteffan Castle also fell in 1146, and the attempt of the Normans and Flemings of Dyfed, led by William and Maurice, sons of Gerald, castellan of Pembroke, and William fitz Hay, to retake it was unsuccessful.[16] Llansteffan controlled the crossing of the Tywi estuary and its capture by the Welsh represented a serious threat to communications with Pembroke. Eastern Dyfed and the Tywi valley were now dominated by the Welsh. Welsh penetration into Dyfed via Ceredigion was further facilitated by a quarrel between William fitz Gerald, lord of Carew and castellan of Pembroke, and Walter fitz Wizo, lord of Daugleddau, in which the Welsh participated with advantage. William appealed for Welsh aid against Walter, the result being the destruction of Walter's castle at Wiston in 1147, which removed yet another obstacle in the path of Welsh expansion.[17] In 1153 Tenby Castle temporarily fell into Welsh hands.[18]

Against this background of Welsh incursions into Norman-held areas of South Wales, Gilbert fitz Gilbert's exercise of the lordship of Pembroke in the period between his creation as earl of Pembroke in 1138 and his death in 1148 is difficult to assess. There is no evidence that he resided at or visited Pembroke in person. The local administration of the lordship of Pembroke appears to have remained in the hands of William fitz Gerald, who succeeded his father as castellan of Pembroke.[19] Charters which Earl Gilbert issued in favour of Worcester Abbey relating to the church of Daugleddau prove that he claimed authority over the Flemings of Rhos and that he clearly expected the archdeacon of St Davids to obey his commands, even if he felt it

---

[15] *Brut Hergest*, 121; *Brut Peniarth*, 54; *Annales Cambriae*, 43.
[16] *Brut Hergest*, 120–3; *Brut Peniarth*, 58; *Annales Cambriae*, 43. William fitz Hay, as a son of Nesta, daughter of Rhys ap Tewdwr, king of Deheubarth, was related to the Geraldines: *Gir. Camb. op.* i. 59.
[17] Lloyd, *Wales*, ii. 502.   [18] Ibid. 503.
[19] See the mandate addressed to William fitz Gerald by Gilbert, earl of Pembroke, ordering him to place the monks of Worcester in possession of the church of Daugleddau: *Worcester cartulary*, 135.

necessary to enlist the support of Theobald, archbishop of Canterbury, in bringing pressure to bear on Bernard, bishop of St Davids.[20] The chief advantage which Gilbert seems to have derived from the earldom of Pembroke was the right to style himself 'comes Gilbertus'.[21]

The accession of Henry II in 1154 did not halt significantly the course of the Welsh advance in South Wales. In 1154 Henry refused to acknowledge Strongbow, who had succeeded to his father Gilbert's lands and titles in 1148, as earl of Pembroke, which meant that responsibility for its administration reverted once more to the Crown.[22] In practice, it can have made little difference to the Marcher men of Pembroke whether a member of the Clare family or the king was lord, since both were, in effect, absentees and the day-to-day responsibility for holding Dyfed against the Welsh had always fallen on the local men. Henry II had the intention of restoring the stable rule which had characterized his grandfather Henry I's reign, and as soon as was practicable he took active measures both to stem the Welsh resurgence and to re-establish royal authority over the Norman settlers in Wales. He began in North Wales in 1157 by organizing a campaign against the most formidable of the Welsh leaders, Owain Gwynedd. Henry's land forces were to be supported by a naval fleet raised in Dyfed, which was to sail to meet him in the north. It proved of little benefit, however, for the ships, having put into Anglesey, were ambushed by the Welsh. Henry fitz Henry, father of Meilir fitz Henry, who was later to take service in Ireland, was killed, while Robert fitz Stephen, son of the castellan of Cardigan, was seriously injured and barely escaped with his life.[23]

Despite the military ineffectualness of Henry II's campaign Owain Gwynedd came to terms, and this in turn persuaded Rhys ap Gruffydd of the Deheubarth dynasty to do so. The terms Rhys agreed to after negotiations with Henry in 1157

[20] *Worcester cartulary*, 135.
[21] If a fifteenth-century transcript of a charter granted by Earl Gilbert may be relied upon, he actually styled himself on occasion 'comes de Weston', taking the name from his demesne manor in Herts.: *Records of the Templars in England in the twelfth century: the inquest of 1185*, ed. B. A. Lees (Records of the Social and Economic History of England and Wales, 9; London, 1935), 218.
[22] See above, ch. 4 nn. 7, 10, 91.
[23] Lloyd, *Wales*, ii. 496–9.

were stiff. Rhys accepted for the moment the confinement of his independent lordship to Cantref Mawr. In June 1158 Earl Roger of Hertford appeared in Ceredigion to claim the Clare inheritance, after an absence of twenty-two years.[24] About the same time Walter Clifford recovered his hold upon Cantref Bychan and Llandovery. Carmarthen also reverted to the Crown and was refortified,[25] while the castles of Llansteffan, Kidwelly, and Tenby also returned to Norman control.

Notwithstanding the agreement of 1157 between Henry and Rhys ap Gruffydd, a stable peace was very far from having been achieved in South Wales. In August 1158 Henry left England for his Continental dominions for a period of nearly four and a half years. A renewal of conflict between Rhys ap Gruffydd and the Normans in South Wales was not long in following. In 1159 Rhys made a general attack upon the castles of Dyfed and besieged the royal stronghold of Carmarthen. The Welsh threat was taken seriously: a strong Norman relieving force was led by Earl Reginald of Cornwall, accompanied by Earl William of Gloucester, Earl Roger of Hertford, Earl Patrick of Salisbury, and Strongbow.[26] Rhys came to terms, but evidence that he was still deemed to be dangerous may be adduced from the large sums spent by the Crown during 1159–62 upon the defence of Walter Clifford's castle of Llandovery, a clear acknowledgement of the fact that an extension of Rhys's power in that direction threatened the security of the entire Welsh March.[27] Llandovery was actually captured by Rhys in 1162.[28] In January 1163 Henry II returned to England, and about April he led a large expedition into South Wales. Rhys offered no resistance and, surrendering himself to the king, returned a prisoner to England with Henry. What was to be done with Rhys seems to have troubled Henry for some weeks, but eventually it was decided to reinstate him in his patrimony of Cantref Mawr on redefined terms of allegiance. At Woodstock in July 1163 Rhys, in company with Owain Gwynedd and Malcolm, king of the Scots, did homage to the king of England

[24] *Brut Hergest*, 138–9; *Brut Peniarth*, 60; *Annales Cambriae*, 48.
[25] The sheriff of Somerset contributed 20 marks towards the cost of the defences of Carmarthen in 1158–9: *Pipe roll 5 Henry II*, 21.
[26] Lloyd, *Wales*, ii. 511.
[27] *Pipe roll 6 Henry II*, 23, 28, 30; *Pipe roll 7 Henry II*, 22, 54; *Pipe roll 8 Henry II*, 56.
[28] *Annales Cambriae*, 49.

and to his son Henry, apparently thereby accepting a status of dependent vassalage.[29] Scarcely was Rhys re-established as lord of Cantref Mawr, however, than he resumed hostilities against the Normans. In 1164 he mounted an attack on Ceredigion, with the consequence that no more than Cardigan Castle and town remained in Norman hands. Shortly afterwards, Owain Gwynedd, who since his negotiations with Henry II in 1157 had kept the peace, joined Rhys in a new offensive against the Normans. Henry recognized the formidable nature of the challenge and made preparations for a large-scale expedition into Wales. Due to the unseasonable inclemency of the weather, the English army was forced to retreat before the main forces had even engaged the enemy. Henry waited for some time at Chester in the hope of attacking the north coast of Wales with a fleet hired in Dublin, but in the end he abandoned the expedition.[30] Henry's proposed campaign of 1165 had been very ambitious indeed. Little of Welsh independence would have been left had the campaign gone as intended, and its failure must have been intensely disillusioning to him.

In March 1166 Henry II sailed for his Continental dominions. With the king's abandonment of his attempt to enforce their submission, the Welsh rulers pursued with renewed confidence their attacks on the Marcher lordships. Rhys was now free to complete the reconquest of Ceredigion. Within a few months he had recaptured the territory which he had been forced to surrender to Earl Roger of Hertford in 1157, crowning his efforts with the demolition of Cardigan Castle. Thereby Clare rule was virtually ended in Ceredigion until after Rhys's death in 1197. Rhys next attacked the Carew lordship of Emlyn and captured its principal stronghold of Cilgerran, taking its constable, Robert fitz Stephen, prisoner. In 1166 the Normans and Flemings of Pembroke twice attempted to recapture Cilgerran, which was an important strategic defence of Pembroke against Welsh attacks from Ceredigion, but on each occasion they were beaten off.[31] Whatever may have been the position of Cantref Bychan since the capture of Llandovery

---

[29] Lloyd, *Wales*, ii. 512–13; Warren, *Henry II*, 162–3.
[30] *Annales Cambriae*, 50; *Brut Hergest*, 144–6; *Brut Peniarth*, 63–4; see above, p. 76.
[31] *Brut Hergest*, 146–9; *Brut Peniarth*, 64; *Annales Cambriae*, 50.

Castle in 1162, it is certain that cantred and castle were now in the hands of Rhys and that the Clifford claims, like those of the house of Clare in Ceredigion, were in abeyance.

It was during this period of successful Welsh incursions into the Norman March in South Wales under Rhys ap Gruffydd, and of royal absence from England, that Diarmait Mac Murchada sought to recruit military aid among the Normans of Dyfed. It has been argued by L. H. Nelson that the positive response of the Cambro-Normans to Diarmait was determined by the course of the Welsh resurgence, and that their intervention in Ireland may be interpreted as the transference of the Norman frontier from Wales, where it was contracting, to an area where it could be opened up again.[32]

There is strong support for Nelson's argument if one attempts to look at the way in which the Welsh revival had affected individual Cambro-Normans who volunteered for service in Ireland. Take the case of Robert fitz Stephen: thanks in large part to the writings of his nephew, Gerald, it is possible at least partially to reconstruct his circumstances before his intervention in Ireland in 1169. According to Gerald of Wales, Robert fitz Stephen had held the two cantreds of Ceredigion and Cemais.[33] This is an exaggeration on Gerald's part. Robert was not himself the principal landholder in either cantred. Ceredigion was the lordship of the Clare earls of Hertford, who, however, were very infrequently resident in the area. Robert's father had been constable of Cardigan Castle in the employ of the Clare family, and Robert took over this function from him. The territory of Ceredigion, with the exception of Cardigan Castle, had been taken by the Welsh in 1136. It was recovered by the Normans in 1158, but recaptured by the Welsh along with the castle in 1165. That Robert held some land in Ceredigion is evidenced by the fact that he is credited with the foundation of the Cistercian monastery of Strata Florida in 1164.[34] Its very foundation perhaps represented an acknowledgement on his part of the difficulty of holding the land against the Welsh. An indication of the changed political circumstances in this area after 1165 is the fact that after

---

[32] Nelson, *Normans in South Wales*, 131–2.
[33] *Gir. Camb. op.* i. 59.
[34] Ibid. iv. 152.

Robert fitz Stephen the principal benefactor of Strata Florida was to be Rhys ap Gruffydd, and the monastery became the preferred place of burial for members of his dynasty.[35]

Robert fitz Stephen, according to Gerald of Wales, also held the cantred of Cemais. In reality, the fitz Martin family held the lordship of Cemais as a dependency of Pembroke.[36] They may be distinguished from the Geraldines by the fact that they were also tenants-in-chief in Devon, Dorset, and Somerset (which may explain why no fitz Martin appears to have volunteered for service in Ireland). That Robert fitz Stephen held land in the lordship of Cemais is evidenced by his grant of the church of Llanfrynach and one hundred carucates of land in Cemais to the Knights Hospitallers at Slebech.[37] When Gerald of Wales asserted that Robert fitz Stephen held Ceredigion and Cemais, what he probably had in mind was that Robert fitz Stephen was the principal resident Norman representative in both areas, actively engaged in attempting to hold the territory against the Welsh. In difficult times the Clare lord of Ceredigion and the fitz Martin lord of Cemais might retreat to their English holdings. Robert fitz Stephen had no such alternative. When Cardigan Castle fell to the Welsh in 1165 he appears to have assumed the role of constable of the castle of Cilgerran, the principal stronghold of Emlyn, for William fitz Gerald, lord of Carew, his relative.[38] Having been taken prisoner at Cilgerran in 1165 by Rhys ap Gruffydd, he was still in captivity when Diarmait Mac Murchada was recruiting troops in South Wales in 1166–7.[39] Volunteering for service in Ireland secured Robert fitz Stephen's immediate release and in the long term won him new lands in Ireland.

Of Gerald's other relations who responded to Diarmait

[35] Dugdale, *Monasticon Anglicanum*, v. 632–3.

[36] G. E. C., *Peerage*, viii. 530–2; J. H. Round, 'The lords of Kemes', in W. Page (ed.), *Family origins and other studies* (London, 1930), 73–102. For the fitz Martin holding in Teignton, Devon, see *Stogursey charters*, ed. T. D. Tremlett and N. Blakiston (Somerset Record Society, 61; London, 1946), 1–2.

[37] R. Fenton, *A historical tour through Pembrokeshire* (Brecon, 1903), 347.

[38] William fitz Gerald, lord of Carew, was also lord of Emlyn: *Gir. Camb. op.* i. 59. Emlyn had been won from the Welsh about 1109 by Gerald of Windsor: Davies, *Conquest*, 86. In 1174, on William's death and the assumption of the lordship by his son, Odo de Carew, Henry II compensated Odo for the loss from 1165 of the castle and lands of Emlyn to Rhys ap Gruffydd with an exchange of land in Braunton in north Devon 'quamdiu Res' fil' Griffini ea habuerit': *Pipe roll 20 Henry II*, 89.

[39] Giraldus, *Expugnatio*, 28–31.

Mac Murchada's appeal for military aid, his uncle, Maurice fitz Gerald, was a younger brother of William fitz Gerald, lord of Carew. According to Gerald, Maurice acquired the cantred of Llansteffan.[40] The lordship of Llansteffan formed part of the assemblage of territories attached to the royal county of Carmarthen. If Maurice was lord of Llansteffan he would have been a tenant of the Crown when he went to Ireland in 1169. Maurice's association with the lordship of Llansteffan is evidenced by a mandate of Bernard, bishop of St Davids (1115–48), ordering him not to interfere with the land called Pentywyn which the bishop had granted to the priory of St John, Carmarthen.[41] Gerald's assertion that Maurice was lord of Llansteffan must, however, be treated with caution in view of his portrayal of Robert fitz Stephen's circumstances in Ceredigion and Cemais, in which he failed to draw a clear distinction between lordship of the entire honour and the holding of knight's fees within it. The reality may be that Maurice was merely a feoffee in the lordship of Llansteffan and possibly castellan of Llansteffan Castle, a role in which the Geraldines were not infrequently found.[42] When Llansteffan Castle fell to the Welsh in 1146 the Norman attempt to recapture it had been led by William fitz Gerald, lord of Carew and castellan of

[40] *Gir. Camb. op.* i. 59.

[41] *Cartularium S. Johannis Baptistae de Carmarthen*, ed. T. Phillips (Cheltenham, 1865), 10; *Episc. acts*, i. 268. As lord of Carmarthen Henry I granted lands at Pentywyn in Llansteffan to the priory of St John, Carmarthen: *The chronicle of Battle Abbey*, ed. E. Searle (Oxford, 1980), 124–5. About 1130 Henry I transferred his original grant from Battle Abbey to Bernard, bishop of St Davids, Battle Abbey receiving compensation: ibid. 134–6.

[42] It is uncertain who was the first Norman lord of Llansteffan. It has been suggested that it was Roger Marmion (d. about 1130), from whom it passed to his son and grandson until the latter, Robert (d. 1181), granted it to his uncle, Geoffrey Marmion. Geoffrey's daughter and heiress was Albrea, or Auberée, wife of William de Camville, who took custody of Llansteffan Castle in right of his wife in the 1190s: R. Griffiths, 'The cartulary and muniments of the Fort family of Llanstephan', *Bulletin of the Board of Celtic Studies*, 24 (1970–2), 311–84 (at 319–22). R. A. Brown listed the castle of Llansteffan as in the possession of de Camville from 1158: 'A list of castles, 1154–1216', in *EHR* 74 (1959), 249–80 (at 271). Brown appears to depend on J. E. Lloyd, *A history of Carmarthenshire* (Cardiff, 1935), i. 284, which stated that in 1158, following the restoration of order in the March, the Welsh ceded the castle to Henry II, who gave it to William de Camville of Devon, husband of de Marmion's daughter and heiress. Unfortunately Lloyd does not provide a source for this statement, and I have been unable to find any evidence proving possession of Llansteffan by the de Camvilles as early as 1158. The de Camvilles (Richard I to 1176 and Richard II thereafter) certainly were Henry's men: Prestwich, 'Military household', 35.

Pembroke, and Maurice, his brother, along with William fitz Hay, lord of St Clears, another dependent lordship of the royal county of Carmarthen.[43] Llansteffan was recovered by the Normans after the recapture of Carmarthen in 1158, but their hold on it remained precarious (it was to be recaptured by the Welsh at least three more times during Gerald's lifetime). Maurice fitz Gerald's association with Llansteffan, in whatever capacity, was also threatened by the Welsh resurgence, particularly after 1165.

Meilir fitz Henry, according to his cousin, Gerald, held Pebidiog and Narberth.[44] This is an exaggeration on Gerald's part, certainly in respect of Pebidiog.[45] The temporal lordship of Pebidiog had been granted by Henry I to Bernard, bishop of St Davids, who installed Meilir's father, a natural son of Henry I, as steward.[46] Meilir may have taken over this function from his father on the occasion of the latter's death in 1157, but by 1176 Bernard's successor in the see of St Davids, David fitz Gerald, brother of William fitz Gerald, lord of Carew, had invested his brother Maurice with the stewardship of St Davids.[47] The precise nature of Meilir's links with Narberth, which was a dependency of the lordship of Pembroke, is not known, but if he was lord of Narberth his overlord from 1154 would have been Henry II (who was his first cousin).[48]

About the origins and circumstances of his immediate family, the de Barrys, Gerald provided little information beyond the fact that his father was lord of Manorbier, which was subordinate to the lordship of Pembroke.[49] The fact that Gerald's father, William de Barry, paid a relief of ten pounds in 1130 for the inheritance suggests a holding of only moderate size within the lordship of Pembroke.[50] This may in part explain why not only the younger son, Robert de Barry, who

---

[43] See above, n. 16.

[44] *Gir. Camb. op.* i. 59.

[45] Pebidiog, however, may be an error for Peuliniog: G. Owen, *The description of Pembrokeshire*, ed. H. Owen, iii (London, 1906), 343.

[46] *Regesta regum Anglo-Normannorum*, ii, no. 1091; *Gormanston reg.* 203.

[47] *Gormanston reg.* 203.

[48] Gruffydd ap Rhys is recorded to have burnt the castle of Narberth in 1116. The next mention of it occurs in 1215: *Castellarium Anglicanum*, ed. D. J. Cathcart King (London, 1983), ii. 395.

[49] *Gir. Camb. op.* i. 21, vi. 92–3.

[50] *Pipe roll 31 Henry I* (London, 1929), 137.

had no expectation of an inheritance, but also William de Barry's heir, Philip, was prepared to take service in Ireland.

The 'Song of Dermot' provides the names of a number of Flemings who volunteered for service in Leinster, notably Richard fitz Godebert and Maurice de Prendergast.[51] About their prior circumstances in Wales no specific information can be recovered, but in general it can be said that the Welsh take-over of Emlyn in 1165 had left the cantreds of Daugleddau and Rhos vulnerable to penetration by the Welsh.

To Nelson's argument concerning the Welsh resurgence as the background to Cambro-Norman participation in Ireland, one may add that it was not only the Welsh who posed a threat to Cambro-Norman activity. From 1154 Henry II himself did so: restoration of royal authority in South Wales was not aimed simply at the Welsh. From Henry's viewpoint it was also intended to include the Cambro-Norman settlers in South Wales. His general policy between 1154 and 1158 of resuming lands and castles must have caused concern even to the lesser Norman landholders in South Wales. The denial of the title earl of Pembroke to Strongbow meant that Henry resumed royal control of the lordship of Pembroke. Unless the Marchers believed, on the one hand, that Henry would curb Welsh activity, and on the other hand, that they would be the direct beneficiaries, in that the king would restore to them what they had lost, they had every reason to look to Ireland when the opportunity arose.

What links did Strongbow have with those who went to Ireland from Pembroke, and what was the reaction to their involvement in Ireland of Henry II, who from 1154 exercised a direct lordship of Pembroke? It is difficult to assess the extent of Strongbow's personal connections with the Norman settlers of Pembroke, of which he was lord between 1148 and 1154. There is no surviving evidence of his direct intervention in Pembroke, and relatively little in the case of his father, Gilbert, who had held the lordship from 1138.[52] Yet there is evidence for Strongbow's involvement with Cambro-Norman intervention in Ireland from the earliest beginnings. Robert fitz Stephen was

---

[51] *Song of Dermot*, ll. 408–10, 455. Gerald was hostile towards the Flemings of Rhos, from whom he had endeavoured unsuccessfully about 1174–6 to exact tithes on wool and cheese: *Gir. Camb. op.* i. 24–8.   [52] See above, pp. 140–2.

accompanied to Ireland in 1169 by Strongbow's uncle, Hervey de Montmorency, whom Gerald of Wales castigated as a spy in the interest of Strongbow rather than a would-be conqueror; this is hardly suggestive of a relationship of trust between Strongbow and Robert fitz Stephen. Raymond le Gros, younger son of William fitz Gerald, lord of Carew, who led a force to Ireland in 1170, was described by Gerald of Wales as a member of Strongbow's *familia*.[53] Since Pembroke was in the hands of the Crown from 1154, Henry was not only king but also immediate lord of those Cambro-Normans from Pembroke who went to Ireland. The king's strained relations with Strongbow, who had been and still claimed to be lord of Pembroke, made the situation peculiarly sensitive for him.

According to Gerald of Wales, Henry II had granted Diarmait Mac Murchada letters patent stating that anyone who wished to go to Ireland to fight on Diarmait's behalf might do so with his permission.[54] Yet, after the Anglo-Norman capture of the city of Dublin in 1170, Henry issued an edict that no ship might carry anything to Ireland from any of the lands subject to his rule, and that all those who had gone there from his dominions should either return before the following Easter, or be completely disinherited and for ever banished from his realms.[55] The implication is that this edict applied whether or not they may be considered to have had Henry's permission.

Henry's edict resulted in the sequestration of Strongbow's estates.[56] But it also affected those Norman settlers from Pembroke who had gone to Ireland. Gerald recounted that while he was at Pembroke waiting to cross to Ireland in 1171,

the English king began to storm at the magnates of South Wales and Pembroke with the direst threats because they had allowed Earl Richard to cross to Ireland by that route. But in the end on royal custodians being assigned to their castles, this stormy bout of temper subsided into calm and his loud thunderings were not followed by the deadly blow of the thunderbolt.[57]

In the case of Robert fitz Stephen, Gerald related that on Henry's arrival in Ireland the men of Wexford, who had captured Robert, delivered him to Henry II, 'on the grounds that

---

[53] Giraldus, *Expugnatio*, 56–7.   [54] Ibid. 26–7.   [55] Ibid. 70–1.
[56] See above, p. 118.   [57] Giraldus, *Expugnatio*, 90–1.

fitz Stephen was the first to enter Ireland without Henry's consent and had presented others with an opportunity for wrong doing'.[58] Initially, Henry consigned Robert fitz Stephen to be held in captivity in Ragnall's tower in Waterford, but at a second meeting Henry restored him his freedom, depriving him, however, of the city of Wexford and the land which had been granted to him by Diarmait Mac Murchada.[59] Before his departure from Ireland in 1172 Henry assigned Robert fitz Stephen to the garrison of the city of Dublin, which he had retained in his own hands.[60] In 1173 Henry summoned Robert to fight in Normandy. After Strongbow's death in 1176, fitz Stephen returned to Ireland in the king's service in the train of William fitz Audelin.[61] Gerald of Wales asserted that fitz Audelin persecuted the Geraldines, and cited by way of illustration that fitz Audelin deprived Robert fitz Stephen of a cantred in Uí Fáeláin which the king had ordered should be restored to him. Robert fitz Stephen apparently had a grant from Henry II of a cantred in Uí Fáeláin in the period 1172–3, but, following Strongbow's service in Normandy in 1173, Henry restored the cantreds of Uí Fáeláin to Strongbow as lord of Leinster.[62] Strongbow must have exercised his dominical right to grant them to his own feoffees. It was not until the council of Oxford, 1177, that Robert received his first permanent endowment in Ireland, a grant from Henry II of a half portion of the kingdom of Cork.[63]

According to Gerald of Wales, Diarmait Mac Murchada had made a joint grant of the city of Wexford and two adjoining cantreds to Robert fitz Stephen and Maurice fitz Gerald.[64] Before his departure from Ireland in 1172, Henry II took the city of Wexford into his own hands.[65] In 1173 the king restored Wexford to Strongbow.[66] It is significant that Robert did not benefit from this restoration and was not subsequently enfeoffed of land in Leinster by Strongbow. Almost certainly this was because of Robert fitz Stephen's association with Henry II after 1172. While Henry was waiting in Wexford for favourable

---

[58] Ibid. 92–3.   [59] Ibid. 94–5.   [60] Ibid. 104–5.
[61] Ibid. 168–73.   [62] Ibid. 172–3; Flanagan, 'Henry II and Uí Fáeláin'.
[63] The text of the charter is printed in G. Lyttelton, *History of the life of King Henry II* (3rd edn., London, 1773), vi. 406–8.
[64] Giraldus, *Expugnatio*, 30–1, 34–5.   [65] Ibid. 94–5.
[66] Ibid. 120–1; *Song of Dermot*, ll. 2902–5.

winds to leave Ireland, he used the time to cultivate a group of royal supporters in Ireland 'to strengthen his party and weaken that of the earl'.[67] Gerald named three individuals whom Henry attracted to his service, Raymond le Gros, Miles de Cogan, and William Maskerell.[68] From the first two names at least, it may be inferred that Henry sought to recruit support among the ranks of those Normans who had already become involved in Ireland before his arrival there in 1171. Since Robert fitz Stephen, like Miles de Cogan, is found in the service of Henry II from 1172 until 1177, it may be assumed that Robert was also among their number.

Reviewing Robert fitz Stephen's career, one can sympathize with Gerald of Wales's viewpoint that his relatives did not reap a just reward for the military service which they had rendered both in South Wales and in Ireland.[69] In Wales Robert fitz Stephen had attempted to hold Ceredigion and Cemais for the Norman interest against the Welsh, with little active support either from the Norman overlords of Ceredigion and Cemais or from the Crown. In Ireland he had been in the van of the re-taking of Uí Chennselaig and the province of Leinster for Diarmait Mac Murchada, yet he ended up holding no land in Leinster. The eventual grant of a moiety of the kingdom of Cork from Henry II in 1177 was speculative: it remained for Robert fitz Stephen to make it operative.

Closely associated with Robert fitz Stephen in Ireland were his nephews, Philip and Robert de Barry, brothers of Gerald of Wales. Robert is mentioned as having participated with fitz Stephen at the siege of Wexford in 1169 and in a raid on Osraige in 1170.[70] Strongbow did not enfeoff either Philip or Robert with lands in Leinster. It was not until fitz Stephen was granted a portion of the kingdom of Cork by Henry II in 1177 and enfeoffed the de Barry brothers that they gained any territorial reward from their military service in Ireland.[71]

---

[67] Giraldus, *Expugnatio*, 102–3.

[68] William Maskerell is otherwise unknown in Ireland. The name Maskerell occurs among the tenants of the senior branch of the Clare family at Cavendish in Suffolk: *Red Book of the Exchequer*, i. 403; *Stoke by Clare cartulary*, ed. C. Harper-Bill and R. Mortimer, ii (Suffolk Record Society: Suffolk Charters, 5; Ipswich, 1983), 184, 290; cf. Ward, 'Fashions in monastic endowment', 437.

[69] Cf. Giraldus, *Expugnatio*, 156–7, 168–9.

[70] Ibid. 32–3, 36–9.

[71] Cf. ibid. 188–9; E. St J. Brooks, 'Unpublished charters relating to Ireland, 1177–

Like Robert fitz Stephen, Maurice fitz Gerald was deprived of his grant of the city of Wexford and two adjoining cantreds, which he had received from Diarmait Mac Murcháda, by Henry II's retention of Wexford as royal demesne in 1172. When Henry restored Wexford to Strongbow in 1173, Strongbow did not subsequently enfeoff or confirm Maurice in possession of any lands in or around Wexford. Maurice fitz Gerald was employed by Henry to man the Dublin garrison before his departure from Ireland in 1172. Like fitz Stephen, he appears to have had a grant from the king of a cantred in Uí Fáeláin in the period 1172–3. Following Henry's restoration of this cantred to Strongbow in 1173, Strongbow granted it to his own feoffee, with the result that Maurice fitz Gerald actually returned landless to Wales. Some time later, however, according to Gerald, Strongbow sent to Wales to request Maurice to return and regranted him the cantred of Uí Fáeláin, which he had originally received from Henry II, and also the castle of Wicklow; at the same time, 'in order that relations between the families should be cemented with more durable links', Strongbow gave his daughter Aline in marriage to Maurice's eldest son, William, and Maurice's daughter, Nesta, became the wife of Hervey de Montmorency.[72] As in the case of fitz Stephen, there would appear to have been tensions in the relations between Strongbow and Maurice fitz Gerald, which in the latter's case, however, were eventually resolved. Small wonder, though, that Gerald of Wales's portrayal of Strongbow is so unfavourable, especially when his principal informant on the early years of Norman involvement in Ireland was his uncle, Robert fitz Stephen.

Another notable absentee from Strongbow's known feudatories in Leinster was Miles de Cogan.[73] Gerald of Wales first mentioned him at the siege of Dublin in 1170, and in very favourable terms. According to Gerald, Strongbow had left Miles de Cogan as *custos* of Dublin after the siege in 1171, but Miles is subsequently named as one of those whom Henry II

82, from the archives of the city of Exeter', *RIA Proc.* 43 C (1935–7), 313–66 (at 341–4); *Reg. St Thomas, Dublin*, 205, 214.

[72] Giraldus, *Expugnatio*, 30–1, 34–5, 104–5; 142–3.

[73] It is significant that he is not listed among Strongbow's feudatories in the *Song of Dermot* (ll. 3024–128), which otherwise gives him prominent mention: ll. 1598–605, 1652, 1674–723, 1807, 1880–928, 1976, 2208, 2275–494, 2759.

attached to the royal interest before his departure from
Wexford in 1172.[74] The 'Song of Dermot' supplies the information that Miles left Ireland with Henry and subsequently
fought on his behalf in Normandy.[75] Along with Robert fitz
Stephen, he returned to Ireland in 1176 in the entourage of
William fitz Audelin and in 1177 was granted a half portion of
the kingdom of Cork.[76] Unlike Robert fitz Stephen, who is not
found in association with Strongbow after 1172, Miles de
Cogan witnessed five charters and his brother Richard witnessed four charters granted by Strongbow in Ireland. The
beneficiaries were St Mary's Abbey, Dublin, Dunbrody
Abbey, Vivien Cursun,[77] the Knights Hospitallers,[78] and
Hamund Mac Turcaill.[79] The charter in favour of Vivien
Cursun was given 'in Hibernia apud Dublin'. The charter in
favour of Hamund Mac Turcaill was issued by Strongbow 'ex
parte regis Anglie', and related to the royal demesne in Dublin.
It is likely that all these charters were issued at Dublin, and that

[74] Giraldus, *Expugnatio*, 66–9, 102–3. Miles de Cogan's daughter subsequently
married Gerald's cousin Ralph, son of Robert fitz Stephen, which probably accounts
for Gerald's favourable notice of de Cogan: ibid. 186–7. Roger of Howden, *Chronica*,
i. 269, described Strongbow invading Ireland 'auxiliante ei Milone de Coggeham viro
bellicoso', but this may have been an afterthought on Roger's part, since there is no
mention of Miles in the equivalent passage in the *Gesta*.

[75] *Song of Dermot*, ll. 2755–9.

[76] Giraldus, *Expugnatio*, 168–9, 182–7, and see above, n. 63. A Miles de Cogan held 2
knights' fees of the earl of Gloucester in 1166: *Red Book of the Exchequer*, i. 291. They
may be located in Penarth, south of Cardiff, at the mouth of the Ely river on the Bristol
channel: *Earldom of Gloucester charters*, no. 14. If this individual was not identical with
the 'Irish' Miles de Cogan, and it cannot be proved that he was, they were certainly
related. The same may be said of the Miles de Cogan who married Christiana Paynell
of Bampton in Somerset, via whom in 1261 a branch of the de Cogan family inherited
Bampton. The Bampton de Cogans acknowledged a relationship with the Irish de
Cogans: E. St J. Brooks, 'The family of de Marisco', *RSAI Jn.* 41 (1931), 22–35 (at 24).
Between 1176 and 1198 Robert, son of Elidor, lord of Stackpole in Pembroke, gave the
church of Trefdant to the see of St Davids for the safety of his own soul and that of Miles
de Cogan: *Episc. acts*, i. 299. Since it postdates Miles's acquisition of the half portion of
the kingdom of Cork, from which Robert son of Elidor also benefited, it does not prove
a connection between Miles de Cogan and Pembroke prior to his involvement in
Ireland. Robert son of Elidor was a witness to Henry II's charter in favour of Miles de
Cogan and Robert fitz Stephen; see above, n. 63. Cf. also his attestation of a grant by
William Not in Cork about 1177–82, in Brooks, 'Unpublished charters', 345. For his
lordship of Stackpole see H. Owen, *Old Pembroke families* (London, 1902), 25.

[77] *Chartul. St Mary's, Dublin*, i. 78–9, 83–4, 258; ii. 152–4.

[78] *Calendar of ancient deeds and muniments preserved in the Pembroke Estate Office, Dublin*
(Dublin, 1891), 11.

[79] M. P. Sheehy, 'The registrum novum: a manuscript of Holy Trinity Cathedral:
the medieval charters', *Reportorium Novum*, 3 (1963–4), 249–81 (at 254).

the de Cogan brothers were members of the garrison there. Miles de Cogan, on the evidence of these charters, must have been in Ireland some time between 1173 and 1176. Nevertheless, Strongbow does not appear to have endowed him with any lands in Leinster.

On Gerald's own admission, Raymond le Gros, a younger son of William fitz Gerald, lord of Carew, came to Ireland in 1170 as a member of Strongbow's *familia*, which is suggestive of Strongbow's contacts with the Cambro-Normans who preceded him to Ireland. In 1171, before Henry II's intervention in Ireland, Strongbow had dispatched Raymond to negotiate with Henry on his behalf. Yet before the king departed from Wexford in 1172 he attempted to detach Raymond from the party of Strongbow.[80] Raymond took service with Henry, for when Strongbow returned from Normandy to Ireland in 1173, having been appointed as Henry's agent in Ireland, Henry gave Raymond to Strongbow once more as his coadjutor, according to Gerald of Wales. Gerald implied rivalry between Hervey de Montmorency and Raymond over the leadership of Strongbow's troops, who preferred Raymond. When Raymond returned to Wales because of the death of his father in 1174, Strongbow, in order to maintain the loyalty of his soldiers, was obliged to secure Raymond's return to Ireland by promising him the hand of his sister Basilia in marriage, which Raymond had apparently requested previously. Raymond subsequently held the position of constable in Strongbow's *familia*, and was enfeoffed by him of Fotharta, Uí Dróna, and Uí Dega.[81]

The differing backgrounds of Strongbow and the Geraldines deserve emphasis. Strongbow's landholdings and interests, unlike those of the Geraldines, were not confined to South Wales. Historians, following the lead of Gerald of Wales, have

---

[80] Giraldus, *Expugnatio*, 56–61, 70–8, 80–1, 102–3, 120–1, 134–9.

[81] Raymond styled himself 'constabularius comitis Ricardi' in a charter in favour of William *monachus*: E. St J. Brooks, 'An unpublished charter of Raymond le Gros', *RSAI Jn.* 69 (1939), 167–9. Cf. also his attestations as 'constable' of charters of Strongbow: *Reg. St Thomas, Dublin*, 369; *Ormond deeds, 1172–1350*, nos. 1, 2; Orpen, *Normans*, i. 394. He is styled 'constable of Leinster' in *Song of Dermot*, ll. 3360–1. According to Gerald, Raymond was deprived of lands both in the vale of Dublin and adjacent to Wexford by William fitz Audelin: Giraldus, *Expugnatio*, 172–3. For his holdings in Fotharta, Uí Dróna, and Uí Dega, see *Song of Dermot*, ll. 3061–9; Roger of Howden, *Gesta*, i. 164; *Chronica*, ii. 134; *Knights' fees*, 27–32.

given prominence to the Cambro-Norman element[82] among the first settlers in Leinster, but the earliest feudatories to whom Strongbow offered grants of land were not drawn exclusively from South Wales. Strongbow's grantees in Leinster reflect his wider geographical interests. His uncle Hervey de Montmorency was among the first to receive a grant of lands in Co. Wexford. The latter's English background is reflected in the fact that he endowed the monastery of Christ Church, Canterbury, with the churches of his Irish lands;[83] and when he planned to found a monastery in Ireland it was from Walden in Essex that the house was to be colonized.[84] Strongbow first offered a portion of Uí Dróna to Peter Giffard of the Giffard line of Fonthill in Wiltshire, and only when the latter apparently failed to take up the grant was Raymond le Gros enfeoffed of Uí Dróna.[85]

A clear case of Strongbow drawing on his English tenants is provided by the Bloets. At least four members of the Bloet family witnessed Irish charters of Strongbow,[86] and at least one

---

[82] Although there is no contemporary justification for the use of this term, it provides a convenient means of distinguishing between those who held land only in Wales and those who had wider interests.

[83] Giraldus, *Expugnatio*, 188–9. When in 1182 Hervey de Montmorency became a monk of Christ Church, Canterbury, his Irish lands passed to that community; cf. *Litterae Cantuarienses*, ed. J. B. Sheppard, iii (Rolls series, London, 1889), pp. xl–xlix.

[84] See H. G. Richardson, 'Some Norman monastic foundations in Ireland', in *Med. studies presented to A. Gwynn*, 29–43. Cf. the charter of Henry II in favour of Stratford Langthorne Abbey in Essex, granted about 1164–6, which was witnessed by Hervey de Montmorency and his nephew Gilbert de Montfichet: *Sir Christopher Hatton's book of seals*, no. 413. William de Montfichet, father of Gilbert, had founded Stratford shortly before his death about 1135–6. William was married to Margaret, sister of Gilbert fitz Gilbert, father of Strongbow, who administered the Montfichet fief during Gilbert de Montfichet's minority: *Red Book of the Exchequer*, ii. 351; *Historia et cartularium monasterii sancti Petri Gloucestriae*, ed. W. H. Hart, ii (Rolls series, London, 1865), 165–75; *Rotuli de dominabus*, 45. Cf. also the charter of Earl Gilbert granting Parndon in Essex 'pro anima Willelmi de Montefichet ex cujus feudo exstitit pars hujus donationis', to which Hervey de Montmorency was a witness: J. H. Round, *Studies in the Red Book of the Exchequer* (London, 1898), 8–9. The *caput* of the Montfichet honour was at Stansted Mountfichet in Essex, and the lands were located chiefly in Essex and Cambridgeshire: Sanders, *English baronies*, 83. Cf. also Hervey de Montmorency's enfeoffment in Uí Bairrche of Osbert son of Robert, whose connections were with Bedfordshire: R. Halstead, *Succinct genealogies of the noble and ancient houses of Alno or de Alneto, etc.* (London, 1685), 446.

[85] The text of Strongbow's charter is in G. Wrottesley, *The Giffards from the Conquest to the present time* (William Salt Archaeological Society, NS 5; London, 1902), 212–13.

[86] *Chartul. St Mary's, Dublin*, i. 78–9, 83–4, 258; ii. 151–4; Wrottesley, *The Giffards*, 212–13; *Calendar of ancient deeds in the Pembroke Estate Office*, 11; Sheehy, 'The registrum novum', 253.

had a grant from him of land in Co. Wexford.[87] Walter Bloet was the most frequent attestor of Strongbow's Irish charters apart from John de Clahull. The Bloets were among the original feoffees of the lordship of Strigoil: in 1086, when Domesday Book was compiled, Ralph Bloet held Hilmartin and Lackham in Wiltshire, Silchester in Hampshire, Hinton (Blewitt) and Yeovilton in Somerset, and Daglingworth in Gloucestershire as a tenant of William of Eu, lord of Strigoil, whose honour was subsequently granted to Walter fitz Richard, whence it came to Strongbow.[88]

Gilbert de Boisrohard, Strongbow's feoffee in Uí Felmeda (barony of Ballaghkeen, Co. Wexford), reflects Strongbow's interests in Normandy and possibly also in Bedfordshire and

[87] *Knights' fees*, 26–7.
[88] *Domesday Book*, i. 47b, 71d, 96c, 166d; see above, p. 113. About 1173–4, Strongbow granted Raglan to Walter Bloet: *Cal. Pat. rolls, Henry IV, 1399–1401*, 181 (inspeximus of charter of confirmation from Henry II, 1174, confirming to Walter Bloet 'villam de Raglan cum omnibus pertinentiis suis quam comes Ricardus filius comitis Gilleberti ei rationabiliter dedit'); cf. Dugdale, *Monasticon Anglicanum*, vi. 2. 1095. In 1138 Morgan ap Owain (d. 1158) of the Gwynllwg dynasty had seized the castle of Usk and established himself as lord of Caerleon: Orderic Vitalis, *Ecclesiastical history*, vi. 518–19. Pipe rolls 2, 3, and 4 Henry II (1155–8) record an annual deduction of 40 shillings from the account of the sheriff of Gloucester for Crown lands held by Morgan or his son in 'Carlion': *The great rolls of the pipe for the second, third and fourth years of the reign of King Henry the Second*, ed. J. Hunter (London, 1844), 49, 100, 167. In 1171 on his way to Ireland Henry II deprived Morgan's brother Iorwerth of Caerleon, but no sooner had Henry moved on to Pembroke than Iorwerth and his sons and nephew mounted a raid on Caerleon Castle: *Brut Peniarth*, 66, 68; *Brut Hergest*, 154–5. The castle withstood the siege, and was provisioned by the king's orders to meet further attacks: *Pipe roll 18 Henry II*, 119. Iorwerth took advantage of the revolt against Henry in 1173 to regain possession of Caerleon on 21 July in that year. This success was followed on 16 August by a great raid on Netherwent, which reached as far as Strongbow's castle at Chepstow: *Brut Peniarth*, 70; *Brut Hergest*, 162–3. Strongbow or King Henry must have taken measures against this Welsh incursion, for soon afterwards the castle of Usk, which the Welsh had held since 1138, was recovered by Strongbow's men: *Pipe roll 20 Henry II*, 22, which records a payment 'in warnis' castelli de Usch quod homines comitis Ricardi ceperat super Walenses'; cf. *Gir. Camb. op.* vi. 60–1. Strongbow's grant of Raglan to Walter Bloet must postdate the retaking of Usk, and represents a reorganization of the Norman frontier in this area. It is noteworthy that in 1173 the Anglo-Norman garrisons at Kilkenny and Waterford were attacked by Domnall Mór Ua Briain, king of Thomond, and the son of Domnall Caemánach Mac Murchada is stated to have revolted against Strongbow and inflicted a defeat on the Normans in Leinster: *Ann. Tig.* This may have been occasioned not merely by Strongbow's absence from Ireland in Normandy but also by a redeployment of some of his resources in Gwent; referring to Strongbow's return to Ireland in 1173, Gerald of Wales stated that 'the Irish had got to hear of the serious disturbances which had lately broken out in the lands across the sea' and in consequence had revolted against Henry II and Strongbow: Giraldus, *Expugnatio*, 134–5.

Buckinghamshire. The surname Boisrohard derives from Bosc-le-Hard, Seine-Maritime.[89] A Robert de Boisrohard witnessed a charter of Strongbow in favour of Foucarmont,[90] which suggests that the family may have been tenants of Strongbow in Normandy. In England a branch of the de Boisrohard family held Oakley and Turvey in Bedfordshire, Clifton Reynes in Buckinghamshire, Strathern in Leicestershire, and Tallington in Lincolnshire of the honour of Belvoir.[91] No de Boisrohard has been traced holding land in England of Strongbow, but Strongbow had connections with Bedfordshire and Buckinghamshire. William of Eu, whose estates formed the nucleus of the honour of Strigoil which Strongbow inherited, held Sundon, Streatley, Millow, Edworth, Holme, Arlesey, and Campton in Bedfordshire.[92] Strongbow had interests in Buckinghamshire also, for he confirmed a grant of William of Dadford granting land in Dadford to Biddlesden Abbey between 1148 and 1154.[93]

Another instance of Strongbow drawing on English associates is his grant of the Duffry and the constableship of Leinster, together with his daughter in marriage, to Robert de Quency.[94] The surname de Quency derived from Quinchy near Béthune in the Pas-de-Calais. In England the only known family of this name held Long Buckby in Northamptonshire of the honour of Chokes.[95] The senior branch of the Clare family

---

[89] L. C. Loyd, *The origins of some Anglo-Norman families* (Harleian Society, 103; Leeds, 1951), 18–19; *Facsimiles of early charters from Northamptonshire*, 88–9. The head of the family in England at the time of Anglo-Norman intervention in Ireland was Simon de Boisrohard, who is recorded in 1166 holding three fees of the honour of Belvoir: *Red Book of the Exchequer*, i. 328. His name occurs on the pipe rolls between 1176 and 1186, and he was succeeded by his son Simon: G. H. Fowler, 'The Drayton charters', *Bedfordshire Historical Record Society*, 11 (1927), 72–3.

[90] *Documents preserved in France*, ed. J. H. Round (London, 1899), no. 183.

[91] Loyd, *Origins*, 18–19; *Facsimiles of early charters from Northamptonshire*, 88–9.

[92] *Domesday Book*, i. 211d–212a. Cf. the confirmation by Strongbow of the church and tithes of Everton, Beds., to St Neots Priory: Ward, 'Fashions in monastic endowment'.

[93] Original charter in Huntington Library, California, Stowe collection, Grenville evidences, box 1; cf. A. R. Wagner, 'A seal of Strongbow in the Huntington Library', *Antiquaries Journal*, 21 (1941), 128–32. I am grateful to the Librarian of the Huntington Library for supplying me with a photocopy of the charter. The date is suggested by the style 'comes Ricardus de Pembroc'. A portion of Dadford manor is subsequently found attached to the honour of Giffard; *VCH Bucks*. iv. 234 n. 65 stated that the confirmation was issued by Strongbow representing the Giffard honour.

[94] *Song of Dermot*, ll. 2741–8, 2805–42, 3030–7.

[95] Loyd, *Origins*, 84; W. Farrer, *Honors and knights' fees*, i (London, 1923), 32–3.

held land in Northamptonshire.[96] There was a marital connection between the Clare and de Quency families. Saher de Quency (died about 1156–8), the first known holder of Long Buckby, married Maud, widow of Robert fitz Richard (died 1136–8), lord of Little Dunmow in Essex, younger son of Richard fitz Gilbert, lord of Clare.[97] In 1166 Saher de Quency II held one and a half knights' fees of new feoffment in Essex of his step-brother, Walter, son of Robert fitz Richard.[98] The precise relationship of Strongbow's feoffee, Robert de Quency, to the lords of Long Buckby is undetermined, but the name Robert certainly occurred in the family.[99] For the important offices of seneschal of Leinster and constable of Leinster, Strongbow chose respectively Hervey de Montmorency and Robert de Quency.[100] After the capture of Waterford in 1171, Strongbow appointed Gilbert de Boisrohard *custos* of Waterford.[101] It is also worth noting that the lands granted by Strongbow to Hervey de Montmorency, Robert de Quency, Gilbert de Boisrohard, and the Bloet family were situated in Uí Chennselaig, that is in the patrimonial kingdom of Diarmait Mac Murchada, and may therefore be presumed to have been among the earliest feoffments which he made. As marshal of Leinster, Strongbow chose John de Clahull, to whom he granted Uí Bairrche.[102] John was the most frequent attestor of Strongbow's Irish charters.[103] His

[96] Cf. the charter granted by Adeliz, wife of Gilbert fitz Richard, lord of Clare, and grandmother of Strongbow, together with her sons, Gilbert (father of Strongbow), Walter, and Baldwin, and her daughter, Rohesia, confirming land in Lowick and Raunds in Northants. to the abbey of Thorney in Cambs.: *Facsimiles of early charters from Northamptonshire*, 52–4; also Dugdale, *Monasticon Anglicanum*, ii. 601–3, where she is styled 'domina de Deneford', that is Denford in Northants. See also Farrer, *Honors and knights' fees*, ii. 210–11.

[97] G. E. C., *Peerage*, xii. 2. 745.

[98] *Red Book of the Exchequer*, i. 349; Sanders, *English baronies*, 129.

[99] Saher de Quency I had a younger brother, Robert, who carved a career for himself in Scotland: G. E. C., *Peerage*, xii. 2. 747–8; G. W. S. Barrow, *The Anglo-Norman era in Scottish history* (London, 1980), 22–3. Saher de Quency IV (inherited 1197, d. 1234/5) also had a younger brother and a son named Robert: G. E. C., *Peerage*, xii. 2. 748, note g.

[100] Hervey styled himself 'marescallus domini regis de Hibernia et senescallus de tota terra Ricardi comitis' in his charter in favour of Dunbrody Abbey: *Chartul. St Mary's, Dublin*, ii. 151–2.

[101] *Song of Dermot*, ll. 2211–14.

[102] Ibid. 3100–3; *Knights' fees*, 56–8.

[103] John attested no less than ten of Strongbow's Irish charters: in favour of William

brother Hugh became the first prior of the preceptory of
Knights Hospitallers founded by Strongbow at Kilmainham.[104]
The surname of Strongbow's feoffee in Uí Muiredaig,
Walter de Ridelsford, is associated with holdings in Yorkshire
and a small fee at Barnetby-le-Wold in Lincolnshire.[105] Since
both the Yorkshire and Lincolnshire fees were held of the
constable of Chester, who in turn held of the honour of
Chester, the Yorkshire and Lincolnshire families of de Ridels-
ford were almost certainly related. The Lincolnshire de Ridelsfords share with the Irish de Ridelsfords the very rare first name
Haket,[106] and Strongbow's feoffee, Walter de Ridelsford,
almost certainly belonged to the Lincolnshire branch: whereas
Strongbow has no known connections with Yorkshire, the
Clare family had interests in Lincolnshire.[107]
    Among Strongbow's other known feudatories were two
'Geraldines', Meilir fitz Henry, to whom he granted Cairbre,
and Miles, son of David fitz Gerald, bishop of St Davids (d.
1176), to whom he granted Uí Eirc in Osraige.[108] William de
Angulo, whom he enfeoffed in Uí Felmeda, derived his name
from the district of Angle on the Castlemartin peninsula in
Pembroke.[109] To Maurice de Prendergast, whose name derived

---

de Angulo and Adam de Hereford (*Ormond deeds, 1172–1350*, nos. 1, 2), Savaric Sellarius (*Reg. St Thomas, Dublin*, 369–70, where he is titled 'marshal'), Vivien Cursun, St
Mary's Abbey, Dublin, and Dunbrody Abbey (*Chartul. St Mary's, Dublin*, i. 83–4, 258;
ii. 153–4), Walter de Ridelsford (Brooks, 'The de Ridelesfords', *RSAI Jn.* 81 (1951),
118 n. 12). Thomas, abbot of Glendalough (*Chart. privil. immun.* 1). Holy Trinity,
Dublin (Sheehy, 'The registrum novum', 253), and the Knights Hospitallers (*Calendar
of ancient deeds in the Pembroke Estate Office*, 11). The name de Clahull is associated with
the honour of Odell in Beds., and in particular with a holding at Preston Capes,
Northants.: Farrer, *Honors and knights' fees*, i. 77; Dugdale, *Monasticon Anglicanum*,
v. 179.

[104] *Reg. Kilmainham*, iv.
[105] Brooks, 'The de Ridelesfords', *RSAI Jn.* 81 (1951).
[106] Ibid.
[107] Baldwin fitz Gilbert de Clare acquired the honour of Bourne, the lands of which
were situated in Lincs., Northants., and Herts., by marriage about 1130: *Facsimiles of
early charters from Northamptonshire*, 18–20; Sanders, *English baronies*, 107.
[108] *Song of Dermot*, ll. 3084–5, 3108–11.
[109] Owen, *Old Pembroke families*, 85–7; on the partition of the estates of Walter
Marshal, earl of Pembroke, in 1247, Richard de Angulo held two knights' fees and
Adam de Angulo one-twentieth of a knight's fee in Pembroke: *Cal. pat. rolls, 1364–7*,
263–4. For the grant of Uí Felmeda see Flanagan, 'Mac Dalbaig'. The de Angulo
family were also enfeoffed by Hugh de Lacy in Mide: William de Angulo's brother
Jocelin was granted Navan, and his son, Gilbert de Angulo, was granted Morgallion:
Song of Dermot, ll. 3140–5. In view of the smallness of their holding in Pembroke, and

from Prendergast, now a suburb of Haverfordwest, Strongbow granted the district of Ferann na gCenél.[110] Thomas le Fleming, to whom he gave Ardree in Uí Muiredaig, can also be associated with Pembroke.[111] Because their names are not sufficiently distinctive, it has not proved possible to trace the background and circumstances of Strongbow's feoffees Adam de Hereford, Robert de Bermingham, and Robert fitz Richard.[112] Reviewing the evidence of Strongbow's subinfeudation of Leinster, it may be said that the Cambro-Normans, although they proved to be a significant element, were not Strongbow's first choice as feoffees in Leinster. He drew rather on his English associates and tenants, though the evidence suggests— witness the case of Peter Giffard—that Strongbow had difficulty in persuading some of them to commit themselves to involvement in Ireland.

What was Henry II's reaction to the intervention of Cambro-Normans from Pembroke in Ireland, and what influence did it have on Henry's policies towards South Wales? After his Welsh campaign of 1165, Henry never again attempted to crush the Welsh by force. When he returned from his Continental dominions in 1171 he pursued an alternative policy of negotiation with the Welsh princes, and notably with Rhys ap Gruffydd of Deheubarth, who, after the death of Owain Gwynedd in 1170, ranked as the foremost Welsh ruler. What brought Henry back to England in 1171 was the progress of Anglo-Norman intervention in Ireland. This is forcibly suggested by the chronology of his itinerary and the mounting of a winter campaign in Ireland: on 3 August 1171 Henry disembarked

the fact that they occur as feoffees of both Strongbow and Hugh de Lacy, and bearing in mind also their later albeit unsuccessful involvement in the attempted Anglo-Norman penetration of Connacht, they may be categorized as true adventurers in Ireland.

[110] *Song of Dermot*, ll. 3106–9.   [111] Ibid. 3072–82; *Knights' fees*, 145–51.

[112] *Song of Dermot*, ll. 3112–14; Giraldus, *Expugnatio*, 194–5. The name Thomas Flandrensis would not in itself be sufficient to indicate a Flemish settler from Pembroke, but he was succeeded by Miles de Staunton, whose name appears to derive from Stainton in the hundred of Rhos near Haverfordwest: Orpen, *Normans*, iii. 215. The names fitz Tancred and Dullard also occur in association with him: *Reg. St Thomas, Dublin*, 168, 289. In 1332 there was a small township called Dollardstown in the manor of Wiston which was held by Walter de Staunton of the lordship of Pembroke: *A calendar of the public records relating to Pembrokeshire*, ed. H. Owen, iii (London, 1918), 135–7, cf. also 87, 94, 102, 106. Robert fitz Richard could have been a member of the extended Clare family. A Peter de Bermingham held 9 fees of the honour of Dudley in 1166: *Red book of the Exchequer*, i. 269; cf. *Sir Christopher Hatton's book of seals*, no. 48.

from Barfleur at Portsmouth, and already by 8 September he was in South Wales awaiting favourable weather in order to cross to Ireland.[113] While in Wales he negotiated a *rapprochement* with Rhys ap Gruffydd, confirming him in possession of Ceredigion, Cantref Bychan, and Emlyn, despite the respective claims of the Clare and Clifford families and William fitz Gerald, lord of Carew, and granting Rhys also the commotes of Ystlwyf and Efelffre, Rhys in return promising payment of tribute in acknowledgement of Henry's overlordship.[114]

How far were developments in Ireland between 1167 and 1171 responsible for Henry's change of policy towards Rhys ap Gruffydd in 1171? Sir John Lloyd suggested that the involvement of Cambro-Normans in Ireland raised the spectacle for Henry of a centre of baronial unrest being established there that would threaten the stability of his dominions, and was construed by him as a more pressing and serious problem than the Welsh incursions into the Norman march in South Wales, and that this occasioned Henry's willingness in 1171 to negotiate with Rhys ap Gruffydd. Lloyd argued that Henry was prepared to tolerate, even to promote, the career of Rhys as a useful check on the activities of the Cambro-Normans, preventing them from using their newly acquired resources in Ireland against the royal interest in South Wales.[115]

By contrast, W. L. Warren has argued that Henry's change of strategy towards the Welsh was determined by the disaster of his expedition to Wales in 1165, and was reached before and independently of developments in Ireland. Warren attributed significance to the fact that at the siege of Chaumont in 1168 Henry was supported by a large force of Welsh mercenaries, interpreting this as indicative of Henry's *rapprochement* with the Welsh princes. According to Warren, it was the change of royal policy towards the Welsh rulers which determined Cambro-Norman involvement in Ireland rather than the reverse: abandoning any hope after 1165 that Henry would assist them to recover the lands lost to the Welsh, the Cambro-Normans eagerly accepted the opportunity afforded them by Diarmait Mac Murchada to remake their fortunes in Ireland.[116]

[113] Eyton, *Itinerary*, 160.
[114] *Brut Peniarth*, 66–7; *Brut Hergest*, 152–5; cf. above, n. 38, for Rhys's taking of Emlyn.   [115] Lloyd, *Wales*, ii. 536–7.   [116] Warren, *Henry II*, 164–5.

The chronology of the Welsh recovery may be said to support Warren's thesis, in so far as the major Welsh gains at the expense of the Norman settlers of Dyfed occurred in the period of 1158–65 and were not in any way redressed by the royal expedition of 1165. On the other hand, the presence of Welsh troops in Henry's army at Chaumont in 1168, in the absence of information about their provenance, is insufficient evidence to prove an alteration in Henry's policy towards the Welsh princes before 1171. Welsh support for Henry at Chaumont may have been determined by the factionalism of Welsh politics rather than a change of English royal policy. About the very time of the siege of Chaumont in 1168, Owain Gwynedd dispatched an embassy to the court of Louis VII offering help in his war with Henry and hostages as a pledge of his good faith.[117] Also worth noting is that between 1165 and 1171 the royal dynasty of Powys was divided in its response to Henry II: while Iorwerth Goch professed allegiance to Henry and was placed by him in possession of the castle of Chirk in April 1166, his nephews, Owain ap Madog and Owain Cyfeiliog, resented his dealings with the English king and drove him out of southern Powys. Within the year, Owain Cyfeiliog had joined forces with the English, and was in turn attacked in the interest of Owain ap Madog by Owain Gwynedd and his son Cadwaladr, and by Rhys ap Gruffydd of Deheubarth, and expelled from his commote of Caereinion. With English help, however, Owain Cyfeiliog was re-established in Caereinion, and thereafter generally supported Henry II.[118] The fact that Rhys ap Gruffydd was prepared to attack Owain Cyfeiliog on Owain ap Madog's behalf in 1167 suggests that Rhys at least had not identified a change of direction in regard to the Welsh rulers on Henry's part.

It was not necessary to be on good terms with the Welsh princes in order to recruit Welsh troops. In 1144 Robert, earl of Gloucester, hired Welsh troops to use against King Stephen.[119] In 1155, at the height of the Welsh resistance, Earl Roger of Hereford employed Welsh troops against Henry II when he attempted to resist royal resumption of the castles of Gloucester

---

[117] Ibid.   [118] Lloyd, *Wales*, ii. 520–1.
[119] Orderic Vitalis, *Ecclesiastical history*, vi. 536; *Gesta Stephani*, ed. K. R. Potter (Oxford, 1976), 172.

and Hereford.[120] Edward I was to use vast numbers of Welsh troops in his conquest of Wales. Another possibility is that the *Walenses* who fought for Henry II at Chaumont in 1168 may simply have been drawn from the counties of Hereford, Glamorgan, or Shropshire: large districts inhabited by Welshmen were attached to these border shires.[121]

There is no firm evidence that Henry II had decided upon a *rapprochement* with the Welsh princes in 1165, and particularly with Rhys ap Gruffydd, nor that such a change of royal policy was apparent to the Marcher men of Pembroke and determined their response to Diarmait Mac Murchada's recruitment of mercenaries in 1166–7. Sir John Lloyd's view is convincing, that developments in Ireland did determine a change in Henry's policy in Wales and materially contributed to the dominance of Rhys ap Gruffydd from the death of Owain Gwynedd in 1170 until his own death in 1197. Intervention in Ireland by a significant number of Norman settlers from South Wales thus had important consequences for the history of the Norman colony and of the Welsh revival in South Wales, and in particular for Rhys ap Gruffydd, in the late twelfth century.

---

[120] Gervase of Canterbury, i. 161.

[121] Cf. the entries on *Pipe roll 34 Henry II*, 8–9, 95, 209–10. Herefordshire was not infrequently referred to as 'in Wales': cf. *The great rolls of the pipe, second, third and fourth years of Henry the Second*, 143; *Red Book of the Exchequer*, iii. 1204; *Domesday Book*, i. 179–186b. For references to Welsh tenants paying rents, often in kind, in Shropshire see *Domesday Book*, i. 255. The area between the Wye and the Usk was attached to Gloucestershire: cf. *Domesday Book*, i. 162b–170b. On the indeterminate boundary between Wales and England between the 11th and 13th centuries see Davies, *Conquest*, 1–7.

PART III

Angevin Kingship and Ireland

6

Henry II's Relations with the Irish Kings, 1171–1172

DIARMAIT Mac Murchada's death in 1171 was the signal for Ruaidrí Ua Conchobair as high-king of Ireland to try to re-assert his authority over Leinster. When Diarmait Mac Murchada had returned to Ireland in 1167 and regained the kingship of Uí Chennselaig, he had been obliged to acknowledge the high-kingship of Ruaidrí Ua Conchobair: Ruaidrí exacted a further submission from him in 1169, when Diarmait was obliged to give him additional hostages, including his son Conchobar.[1] Once Mac Murchada had augmented his military strength with the arrival of significant numbers of mercenaries, and particularly of Strongbow after August 1170, he not only set about re-establishing and consolidating his former position as provincial king of Leinster, but also embarked on an expansionist policy beyond Leinster into Mide. This was a direct challenge to the high-kingship of Ruaidrí Ua Conchobair. Diarmait was thereby deemed by Ruaidrí to have repudiated his former submission: in 1170 Ruaidrí executed the hostages whom he held in custody from Mac Murchada.[2] Ruaidrí could no longer be regarded as overlord of the province of Leinster, ᴗnd Mac Murchada himself was now a serious contender for the title of high-king.

When Mac Murchada died at Ferns in the spring of 1171, Ruaidrí Ua Conchobair immediately mounted a military expedition against Strongbow, which may be interpreted as an attempt to regain acknowledgement of his high-kingship from the new lord of Leinster. According to the 'Song of Dermot', Strongbow offered to acknowledge Ruaidrí Ua Conchobair as high-king if the latter would recognize Strongbow as lord of Leinster.[3] Ruaidrí, however, was willing to

---

[1] See above, ch. 3, pp. 96–7, 99 and nn. 52, 62.
[2] *Ann. Tig., AU, AFM* 1170; see above, ch. 3 n. 83.
[3] *Song of Dermot*, ll. 1798–876.

concede to Strongbow lordship only of the Hiberno-Norse towns of Dublin, Wexford, and Waterford. Since agreement could not be reached, Ruaidrí besieged Strongbow at Dublin for almost two months until the Anglo-Norman garrison managed to make a sudden sortie from the city, surprise the high-king and his army, and rout him. It was a significant defeat: the high-king had attempted to assert lordship over Strongbow and had failed. Control of Dublin in 1171 was the crucial turning-point for Strongbow's assertion of lordship over Leinster, as it had been for Ruaidrí Ua Conchobair in 1166, and for Mac Murchada in 1170.[4]

News of the siege of Dublin, and of Strongbow's humiliation of the high-king of Ireland, must have reached England and the notice of Henry II relatively quickly via the trading contacts between Dublin and Bristol and Chester. Henry had betrayed anxiety about Strongbow's intended intervention in Ireland even before he had departed in 1170. Strongbow's defeat of the high-king can only have contributed further to Henry's disquiet. Strongbow was now a lordless man in Ireland. His succession to the lordship of Leinster would not have posed such a serious threat to Henry if he could have relied on the high-king to exercise effective control over Strongbow's activities. After the siege of Dublin in 1171 it must have appeared to Henry that Strongbow had a free hand in Ireland. Despite the assurances which Strongbow was prepared to make to Henry via his messengers and in person, Henry judged that his personal intervention in Ireland had become necessary.

The most expansive contemporary assessment of the reasons why Henry II decided to go to Ireland in 1171 was given by the monk Gervase of Canterbury.[5] Henry went to Ireland, according to Gervase, firstly because Strongbow had gone there, and Strongbow had done so because he had incurred the anger of

---

[4] Robert of Torigny consistently referred to Diarmait Mac Murchada as king of Dublin, and related Strongbow's successes in Ireland in terms of his take-over of the cities of Dublin and Waterford: Robert of Torigny, 252, 270. This may reflect the importance which Henry II assigned to the Irish towns, for Robert may have seen the dispatch which he stated Henry sent from Ireland to the young King Henry in Normandy. Cf. also Roger of Howden, *Chronica*, i. 269, who said of Strongbow that 'facta concordia cum rege Diviliniae, filiam illius in uxorem duxit cum regno Diviliniae', and Ralph of Diss, i. 407, who described Diarmait Mac Murchada as king of the people of Dublin.

[5] Gervase of Canterbury, i. 234–5.

the king to such an extent that neither he, nor anyone interceding on his behalf, was able to placate Henry, nor was Strongbow allowed to enjoy his lawful possessions in peace.
Accordingly, Strongbow sought and obtained the king's
licence to go to Ireland. Gervase made no mention of Diarmait
Mac Murchada's offer to Strongbow of the kingdom of
Leinster; he related merely that Strongbow sent his uncle,
Hervey de Montmorency, on an exploratory mission to Ireland, and when the latter had reported back to him, they journeyed together to that country. Once there, Strongbow began to
plunder the Irish countryside, which was spacious but not
much cultivated, and to wipe out the simple inhabitants. Having taken possession of the city of Dublin, he began to make frequent attacks on the Irish. The Irish kings and their people
were goaded into retaliation, but when they could not get the
better of Strongbow's forces they sent messengers to the king of
England, urging him to come to Ireland to protect them
against Strongbow, and to accept the overlordship of Ireland.
Then Strongbow, fearing that he might lose all that he had
gained, sent messengers to the king offering to hold his Irish
acquisitions from him.

According to Gervase, Henry went to Ireland firstly because
Strongbow had gone there, and secondly and consequentially
because the Irish had invited Henry to do so. This information
was derived from some acknowledged but unspecified source,
'ut fertur', as Gervase put it. But in Gervase's opinion, 'ut
aestimo', Henry's most important reason was to avoid the
proclamation of a papal interdict following the murder of Thomas Becket. Gervase's account thus far is independent of the
other Anglo-Norman chroniclers who recorded the English
king's intervention in Ireland, none of whom mentioned an
Irish embassy to Henry. Thereafter, Gervase's description of
Henry's stay in Ireland is perfunctory, an abbreviated borrowing from Roger of Howden. Gervase was not particularly interested in Henry's subsequent activities in Ireland. His main
concern was his monastery of Canterbury and its martyr,
Thomas Becket, and it is likely that Gervase would not have
dwelt on Henry's supposed reasons for intervention in Ireland
were it not for the fact that the king was at that time under
threat of excommunication because of the murder of Becket.

Most interesting is Gervase's assertion that Strongbow only offered the overlordship of his Irish acquisitions to Henry II after the Irish had made overtures to Henry. Gervase's account, which was written about 1188, deserves serious consideration, because of his access at Canterbury to the very man who had negotiated with Henry on behalf of Strongbow in 1171, namely Hervey de Montmorency. Hervey became a monk of Canterbury, in 1179 according to the annals of St Mary's Abbey, Dublin, around 1182–5 according to Gerald of Wales.[6] Upon his reception into the monastic community, Hervey gave to Canterbury the lands which he had acquired in south Leinster.[7] The only individuals named by Gervase of Canterbury in his account of Henry II's intervention in Ireland, apart from the king, were Strongbow and Hervey de Montmorency. Strongbow is first mentioned as the nephew of Hervey, a slightly odd way of introducing him, and Hervey then as Strongbow's uncle. The obvious conclusion is that Hervey was given this prominence because he, as Gervase's fellow monk, was Gervase's source.

There can be little doubt that the expansionist activities of Diarmait Mac Murchada and Strongbow beyond the confines of Leinster from 1170 onwards would have caused considerable concern to the Irish of the adjacent kingdoms. Beyond Leinster the most immediately involved were the Munster kings, by the annexation of the city of Waterford. Waterford had been subject to the overlordship of the Dál Cais dynasty from AD 984 until the collapse of the high-kingship of Muirchertach Ua Briain in 1114. Thereafter, Waterford and the adjacent kingdom of Déise came under the control of the Mac Carthaig kings of Desmond. From 1133 onwards their influence in that region was challenged by Diarmait Mac Murchada.[8] In 1137 Waterford was besieged by Mac Murchada, who received the hostages of Déise on the same occasion.[9] It is significant that Diarmait Mac Carthaig, king of Desmond, was the first Irish king to make submission to Henry II when he landed at Water-

---

[6] *Chartul. St Mary's, Dublin*, ii. 304–5; Giraldus, *Expugnatio*, 188–9.

[7] *Litterae Cantuarienses*, ii, pp. xl–xlix; see above, ch. 5 n. 83.

[8] See H. A. Jefferies, 'Desmond: the early years, and the career of Cormac Mac Carthy', *Cork Hist. Soc. Jn.* 81 (1983), 81–284.

[9] *AFM* 1137; cf. *Ann. Clon.* 194.

ford in 1171. Diarmait Mac Carthaig would certainly have had reason to make overtures to Henry.

The 'Song of Dermot' provides corroborative evidence for embassies from Ireland to Henry II before his arrival in that country. It recounts that, while Henry was at Pembroke Castle waiting to cross over to Ireland, he was visited by a deputation of twelve men from Wexford, who reported that they had taken Robert fitz Stephen prisoner, and were willing to deliver him into Henry's custody.[10] This implies that there was foreknowledge in Ireland of Henry's imminent arrival, and that the visit was viewed by at least some as a punitive expedition against the Anglo-Normans. We cannot tell how many other deputations from Ireland Henry may have received between 1166–7, when Diarmait Mac Murchada had first approached him, and his arrival in Ireland in October 1171, but what little evidence there is suggests that at least some individuals in Ireland were expecting Henry and interpreted his intervention as being to their advantage, as a mission which would regulate relations between them and the Anglo-Normans.

Apart from Gervase of Canterbury, Henry II's expedition to Ireland received mention from Robert of Torigny, William of Newburgh, Ralph of Diss, Roger of Howden, and, of course, Gerald of Wales. Of these accounts that of Robert of Torigny is the shortest; he merely mentioned that Henry crossed to Ireland on 17 October 1171 and that the details of his journey and reception in that country could be read in the dispatches which Henry sent to his son, the young King Henry, in Normandy.[11] William of Newburgh, writing in the north of

[10] *Song of Dermot*, ll. 2500–78. The author of the Song styled the deputation from Wexford 'traitors'. I have presumed them to be Irish, and not Normans, since they accused Robert fitz Stephen of coming 'to Ireland to cause our destruction' and of laying waste 'our country'. An entry on the pipe roll of 1172–3 recorded expenses of £2. 6s. 7d. for 11 nights stay at Winchester by 'Morchard'' and the burgesses of Wexford, and expenses of £20. 14s. 11d. for robes given to 'Morchard'' and the burgesses: *Pipe roll 19 Henry II*, 51. The form *Morchard'* could stand for the surname Mac Murchada, or the first name Murchad (in which case he may have been the brother of Diarmait Mac Murchada), or the first name Muirchertach (in which case he may have been Diarmait's nephew): see above, p. 109. Wexford was retained by Henry II as royal demesne until its restoration to Strongbow in 1173: Giraldus, *Expugnatio*, 120–1; *Song of Dermot*, ll. 2902–5.

[11] Robert of Torigny, 252. Henry II was punctilious about treating his son as a king after his coronation in 1170, hence probably the dispatches. Cf. A. Heslin, 'The coronation of the young king in 1170', *Studies in Church History*, 2 (1965), 165–78.

England at some distance from the royal court, recorded how Henry crossed to Ireland with a large army and obtained the submission of the Irish kings without bloodshed and by the mere force of his reputation, and, having disposed of affairs to his satisfaction, returned in safety to England.[12] Roger of Howden's and Ralph of Diss's accounts are those of historians chronicling the movements of the court and the actions of the king.[13] Gerald of Wales wrote of Henry's visit within the context of his narrative history of the English in Ireland.

The Anglo-Norman accounts have in common an emphasis on Henry II's relations with the Irish rather than his Anglo-Norman subjects in Ireland, and particularly on the submissions of a number of Irish kings to Henry. While the Anglo-Norman chroniclers, with the exception only of Robert of Torigny, recorded a form of submission made by the Irish kings to Henry II, they did not all describe that submission in the same terms. Roger of Howden and Ralph of Diss stated that the Irish kings gave homage and swore fealty to Henry, Gervase of Canterbury mentioned only fealty, William of Newburgh spoke of subjection, and Gerald of Wales of fealty and submission under solemn oath. Additional incidental details about the submissions were provided by a number of chroniclers. Gerald of Wales described a number of the Irish kings who had submitted to Henry departing 'cum regiis donariis et honore'.[14] Roger of Howden depicted the submissions of the kings taking place at the Christmas feast at Dublin, in a palace which was constructed specially for Henry by the Irish kings 'according to the custom of the country'.

The Anglo-Norman accounts of the submissions of the Irish kings have been variously interpreted by historians. Orpen, MacNeill, Curtis, Poole, Barlow, and Otway-Ruthven assumed that the Irish kings entered into a full feudal relationship with Henry II by performing homage and fealty.[15] W. L. Warren challenged this view, arguing that the Irish kings swore only fealty and did not render homage, the essential difference

---

[12] William of Newburgh, i. 169.

[13] Roger of Howden, *Gesta*, i. 24–5; *Chronica*, ii. 29–30; Ralph of Diss, i. 348.

[14] Giraldus, *Expugnatio*, 94–5.

[15] Orpen, *Normans*, i. 264–5, 283–4; MacNeill, *Phases*, 311–12; Curtis, *Med. Ire.* 56–7, 61–4; Poole, *Domesday Book to Magna carta*, 308; F. Barlow, *The feudal kingdom of England, 1014–1216* (London, 1955), 335; Otway-Ruthven, *Med. Ire.* 49–50.

between the two acts being that, whereas fealty was an oath of personal allegiance to the individual, homage created a tenurial link between lord and vassal, which, Warren held, was not created between the Irish kings and Henry II in 1171.[16]

Historians have approached the problem of the nature of the submissions of the Irish kings to Henry II from the standpoint of Anglo-Norman institutions; if they have differed in their interpretations, it is over what type of feudal relationship was involved, homage or fealty. The incidental details of the chroniclers' accounts have received little attention. Roger of Howden's description of the Christmas court of Henry II at Dublin has been treated simply as a social event, and the fact that Henry had a palace constructed for him according to the native custom has been interpreted as Henry 'trying to please his new vassals by showing an appreciation of native craftsmanship'.[17] The submissions have not been considered in the context of Irish social or political institutions, of whether homage or fealty would have been meaningful concepts to the Irish kings.[18]

The Irish annals are in agreement with the Anglo-Norman chroniclers in recording the submissions of a number of Irish kings to Henry II. While the accounts of the Anglo-Norman chroniclers can be shown to be contemporary, or nearly contemporary, with Henry's visit to Ireland, this is not the case with all the entries in the Irish annals. The majority of the annals survive only in later copies and, although the entries could have been written up originally as the events took place, they may have been altered—reworded, expanded, shortened, suppressed—on each subsequent occasion when the annals were recopied. It cannot be assumed that the wording of an entry, as it now survives, was contemporary with the events which it recorded. The submissions of Irish kings to Henry II do not appear to have been a politically sensitive issue for the contemporary twelfth-century Irish annalist, but they were to become so in the light of the subsequent history of the English colony in Ireland.[19]

[16] Warren, *Henry II*, 201–2.   [17] Orpen, *Normans*, i. 267.

[18] Fealty and homage were not necessarily feudal concepts, but in relation to the Irish kings they have not been considered in other than a feudal context.

[19] *Ann. Inisf.*, *AU*, *Ann. Tig.*, *ALC*, *Misc. Ir. annals* record the submissions of the Irish kings. *AFM* do not, a deliberate suppression by the seventeenth-century

Only one set of annals which covers the twelfth century survives in a contemporary manuscript, namely the Annals of Inisfallen, which are of Munster provenance. The following entry is a contemporary record of Henry II's arrival in Ireland and the submissions of two Munster kings: 'The son of the Empress [Henry II] came to Ireland and landed at Waterford. The son of Cormac [Diarmait Mac Carthaig, king of Desmond] and the son of Toirdelbach [Domnall Mór Ua Briain, king of Thomond] came into his house there and he proceeded thence to Dublin where he remained for the winter.'[20] The annalist did not necessarily expect his readers to interpret the statement literally that Diarmait Mac Carthaig and Domnall Mór Ua Briain entered Henry's house at Waterford: to state that one king had entered the house of another was for him the equivalent of stating that one king had recognized the superiority of another. He meant the reader to understand by it that these two kings had submitted to Henry at Waterford.

In order to appreciate the significance of stating that one king had entered the house of another, and, more importantly, the institution which it denoted, it is necessary to examine the nature and form of submission within the Irish polity. Only by doing so can the motives be evaluated which led a number of Irish kings to submit to Henry II in 1171.

POLITICAL SUBMISSION IN PRE-NORMAN IRELAND

D. A. Binchy described the ritual of entry by one king into the house of another to signify submission as having 'all the marks of antiquity'.[21] This may be so, but the first record of the procedure in a historical context occurs in 1059 in the Annals of Inisfallen. In that year Donnchad, son of Brian Bóruma, king of Dál Cais and claimant to the kingship of Munster, is stated to

compilers of a fact which was politically unpalatable to them. An instance of tampering with contemporary accounts bearing on the arrival of the Anglo-Normans by subsequent compilers is the conflicting death notices of Diarmait Mac Murchada, king of Leinster: see Giraldus, *Expugnatio*, 304 n. 104, to which should be added the most important contemporary obit in *Ann. Inisf.* 1171. 2.

[20] *Ann. Inisf.* 1171. 5. Cf. p. xxxv, 'The annals for 1170 and 1171 appear as if they were entered each at the end of its year.'

[21] Binchy, *Celtic and Anglo-Saxon kingship*, 31.

have entered the house of Áed Ua Conchobair, king of Connacht. The Annals of Tigernach and the *Chronicon Scotorum* under the same year recorded that Donnchad gave hostages to the king of Connacht.[22] These parallel entries provide the means of interpreting as an act of submission the statement in the Annals of Inisfallen, that Donnchad entered the house of Ua Conchobair.

The typical expression until the eleventh century by which annalists recorded the submission of one king to another was by the taking of hostages. The taking of hostages was recorded in the annals from the late eighth century onwards with a simple formula such as 'A took hostages from B', or 'B gave hostages to A'.[23] In 1059 the formula that one king entered the house of another to indicate submission was used for the first time in the Annals of Inisfallen. Thereafter, this phrase was used in preference to accounts of the taking of hostages in the Annals of Inisfallen; and it also began to be used in other sets of annals to indicate submission, sometimes in conjunction with a record of the exaction of hostages.[24] If the ritual of entry into the house of another as a recognition of superiority was a very ancient one, as Binchy argued, the annalistic evidence suggests that it acquired increasing importance from the mid eleventh century onwards and, in consequence, caused a modification of annalistic literary conventions.

Since the change in annalistic terminology first occurred in the Annals of Inisfallen, a source of Munster provenance, it is natural to seek a specific political context in Munster to

[22] For the background to Donnchad's submission to the king of Connacht see Ryan, 'The O'Briens in Munster', 145.

[23] According to an 8th-century law tract on status, the concrete evidence of a king's sovereignty was that he should 'carry off many hostages' from the territory owing allegiance: *Crith gablach*, ed. D. A. Binchy (Dublin, 1941), 18 (l. 460), 96. In one Irish *Fürstenspiegel* 'the chief who has not hostages in keeping is as ale in a leaky vessel': T. O'Donoghue, 'Advice to a prince', *Ériu*, 9 (1921), 43–54 (at 45). These refer to the hostages which the king exacted within his own *tuath*. The earliest entry in the annals of the taking of hostages by one king from another is *AU* 778. 10 = 799. The entry of 721 in *AU* and *Ann. Inisf.* is retrospective: Byrne, *Ir. kings*, 208.

[24] *Ann. Inisf.* 1059. 7, 1070. 9, 1072. 6, 1081. 5, 1092. 5, 1093. 11, 1095. 6, 1120. 4 (lacuna 1130–58), 1165. 2, 1171. 5, 1203. 3, 1206. 7, 1209. 2, 1210. 2; *AU* 1063. 4, 1076. 4, 1114. 3, 1122. 3 (lacuna 1132–54), 1156, 1157, 1166, 1167, 1168; *Ann. Tig.* 1059, 1060, 1079, 1122, 1123, 1125, 1126, 1161, 1166, 1167, 1170, 1171; *Chron. Scot.* 1057 (= 1059 *Ann. Inisf.*), 1058, 1076, 1111, 1116 (lacuna 1132–40 and termination 1150); *ALC* 1063, 1076, 1114, 1122, 1132 (lacuna 1138–70); *Misc. Ir. annals*, 1117. 4, 1123. 3; *Ann. Boyle*, 1196; *AFM* 1132, 1137, 1149, 1150, 1151, 1153, 1161, 1165, 1166, 1171, 1189.

account for the change. The entries in the Annals of Inisfallen as far as 1092 comprise an abbreviated transcript of an earlier exemplar; from 1092 onwards begin a series of annual entries by contemporary or almost contemporary annalists.[25] The entries for the period 972–1092 form a subsection of the pre-1092 transcript and correspond with the growth of the supremacy of the Dál Cais dynasty and the advent of Brian Bóruma. The hegemony of Brian and his successors is reflected throughout, while the material in general is characterized by an increase in recorded events other than obits, and a less abbreviated form of entry, particularly for those of Munster interest. There is increasing evidence of obviously contemporary notices, for example those of natural phenomena, hostings, the taking of hostages, contests for abbacies, and the like. There are also some changes in wording.[26] Throughout the 972–1092 section the average number of entries shows a marked increase. From 1000 to 1050 the annual average of entries is about twice that for the period 970–1000. From about 1052 to 1092 they tend to increase in length, but are proportionately fewer than in the first half of the century, and those of Munster interest now account for about three-quarters of the total. The first identifiable stratum appears to have been compiled in the monastery of Emly about the end of the tenth century, whence it was continued probably at Toomgraney, Co. Clare. This text in turn seems to have been transcribed some time after the middle of the eleventh century at Killaloe, the chief ecclesiastical centre of the Dál Cais dynasty. For the contemporary section which follows from 1092 onwards, the weight of evidence suggests that the manuscript was transferred from Killaloe to the church of Lismore in or about 1119 and written up there until about 1130, when the codex passed from east to west Munster, where it appears to have been continued at the monastery of Inisfallen. Events of Desmond and western Munster are thereafter given chief prominence and, in general, the Mac Carthaig replace the Uí Briain as the most noticed family.

The change in terminology in regard to submission occurs in

---

[25] *Ann. Inisf.*, pp. x–xxx. See also A. Gwynn, 'Were the "Annals of Inisfallen" written at Killaloe?', *N Munster Antiq. Jn.* 8 (1958–61), 20–33.

[26] For instance the Irish *bás* makes its first appearance at AD 980, and thereafter tends to oust the Latin *mors*: *Ann. Inisf.*, p. xxv.

the Annals of Inisfallen in a section which shows a bias in favour of the Dál Cais dynasty. It is possible that the emphasis on entry by one king into the house of another as a means of expressing submission should be associated specifically with the Dál Cais dynasty. Two entries in the Annals of Inisfallen which pre-date the adoption of the new formula in 1059 recorded the attendance of individuals at the Dál Cais court at Kincora. In 1011, after a co-ordinated military and naval expedition against Ua Máel Doraid, king of Cenél Conaill, which secured his submission, Brian Bóruma is stated to have brought the king of Cenél Conaill back to Kincora, where Ua Máel Doraid accepted a large stipend from him and 'made complete submission to him'. In 1026 it is recorded that the *comarba* of Armagh, the chief ecclesiastic of the Irish Church, and the king of Osraige celebrated Easter with Donnchad, son of Brian Bóruma, at Kincora. The attendance of the king of Osraige at Kincora in 1026 followed a military expedition by Donnchad into Leinster, during which he had received hostages from the king of Osraige. These accounts of guests in attendance at the Dál Cais royal residence at Kincora in 1011 and 1026 could be said to record implicitly the entry of these individuals into the house of Brian Bóruma and his son Donnchad.

Between 1026 and 1059 there are only two entries in the Annals of Inisfallen bearing on submission: the taking of hostages from Leinster and Osraige by Donnchad, son of Brian Bóruma, is recorded in 1049, and his inability to take hostages from Ua Conchobair of Connacht is mentioned in 1051. In 1059 occurs the first use in the Annals of Inisfallen of the formula of entry by the submitting king into the house of the superior as a means of indicating submission: 'Brian's son [Donnchad] went into the house of Ua Conchobair of Connacht and he [Donnchad] obtained his demand from him [Ua Conchobair], including valuables, treasures and recognition and was detained there from Shrovetide till Easter.'[27] From 1059 onwards, entry by a submitting king into the house of the superior is almost invariably used in the Annals of Inisfallen to indicate submission, replacing the earlier practice of recording the giving or taking of hostages.

[27] *Ann. Inisf.* 1059. 7.

In support of a connection between the emergence of this formula and the Dál Cais dynasty is its occurrence also in Dál Cais pseudo-historical literature, such as *Cogadh Gaedhel re Gallaibh* and material in *Leabhar Muimhneach*.[28] These are later in date, however, than the appearance of the formula in the Annals of Inisfallen. The earliest extant recension of *Cogadh Gaedhel re Gallaibh* was compiled in the twelfth century from material which included the Annals of Inisfallen.[29] It is a characteristic of *Cogadh Gaedhel re Gallaibh* that it builds incidents of political significance around visits of guests, notably the king of Leinster, to the court of Brian Bóruma at Kincora.[30]

Is it arguable that Brian Bóruma may have developed a procedure of entry into his house as a ceremony specifically designed to indicate submission to the claimant to the high-kingship of Ireland, an office which Brian Bóruma had been the first to take from the Uí Néill dynasty, and which Brian's successors sought to retain?[31] Is it possible that just as Brian Bóruma acknowledged the ecclesiastical supremacy of the *comarba* of Armagh by staying a week at Armagh in 1005, so a visit to Brian's royal residence at Kincora was deemed to be a public recognition of his high-kingship or that of his successors?[32] Elsewhere in Europe during this period, the recording of the attendance of subordinates at the court of a superior was a characteristic of claims to overlordship, of imperializing tend-

---

[28] On its compilation see P. Walsh, 'An Leabhar Muimhneach', *IHS* 3 (1942), 135–43. Cf. the anecdote about the alleged submission of the Eóganachta Áed son of Crimthann to the Dál Cais Áed son of Conall, intended to justify the Dál Cais in taking the kingship of Cashel in 964: *Lr Muin.* 88; R. Thurneysen, 'Colmán mac Lénnéni and Senchán Torpéist', *ZCP* 19 (1932), 193–209. It is difficult to date the compilation of this anecdote, but like *Cog. Gaedhel*, it links Colmán mac Lénnéni with the Dál Cais, making him prophesy the Dál Cais kingship of Cashel: *Cog. Gaedhel*, 84–7.

[29] See R. H. Leech, 'Cogadh Gaedhel re Gallaibh and the annals of Inisfallen', *N Munster Antiq. Jn.* 11 (1968), 13–21.

[30] *Cog. Gaedhel*, 107, 119, 123, 127.

[31] Suggested by T. M. Charles-Edwards in 'The date of the four branches of the Mabinogi', *Cymrrod. Soc. Trans.*, session 1970, part ii, 263–98 (at 297). Charles-Edwards was misled by the inaccurate footnote in *Ann. Inisf.* to interpret *Ann. Tig.* 1059 in the opposite sense to its real meaning.

[32] Cf. *Fled Dúin na nGéd*, which depicted Domnall mac Áed mac Ainmire as high-king of Ireland summoning the rulers of the five provinces of Ireland, with their kings, *tóisig*, and *óchtigern*, to a feast: *The banquet of Dun na n-Gedh and the Battle of Magh Rath*, ed. J. O'Donovan (Irish Archaeological Society, Dublin, 1842), 22–3; *Fled Dúin na nGed*, ed. P. Lehmann (Dublin, 1964), l. 194.

encies. This was especially true of the Anglo-Saxon kings. It is not impossible that Brian borrowed ideas for his high-kingship from the royal house of Wessex, which was in the process of converting itself not only into sole kings of England but also overlords of Britain. It has been suggested that Brian's use of the title 'imperator Scottorum' in 1005 was influenced by the adoption of the title 'imperator Romanorum' by the Ottonian royal house in 996,[33] but it is equally redolent of the high-flown contemporary titles used of the West Saxon royal house.[34] *Cogadh Gaedhel re Gallaibh*, the pseudo-historical account of Brian's heroic struggle against the Vikings, was partly modelled on Asser's life of Alfred.[35] Although the extant text of *Cogadh Gaedhel re Gallaibh* is a twelfth-century redaction, it is not impossible that the model was borrowed and a prototype composed during or shortly after the lifetime of Brian Bóruma.

An entry in the Annals of Inisfallen for 1072, which stated that the son of Ua Máel Sechlainn, king of Mide, Gofraid, king of Dublin, and Domnall Mac Gilla Pátraic, king of Osraige, 'entered the house' of Toirdelbach Ua Briain, king of Munster, and 'gave acknowledgement and high-kingship to him', might be said to support the view that a ceremony was promoted by the Dál Cais dynasty as a specific recognition of high-kingship. But even if it may have been initiated, or elaborated upon an older institution, by the Dál Cais dynasty for this purpose, it was not subseqently the case that every king with whom this form of submission was associated was a claimant for the office of high-king. This could have been a consequence of the failure of Brian Bóruma's successor Donnchad, to achieve the high-kingship. On the other hand, the apparently increasing importance of entry by one king into the house of another as a form of submission from the mid eleventh century onwards may simply be associated with a general intensification of overlordship rather than specifically with the high-kingship. In addition to giving hostages, the subordinate king may have been summoned to the court of his superior to demonstrate his submission on a more ceremonial public occasion, when a large

[33] A. Gwynn, 'Brian in Armagh, 1005', *Seanchas Ardmhacha*, 9 (1978–9), 35–50 (at 32).

[34] See above, pp. 41–4.

[35] D. Ó Corráin, 'Caithréim Chellacháin Chaisil: history or propaganda', *Ériu*, 25 (1974), 1–69 (at 69).

number of the king's clients and subjects would have been present.

Once annalists regularly begin to use the formula 'A went into the house of B' as a synonym for submission, it can no longer be taken literally, that is it cannot be assumed that in each case the submitting king travelled to the house of the superior for the actual ceremony of submission. The formula becomes a convenient annalistic shorthand for submission. That the submitting king did not invariably make a journey to the superior's residence is suggested by the occasional occurrence of an alternative formula, 'A joined the assembly of B', indicating an act of submission at the itinerant court of a superior king who had either invaded or was on peaceful circuit within the subordinate's kingdom.[36]

A number of entries in the annals link entry into the house of a superior king with the bestowal of gifts on the submitting king.[37] The notion of reciprocal relations being created by the formalized exchange of gifts, or a relationship of submission being initiated by the acceptance of a gift without immediate or like reciprocation, is familiar to anthropologists.[38] That the exchange of gifts was formalized in Irish society is evidenced by the use of a number of technical terms, such as *rath* and *tuarastal*, for the gifts bestowed by a superior king on a submitting king. While the term *rath* could be used in other senses besides that of ceremonial gifts, *tuarastal* was used exclusively to denote ceremonial gifts from the eleventh century onwards. It is in the eleventh century that the term *tuarastal* first appeared in the annals in association with submission: the earliest annalistic occurrence is in the Annals of Ulster in 1080.[39] The Annals of

---

[36] *Ann. Inisf.* 1093. 2; *AU* 1114. 3, 1156, 1165; *Misc. Ir. annals*, 1118. 3; *AFM* 1115; cf. *Cog. Gaedhel*, 155. On the term *airecht* see *RIA Contrib.* A, fasc. 1, col. 195; *Críth gablach*, 73.

[37] *Ann. Inisf.* 1011. 5, 1059. 7, 1070. 9, 1081. 5, 1095. 6, 1120. 4, 1225. 2; *AU* 1080. 6, 1083. 6, 1084. 4, 1166; *Chron. Scot.* 1058, 1063; *ALC* 1083, 1084; *Ann. Tig.* 1060, 1151, 1166, 1167; *AFM* 1154, 1166.

[38] M. Mauss, *The gift: forms and function of exchange in archaic societies* (London, 1969), 72; E. Benveniste, *Indo-European language and society* (London, 1973), 53–83, for the close connection between hospitality and the exchange of gifts.

[39] *Tuarastal* derives from *fresndal/frestal*, 'attending', verbal noun of *frestlaid/frisindlea*, 'serves', 'waits on'. There is no occurrence of *tuarastal* in the sense of stipend in the law tracts. It does, however, occur with this meaning in *The poems of Blathmac son of Cú Brettan*, ed. J. Carney (Ir. Texts Soc. 47; Dublin, 1964), 48–9, to which Carney would assign a 9th-century date.

Inisfallen s.a. 1059 and the Annals of Tigernach s.a. 1060, however, recorded bestowals of gifts on the occasion of submission without the use of the term *tuarastal*; the bestowal of ceremonial gifts may also be inferred from an entry in the Annals of Inisfallen s.a. 1011.[40] It is noteworthy that within a few decades of literal recordings of the bestowal of gifts, the term *tuarastal* began to be used in a technical sense by the annalists. This development seems to parallel the literal recording of the presence of subordinates at the court of a superior in the Annals of Inisfallen in 1011 and 1026, which was followed in 1059 by the adoption of a formula expressing submission by entry into the house of another. The emergence in the annals of the formula expressing submission by entry into the house of another and of the technical term *tuarastal* broadly coincide around the mid eleventh century.

Literary sources, roughly contemporaneous, support the annalistic evidence for an association between submission by entry into the house of another and the bestowal and acceptance of ceremonial gifts. An incident from the twelfth-century *Cogadh Gaedhel re Gallaibh* serves as an illustration.[41] Brian Bóruma had defeated Máel Mórda, king of Leinster, who is subsequently depicted as a guest in Brian's house at Kincora. A dispute arose between Murchad, son of Brian Bóruma, and Máel Mórda over a game of chess. Murchad lost to Máel Mórda and took his revenge by accusing him of cowardice at the battle of Glenn Máma. 'Máel Mórda was angered and retired to his sleeping apartment without permission, without taking leave.' When Brian heard of his departure he hurriedly sent a messenger to detain him 'so that he could speak to him,

---

[40] *Ann. Inisf.* 1011. 5: 'Sluaged mór la Brian co Cenel Conaill eter muir 7 tír co tanic Hua Maíl Doraid, rí Ceneúil Chonaill, lais Cend Corad 7 co ruc innarad mór o Brian 7 co tuc a ogréir do Brian.' *Ann. Inisf.* 1059. 7: 'Mac Briain do dul co tech Hui Chonchobuir Connacht co tuc a réir huad eter séotu 7 muíne 7 additin 7 coro astad and ó Init co Caisc.' *Ann. Tig.* 1060: 'Mac Briain do dul a teach maic Mail no mbo co tuc seoit 7 maine imda dó.'

[41] *Cog. Gaedhel*, 142–56, cf. 50, 132, 136, 210. In *Aided Guill Meic Carbada* the acceptance of *tuarastal* is equated with submission: W. Stokes, 'The violent deaths of Goll and Garb', *Rev. Celt.* 14 (1893), 396–449 (at 106–7, 410–11). For its 12th-century date see R. Thurneysen, *Die irische Helden- und Königsage bis zum siebzehnten Jahrhundert* (Halle, 1921), 485–9; P. Mac Cana, 'The influence of the Vikings on Celtic literature', in B. Ó Cuív (ed.), *The impact of the Scandinavian invasions on the Celtic-speaking peoples* (Dublin, 1975), 78–118 (at 82).

so that he should carry away with him cattle and *tuarastal*. Máel Mórda, however, killed the messenger and instigated a revolt of the men of Leinster against Brian Bóruma because of the insult he had received while a guest in his house.

The association of *tuarastal* with political submission led to a further development in the annals: by the twelfth century acceptance of *tuarastal* was beginning to be used as an alternative annalistic catch-phrase for political submission. Of course, an argument *ex silentio* from the annals is dangerous. It is possible that earlier annalists merely chose not to record submissions by entry into the house of another or the bestowal of *tuarastal*. But such an omission would in itself surely be significant. The origin of both customs as social institutions may date back to long before the eleventh century.[42] Annalistic usage, however, appears to reflect their increasing significance in the context of political overlordship from the eleventh century onwards.

What was the nature of the submission signified by the entry into the house, or itinerant court, of a superior and the acceptance of ceremonial gifts? Was there a difference between it and the form of submission expressed by annalists as the giving or taking of hostages? In medieval society political relationships were conceived of primarily as personal relationships; there was no clear-cut division between private and public business, between the personal and political relations of kings. In feudal society the dependence of one ruler on another, and of subjects on their king, was expressed visibly by the performance of symbolic mimes borrowed from the ceremony between a vassal and his lord. As in feudal society, so in Irish society there were similarities between the relationship of a lord and his client and that of a superior king and his subordinates.

There existed in early Irish society a form of clientship which was a variant of the relationship between lord and vassal that was a basic institution of early medieval Europe. Clientship

---

[42] Cf. the (?mid-6th-century) legislation of the so-called 'first synod of Patrick', forbidding the Christian community to accept alms from pagans: *The Irish penitentials*, ed. L. Bieler (Scriptores Latini Hiberniae, 7; Dublin, 1975), 56, and the emendation suggested by Charles-Edwards, 'The social background to Irish *peregrinatio*', 56. For the antiquity of the concept of a poem as a gift by the poet to his patron and the reciprocal reward required from the patron, see C. Watkins, 'The etymology of Irish *duán*', ibid. 270–7.

permeated the economic, social, and political structures of pre-Norman Ireland.[43] It provided an important means of material exchange. It helped to determine social status: the status of the nobility depended in part on the number of their clients. Clientship provided a network of political alliances between kings, with exchanges of military alliances, protection, and goods. A theoretical description of clientship in Ireland may be reconstructed from a number of eighth-century law tracts dealing directly with or touching on the institution.[44] The relationship operated among the nobility and free commoners, and was created most commonly not by the advance of a fief of land, as in feudal society, but by a fief of movable goods, usually livestock. There were two forms of clientship, free clientship, or *saerrath*, and base clientship, termed *giallnae* or *aigillne* (later, by an analogical formation with *saerrath*, also termed *daerrath*).[45] Despite the terminology 'free' and 'base', only free men participated in both forms of clientship; the distinction was between a looser and a more binding relationship, not between a difference in the free or unfree status of the participants.

The laws do not assume that clientship was universal among commoners and nobles; they allow for a proportion of the free population to be outside all clientship ties. In theory, each individual could choose whether or not to enter into clientship, although it may be doubted whether independence was, in fact, a real option. Lord or client could terminate the relationship in order to choose a new partner. However, unilateral termination of clientship entailed penalties, which varied with individual circumstances and were more severe for the client than the lord. Indeed, the penalties were such as would have

---

[43] M. Gerriets, 'The organization of exchange in early Christian Ireland', *Journal of Economic History*, 41 (1981), 171–8, and 'Economy and society; clientship according to the Irish laws', *Cambridge Medieval Celtic Studies*, 6 (1983), 43–61; N. T. Patterson, 'Material and symbolic exchange in early Irish clientship', *Proceedings of the Harvard Celtic Colloquium*, 1 (1981), 53–61.

[44] R. Thurneysen, 'Aus dem irischen Recht I: das Unfrei-Lehen' [= Cáin aigillne], *ZCP* 14 (1923), 335–94, = *Corpus iuris Hibernici*, ed. D. A. Binchy (Dublin, 1978), v. 1178. 34–1781. 31, and 'Aus dem irischen Recht I' [= Cáin saerraith], *ZCP* 15 (1924), 238–60, = *Corpus*, vi. 1770. 15–1778. 33; *Críth gablach*, ed. Binchy, = *Corpus*, ii. 777. 1–779. 21; *Di dligud rath ocus somuine la flaith*, in *Senchas Már*, 5–7, = *Corpus*, ii. 432. 21–436. 32.

[45] This term occurs only in the later glosses and commentaries.

discouraged a client from abandoning a lord unless his performance was blatantly unsatisfactory or the new lord was
superior in clearly discernible ways.

The typical base client in the law tracts was depicted as the
bóaire, a prosperous farmer, with his own land obtained from
his family inheritance. A lord supplemented a client's possession of cattle by advancing him a fief of more cattle (occasionally land or tools). In return, the client rendered certain services
to the lord. These consisted of the provision of food renders,
which were partly paid in produce to the lord and partly
exacted by the lord as hospitality for himself and his retinue at
certain times of the year, and of personal service. Personal
service comprised military service, the obligation to accompany
the lord on a hosting or go to his defence when attacked, and
labour service, the obligation to provide labourers to work in
the lord's fields at harvest-time, to fortify his dwelling, and to
erect his burial mound at death. The lord's obligation to
protect his client is implicit in his right to collect one-third of
any compensation, or *éric*, paid for the injury or death of the
client.[46]

The law tract on free clientship is fragmentary, and the
paucity of the evidence makes it difficult to isolate the essential
differences between the two forms of clientship. One of the
characteristics, however, which distinguished the free from the
base client was that the free client could more easily end his
relationship with his lord: the relationship was termed 'free'
because the client and the lord could each terminate the
contract with less difficulty and disadvantage. As in base, so in
free clientship, the client received the protection of his lord and
was obliged to go to his lord's defence and to render him
personal service. The economic distinctions between base and
free clientship within the *tuath* in respect of the fief advanced
and the renders returned have been discussed by M. Gerriets
and N. T. Patterson.[47] The social and political implications of
the distinction between base and free clientship have received
less attention. The free client might form part of the honorary
retinue of the lord, including occasions when the lord exacted

---

[46] *Crith gablach*, l. 85.
[47] See above, n. 43.

hospitality from his base clients,[48] and might be a guest in the house of the lord. This social distinction between base and free clientship is highlighted by the legal maxim in the law tract *Cáin saerraith*, which stated that the greatest burden incurred by the free client was the duty of personal service and homage to the lord.[49] One important social difference between free and base clientship, therefore, in so far as the fragmentary law tracts afford evidence, was the free client's privilege (or burden) of *Tischgesellschaft* with the lord.[50]

The legal term for base clientship was *giallnae*, or *aigillne*, literally 'hostageship'. It is not immediately apparent why it was so called, since neither the client, nor anyone else on his behalf, gave a hostage to the lord. The giving of hostages was, however, a sign of submission in the sphere of political relations, and it is possible that *giallnae*, when applied to base clientship, was used in the sense of submission. This is suggested by the fact that, in addition to the fief of cattle, the lord paid *sét turchluide*, literally 'chattels of subjection', to the base client, a sum equivalent to the client's honour-price, apparently in order to qualify for a portion of any legal compensation paid to his client.[51] Base clientship seems to have been interpreted as analogous to a form of political submission. In the political sphere subjection was marked by the giving of hostages. For the base client the mark of defeat, or subjection, was the purchase of his honour-price, which seems to have been thought of as providing the lord with the equivalent of a hostage for the client's good behaviour.

If base clientship was literally termed 'hostageship' by analogy with a form of political subjection, was there a form of political submission analogous to the institution of free clientship? A duality between free and base clientship and two differently perceived kinds of political relationships can be demonstrated. The Book of Rights, a twelfth-century, pseudo-historical compilation, which details the obligations

[48] On the lord's right to hospitality see D. A. Binchy, 'Aimser Chue', in *Féil-sgríbhinn Eóin Mhic Néill*, 18–22.
[49] Thurneysen, 'Aus dem irischen Recht II', 240.
[50] Cf. also *Crith gablach*, l. 593.
[51] *Turchluide* is presumed to derive from a compound of the verb *clód*, 'vanquishes', 'conquers', 'defeats': Thurneysen, 'Aus dem irischen Recht I', 340; cf. *Contributions to a dictionary of the Irish language, to–tu* (Dublin, 1948), 337.

and counter-obligations which operated between overkings and subordinate kings, divided subordinate kingdoms into two categories, *saertuatha*, literally 'free kingdoms', and *daertuatha*, literally 'base kingdoms'.[52] This categorization was modelled on the distinction between free and base clientship. The chief material difference between the so-called free and base kingdoms in the Book of Rights was that the free kingdoms received stipend from, but were not required to pay tribute to, the overking. They were obliged to acknowledge his suzerainty by accepting his stipend, but were not required to pay him tax or tribute. The so-called base kingdoms, on the other hand, received stipend from and had to pay tribute to the overking.

The justification used by the Book of Rights for classing a particular kingdom as 'free' or 'base' was genealogical. Those subkingdoms whose kings shared a common ancestor, real or fictitious, with the overking were categorized as free; subkingdoms whose kings could not claim a common descent with the overking were classed as base. This distinction must, in some cases at least, be spurious, since the genealogical tradition on which it was based was itself unreliable: the genealogies were frequently altered to suit changed political circumstances, to justify the replacement of one dynasty by another, or to justify a shift in political alliances. Where the Book of Rights undoubtedly reflected reality was in acknowledging that the degree of lordship which an overking could exercise varied from one subordinate to another. Political relationships were, in reality, determined by the practical considerations of what the overking could exact and the subordinate king bring himself to concede, or by precedent established by the predecessors of either party. If necessary, the genealogists were prepared to alter the genealogical tradition to suit changed political circumstances. These often falsified genealogies formed the starting-point for the compiler of the Book of Rights, who added another pseudo-historical dimension by dividing subkingdoms into free and base categories, borrowing his distinctions from the institution of clientship.

[52] *Bk Rights*, ed. Dillon, ll. 687, 770, 1345, 1620. The terms *saerchlann* and *daerchlann*, ll. 1670, 1672, 1684, *daerfine*, l. 1651, *saerchís*, l. 1668, *daerchís*, l. 1674, are also used. See also review by F. J. Byrne in *Studia Hib.* 5 (1965), 155–8; also his *Ir. kings*, 45–6.

Since the political theorist, or pseudo-historian of the Book of Rights used the analogy of free and base clientship to describe political relationships between an overking and his subordinates, it is possible that it may have been used in other similar contexts, that it may also have influenced the theory or symbolism of public ceremonies of political submission.[53] The function of the synthetic historian in pre-Norman Ireland was precisely to create or contribute to the elaboration of such ceremonies. The term *aicillne* implies a loose analogy between political submission by the giving of hostages and base clientship. Is it possible that a form of political submission which was considered analogous to free clientship was publicly and ceremonially expressed by entry into the house of the superior? Entry into the house of another implied the acceptance of hospitality at the overking's table. One of the ways in which the free client was distinguished from the base client was in his privilege or duty to partake of his lord's hospitality, either at the lord's table or that of his base clients. The description of the seating arrangements of a king's house in *Críth gablach*, an eighth-century law tract on status, allowed for the placing and entertainment of a king's free clients but made no mention of his base clients.[54] The acceptance of hospitality was one feature which may be assumed to have been common to the free client and the subordinate king submitting to a superior by entering into his house.

A king who entered the house of another might also be offered and be obliged to accept gifts. This feature could also be construed as having a link with the institution of free clientship. The Book of Rights gives details of the ceremonial gifts, termed *tuarastal*, offered by the high-king and the provincial kings to their subordinates. Although a twelfth-century compilation, the Book of Rights had antecedents as a literary genre: an earlier, less elaborate text dating from the eighth or ninth century listed the mutual obligations between the overking of Cashel and his subordinate kings, and in this text the equivalent term to *tuarastal* was *rath*.[55] Significantly, in the law tract

---

[53] Cf. the revivals of Óenach Tailten: see below, pp. 193–4. In 1033 Donnchad Mac Gilla Pátraic, king of Osraige, celebrated the Óenach Carman on assuming the provincial kingship of Leinster: *AFM*.   [54] *Críth gablach*, l. 593.

[55] Only one section has been edited without translation, in *Irish texts*, ed. J. Fraser *et al.* (London, 1931), i. 19–21. Large portions, however, are discussed and paraphrased

Cáin saerraith, *rath* was the term used for the fief of stock advanced by the lord to the client in free clientship, whereas the analogous term used in *Cáin daerraith* was *taurcrech*. The apparent association of *rath*, alias *tuarastal*, with free clientship provides another possible link between submission by entry into the house of another and free clientship.[56]

If there was a difference between submission by the giving of hostages and submission by entry into the house of another, it may perhaps be sought in the differences which characterized free and base clientship. Free clientship was a more honourable and voluntary relationship in so far as it did not imply the same degree of economic dependence and brought closer social contact with the lord. Entry into the house of a superior king, and the acceptance of hospitality and gifts, can be construed as a more honourable form of submission than the exaction of hostages, which usually resulted from a military defeat.[57] Submission by entry into the house of another king could be offered voluntarily and without prior military hostilities.

It would be dangerous to stress a clear-cut difference between submission by the handing over of hostages and submission by entry into the house of the superior king. Both acts might constitute aspects of a particular submission. This is suggested by entries in the annals which state at one and the same time that a king both gave hostages and entered the house of the superior king. Occasionally, a particular submission is recorded in one set of annals by the giving of hostages and is described in another as the submitting king entering the house of the superior. Nevertheless, the symbolic gestures of the ceremony of submission by entry into the house of another would appear to have been designed to convey the impression

in L. Ó Buachalla, 'Contributions towards the political history of Munster, 450–800 A.D.', *Cork Hist. Soc. Jn.* 56 (1951), 87–90; 57 (1952), 67–86; 59 (1954), 111–26; 61 (1956), 89–102. Cf. also the poem on the reciprocal duties of the Airgialla and the king of the northern Uí Néill: M. O'Daly, 'A poem on the Airgialla', *Ériu*, 16 (1952), 179–88), on which the Book of Rights drew.

[56] The Book of Rights supports an interpretation of free clientship as a more honourable and voluntary relationship, firstly because the kingdoms classed as free do not pay tribute, and secondly by the actual kingdoms which are placed in this category, for they were precisely those whose relations to the overkings were politically the most sensitive.

[57] Cf. the phrase *giallad fri claidib*, literally 'submission at the sword's point': *RIA Contrib.*, fasc. G, 78–9.

of a more honourable form of submission than that made simply by the handing over of hostages, and could, if political circumstances required it, be so interpreted.

The Book of Rights indicates what some of the obligations resulting from submission were thought to consist of by the twelfth century. One obligation of a subordinate king, according to the Book of Rights, was to provide military aid for his superior in time of war. Just as the client—base or free—was bound to go to the aid of his lord with military assistance, so the subordinate king was supposed to support the overking when summoned to take part in his campaigns. How onerous the subordinate's military duties would be and how frequently he could be summoned depended on whether his kingdom was classed as 'free' or 'base'. Broadly speaking, the more important the political status of the subordinate kingdom the less were the demands made upon it by the superior king. According to the Book of Rights, the king of Airgialla could only be summoned for military service by the high-king every third year, and only for a period of six weeks excluding spring and autumn, and compensation for any loss of life incurred would have to be paid by the high-king.[58] None of these details can be relied upon, but the general impression that the demands of the superior king were modulated by political exigency, by the relative power of the subordinate king, and the degree to which the overking desired or required public recognition, is undoubtedly true. The Book of Rights conveys some impression of the kind of negotiations which might be conducted before a king would recognize the superiority of another. The limitations placed on the military service required from the king of Airgialla were such as to render his contribution to the military standing of the high-king negligible. But if the high-king could only secure public submission from a subordinate by acceptance of such minimal terms, he had little option but to agree, if it was essential that the subordinate king should be seen to be in a client relationship with him.

The most detailed description of a military muster summoned by an overking is contained in *Caithréim Cellacháin Chaisil*, a pseudo-historical tract, which is roughly

---

[58] *Bk Rights*, ed. Dillon, 72–3.

contemporaneous with the Book of Rights.[59] The king of Cashel is depicted summoning his subordinate kings for battle against the Vikings in defence of the province of Munster. Defensive roles were assigned to the border subkingdoms; the remainder were to muster a specified number of battalions of soldiers or ships. It would be rash to place credence on the details, but the annals bear testimony to specific military roles, such as leader of the cavalry, or admiral of the fleet, being assigned by overkings to subordinates by the twelfth century and being held in succession by individuals from the same family.[60] Subordination obviously was no longer negotiable. Such was the degree of dependency that the subordinate kings had been assigned honorary hereditary offices within the household of the overking. In other cases, however, the annals reveal that an overking might have to exact hostages from subordinate kings on the eve of a military campaign in order to ensure their participation.

Another possible consequence of submission was the payment of tribute. The Book of Rights purports to list the tributes due to the overking of Cashel and the high-king of Ireland from subordinate kings. Items listed as tributes include cattle, cloaks, bars of iron, and flitches of bacon. In practice, as references to cattle-raids in the annals suggest, cattle must have been the main form of tribute. Such raids were often another extension of the civil order into the political sphere; they reflect the process of *athgabáil*, a legal remedy whereby the litigant could forcibly retrieve his property, or what was owing to him, having given due notice of his intention to do so.[61] Stipends, on the other hand, according to the Book of Rights, were more likely to be proffered as horses, cloaks, military accoutrements, personal ornaments, drinking-horns, goblets, and chess sets, thus emphasizing the ceremonial, or more honourable, nature of the gifts.[62]

---

[59] *Caithréim Cellacháin Caisil*, ed. A. Bugge (Christiania, 1905), 28–9.

[60] Cf. *Ann. Tig.* 1132; *AU* 1170.

[61] See D. A. Binchy, 'Distraint in Irish law', *Celtica*, 10 (1973), 22–71; 'A text on the forms of distraint', ibid. 72–86.

[62] The stipends paid in 1166 by Ruaidrí Ua Conchobair, king of Connacht, on his assumption of the high-kingship, included, in addition to cattle, 200 coloured garments to the men of Cenél Conaill, 40 coloured garments to the men of Munster, 25 horses to Mac Gilla Pátraic, king of Osraige, and 700 horses to Mac Carthaig, king of Desmond: *Ann. Tig.*; cf. *Aisling Meic Conglinne*, ed. K. Meyer (London, 1892), 56–7, 108–11.

A form of tribute enjoyed by the petty king within the *tuath* was refection, the right to undertake at certain times of the year a circuit of his kingdom, accompanied by his household, and to exact hospitality from his subjects. By the twelfth century kings were circuiting not just their patrimonial kingdoms but the wider areas over which they were claiming hegemony.[63] In 1101 the annals recorded that Muirchertach Ua Briain, king of Munster and high-king of Ireland, hosted into the north of Ireland, and, having demolished the northern Uí Néill fortress of Ailech, 'marched around Ireland and gave neither hostages nor pledges'.[64] In 1140 a circuit of Conmaicne by Donnchad Ua Cerbaill, king of Airgialla, was recorded, during which he levied a large prey of cattle.[65] In 1177 a circuit of west Connacht undertaken by Ruaidrí Ua Conchobair, king of Connacht, was noted.[66]

The Book of Rights is prefaced by a description of a hegemonial circuit of Ireland undertaken by the king of Cashel as high-king, which may reflect Muirchertach Ua Briain's circuit of Ireland recorded in the annals in 1102.[67] The twelfth-century pseudo-historical tract *Cogadh Gaedhel re Gallaibh*, written on behalf of the Dál Cais dynasty, depicted Brian Bóruma making a similar circuit of all Ireland as high-king.[68] A twelfth-century poem about a tenth-century king of Cenél nEógain, Muirchertach mac Néill, anachronistically represented him making a circuit of all Ireland to assert his authority as high-king. The poem was composed as an encomiastic tribute

---

[63] The earliest circuits of political significance recorded in the annals occur in ecclesiastical rather than secular contexts. Circuits of the *comarba* of Armagh to enforce subjection to Armagh and collect tribute are recorded from the 9th century: *AU* 836. 4, 960. 4, 973. 5, 993. 8, 1021. 5, 1050. 6, 1068. 2, 1092. 6, 1094. 6, 1106. 6, 1108. 3, 1110. 12, 1116. 1, 1120. 4; *AFM* 1133, 1134, 1136, 1138, 1140, 1150, 1151; *AU* 1161, 1162, 1172.

[64] *Ann. Tig.*

[65] *Misc. Ir. annals*, 1140. 2. Conmaicne was a satellite kingdom of Bréifne. Ua Cerbaill made his circuit at the expense of Tigernán Ua Ruairc, king of Bréifne, which is why the annalist found it worthy of record.

[66] *Ann. Tig.* West Connacht was originally considered to be beyond the kingdom of Connacht, literally 'west of Connacht'. In the 11th century this hitherto sparsely populated region had been colonized by the Uí Briúin Seola (12th-century surname Ua Flaithbertaig), who had been displaced from the plains around Tuam by the more powerful Uí Briúin Aí (12th-century surname Ua Conchobair) and had been excluded from participation in the overkingship of Connacht. The recording of Ruaidrí Ua Conchobair's unopposed circuit of west Connacht in 1177 was a way of expressing his assertion of overlordship over Ua Flaithbertaig.

[67] *Bk Rights*, ed. Dillon, 5–13. [68] *Cog. Gaedhel*, 135–7.

to Muirchertach Mac Lochlainn, king of Cenél nEógain (from 1145) and high-king of Ireland (1156–66).[69] It purports to describe a journey which the tenth-century Muirchertach, who in reality was never in contention for the high-kingship, undertook around Ireland, the royal residences where he enjoyed hospitality and bestowed *tuarastal*, and the kings from whom he took hostages. Other twelfth-century pseudo-historical sources made less ambitious claims for other kings. *Caithréim Cellacháin Chaisil*, the riposte of the Eóganachta dynasty to *Cogadh Gaedhel re Gallaibh*, depicted Cellachán, the tenth-century king of Cashel, on a circuit of Munster.[70] The twelfth-century satirical poem *Aisling Meic Conglinne* described Cathal mac Finguine, the eighth-century king of Cashel, on circuit in the kingdom of Uí Echach.[71] These works describe events of an earlier period in an anachronistic and often fictitious fashion, but they reflect twelfth-century preoccupations with wider claims to political hegemony and intensification of overlordship over subordinate kingdoms.

The Book of Rights provides some incidental details about the hegemonial circuit: it envisages that the retinue of a king on circuit beyond his patrimonial kingdom will consist of his political subordinates. Subordinates are depicted as meeting the overking at the boundaries of their kingdoms, accompanying him during his circuit of their territory, and escorting him on his departure to another border, where he would be met by the king of the adjoining kingdom.[72] In addition to providing an opportunity for the exaction of tribute and the bestowal of *tuarastal*, the hegemonial circuit was a suitable occasion for the performance of personal service by subordinate kings.

[69] J. O'Donovan, 'The circuit of Ireland by Muircheartach mac Neill, prince of Aileach', in *Tracts relating to Ireland* (Dublin, 1841), i. 24–68; *Móirtimchell Éirenn uile dorigne Muirchertach mac Néill*, ed. E. Hogan (Dublin, 1901).

[70] *Caithréim Cellacháin Caisil*, 4, 30.

[71] *Aisling Meic Conglinne*, 9.

[72] On the significance of the boundary area see P. Ó Riain, 'Boundary association in early Irish society', *Studia Celtica*, 16 (1972), 12–29, and 'Battle site and territorial extent in early Ireland', *ZCP* 33 (1974), 67–80; D. Ó Corráin, 'Aspects of early Irish history', in B. G. Scott (ed.), *Perspectives in Irish archaeology* (Belfast, 1974), 64–75 (at 64–6). Cf. *AU* 1156, which describes the king of Osraige meeting Muirchertach Mac Lochlainn, king of Cenél nEógain and claimant to the high-kingship, at Clár Dairi Máir on the boundary of Osraige and submitting to him there. For the border location of Daire Már see F. J. Byrne, 'Derrynavlan: the historical context', *RSAI Jn.* 110 (1980), 116–26 (at 120).

Personal service by the free client to his lord included attendance at the latter's feasts. The king who was subordinate to another was also expected to attend the overking's feasts. Such occasions were used to demonstrate influence and wealth by the overking. One occasion for the public celebration of a royal feast was provided by the *óenach*, or assembly of the people of a *tuath*, convened by the king at regular intervals, during which public business was transacted.[73] At an *óenach* a king could pledge his subjects to observe certain public obligations, such as military hostings, or special ordinances enacted to meet grave emergencies, or the endorsement of treaties concluded with other kings. The *óenach* originally consisted exclusively of the assembly of a particular *tuath* or dynastic federation, but by the twelfth century the *óenach* had also been adapted to a wider political context and was being used as a means of asserting overkingship.

A well-documented assembly of the early Irish period was Óenach Tailten, the chief gathering of the Uí Néill dynastic federation.[74] When the synthetic historians of the eleventh and twelfth centuries associated the kingship of Tara, originally the overkingship of the Uí Néill federation, with the high-kingship of Ireland, Óenach Tailten, like Tara, also came to be invested artificially with a national character. Hence the attempt in 1120 by Toirdelbach Ua Conchobair, king of Connacht and claimant of the high-kingship, and by his successor Ruaidrí Ua Conchobair in 1167 and 1168, to convene the Óenach Tailten.[75] These two aspirants to the high-kingship, or their political advisers, had been persuaded by the propaganda of the pseudo-historians into believing that the convening of Óenach Tailten would be a public assertion and demonstration of high-kingship. The attempt to transform the Óenach Tailten into a national assembly is, like the concept of a hegemonial circuit of all Ireland, another illustration of political theorists in twelfth-century Ireland manufacturing national institutions for an embryonic national monarchy.

The Óenach was an ancient feast which had survived from the prehistoric period. The Church added other occasions for

---

[73] *Críth gablach*, 102.
[74] D. A. Binchy, 'The fair of Tailtiu and the feast of Tara', *Ériu*, 18 (1958), 113–38.
[75] *Ann. Tig.* 1120, 1167, 1168.

the celebration of royal feasts, especially at Christmas, Easter, and Whitsun, which both the ecclesiastical and secular law tracts designated as the three most solemn festivals of the year.[76]

Irish kings appear to have shared with their Anglo-Saxon counterparts the celebration of royal feasts on these solemn Christian festivals. In 1026 the Annals of Inisfallen noted the guests whom Donnchad, son of Brian Bóruma, entertained at Kincora during the Easter festival.[77] There are also references in the twelfth century to the erection of temporary banqueting-halls known as Easter houses, which were built by Irish kings for the duration of the festival.[78] The royal celebration of Christmas is less well documented in the pre-Norman period, although there is evidence for the importance of the royal Christmas feast in post-Norman Ireland. The best-documented example is the feast held at Christmas 1351 by Uilliam Buidhe Ua Cellaig, king of Uí Maine, to which the poets of Ireland were invited to pit their skills against one another.[79] That this was almost certainly also a practice of an earlier period is suggested by Welsh evidence which bears witness to the importance of the Christmas royal court in the twelfth century. *Brut y Tywysogyon* recorded the Christmas celebration in 1109 of Cadwgan ap Bleddyn, prince of Powys, 'for the leading men of his land', and of Rhys ap Gruffydd at Ceredigion in 1176, 'to which the poets of all Wales, as well as England, Scotland and Ireland were invited'.[80] It may be inferred that Christmas, no less than Easter, and probably also Whitsun, provided occasions for royal feasts in pre-Norman Ireland at which a subordinate king might be expected to attend the court of his superior.[81]

---

[76] *The rule of Tallaght*, ed. E. Gwynn (Dublin, 1927), 63–87; *Studies in Ir. law*, 19, 23; *Anc. laws Ire.* iii. 18, 19 = *Corpus iuris Hibernici*, ii. 524. 8.

[77] *Ann. Inisf.* 1026. 3, 1059. 7; Magnus, king of Norway, is reputed to have sent his shoes to Muirchertach Ua Briain, king of Munster and high-king of Ireland, 'instructing him to carry them above his shoulders through the middle of his house on Christmas day in full view of his envoys, that he might understand from that that he had subjected himself to King Magnus': *Chronica regum Mannie*, 35.

[78] See below, pp. 203–4. Cf. *Bk Rights*, ed. Dillon, l. 2075, which lists as stipend to the king of Uí Chonaill the Easter raiment from the king of Cashel.

[79] *AU, Ann. Clon., Ann. Conn., AFM.* Cf. E. Knott, 'Filidh Éireann go haointeach: Ó Ceallaigh's Christmas feast to the poets of Ireland, A.D. 1351', *Ériu*, 5 (1911), 50–69. Cf. also *NHI* iii. 523.

[80] *Brut Hergest*, 54–5, 166–7; *Brut Peniarth*, 28, 71.

[81] Cf. the detailed evidence for the celebration of Easter, and to a lesser extent

An element of the personal service which a free client was bound to render to his lord was *urérge*, literally 'rising up before', an act of homage or public recognition of their relationship.[82] *Urérge* might also be performed by a subordinate king to a superior. In the ninth-century tract on the mutual obligations between the king of Cashel and his subordinate kings it is stated that the king of Múscraige sat next to the king of Cashel unless the kings of Uí Fidgente, Irluachra, or Raithlind were present, when 'he raises his knee before them'—a polite way of indicating that the king of Múscraige came fourth in order of precedence at the court of the king of Cashel, but was still equal in rank to the other three kings.[83] The compiler emphasized that the king of Múscraige merely raised his knee, that is curtsied, to these kings but did not have to 'rise up' before them, the implication being that in other circumstances he might expect to do so.

Since *urérge* was performed both within a formal client relationship and as a ceremonial greeting among kings on public occasions, it may be assumed that it was an element of public ceremonies of political submission. In the description in the law tracts of the initiation of a client relationship between lord and vassal, the performance of *urérge* is associated with the oath of personal loyalty sworn by the client to his lord. There is evidence to suggest that a similar oath was taken by a submitting king. The twelfth-century Book of Rights remarks of a sub-king of Cashel that he is not required to give hostages to the king of Cashel, but only an oath 'under the hand of the king of Cashel'.[84] Of the king of Airgialla it is stated that the personal surety given by him to the high-king may not be held in fetters or chains: he is only required to 'swear under the king's

Christmas, by the 10th-century Ottonian kings at specific centres: K. Leyser, *Rule and conflict in an early medieval society: Ottonian Saxony* (London, 1979), 90–1.

[82] Thurneysen, 'Aus dem irischen Recht II', 240. An inferior stood in the presence of his superior. A king was supposed to rise to greet a bishop to indicate the superiority of ecclesiastical over secular rank: *Críth gablach*, 24. In return the bishop raised his knee to the king in a curtsy to imply equal status, for individuals of equal rank raised a knee to one another in salutation. The pagan poet Dubtach maccu Lugair is depicted rising up publicly before Patrick when he converts to Christianity: *The Patrician texts in the Book of Armagh*, ed. L. Bieler (Scriptores Latini Hiberniae, 10; Dublin, 1979), 92–3; *Trip. life*, ed. Stokes, i. 53.

[83] *Irish texts*, ed. Fraser *et al.*, i. 20. 9.

[84] *Bk Rights*, ed. Dillon, 31, 35.

hand'.[85] A description of the inauguration of the king of Cashel in the twelfth-century pseudo-historical *Caithréim Cellacháin Chaisil* depicted the subkings of Munster placing their hands in his hands as part of the ritual, and re-enacting the ceremony as a demonstration of their loyalty before being led into battle by him.[86]

Literary texts depict hypothetical situations, but the phrase is used also in connection with named individuals in historical sources of the eleventh and twelfth centuries. In the regnal list of the kings of Leinster, Murchad son of Diarmait mac Máel na mBó, who ruled in association with his father, was described as king of Leinster *ri láim a athar*, 'under the hand of his father'.[87] In 1039 the death of Donnchad Ua Ruairc, king of east Connacht *fri láim a athar*, that is, under the hand of his father, Art Ua Ruairc, king of the whole province of Connacht, is recorded.[88] In 1118, when Toirdelbach Ua Conchobair, king of Connacht, invaded Leinster and in virtue of his claim to the high-kingship left Énna son of Donnchad in the kingship of Leinster and of Dublin, Énna was described as king under the hand of Toirdelbach.[89] In 1127 Conchobar and Toirdelbach Ua Briain, princes of the Dál Cais dynasty, 'revolted' against Toirdelbach Ua Conchobair, king of Connacht and high-king, and went to the church of Lismore, where they 'clasped hands with' Cormac Mac Carthaig and persuaded him to accept the provincial kingship of Munster.[90] Earlier in the same year they had submitted to Toirdelbach Ua Conchobair, and their offer of the kingship of Munster to Cormac was in defiance of their submission to Toirdelbach Ua Conchobair. Their clasping of hands with Cormac Mac Carthaig denoted a transfer of allegiance. In 1152 Diarmait Mac Carthaig, king of Desmond, and Toirdelbach Ua Briain, king of Thomond, rivals for the provincial kingship of Munster, each intervened in the kingdom of Ciarraige in support of rival candidates for the kingship, Diarmait Mac Carthaig securing the installation of his nominee, whom he left 'under his own hand over the territory'.[91]

From these instances it may be concluded that the overking

---

[85] *Bk Rights*, ed. Dillon, 73–5.
[86] *Caithréim Cellacháin Caisil*, 4, 30; cf. *Cog. Gaedhel*, 131–2.
[87] *Bk Leinster*, i. 183; *AFM* 1070; see above, pp. 10, 88.
[88] *AFM*. [89] *Misc. Ir. annals*, 1119. 2.
[90] *Ibid.* 1126. 11. [91] *Ibid.* 1152. 1.

could exact an oath of loyalty from his subkings, and that it was
sworn at a public ceremony not dissimilar to that of feudal
society where lord and vassal clasped hands.

A number of formal elements which might signify a political
relationship between kings in pre-Norman Ireland have been
identified: the giving of hostages, entry into the house of the
superior, acceptance of hospitality and of ceremonial gifts or
tuarastal, performance of military service and personal service,
which might include attendance at the superior's court and
public celebrations, membership of his retinue when on
circuit, an act of homage, an oath of loyalty, payment of tribute.
Depending on the relative power of the overking and the subordinate king, some or all of these elements, and in varying
degrees, might be involved.

There remains the problem of the stability and legal force, if
any, of such relationships in pre-Norman Ireland, and the
penalties for their repudiation. As in feudal society, so in Irish
society the customary law which determined relations between
a lord and his vassal provided an analogue for relationships
between rulers. In feudal society the customs which developed
at the most basic level of lordship were gradually extended
upwards until they came to include the supreme overlord, the
king. The obligations and legally binding force which existed
in the contract between lord and vassal came to be applied
gradually also to the relations between a king and even the
most powerful of his subjects, men who sometimes had as
much resources in land and movable wealth at their disposal as
the king himself. The obligations between the king and the
more powerful of his vassals, which had initially been dictated
by political expediency, became increasingly less negotiable
and more legally binding, with ever more precisely defined
penalties for transgressions. Such a development was not
inevitable, however, and might be reversed in unfavourable
political circumstances.

In twelfth-century pre-Norman Ireland, relationships
between rulers were tending to acquire the strict obligations of
clientship which obtained between lord and vassal. Many of
the achievements of overkings in twelfth-century Ireland
required consolidation before the sanction of customary law,

which determined rights and obligations of lordship at the lower levels of society, could be applied systematically at the higher levels and ultimately at the highest level of the high-kingship. Relations between overkings and subordinate kings were still determined by the political realities of power and military force. A king might receive the submission of another, and he might do so symbolically according to a procedure which normally established a legally binding client relationship between a lord and vassal, but if the overking's power declined, or that of his subordinate increased sufficiently, the latter might repudiate his submission and refuse observance of the obligations it might have entailed. Overkings in twelfth-century Ireland did retaliate against those who, having acknowledged their authority, then rejected it, by attempting to deprive them of political office, and even banishing them from their kingdoms, but such remedies depended on the power of the overking to carry them out effectively.[92] Overkings up to and including the high-king were vigorously claiming certain rights of lordship as their legal due. In practice, these could only be exercised by force or the latent threat of it. Given political stability, the relationship between force and legality might change in favour of legality. The beginnings of such a development are discernible in Ireland on the eve of Anglo-Norman intervention.

The fact that an individual might enter into a client relationship with more than one lord complicated the development of legally binding relationships between rulers. The eighth-century law tracts specified varying services which the client had to perform to his first lord, who took precedence, his second lord, third lord, and so on. This was regulated, in theory at any rate, by the fact that a client could not accept a larger fief from any subsequent lord than he had received from his first lord. In relationships between rulers it would have been even more difficult to determine precedent rights of lordship.

In pre-Norman Ireland the variety of ways by which submis-

---

[92] Some of many references to revolts against overkings by subkings include *An. Inisf.* 1093. 7, 1118. 7, 1127. 4; *Ann. Tig.* 1115, 1124, 1125; *AU* 1127; *Misc. Ir. annals*, 1115. 2, 1124. 2, 1125. 1, 1126. 11; *AFM* 1170. For some references to depositions or banishment by overkings of those who had previously submitted to them cf. *Ann. Inisf.* 1077, 1093, 1094, 1105, 1124, 1166; *Misc. Ir. annals*, 1119, 1120. 3, 1125. 2, 1126. 5.

sion could be made by one king to another, and the varying consequences, reflect the variety of relationships which could be entered into and the degree of subjection which might ensue from them. An overking might exercise an effective and stable overlordship over his petty kings, a relationship which might be of long standing and inherited from predecessors, and which had binding mutual obligations. Between kings of more equal power, however, there was a form of submission which may have been modelled loosely on the institution of free clientship, but which was negotiable and determined by the power and status of the parties involved, with the emphasis on honour and status, friendship and alliance, and with the resultant obligations left deliberately vague and ambiguous.

THE IRISH CONTEXT OF THE SUBMISSIONS OF
THE IRISH KINGS TO HENRY II IN 1171–1172

The Irish annalists recorded the submissions of the Irish kings to Henry II in 1171–2 in the same terminology as they used for submissions between kings in pre-Norman Ireland. Chroniclers writing in England expressed the submissions of the Irish kings in the terminology of their own society. To what extent can the Irish and English accounts be reconciled, and do the differences in language and terminology reflect a fundamental difference in the nature of political submission in the two societies?

The Annals of Inisfallen, which provided an indubitably contemporary account, stated that when Henry II landed at Waterford, Diarmait Mac Carthaig, king of Desmond, and Domnall Mór Ua Briain, king of Thomond, went into his house there, that is made submission to him. A regional compilation concerned primarily with events in or affecting Munster, the Annals of Inisfallen recorded only the submissions of the two most prominent Munster kings. Bearing this limitation in mind, how does its account compare with that of the English chroniclers?

Gerald of Wales's version comes closest to that of the Annals of Inisfallen: Diarmait Mac Carthaig came to meet Henry II at Waterford and of his own volition made submission, swore an oath of loyalty, promised to pay an annual tribute, and gave hostages as a guarantee of his good faith. Henry then journeyed in the direction of Cashel, and Domnall Mór Ua Briain came to meet him at a point on the bank of the river Suir, made submission, promised tribute, and displayed his loyalty to the king.[93] There is a discrepancy between this account and the Annals of Inisfallen, which stated that both kings made submission at Waterford, whereas Gerald recounted that Domnall Mór Ua Briain met Henry at the river Suir. The entry in the Annals of Inisfallen is abbreviated, however, and there is no reason to doubt Gerald's more detailed account that Domnall Mór Ua Briain met Henry at the Suir, especially as it can be reconciled with a known Irish practice: according to the Book of Rights it was usual for a king to meet a superior, whom he intended to acknowledge, at the border of his kingdom.[94] Waterford, where Diarmait Mac Carthaig, king of Desmond, came to meet Henry, was on the border between Desmond and Leinster. The river Suir, where Gerald said Domnall Mór Ua Briain met Henry, marked another boundary between Munster and Leinster, as Gerald himself tells us in another passage, where he described how Ua Fáeláin, king of Déise, 'crossed the river Suir which runs under the walls of Waterford on the east side dividing Desmond from Leinster'.[95] Gerald then described how, as Henry journeyed towards Dublin, two other kings came to meet him, namely the kings of Déise and Osraige, whose kingdoms lay along the route to Dublin. They agreed to the payment of tribute and swore oaths of loyalty, and, added Gerald, accepted gifts from Henry,[96] all elements of submission in pre-Norman Ireland.

Gerald's account is reminiscent of the description of the circuit of the king of Cashel as high-king in the Book of Rights, where, as he crossed a political boundary, he was depicted being met by the king into whose territory he was entering. The Irish kings could have interpreted Henry's journey through Leinster as a circuit: wittingly or unwittingly, his route from Waterford to Dublin and back to Wexford did form a circuit of

[93] Giraldus, *Expugnatio*, 92–5.
[94] See above, p. 192.
[95] Giraldus, *Expugnatio*, 56–7.
[96] Ibid. 94–5.

Leinster; he even travelled in the approved Irish manner of going *deiseal*, or clockwise, around the province![97]

Gerald recorded the submissions of the kings of north Leinster and those from beyond Leinster as having taken place at Dublin.[98] Disappointingly, he provided less detailed information about them. By contrast, Roger of Howden centred his account of the submissions of the Irish kings around the Christmas feast celebrated by Henry at Dublin.[99] Christmas was an important festival for the itinerant Angevin court, and the venue for its celebration is noted for almost every year of Henry's reign by the Anglo-Norman chroniclers.[100] The Anglo-Norman kings inherited from their Anglo-Saxon predecessors the custom of holding their most important royal assemblies of the year at the festivals of Christmas, Easter, and Whitsun.[101] Prominent nobles and ecclesiastics were generally summoned by the king, and the occasion was frequently used to hold a great council or ecclesiastical synod or both. The royal dignity was emphasized on these occasions by the ceremony of crown-wearing. It was doubtless to stress the *regia potestas* that Roger of Howden usually accorded Henry the title of fitz Empress when describing the king's celebration of Christmas, as he did in the case of the Christmas court held at Dublin.

After the Norman Conquest of England the household of the Norman dukes merged with the court of the Anglo-Saxon kings. The Christmas court became a suitable occasion for the performance of feudal duties by the king's vassals. William, king of the Scots, who by the terms of the treaty of Falaise, 1174, had become the liege man of Henry II, attended Henry's Christmas court at Nottingham in 1179. William's brother David, who, as earl of Huntingdon, owed homage for the lands which he held of Henry in England, attended Henry's Christmas court in 1184 and 1186.[102] In 1182 at the Christmas

---

[97] S. Ferguson, 'On the ceremonial turn called "Desiul"', *RIA Proc.*, 2nd ser., 1 (1879), 355–64.   [98] Giraldus, *Expugnatio*, 94–5.

[99] Roger of Howden, *Gesta*, i. 24–5; *Chronica*, ii. 29–30.

[100] During a reign of 34 years Henry celebrated Christmas in at least 24 different places: Warren, *Henry II*, 302.

[101] F. Liebermann, *The national assembly in the Anglo-Saxon period* (Halle, 1913), 48–9, 52, 58; E. H. Kantorowicz, *Laudes regiae* (Berkeley, 1946), 178–9.

[102] Eyton, *Itinerary*, 229, 259, 275; A. O. Anderson, 'Anglo-Scottish relations from Constantine II to William', *Scot. Hist. Rev.* 42 (1963), 1–20.

celebrations at Caen, William de Tancarville, the chief chamberlain, who had become estranged from the king, arrived to perform his customary service of washing the king's hands and forcibly removed the silver bowl from the man who had taken his place, defending his intrusion by stating that he wished to do no more than perform his hereditary duty.[103] At the Christmas feast of 1186 the earls of Leicester, Arundel, and Norfolk performed their respective household duties at the royal table as stewards and butler to the king.[104]

From Henry's viewpoint the Christmas feast at Dublin would have been a very suitable occasion on which to receive the submissions of those Irish kings who had not met him on his journey from Waterford to Dublin. For a court historian like Roger of Howden it formed a suitable focus for an account of the submissions of the Irish kings. In this way the different treatment of the submissions of the Irish kings by Gerald of Wales and Roger of Howden may be reconciled.

If Christmas was a suitable occasion for receiving submissions from Henry's viewpoint, it was also from the standpoint of the Irish kings an appropriate occasion on which to proffer submission. In pre-Norman Ireland, Christmas, Easter, and Whitsun also ranked as important feasts. There is indisputable documentary evidence in the case of Easter, at least, that political subordinates might celebrate Easter at the court of their superior.[105] If Gilbert, bishop of Limerick, may be relied upon, the Irish were familiar with the tradition of solemn crown-wearing at Christmas, Easter, and Whitsun: in his tract *De statu ecclesiae*, Gilbert stated that it was the prerogative of an archbishop to place the crown on the head of the king at those three festivals.[106]

A unique detail of Roger of Howden's description of the Christmas feast at Dublin is his statement that the Irish caused a palace to be constructed for Henry II out of wattles 'according to the custom of the country'.[107] In the *Gesta*, which is the

---

[103] Walter Map, *De nugis curialium*, ed. M. R. James (Oxford, 1914), 242–6.
[104] Eyton, *Itinerary*, 275.　　　　　　　　　　　　　　　　[105] See above, p. 177.
[106] Ussher, *Works*, iv. 509. Gilbert of Limerick's statement may be a borrowing from a foreign source, but there is other evidence that 12th-century Irish kings were familiar with crowns: *Caithréim Cellacháin Caisil*, 4, §7; *RIA Contrib. dict.* s.n. *mind*, 144.
[107] There is ample evidence for the use of wattles in buildings both among the Irish and the Hiberno-Norse of Dublin in the 11th and 12th centuries: H. Murray, 'Docu-

earlier and more detailed account, the palace is said to have been constructed for Henry's use by the Irish kings and the richer men from wattles 'ad morem patriae illius'; in the later condensed *Chronica* the palace is stated to have been of wattles 'ad modum patriae illius constructum', with no mention of the role of the Irish kings. The use of the generally abstract *mos*, 'practice', 'custom', in the account in the *Gesta* suggests that the phrase referred to the political significance of the act of construction rather than the building techniques employed, that it should be construed as referring to the whole sentence.[108]

The act of construction of such a palace can be related to a practice of pre-Norman Irish society. Irish literary sources contain many descriptions of the erection of temporary halls for great feasts.[109] Such a temporary feasting-hall was sometimes termed a *tech midchuarda*, literally a 'house of mead circuits'. The twelfth-century Book of Leinster contains a text, *Suidigud Tigi Midchuarda*, which describes the seating arrangements in order of precedence for the guests in such a hall; it is even accompanied by a diagram.[110] The metrical *Dindshenchas*, another twelfth-century compilation, has a detailed description of Cormac mac Airt's feasting-hall at Tara.[111] Although it is a figment of the poet's imagination, in part inspired by the biblical account of Solomon's house and temple, there is little doubt that a genuine tradition of erecting feasting-halls underlies such literary descriptions.

A temporary structure which is documented in the annals, as distinct from literary sources, is the Easter house, or *tech Cásca*, a special dwelling built by Irish kings, sometimes within the confines of a monastic settlement, for use during the period of

mentary evidence for domestic buildings in Ireland c. 400–1200 in the light of archaeology', *Medieval Archaeology*, 23 (1979), 81–97; cf. *Aisling Meic Conglinne*, 52–3.

[108] Cf. Roger of Howden, *Gesta*, i. 270, *Chronica*, ii. 254, where he described Hugh de Lacy's marriage to the daughter of the king of Connacht 'secundum morem patriae illius'.

[109] The most notable is that in the 'Feast of Bricriu', a saga of the Ulster cycle, which opens with an elaborate account of a hall specially constructed by Bricriu to entertain Conchobar mac Nessa, king of Ulster: *Fled Bricrend*, ed. G. Henderson (Ir. Texts Soc. 2; Dublin, 1899), 2–5.

[110] *Bk Leinster*, i. 116–20; translation in G. Petrie, 'On the antiquities of Tara hill', *RIA Trans.* 18 (1837), 199–204; diagram in *Facs. nat. MSS Ire.* ii, pl. 53.

[111] *The metrical Dindsenchas*, ed. E. J. Gwynn, i (Dublin, 1903), 28–37.

Lent and Easter.[112] Given the association of Christmas with Easter and Whitsun as the most important festivals of the year, given the historical evidence of a temporary structure erected specifically for the Easter period, and of Easter as a suitable occasion for the entertainment of clients and the acceptance of their submission, as evidenced in the case of Brian Bóruma and his successors, it is probable that the construction of a temporary palace was also a feature of royal celebrations at Christmas.

In the *Gesta* description of the Christmas feast at Dublin, the Irish kings 'and richer men' are specifically associated with the building of the temporary banqueting-hall for Henry's use. That this detail may be significant is suggested by a passage in the Branwen tale, one of the four branches of the *Mabinogion*, which relates how Matholwch, king of Ireland, sought Branwen, sister of Bendigeidfran, the king of the island of Britain, in marriage. On her arrival in Ireland, Branwen was dishonoured by being obliged to perform menial tasks. When this came to the attention of Bendigeidfran he mounted an invasion of Ireland to revenge her honour and that of the son whom she had borne to Matholwch. Matholwch was obliged to sue for peace. The first offer which he made to Bendigeidfran was to hand over the rule of Ireland to his son. This, however, was regarded as insufficient compensation by Bendigeidfran, and Matholwch sought counsel on the formulation of another proposal. His councillors advised him 'to prepare a better answer', to offer to build a house for Bendigeidfran

so that he and the men of the Island of the Mighty [Britain] may be contained in the one half of the house and thyself and thy host in the other, and give over thy kingship to his will and do him homage. And by reason of the honour in making the house, for he had never had a house in which he might be contained, he will make peace with thee.[113]

The Branwen tale implies that the construction of the house would be a particular honour to the king of Britain since he had not previously had a house which could accommodate him. This hardly seems a sufficient explanation of why Matholwch

---

[112] *AU* 1119, 1124; *Misc. Ir. annals*, 1147. 3, 1165. 2; *AFM* 1201.

[113] *Branwen verch Llyr*, ed. D. S. Thomas (Dublin, 1961), 12–13; translation from G. Jones and T. Jones, *The Mabinogion* (London, 1974), 35.

and his advisers considered the building of a house would be a substantial improvement on their first offer to the king of Britain. The Branwen tale is acknowledged to have been influenced by Irish story-telling techniques and to have drawn directly on Irish material.[114] Although the date of composition of the tale is a matter of dispute among Celtic scholars, for present purposes it is sufficient to note that the *termini ante et post quem* fall between the eleventh and thirteenth centuries.[115] It could be that the Welsh author of this tale borrowed Irish material, which he only partially understood, and that behind his account lies a description of a ceremony of submission associated with the entry of one king into the house of another in pre-Norman Ireland.

The Branwen tale prompts the question of whether participation in, or contribution towards, the construction of a house by the submitter could upon occasion form part of a ceremony of submission. It would certainly have been appropriate on an occasion when the ceremony of submission took place outside the superior's own kingdom, as in the case of the king of Britain in Ireland in the Branwen tale, or of Henry II in Ireland in 1171. Bearing in mind the description in the Book of Rights of a circuit made by the high-king of Ireland and the obligation of the subordinate kings, through whose kingdoms he circuited, to entertain him, it is conceivable that temporary halls were constructed by the lesser kings for the entertainment of their superiors. In the twelfth-century poem *Aisling Meic Conglinne*, Cathal mac Finguine, king of Munster, is depicted on circuit in the subkingdom of Uí Echach, and Pichán mac Máelfind, king of Uí Echach, complains to the poet how troublesome it is to have to entertain Cathal because he has been obliged to erect a house to entertain him, which, we are told incidentally, was situated on the border of Uí Echach and Corco Laigde, presumably at the point of entry into Uí Echach where Pichán was to receive the king of Munster.[116]

---

[114] P. Mac Cana, *Branwen daughter of Llyr* (Cardiff, 1958).

[115] See Charles-Edwards, 'The date of the four branches of the Mabinogi'. Cf. also his 'Honour and status in some Irish and Welsh prose tales', *Ériu*, 29 (1978), 123–41.

[116] *Aisling Meic Conglinne*, 42–4. In the 9th-century tract *Dál Caladbuig*, the Dál Caladbuig are required to build the house of their overking: *Irish texts*, ed. Fraser, i. 19, §2. Cf. the erection of a palace in recognition of kingship in early Mediterranean cultures. A specific parallel with Irish evidence has been drawn by Heinrich Wagner,

That the construction of a building for a superior king may have been a public recognition of his kingship is suggested by *Crith gablach*, an eighth-century law tract on status, which described the dwelling, or fortress, and the palace, or royal banqueting-hall, of a king and distinguished them as two separate buildings, the latter being a temporary construction. The status of the king was differentiated from his nobles by the size and splendour of his fortress and banqueting-hall.[117] *Crith gablach* provides no details about the construction of the banqueting-hall, but the king's fortress is said to be constructed by his base clients, and the number of ramparts which surround it is interpreted as a visible expression of the number of base clients who built it.

It may be that the construction of the banqueting-hall for the celebration of Henry II's Christmas feast at Dublin, which Roger of Howden attributed to the Irish kings, should also be interpreted as constituting an element of the ceremony of submission. Roger of Howden described the banqueting-hall as a *palatium regium*. From Henry's point of view a *palatium* was a symbol of wealth and power.[118] *Palatium*, rather than *domus*, even has an imperial flavour. Charlemagne had *palatia*, as did the Ottonian emperors in Germany.[119] Although the structure built for Henry at Dublin may have been made of wattles, the fact that it was styled a *palatium* suggests grandiose claims, and that its significance lay in the act rather than the manner of its construction. There is little doubt that the festivities at Dublin made an impression on chroniclers writing in England. Roger of Howden's description of the palace built by the Irish kings for Henry must ultimately derive from a firsthand account of the event; it may have been drawn from some form of dispatch, such as Robert of Torigny tells us Henry II sent from Ireland to the young King Henry, his son, in Normandy, and if so, it would reflect Henry's interpretation of the event.[120]

Although Gerald of Wales devoted less attention than Roger

'Der königliche Palast in keltischer Tradition', *ZCP* 33 (1974), 6–14; 'Near eastern and African connections with the Celtic world', in R. O'Driscoll (ed.), *The Celtic consciousness* (Mountrath, 1982), 51–67.

[117] *Crith gablach*, 22–3.
[118] Cf. William Rufus's erection of Westminster Hall: Barlow, *William Rufus*, 132–3, 371–2.
[119] Leyser, *Rule and conflict*, 90–1.   [120] Robert of Torigny, 252.

of Howden to the submission of the Irish kings at Dublin, he nevertheless bears out Roger's account of the importance of the Christmas feast. Commenting on its sumptuousness, Gerald described how the Irish kings were impressed, and provided the incidental detail that at the wish of Henry, 'regia voluntate', they ate cranes' flesh for the first time, 'a meat which they had hitherto loathed'.[121] That Gerald's account was accurate in this detail is suggested by the manner in which cranes are portrayed as cult objects on early Celtic iconographic material. Even more telling in view of Gerald's remark is a Scottish folk tradition which preserves a belief that the flesh of a crane had the power of causing the death of anyone who dared to consume it. The Irish language, which has taboo names for the crane, such as *Máire fhada*, *Sadhbh fhada*, and *Síle na bportach* (Sheila of the bogs), also lends credence to Gerald's story.[122]

From the evidence of the Irish annals and the accounts of Anglo-Norman chroniclers it is beyond doubt that the Irish kings made submission to Henry II and that they did so wittingly in terms of their own institutions. Typical elements of a public ceremony of submission in pre-Norman Ireland were present. Diarmait Mac Carthaig, king of Desmond, came to meet Henry at Waterford on the border between Desmond and Leinster, Domnall Mór Ua Briain, king of Thomond, came to meet him at the river Suir which delineated a boundary between Munster and Leinster; the kings of Déise and Osraige met Henry as he progressed through their territories, accepted gifts, and promised tribute. Other kings attended Henry's Christmas court at Dublin, as they might have done in the case of an Irish overking. They entered the house of King Henry and accepted his hospitality; in doing so they made submission, and they may even have caused the erection of the palace at Dublin for that very purpose.

---

[121] Giraldus, *Expugnatio*, 96–7. On the significance of *regia voluntas* see Jolliffe, *Angevin kingship*, 60–86.

[122] See H. Wagner, 'Zur Bezeichnung des Kranichs im Keltischen', *ZCP* 29 (1962–4), 301–4; A. Ross, *Pagan Celtic Britain* (London, 1967), 6–14.

THE ANGEVIN CONTEXT OF THE SUBMISSIONS
OF THE IRISH KINGS TO HENRY II IN
1171–1172

Although the accounts by Gerald of Wales and Roger of
Howden provided incidental information, which may be
reconciled with Irish evidence on submission in pre-Norman
Ireland and help to substantiate that the Irish kings made a
form of submission to Henry II which was comprehensible to
them in terms of their own institutions, it would be wrong to
leave the impression that this was understood also by those
Anglo-Norman chroniclers who commented on the submissions of the Irish kings. Gerald of Wales very clearly described
oaths of fealty taken by a number of Irish kings, as well as an act
of submission. Of the submission of Diarmait Mac Carthaig,
king of Desmond, Gerald of Wales wrote: 'tam subjectionis
vinculo quam fidelitatis sacramento ... se Anglorum regi
sponte submisit.' Of Domnall Mór Ua Briain's submission:
'impetratoque pacis beneficio, constituto similiter regni sui
tributo firmissimis subieccionis vinculis se quoque regi fidelem
exhibuit.' Of Máel Sechlainn Ua Fáeláin, king of Déise, and
Domnall Mac Gilla Pátraic, king of Osraige: 'sponte submis-
sis'. Of the remaining kings who submitted at Dublin: 'sub
fidelitatis et subieccionis obtentu ... firmissimis se fidelitatis et
subieccionis vinculis innodavit.' And the chapter relating to the
submissions was headed 'et tam Dermitio Corcagiensi quam
Duvenaldo Limericensi cum universis australis Hiberniae
principibus se regi sponte subdentibus.'[123] William of Newburgh
described Henry II as having subjugated the Irish kings.[124]
Gervase of Canterbury named four Irish kings who swore fealty
to Henry.[125] The letter which Pope Alexander III wrote to the
Irish bishops in 1172 exhorted them to ensure that the Irish
kings remained faithful to the oaths which he had been
informed they had sworn.[126] The letter of procuration given to
William fitz Audelin by Henry II in 1173 was addressed,
among others, to the kings of Ireland and spoke of the 'fidem

---

[123] Giraldus, *Expugnatio*, 12–13, 93–5.
[124] William of Newburgh, i. 169.
[125] Gervase of Canterbury, i. 235.
[126] Sheehy, *Pontificia Hib.* i. no. 5.

quam mihi debetis'.[127] On the other hand, Ralph of Diss explicitly mentioned an act of homage done by three Irish *reguli*,[128] and Roger of Howden in the *Gesta* account stated that the Irish kings swore fealty to Henry 'et homines ejus devenerunt de omnibus tenementis suis', although he omitted reference to the tenurial tie in his revised *Chronica*.[129]

It is possible to reconcile the Anglo-Norman chroniclers' accounts of an oath of fealty sworn by the Irish kings to Henry II with a constituent element of submission in pre-Norman Ireland. An oath of loyalty was one element which established a mutual contract between a lord and client; it might also form part of the public ceremony of submission by one king to another, and was also sworn on other relevant occasions such as the eve of battle.[130] Between kings of equal, or near equal, power, mutual oaths were sworn as a means of avoiding or terminating hostilities. Since the sanction of customary law did not apply to political relations between kings, resort was frequently made to solemn oaths sworn publicly and guaranteed by ecclesiastics, the custodians of the relics on which the oaths were generally taken, who were entitled, in theory, as clerics to exact legal compensation for the violation of their suretyship. The twelfth-century annals attest to the public swearing of oaths and the making and breaking of numerous peace treaties and concords concluded between Irish kings with ecclesiastics acting as oath-helpers.[131]

Bearing in mind the frequent resort to oaths in a political context in pre-Norman Ireland, the statement of the Anglo-Norman chroniclers that the Irish kings swore an oath to Henry II is plausible and is supported by the testimony of the letter of Pope Alexander III to the Irish bishops. The ceremony must have been much the same in externals, whether it was

---

[127] *Recueil des actes de Henri II*, ed. Delisle and Berger, i, no. 310.
[128] Ralph of Diss, i. 348.
[129] Roger of Howden, *Gesta*, i. 24–5; *Chronica*, ii. 29–30.
[130] See above, pp. 195–7.
[131] Cf. *AU* 1097. 6, 1099. 7, 1101. 8, 1102. 8, 1105. 3, 1107. 8, 1109. 5, 1113. 7, 1126. 8, 1128. 5, 1156, 1160, 1166; *Ann. Tig.* 1113, 1116, 1120, 1134, 1136, 1143, 1144, 1152, 1155, 1157, 1161, 1162, 1166, 1168; *Chron. Scot.* 1090, 1130, 1143, 1148; *Ann. Inisf.* 1091. 2, 1093. 4, 1116. 3, 1120. 5; *Misc. Ir. annals*, 1114. 2, 1116. 1, 1117. 1, 1134. 5, 1147. 4, 1153. 1, 1165. 2. Malachy of Armagh's role as a peace negotiator was stressed by Bernard of Clairvaux in his biography and in the sermon which he preached on the saint's anniversary: Bernard, *Life of St Malachy*, 103–5, 154; vi. 1. 51.

performed in accordance with contemporary Irish or Anglo-Norman practice, even if the consequences for breach of oath may not have been identical in both societies. Gerald of Wales accused the Irish of being oath-breakers.[132] The twelfth-century Irish annals give some substance to his accusations: the swearing of oaths in political contexts appears to have been debased by a combination of over-use and ineffective sanctions, for the only certain punishment for the violator was ecclesiastical censure.

The oath sworn by the Irish kings to Henry II may also be placed in an Anglo-Norman context. It was described by the Anglo-Norman chroniclers as an oath of fealty. An oath of fealty was an element in the formation of the feudal relationship between a lord and vassal. It could have another connotation when sworn to the king of England. There was a distinction between swearing an oath of fealty to one's lord and taking an oath of fealty to the king, although in some instances they might be one and the same person. The oath of fealty sworn to the king of England originated from the oath of loyalty which the Anglo-Saxon king had been entitled to exact from all his subjects. In 1086 William the Conqueror exacted an oath on the plain of Salisbury, not just from his tenants-in-chief, to whom he was immediate lord, but also from their principal tenants.[133] In 1166, after Henry II had commissioned a survey of knight service owing to the Crown, an oath of fealty was secured not only from his tenants-in-chief but from the knightly class about whom he had ascertained information: knights were made to take individual and direct oaths of allegiance to the king irrespective of whether or not they held in fee of him.[134] The assize of Northampton in 1176 was to extend the oath of fealty even further, ordering that it should be taken from all subjects, from earls to villeins, if they wished to stay in the kingdom, 'et qui facere noluerit fidelitatem tanquam inimicus domini regis capiatur'.[135]

In order to clarify the possible Anglo-Norman context in which the Irish kings could have sworn fealty to Henry II it is

[132] *Gir. Camb. op.* v. 165.
[133] *Anglo-Saxon Chronicle*, s.a. 1086.
[134] G. W. S. Barrow, *Feudal Britain* (London, 1956), 149.
[135] Roger of Howden, *Gesta*, i. 110.

necessary to consider at the same time the question of homage which Ralph of Diss stated, and Roger of Howden implied, was performed by some Irish kings to Henry. Typically, homage created a tie between a lord and vassal based on the tenure of land in return for military service. But as in the case of fealty, a distinction may be drawn between homage made to one's lord and liege homage rendered to the king. According to Glanvill, homage could be given to the king without receipt of a reciprocal grant of land, without the creation of the typical vassalic relationship.[136] Homage done to the king, as king rather than lord, came to be known in England as liege homage.

The origins of liege homage lay in France, where its development stemmed from the fact that the strict ties of vassalage were compromised when vassals began to do homage to more than one lord, creating the likelihood of a conflict of loyalties whereby a vassal might be faced with the choice of having to go to war against one of his lords in defence of another.[137] Liege homage designated one lord among several as liege lord, whom a vassal would have to serve with the full strictness that had been characteristic of primitive vassalage. Two degrees of homage between a lord and vassal were thus possible, of which liege homage was supposedly the stronger. On the Continent, liege homage gradually succumbed to a similar debasement to that which had occurred with vassalic homage, namely that it became possible to perform liege homage to more than one lord. The original purpose of the institution was thereby negated, and the term liege homage lost its distinctive meaning and came to be applied indiscriminately to ordinary homage.

The Normans introduced the concept of liege homage to England, where it underwent a different evolution. The degenerative process, whereby a vassal might swear liege homage to more than one lord, did not develop: in England the king managed to establish a virtual monopoly of liege homage. If Glanvill may be believed, it did not necessarily imply that the performer of the act held lands as a vassal from the king.[138]

Homage performed between rulers has to be placed in yet

[136] Glanvill, ix. 1–3, 109.
[137] F. L. Ganshof, *Feudalism* (2nd edn., London, 1964), 103–6; M. Bloch, *Feudal society* (2nd edn., London, 1962), i. 211–19.
[138] F. Pollock and F. W. Maitland, *The history of English law before the time of Edward I* (2nd edn., Cambridge, 1898, repr. 1968), i. 298–9.

another category. It did not necessarily involve the full range of feudal obligations that followed from vassalic homage. A form of homage might operate between rulers known as *hommage de paix*, or *hommage en marche*.[139] This homage is best documented in the context of relations between the Capetian kings and the Norman dukes, but it also operated between, among others, the dukes of Normandy and the counts of Anjou, Maine, and Brittany. The predominant characteristic of *hommage de paix*, or *hommage en marche*, was the meeting of two rulers to negotiate peace, often on neutral ground. It was frequently performed at the conclusion of hostilities. The rights conferred on the party to whom such homage was offered were very much a matter of interpretation. Generally, it gave the superior only the vaguest overlordship of honour and left the vassal in virtual independence. Whether or not such an act proved of lasting significance depended on the interpretation which either party was able subsequently to impose on it or deny to it. This was dictated by the realities of political power. The primary purpose of the ceremony was the creation, or re-establishment, of peace, and this took priority over the political subordination of one party to the other. The ambiguity of the relationship left scope for subsequent definition and reinterpretation. This was similar to political submission between the more powerful overkings in twelfth-century Ireland. It was precisely in the twelfth century, however, that on the Continent the flexibility for political manœuvre in relations between rulers was becoming restricted: the more malleable practices of an earlier age were being set into hard and fast rules before the advance of the clarifying, codifying, and systematizing lawyers of the schools and universities. The advantage lay with the party who could realize as much potential as possible from a relationship at a time when the lawyers might gratuitously freeze it, if not actually invest it with greater significance.

The homage relationship between the Capetian kings of France and the dukes of Normandy serves as an illustration.[140] It also sheds light on Henry II's own attitude towards the per-

---

[139] J. F. Lemarignier, *Recherches sur l'hommage en marche et les frontières féodales* (Lille, 1945).

[140] What follows relies heavily on C. W. Hollister, 'Normandy, France and the Anglo-Norman *regnum*', *Speculum*, 51 (1976), 202–42.

formance of homage between rulers. As a result of the Norman Conquest of England the dukes of Normandy acquired the title and dignity of kings of England. As kings of England they recognized no superior authority, but as dukes of Normandy they continued to owe homage to the kings of France. After the Norman Conquest of 1066 they demonstrated a reluctance to render that homage. This was partly due to a conviction that homage of any sort compromised the royal dignity. Their royal status attained in England was used as a justification for withholding homage. In reality, it was their greater wealth and power compared with the Capetian kings which enabled the Anglo-Norman kings to indulge such convictions.

For a time it looked as if the Norman dukes would succeed in gaining complete independence of the Capetian kings under the pretext of the dignity of the English Crown. The height of Norman ducal independence of the kings of France was reached during the reign of Henry I (1100–35), but it was to be jeopardized by his nephew William Clito's pursuit of a claim to the Norman duchy with Capetian support from 1114 onwards, and by the political instability which followed Henry's death in 1135. The disputed succession to the crown of England after his death drove the rival parties, in their capacities as dukes of Normandy, to seek the support of the French Crown. The effect of each new appeal was to emphasize and redefine the feudal link between the Capetian king and the duchy of Normandy, which had been steadily eroded from the time of the Norman Conquest of England. William Clito's attempt to take Normandy forced Henry I to allow his own son William to do homage to Louis VI for Normandy in 1120. King Stephen was driven to make a similar concession in 1137, when he allowed his son Eustace to do homage to Louis VI for Normandy in the face of the rival claims of Matilda and her husband, Geoffrey, count of Anjou. When Geoffrey, count of Anjou, gained possession of Normandy in 1144 he, in turn, rendered homage for Normandy to Louis VII because of the conflict with King Stephen.

The Angevin claim and eventual succession to the English throne in 1154 was an important factor in causing the feudal link between the Norman dukes and the Capetian kings to be invested with increased significance. By 1154 the feudal bond between the counts of Anjou and the Capetians was stronger than between the latter and Normandy.[141] The Angevins did not display the same sensitivity as previous rulers of the Anglo-Norman state about the performance of homage to the French king. When Henry succeeded his father as count of Anjou in 1151 he did homage for both Anjou and Normandy to Louis VII; furthermore, it was the first certain instance of a Norman duke performing the ceremony at Paris rather than the traditional location near Gisors on the border between Normandy and Capetian territory. Henry set an even greater precedent in 1156 when he performed homage for Normandy after he had been crowned king of England; he was the first English king to do homage for Normandy after the assumption of the royal dignity, and he repeated the act in 1183.

That King Henry was less sensitive about performing homage as duke of Normandy to the kings of France was dictated partly by the practical difficulties which he experienced in administering his vast inheritance and acquisitions by marriage. His accession added Anjou, Maine, Touraine, and Aquitaine to the Anglo-Norman *regnum*. In attempting to govern these diverse territories Henry was faced with a much greater challenge than the more compact Anglo-Norman unit had presented to his predecessors. The Norman Conquest had created an artificial degree of conformity between Normandy and England, which could not be imposed on Henry's other dominions; a policy of full integration of the Angevin territories into the Anglo-Norman state was impossible. His response was to retain the separate identities of his dominions, even to emphasize them. Henry's use of the multiple titles 'rex Anglorum, dux Normannorum et Aquitanorum, et comes Andegavorum' may be contrasted with that of Henry I, who used the title of 'rex Anglorum' and eschewed that of 'dux Normannorum'.

The danger of Henry II's policy was that the autonomy of the Norman duchy *vis-à-vis* the Capetian kings might be eroded by assimilation to the less autonomous position of Henry as duke of Aquitaine or count of Anjou. He was aware of this drawback, and tried to arrest its development by performing separate acts of homage for each of his Continental domin-

[141] Powicke, *The loss of Normandy*, 13–14.

ions, but he was not entirely successful. In 1183, following the revolt of his sons, he was obliged to swear a single act of homage to Philip Augustus for all his Continental holdings.[142] Henry's successors were made to yield even more to the growing ambitions of the Capetians as feudal suzerains, until in 1204 Philip Augustus was able to effect the confiscation of Normandy and Anjou on the pretext of the defiance of his feudal obligations by King John.

It would be wrong to overestimate the degree of overlordship which Henry II conceded to the Capetians during his lifetime. Despite his acts of homage to the French king, Normandy's domestic government remained as autonomous as previously; Capetian kings continued their traditional policy of non-intervention in the domestic affairs of the duchy. Henry managed to retain a sufficient degree of ambiguity in the relationship to allow him room for manoeuvre for the duration of his reign. An instance of that ambiguity is provided by the treaty of Ivry of 1177, in which Henry's earlier acts of homage to the French king were acknowledged by reference to Louis VII as Henry's *dominus* and to Henry as Louis's *homo et fidelis*.[143] The negotiations, however, were conducted on the border of Normandy by arbitration in the manner of rulers of sovereign states, and not at the court of the Capetian king. There is no doubt, however, that Henry II was prepared to concede more than his Anglo-Norman predecessors had done on the question of homage to the Capetians, and that his accession compromised their policy of detaching Normandy from the French Crown and attaching it more firmly to the English kingdom.

Henry II's homage to the French Crown did not diminish his status as king of England, but even in respect of England he appears to have been less cautious than his royal predecessors in his willingness to recognize a superior political authority. A letter sent by Henry to the Holy Roman Emperor, Frederick Barbarossa, in 1157 ran:

We place our kingdom and everything subject to our rule anywhere at your disposal and entrust it to your power so that all things shall be arranged at your nod and that the will of your *imperium* shall be done

---

[142] Roger of Howden, *Gesta*, i. 306.
[143] Hollister, 'Normandy', 238.

in everything. Let there be then between us and our peoples an indivisible unity of peace and love and of safe commerce, yet in such a way that the authority to command shall go to you who hold the higher rank and we shall not be found wanting in willingness to obey.[44]

The background to this missive was a demand from Frederick Barbarossa for the return to Germany of a relic which had once belonged to the German imperial treasury, a request to which Henry refused to accede. The fulsome compliments were designed to soften the blow of refusal, and were doubtless not envisaged by Henry as having any practical effect. Nevertheless, it must have been useful propaganda for the German royal house. The compromising tenor of Henry II's rhetoric in 1157 may have been used in 1193–4 to persuade Richard I to do homage to the emperor for the kingdom of England. Although even this act never invested the emperor with authority in England, there were some contemporaries prepared to countenance his claims to overlordship there: when in 1215 Pope Innocent III referred to King John as a vassal of the Roman Church at the fourth Lateran council, the archbishop of Mainz objected on the grounds that the kingdom of England belonged to the imperial power. Although Henry II's letter of 1157 to Frederick Barbarossa may not have formed the origin of this belief, it could certainly have been used to advance it.

Henry also appears to have been prepared to concede a certain degree of overlordship in his dominions to the pope. The text of a letter addressed to Alexander III (1159–81) survives in which Henry bound himself to the pope as his overlord 'quantum ad feudatarii juris obligationem'. Doubts have been expressed about the authenticity of the text, but even if it was not genuine, it was in circulation during Henry's lifetime, by 1184 at the latest, which suggests that the sentiments at least were familiar to Henry's contemporaries.[145]

Henry II's letters to Frederick Barbarossa and to Pope Alexander III (if genuine) have to be seen in the context of diplomatic negotiations and alliances. The language of twelfth-century diplomacy was sonorously grandiloquent. It would be

---

[144] K. Leyser, 'Frederick Barbarossa, Henry II and the hand of St James', *EHR* 356 (1975), 481–506 (at 482–3).
[145] Ibid. 505 n. 2.

naïve to attribute too much significance to them. They serve, however, as a very useful reminder that the language of lordship and of vassalage cannot be interpreted literally when it occurs in an essentially political context, and that the mutual obligations which normally obtained between lord and vassal cannot necessarily be presumed to have operated.

This is apparent not only from the acts of homage performed to the French king by Henry II, and from rights to an overlordship of England which he may have been prepared to concede on parchment to the German emperor or the pope, but also from the acts of homage which he received as king of England from the kings of Scotland and Wales. The relationships of the Norman kings of England with the kings of Scotland and Wales had originated in the pre-Norman era, in the period when the West Saxon royal dynasty had not merely established itself as kings of England but also claimed an overlordship of Britain. They had not, therefore, originally been expressed, either ceremonially or verbally, as feudal relationships. The practical consequences of the submission of Scottish and Welsh rulers to the Anglo-Saxon kings had been minimal, amounting to little more than an acknowledgement of their position as the weaker parties in an alliance of friendship. Initially, the Anglo-Norman kings were content with an acknowledgement of their overlordship by the Scottish and Welsh rulers in the manner which had obtained in the pre-Conquest period. It was inevitable, however, that the Norman kings would gradually seek to have that relationship expressed ceremonially and publicly in accordance with contemporary Anglo-Norman practice, and, by the same token, attempt to strengthen the nature and degree of subordination. In the early years of his reign Henry II gave a military demonstration in Wales of his power which was sufficiently convincing to persuade a number of Welsh kings to do homage to him in 1157, the first known occasion of a feudal act of homage between a Welsh ruler and the king of the English.[146] Acts of homage were again performed by the Welsh kings to Henry at Woodstock in 1163. If he interpreted their actions in 1163 as implying a full feudal relationship of homage

[146] See A. J. Roderick, 'The feudal relations between the English Crown and the Welsh princes', *History*, 37 (1952), 201–12; Warren, *Henry II*, 153–69; S. B. Chrimes, *King Edward I's policy for Wales* (Cardiff, 1969), 1–6.

for their lands, he had too many preoccupations subsequently to devote sufficient time and energy to asserting effective lordship in Wales. The consequence was that the initiative for interpreting the relationship between the Welsh rulers and Henry lay with the Welsh kings. Henry acknowledged as much by conceding a redefinition of relations in 1177, where only two Welsh rulers, Dafydd, styled 'king of North Wales', and Rhys, styled 'king of South Wales', swore oaths of fealty and rendered him homage. From the remaining Welsh kings he merely accepted oaths of fealty.[147] Henry, in other words, recognized the sovereignty of these two rulers in North and South Wales in their own lordships and envisaged that any subsequent relations with the Welsh would be negotiated through them. This arrangement endured for the remainder of Henry's reign. The nature of the liege homage performed by the two Welsh rulers in 1177 is complicated by the fact that Henry made a grant to Dafydd of Ellesmere and to Rhys of Maelienydd. Did their acts of liege homage relate only to these grants of land, which they held thereafter as tenants-in-chief of Henry?[148] Or was their liege homage also intended to regulate the political relationship between Henry and the kingdoms of North and South Wales? The acts of homage made in 1177 did not compromise their authority within their kingdoms. The paradox is that, although liege homage ought to have bound its performer more securely to his lord, the net effect, when it operated in a political context, was often to allow to the vassal a greater degree of independence than would have obtained with vassalic homage.

The Anglo-Norman kings also inherited an ill-defined relationship with the Scottish kings.[149] The indeterminate nature of the border between England and Scotland provided scope for political manœuvre. The Scottish kings were, in certain circumstances, prepared to trade acknowledgement of the

---

[147] Roger of Howden, *Gesta*, i. 159, 162.

[148] Michael Richter argued that Dafydd and Rhys received lands outside their own territories in exchange for fealty and homage, which was not performed for their principalities, and that this arrangement was meant to emphasize their status as independent rulers of North and South Wales; M. Richter, 'The political and institutional background to national consciousness in medieval Wales', *Hist. Studies*, 11 (1978), 37–55 (at 42).

[149] See Anderson, 'Anglo-Scottish relations'; Warren, *Henry II*, 169–87.

superiority of the kings of England for recognition of their lordship in the ill-defined border territory, both before and after the Norman Conquest of England.[150] The natural development that the Anglo-Norman kings would seek to have submissions made to them by Scottish rulers performed ceremonially in a feudal manner was accelerated both by the general Normanizing policy of King David (1124–53), and by the fact that David from before his accession as king of Scotland held the honour of Huntingdon in right of his wife and had done homage to the king of England as a tenant-in-chief. This helped the Anglo-Norman kings both to retain the relationship with the Scottish kings which they had inherited from the pre-Conquest period, and to attempt to translate that relationship into a feudal context.

Nevertheless, the precise nature and scope of the relationship remained ambiguous. The act of homage performed by Malcolm IV (1153–65) to Henry II at Chester in 1157 'in such fashion as his grandfather had been the man of the older king Henry saving all his dignities' is a good illustration.[151] In what precise fashion Malcolm's grandfather Edgar (1097–1107) had been considered the man or vassal of Henry I (1100–35), and what dignities were safeguarded in 1157, it is impossible to determine. If the saving clause deprived the act of most of its legal context, this, as Barrow has argued, was probably deliberate.[152] The reason adduced by William of Newburgh for Malcolm's acquiescence to the act of homage in 1157 is noteworthy: William drew attention to the difficulty of determining the nature of the oath sworn by Edgar, and implied in fact that Malcolm owed nothing by it, but that he conceded an act of homage in 1157 'because he prudently considered the king of England had the better of the argument by reason of his much greater power'.[153] In 1163 Malcolm was summoned to Henry II's court at Woodstock to renew his homage to Henry and to give homage to Henry's son, the younger Henry, and was required as well to surrender hostages in order that he

---

[150] See G. W. S. Barrow, 'The Anglo-Scottish border', *Northern History*, 1 (1966), 21–42.

[151] Roger of Howden, *Chronica*, i. 216.

[152] *Regesta regum Scottorum*, ed. G. W. S. Barrow, i (Edinburgh, 1960), 9–10.

[153] William of Newburgh, i. 105–6.

might retain his border castles. According to Robert of Torigny, Malcolm agreed to these conditions so that 'peace might be preserved'.[154]

Malcolm's successor, William, was obliged to concede much more to Henry II after his support of the abortive rebellion of 1173 and his ignominious capture. The price of his release was the harsh and unambiguous terms of the treaty of Falaise in 1174: King William became the liegeman of Henry in respect of the kingdom of Scotland and of all his other lands; Henry reserved the right to demand liege homage and fealty from such other men who held lands of the Scottish king as he wished to select; the Scottish Church was to make submission to the English Church, and its bishops were required to place William's dominions under interdict if he broke fealty; William was obliged to cede the castles of Lothian to Henry.[155] In practice, this last was the only stipulation of the treaty that was put into effect. William's authority in Scotland was not in fact compromised by the treaty of Falaise. Although Henry did intervene subsequently in Scotland on three occasions, it seems to have been by invitation, in response to appeals made to him as ultimate overlord. The terms of the treaty of Falaise in regard to the Scottish Church proved impossible to implement. Within months of Henry II's death in 1189, King William was able to purchase release from the obligations of the treaty from King Richard I.

The acts of homage performed by the Scottish kings in 1157, 1163, and 1174 were conceded at times when the political initiative lay with Henry II. The negotiation of peace rather than the initiation or affirmation of a feudal contract was the immediate objective of both parties. Undoubtedly there was political advantage in the situation for Henry, especially after the treaty of Falaise in 1174, but he showed little interest in realizing it.

In sum, the terms homage or liege homage were used frequently to characterize a political or diplomatic relationship between rulers of autonomous territories, rulers, however, who

---

[154] Robert of Torigny, 218; Ralph of Diss, i. 311. Roger of Howden made no mention of an act of homage in 1163, only that a firm peace was made between Henry II and Malcolm: Roger of Howden, *Chronica*, i. 219.

[155] *Anglo-Scottish relations, 1174–1328: some selected documents*, ed. E. L. G. Stones (London, 1965), 1–5.

were not equals in military strength or political power, a fact which was acknowledged publicly by the weaker party with a ceremonial act of homage. Relationships between rulers which were expressed ceremonially as feudal vassalic relationships cannot be presumed to have had the consequences which proceeded from such ceremonies between a lord and his vassal. The long-term effects of such an act of homage were determined by the political pressure which might be exerted subsequently by either party to intensify or minimize the relationship.

In considering the submissions of Irish kings to Henry II in 1171–2, and the assertion by a number of Anglo-Norman chroniclers that some of the Irish kings performed homage to him, there are a variety of contexts in which they might have done so. The Irish kings could have performed homage to Henry as king rather than as lord. Homage to the king might be distinguished by the use of the term liege homage, although, as Glanvill's usage about 1176 suggests, it might still simply be referred to as homage. Liege homage might be made to the king of England by subjects, who did not necessarily hold land of him directly as tenants-in-chief, but were vassals of other lords; or it might be rendered to him in a more political or diplomatic context, as is illustrated by Henry's relations with the Welsh and Scottish rulers, who did not necessarily thereafter hold their lands as fiefs from him.

An act of homage by an Irish king to Henry in 1171–2 need not necessarily have established a tenurial relationship between them. It could have been interpreted as signifying only the ceremonial public establishment of peaceful relations between rulers of unequal power. The status and power of those Irish kings who submitted to Henry varied considerably. This is obscured in part by the practice in pre-Norman Ireland of continuing to accord the title of king to individuals who, in fact, by the twelfth century exercised few regalian rights. The power and importance of Diarmait Mac Carthaig, king of Desmond, was much greater than that of Ua Cathasaig, king of Saithne, each of whom is recorded to have submitted to Henry II.[156] Whereas Mac Carthaig might have submitted to

[156] See Appendix 2.

Henry as a ruler entering into a treaty of friendship with a superior king, in a manner similar to the way in which the Welsh rulers did so, the so-called king of Saithne was little more than lord of an estate, a former petty kingdom, which had been absorbed into the Hiberno-Norse kingdom of Dublin.[157] It cannot be assumed that the consequences of submission to Henry II were identical for each of the Irish kings.

Roger of Howden, in the *Gesta* account, stated explicitly that the Irish kings 'homines ejus devenerunt de omnibus tenementis suis', although he modified this in the shortened *Chronica* version, omitting any reference to a tenurial link.[158] Can Roger of Howden's assertion that the Irish kings performed homage for their lands, that is that they became vassals, or tenants-in-chief, of Henry II, be substantiated? The problem may be approached by considering the position of those kings of Leinster who are recorded to have submitted to Henry in 1171–2, namely the kings of Uí Muiredaig, Uí Fáeláin, Uí Felmeda, and Osraige.[159] In the immediate pre-Norman period these kings were subordinate to the provincial king of Leinster. If Henry recognized Strongbow as lord of Leinster in 1171–2 in succession to Diarmait Mac Murchada, then Strongbow, and not Henry, ought to have been the immediate lord of these kings. If Henry accepted homage for their lands from those kings, the rights of Strongbow as lord of Leinster would have been diminished greatly. It is not impossible that Henry initially may have contemplated a policy of entering into a tenurial relationship with a number of Irish kings within Leinster as a possible counterweight to Strongbow's influence there. It is more likely however, that Henry regarded the submissions of the kings of Leinster as a recognition not of direct lordship but of overlordship from subordinates of the lord of Leinster, just as Henry might exact fealty or homage not merely from his tenants-in-chief but also from their principal subtenants.

Henry reserved portions of the kingdom of Leinster as royal demesne, notably the cities of Dublin and Wexford with the adjacent hinterland which had been attached to them in the

---

[157] For territorial expansion of the Hiberno-Norse kingdom of Dublin into north Co. Dublin, cf. above, p. 62.

[158] *Gesta*, i. 25; *Chronica*, ii. 30, which omitted the phrase 'de omnibus tenementis suis'.

[159] See Appendix 2.

pre-Norman period. Among the kings who submitted to Henry at Dublin were Mac Gilla Mo Cholmóc, king of Uí Dunchada, and Ua Cathasaig, king of Saithne. Both these petty Irish kingdoms had been absorbed into the Hiberno-Norse kingdom of Dublin in the immediate pre-Norman period. Consequently they formed part of Henry's demesne of Dublin after 1172. The Mac Gilla Mo Cholmóc family did, in fact, become tenants-in-chief of the English king after 1171–2, adopting the name fitz Dermot. They retained lands in the county of Dublin as late as 1400.[160] Little is known of the fate of the Uí Cathasaig after Anglo-Norman intervention; the apparently peaceful death of Imar Ua Cathasaig, lord of Saithne, is recorded in 1179.[161] According to Gerald of Wales, Hugh de Lacy attempted to appropriate Saithne for his own use, but it was restored to the royal demesne of Dublin by Henry II's agent, Philip of Worcester, about 1184–5.[162] From the all too sparse charter evidence, at least one pre-Norman landholder in the vicinity of Saithne can be shown to have retained lands as a tenant of the English Crown after 1172, namely the Welsh royal house of Gwynedd, descendants of whom, known as the fitz Rerys, continued to hold land in north Co. Dublin into the eighteenth century.[163] It is possible that Mac Gilla Mo Cholmóc, king of Uí Dunchada, and Ua Cathasaig, king of Saithne, could have sworn fealty and done homage to Henry II 'de tenementis suis'. This may also have been the case within the royal demesne of Waterford, and of Wexford until the restoration of the latter to Strongbow in 1173. Only Roger of Howden listed Ragnall, Hiberno-Norse king of Waterford, as having submitted to Henry in 1171–2. Ragnall could have sworn fealty and done homage to Henry for his landholdings. There is possible evidence of a direct dominical relationship between Henry and the men of Wexford on the pipe roll of 1172–3, which recorded gifts made to 'Morchard'' and the men of

---

[160] *Chartul. St Mary's, Dublin*, i. 31–5; *Crede mihi*, 67; *Reg. St John, Dublin*, 239; *Cal. doc. Ire., 1171–1251*, nos. 356, 569; J. T. Gilbert, *A history of the city of Dublin*, i (Dublin, 1854), 230–5.

[161] *AFM.*

[162] Giraldus, *Expugnatio*, 198–9. Saithne had been a subkingdom of Mide before its incorporation into the kingdom of Dublin, and Hugh de Lacy, as lord of Mide, may have used this to justify its appropriation.

[163] See Curtis, 'The Fitz Rerys'.

Wexford by Henry.[164] Roger of Howden's information about Henry's Irish expedition derived from royal officials, or their records. His statement that the Irish kings swore fealty and became the men of Henry II 'for their lands' may have substance in the case of those kings whose lands fell within the areas designated by Henry as royal demesne. But it cannot have been true of all the kings who submitted to Henry.

If the king of Mide swore fealty and became the man of Henry II for his lands, then Henry's grant of the kingdom of Mide to Hugh de Lacy on the eve of his departure from Ireland would have been irresponsible in the extreme, in that it would have gratuitously exacerbated political instability in an already highly volatile area. There would be little point in Henry requesting Pope Alexander III to exhort the Irish kings to observe oaths of loyalty sworn to him if he were blatantly prepared to violate his obligations to them as lord. Henry's grant of the kingdom of Mide to Hugh de Lacy is intelligible only if it is presumed that the king of Mide made a personal submission to Henry as a superior king rather than as his feudal lord. It can be argued that Henry, nevertheless, had no right to grant the kingdom of Mide to Hugh de Lacy after he had accepted a submission from the king of Mide. There was a difficulty, however, for Henry in determining which individual actually was the recognized king of Mide in 1171–2. In the immediate pre-Norman period Mide had been partitioned frequently, by the external intervention of claimants to the high-kingship, among a number of individuals, some of whom did not even belong to the royal dynasty of Mide.[165] Diarmait Mac Murchada had been the beneficiary of one such partition, effected by Toirdelbach Ua Conchobair, king of Connacht and high-king, in 1144; on that occasion Diarmait was apportioned the eastern half of Mide, while Tigernán Ua Ruairc, king of Bréifne, was allotted the western half. Diarmait Mac Murchada had intervened in Mide for the first time in 1138 and was to do so again in 1152, 1156, 1157, and 1161.[166] Even more

---

[164] See above, n. 10. In 1173 Wexford was restored to the lordship of Strongbow: see above, p. 122.

[165] Mide was partitioned in 1094, 1125, 1143, 1144, 1150, 1152, 1161, 1162, 1163, and 1169: *Ann. Tig.* 1094, 1161, 1162, 1163; *AU* 1125; *Chron. Scot.* 1143; *AFM* 1125, 1143, 1144, 1150, 1152, 1162, 1163, 1169.

[166] *Ann. Tig.* 1152; *AFM* 1138, 1152, 1156, 1157, 1161. Ua Máel Sechlainn, king of

importantly, after Strongbow's arrival in Ireland in 1170, Mac Murchada resumed his earlier activities in Mide, as a result of which he received the submission and hostages of Domnall Bregach Ua Máel Sechlainn, styled king of East Mide.[167] According to the Book of Leinster and the 'Song of Dermot', Diarmait Mac Murchada was king of Mide as well as of Leinster when he died in 1171.[168] Strongbow could have argued a case for his succession in Mide in right of his wife. Domnall Bregach Ua Máel Sechlainn, who submitted to Diarmait Mac Murchada in 1170, was recognized only as king of eastern Mide; the western half was under the control of his brother Art.[169] Henry II was faced with at least two rival claimants for the kingship of Mide from within the Clann Cholmáin royal dynasty, and an external challenge from Tigernán Ua Ruairc, king of Bréifne, as well as a claim from Strongbow in right of Diarmait Mac Murchada's and his own military intervention in Mide.[170] It is not known which of the Ua Máel Sechlainn kings submitted to Henry in 1171–2, though the probability is that it was Domnall Bregach Ua Máel Sechlainn. Small wonder that in the circumstances Henry decided to grant the

Mide, is named by the 'Song of Dermot', ll. 136–7, among the traitors who abandoned Diarmait Mac Murchada in 1166. Donnchad Ua Cellaig of the Brega dynasty had been fostered in Uí Chennselaig: *AFM* 1169. Cairpre, a portion of the kingdom of Mide, had been annexed to Leinster prior to Anglo-Norman intervention. A detailed account of 12th-century pre-Norman Mide would illustrate the point more forcefully.

[167] *Ann. Tig.* 1170.

[168] *Song of Dermot*, ll. 16–19; *Bk Leinster*, i. 184, which described Diarmait Mac Murchada as king of Leth Mogha and Mide.

[169] *Ann. Tig.* 1170, 1173; *Misc. Ir. annals*, 1171. 4, 1185. 1; *AU* 1170; *Ann. Inisf.* 1173. 7.

[170] Ua Ragallaig of Tír Briúin is listed among those Irish who were loyal to Strongbow and fought alongside the Anglo-Normans at the siege of Dublin: *Song of Dermot*, ll. 1740, 1788, 1909. The Uí Ragallaig were a branch of the Uí Briúin Bréifne, collateral in descent with the Uí Ruairc. As the Uí Ruairc advanced into eastern Mide in the late 11th century, the Uí Ragallaig were installed by them as lords of the newly annexed Mide subkingdom of Gailenga, but the collaboration between Tigernán Ua Ruairc and the Uí Ragallaig collapsed about 1160: Mac Niocaill, *Notitiae*, 26–33; *Misc. Ir. annals*, 1126–8; *AU* 1161; *ALC* 1128; *Ann. Tig.* 1155, 1161; *AFM* 1128, 1154, 1155, 1157. Cf. Ó Corráin, *Ireland before the Normans*, 170. Some of the Uí Ragallaig must then have taken refuge with Diarmait Mac Murchada, as the most prominent opponent of Tigernán Ua Ruairc's expansion in Mide. Strongbow inherited Diarmait's enemies and allies; hence Ua Ragallaig is found fighting alongside Mac Murchada and Strongbow against Ua Ruairc. This serves as an indication of Strongbow's inevitable involvement in the politics of east Mide.

kingdom of Mide 'as it had been held by Murchad Ua Máel Sechlainn' (d. 1153) to Hugh de Lacy.[171]

According to Gerald of Wales, when Diarmait Mac Carthaig, king of Desmond, and Domnall Mór Ua Briain, king of Thomond, submitted to Henry, each promised to pay him tribute at an agreed annual rate. Gerald did not mention a proffer of tribute from any of the other Irish kings who submitted to Henry. In the case of Diarmait Mac Carthaig he distinguished his submission from that of Domnall Mór Ua Briain by adding that Diarmait gave hostages in guarantee of payment. Gerald's account appears to be accurate in detail, for the pipe roll of 1171–2 records an account of 6 pounds by the sheriff of Winchester for the delivery of the son of the king of Cork, who was a hostage, and an account by the sheriff of Southampton of 6 shillings and 6 pence for one night's maintenance of the son of the king of Cork.[172] The fate of Mac Carthaig's son thereafter is not known, nor is there any evidence of whether tribute was subsequently paid by Diarmait Mac Carthaig to Henry II. But even if it was, this would not necessarily imply that Diarmait had performed homage and fealty for his lands to Henry. The initiative for establishing a relationship with Henry and the proffer of payment of tribute may, in any case, have lain with Diarmait Mac Carthaig rather than with Henry. The purpose of Mac Carthaig's submission may have been to reject publicly the high-kingship of Ruaidrí Ua Conchobair. This may have been equally true of Domnall Mór Ua Briain, who had entered into an alliance with Diarmait Mac Murchada[173] as a

---

[171] Orpen, *Normans*, i. 285–6. Mide was defined in the treaty of Windsor as 'sicut unquam Murchat Ua Mailethlachlin eam melius et plenius tenuit': Appendix 3, clause 8. This suggests a detailed enquiry by Henry II into the state of the kingdom of Mide in the immediate pre-Norman period.   [172] *Pipe roll 19 Henry II*, 51–3.

[173] Órlaith, daughter of Diarmait Mac Murchada, was married to Domnall Mór Ua Briain, probably on or shortly after his accession as king of Thomond in 1168: see above, pp. 96, 98–9. Diarmait's alliance with Domnall Mór Ua Briain may be contrasted with the alliance of his brother Murchad's family with Diarmait Mac Carthaig, king of Desmond, the traditional enemy of Domnall Mór Ua Briain. Órlaith, sister of Diarmait Mac Carthaig, king of Desmond, was the wife of Diarmait son of Muirchertach, styled king of Leinster: Dobbs, 'The Ban-Shenchus', *Rev. Celt.* 48 (1931), 234. Diarmait son of Muirchertach may be identified as Diarmait Muimnech mac Muircertaigh na maor m. Murchada m. Donnchada m. Murchada (*a quo* Mac Murchada): 'The O Clery book of genealogies', ed. Pender, 129. When Domnall Mór Ua Briain submitted to Henry II in 1171–2 he was related by marriage to, and in alliance with,

direct challenge to the high-kingship of Ruaidrí Ua Conchobair.

The kings of Bréifne, Airgialla, and Ulaid also submitted to Henry II. When Henry negotiated the treaty of Windsor in 1175 with Ruaidrí Ua Conchobair, king of Connacht and claimant to the high-kingship, Henry acknowledged the overlordship of Ua Conchobair over Ireland, excepting the provinces of Leinster and Mide, and the cities which he had retained as royal demesne. Henry was thereby assigning to Ruaidrí Ua Conchobair overlordship of the kings of Desmond, Thomond, Bréifne, Airgialla, and Ulaid, each of whom had submitted to him in 1171–2. This further indicates that a tenurial relationship had not been created by the submissions of these kings to Henry.

The balance of the evidence of the Anglo-Norman chroniclers strongly suggests that from Henry's point of view, and that of the better-informed sources in England, the submissions of the Irish kings were considered in terms of fealty alone, with no imposition of service quotas, apart from payment of some tribute in the case of some individuals.

What consequences did the Irish kings, on the one hand, and Henry II, on the other, consider would follow from their submissions? Considering the submissions in the context of pre-Norman twelfth-century Ireland, it may be said that political submission, although it might be symbolically modelled on the relationship between a lord and a client, cannot be interpreted as a legal contract with precisely defined mutual obligations and penalties for infringement. The consequences of submission between rulers were dictated by political exigencies, by the military strength of the individual parties, and by the degree to which they required one another's support, not by a customary or legal code of conduct. The consequences of submission by Irish kings to Henry II might vary, depending on whether the lands of the Irish king were situated in an area retained by Henry as royal demesne, an area of Anglo-Norman settlement over which Henry claimed a feudal overlordship, or areas contiguous to or more distant from Anglo-Norman settlement. If the submissions are considered

Strongbow, whereas Diarmait Mac Carthaig was related by marriage to the lineage of Murchad Mac Murchada.

from the standpoint of the Irish kings, and especially of those kings from beyond Leinster and Mide who were not immediately affected by Anglo-Norman intervention, such as the kings of Ulaid and Airgialla, who voluntarily proferred submission, and if an analogy between voluntary submission and free clientship is accepted, the primary purpose would have been the establishment of friendly relations and the prevention of possible hostilities, without entailing binding political or economic concessions to Henry. An important consideration for some kings at least must have been that their submission to Henry signified also their formal rejection of the high-kingship of Ruaidrí Ua Conchobair.

It would appear that Henry II was more acute in his estimation of the submissions of the Irish kings than the contemporary Anglo-Norman chroniclers who recorded them. Henry's own relations with the kings of France, Scotland, and Wales may have helped his understanding of the nature of political submission in an Irish context. Even if the submissions of the Irish kings to Henry are viewed in an Angevin context, the same qualificàtion may be made as in the case of political submission in pre-Norman Ireland, namely that the consequences of acts of submission, when performed between rulers, were governed by political and diplomatic considerations.

The Treaty of Windsor, 1175

DURING his expedition to Ireland in 1171–2 Henry II received the submissions of the majority of Irish overkings, excluding only the overking of Cenél nEógain and Ruaidrí Ua Conchobair, provincial king of Connacht, who also claimed the high-kingship of Ireland. On the testimony of the court chronicler, Roger of Howden, Henry was dissatisfied that he had not secured the submission of Ruaidrí Ua Conchobair and would have mounted a military campaign against him in the summer of 1172, had he not been obliged to leave Ireland because of the suspected disloyalty of his son, the young King Henry, and the advent of papal legates to negotiate a reconciliation with Henry following the murder of Archbishop Thomas Becket.[1] Henry's failure to reach an accommodation with Ruaidrí in 1171–2 was rectified by the treaty of Windsor concluded between the two kings in October 1175. Henry's intention of dealing with Ruaidrí may have been quickened by Ruaidrí's campaign against the Anglo-Normans in Mide in 1174, during which the Anglo-Norman fortifications under construction at Trim and at Delvin were destroyed and by the military assistance afforded Domnall Mór Ua Briain, king of Thomond, later in the same year by Ruaidrí's son, Conchobar Máenmaige, which resulted in an Anglo-Norman defeat at the battle of Thurles.[2] According to the 'Song of Dermot', Ruaidrí was accompanied on the expedition to Mide not merely by the subkings of Connacht, but also by Ua Máel Sechlainn, king of Mide, Ua Ruairc, king of Bréifne, Ua Máel Doraid, king of Cenél Conaill, Mac Duinn Sléibe, king of Ulaid, Ua Cerbaill, king of Airgialla, and Ua Néill, king of Cenél nEógain. On Gerald of Wales's testimony Ruaidrí, 'having completely devastated

---

[1] Giraldus, *Expugnatio*, 103–4; below, n. 11.

[2] *Song of Dermot*, ll. 3230–332; Giraldus, *Expugnatio*, 140–1; *Ann. Tig.* 1174; *AFM* 1174. It is perplexing that none of the Irish annals record Ruaidrí Ua Conchobair's expedition to Mide.

Mide, had now overrun the territory of Dublin itself': even Henry's royal demesne was under threat. Ruaidrí Ua Conchobair appeared to be regaining the initiative as overking of Ireland. This forms the Irish background to the treaty of Windsor.

The Angevin context for the negotiation of the treaty in 1175 was Henry's successful suppression of the revolt of 1173–4, following which Henry sought to regularize relations with Wales, Scotland, and Ireland before his departure for his Continental dominions. He did so with the Welsh at Gloucester in June 1175, with the Scottish king at York in August 1175, and with Ruaidrí Ua Conchobair as claimant to the high-kingship of Ireland at Windsor, October 1175.[3]

The text of the treaty of Windsor is known only through a transcript made by Roger of Howden.[4] This is a reliable source: Roger of Howden has preserved the texts of many other official documents to which he appears to have had ready access.[5] It is possible to deduce some information about the form of the original document from the diplomatic of the extant text: it was executed as a *finis et concordia*, a final concord, issued in the joint names of the contracting parties, and reached after an implied period of negotiation. Two exemplars would have been made and sealed interchangeably: the exemplar with the seal of Henry II attached would have been given to Ruaidrí Ua Conchobair, and the exemplar with Ruaidrí's seal would have been retained by Henry.[6]

A notable feature of this treaty was the fact that it was not negotiated in person by the principals. Ruaidrí Ua Conchobair was represented at the court of Henry II by Cadla Ua Dubthaig, archbishop of Tuam, Cantordis, abbot of Clonfert, and Master Laurence, styled his chancellor. The latter would have had custody of Ruaidrí's seal. Little is known of the mechanics of negotiation by proxy at this period. As in so many

---

[3] Roger of Howden, *Gesta*, i. 92–103; Warren, *Henry II*, 143.

[4] Appendix 3; Roger of Howden, *Gesta*, i. 102–3; *Chronica*, ii. 84–5; English translation in Curtis and McDowell, *Ir. hist. docs.* 22–4.

[5] Roger of Howden was a royal clerk from 1174 to 1189–90 who wrote up events at court during this period in diarial form more or less as they occurred: D. Corner, 'The *Gesta regis Henrici secundi* and *Chronica* of Roger, parson of Howden', *IHR Bull.* 56 (1983), 126–44.

[6] P. Chaplais, 'English diplomatic documents to the end of Edward's reign' in D. A. Bullough and R. L. Storey (edd.), *The study of medieval records: essays in honour of Kathleen Major* (London, 1971), 22–56.

other areas of thought, it was precisely in the twelfth century that the medieval theory of representation of one individual by another was being formulated and applied to the sphere of diplomatic relations. Such evidence as there is suggests that rulers usually appointed representatives to conduct preliminary discussions on their behalf. The detailed clauses of a treaty were worked out and agreed upon in advance in joint discussion between the representatives of the two parties. It is not known whether these representatives were appointed in writing, and if so what form it took, and whether they had full powers to negotiate, or had to refer back to their principals at every stage in the negotiations. Eventually, the principals themselves would have met to conclude the treaty. By the thirteenth century the principle that valid treaties could be entered into by proxies, duly appointed for that purpose by both sides, had won general acceptance; thereafter meetings between heads of state for the making of treaties became less common.

The treaty of Windsor would appear to be one of the earliest examples of an agreement involving the king of England where the principals did not meet personally: Ruaidrí Ua Conchobair was not present at Windsor in 1175. In 1176–7 a treaty was negotiated by proxy for Henry II with William II, king of Sicily, to arrange a marriage with Henry's daughter. The chroniclers provide some information about the procedure adopted on that occasion. Sicilian *nuncii* negotiated on King William's behalf in England and took oaths on his soul, and English *nuncii* negotiated on Henry's behalf in Sicily, where they took oaths on his soul.[7] These *nuncii* were almost certainly empowered by written grants of procuration. The distinctive feature of such grants was a clause promising ratification ('de rato' or 'de rati habitione'). Henry's appointment of William fitz Audelin as his representative in Ireland in 1173 took the form of a procuration:

Sciatis me, Dei gratia, salvum esse et incolumem, et negotia mea bene et honorifice procedere; ego vero quam cito potero vacabo magnis negotiis meis Hibernie. Nunc autem ad vos mitto Willielmum filium Adelmi, dapiferum meum, cui commisi negotia mea tractanda et agenda mei loco et vice. Quare vobis mando et firmiter

---

[7] Ibid. 25.

precipio quod ei, sicut michimet, intendatis de agendis meis, et faciatis quicquid ipse vobis dixerit ex parte mea, sicut amorem meum habere desideratis, et per fidem quam mihi debetis. Ego quoque ratum habebo et firmum quicquid ipse fecerit tanquam egomet fecissem et quicquid vos feceritis erga eum stabile habebo.[8]

Henry's envoys in Sicily in 1176–7 may have had with them a procuration of a similar kind to that which empowered William fitz Audelin to act in Ireland in 1173. Although the earliest certain reference to English diplomatic representatives being appointed by letters of procuration occurs in 1193 during the negotiations between King Richard I, while he was in captivity in Germany, and King Philip Augustus of France, there is evidence for the use of procurations for domestic business in England during Henry II's reign.[9]

Did English *nuncii* travel to Connacht prior to the treaty of Windsor, and with what powers? What powers did Ruaidrí Ua Conchobair grant to his negotiators at Windsor in 1175, and were they defined in writing? Had Ruaidrí consented to ratify whatever was negotiated on his behalf, or did his representatives have to refer back to him for his approval? Were Ruaidrí's negotiators empowered to swear oaths on his behalf in England in 1175?

Such questions are prompted by the opening clause of the treaty of Windsor, which referred to Ruaidrí Ua Conchobair as the liege man of Henry II. *Homo* implies *homagium*, that Ruaidrí had made an act of homage to Henry, although this is not explicitly stated. The only known occasion on which Ruaidrí could have done so in person was during Henry's visit to Ireland in 1171–2. Gerald of Wales claimed that Ruaidrí made submission to Henry while he was in Ireland. According to Gerald, a meeting was arranged at the river Shannon on the borders of the kingdoms of Connacht and Mide between Ruaidrí Ua Conchobair and William fitz Audelin and Hugh de Lacy as the representatives of Henry II, and there Ruaidrí

---

[8] *Recueil des actes de Henri II*, ed. Delisle and Berger, i, no. 310, which depends on Rymer's *Foedera*, which, in turn, derives from BL Cott. Titus B. XI, fo. 90; Orpen, *Normans*, i. 312–13. An apparently independent version of the text is to be found in Oxford: Bodl. Rawl. B. 499, fo. 55, with the difference that Henry II is styled king of England 'Dei gratia' and 'dominus Hybernie', which is not otherwise known in a charter of Henry II.

[9] Chaplais, 'English diplomatic documents', 26.

made submission (Gerald made no mention of homage).[10] But Roger of Howden, Ralph of Diss, and Gervase of Canterbury explicitly stated that Ruaidrí had refused to submit to Henry.[11] The Irish annals, which make no mention of Ruaidrí's submission in 1171–2, are crucial in assessing the accuracy of Gerald's account. It might be argued that the submission of the high-king was deliberately suppressed as politically embarrassing, except that the annalists, including the Annals of Tigernach, whose compiler at this period was favourable to the Connacht royal dynasty, revealed no such reticence in recording the submissions of the other Irish kings to Henry II, which were equally to the discomforture of Ruaidrí, whose authority the Irish kings who submitted to Henry were thereby implicitly rejecting.

The only possible credence which might be accorded to Gerald's account is that it is conceivable that a meeting did take place between Ruaidrí Ua Conchobair and representatives of Henry, by way of preliminary negotiations for the treaty of Windsor, although in that event it would be more reassuring if William fitz Audelin and Hugh de Lacy, the negotiators named by Gerald, were witnesses to the eventual treaty document.[12] Gerald's description of a meeting taking place between Ruaidrí and representatives of Henry on the border between Connacht and Mide is plausible, since this was an attested Irish practice. It was one of which Gerald, however, was consciously aware, as is apparent from his description of the submissions of Diarmait Mac Carthaig and Domnall Mór Ua Briain to Henry;[13] indeed he was familiar with the practice also in a Welsh context.[14] He could therefore have invented this detail.[15] Historians have held that Gerald fabricated the account of the submission of Ruaidrí

---

[10] Giraldus, *Expugnatio*, 94–5.

[11] Roger of Howden, *Gesta*, i. 25–6; *Chronica*, ii. 30; Ralph of Diss, i. 348; Gervase of Canterbury, i. 235.

[12] Their absence is the more striking since both appear to have been in England around the time of the negotiation of the treaty of Windsor, where they witnessed a charter of Henry II in favour of Hamund Mac Turcaill at Woodstock and in favour of St Mary's Abbey, Dublin at Feckenham: Sheehy, 'The registrum novum', 253; *Chartul. St Mary's, Dublin*, i. 79–80. Cf. Eyton, *Itinerary*, 191–6.

[13] See above, pp. 199–201.

[14] Cf. *Itinerarium Kambriae*, ii. 12, in *Gir. Camb. op.* vi. 142.

[15] For another possible instance of Gerald's use of a 'verification factor' see above, ch. 1 n. 130.

Ua Conchobair to Henry in 1171–2 to conceal what he considered a major limitation of Henry's otherwise successful negotiations with the Irish kings, namely the fact that Henry had not gained the submission of the claimant to the high-kingship.[16] It must certainly occasion suspicion that Gerald made no mention of the treaty of Windsor. He appears to have deliberately suppressed any knowledge of Henry's negotiations with Ruaidrí in 1175; this may have been necessitated by his previous account of the submission of Ruaidrí in 1171–2.[17]

If Ruaidrí Ua Conchobair did not render homage in person to Henry II in 1171–2, or at any other point before 1175, did he then become the liege man of Henry in virtue of the treaty of Windsor, which was negotiated by proxy? The evidence suggests that he did so. It serves as a salutary warning of the impossibility of strict legal interpretations of acts such as homage and fealty between rulers when they occur in the context of diplomatic or political negotiations. The supposedly most solemn act of homage, which a vassal might swear to a particular lord only once in his lifetime, could apparently be made by proxy.

The treaty of Windsor may be compared on this point with the treaty of Falaise, negotiated two months earlier, in which King William of Scotland likewise was referred to as the *homo ligius* of Henry II.[18] King William certainly did homage to the young King Henry, and William's heirs were to do homage to Henry's heirs. Although historians have assumed that King William also did homage to Henry II, this, however, is not specifically stated in the treaty of Falaise.

The distinction between vassalic homage and liege homage between rulers is evidenced by the detailed provisions of the treaty of Windsor. Vassalic homage created a tie between lord and vassal based on the tenure of land held in return for specified service, typically military service. The treaty of Windsor, however, does not state that Ruaidrí Ua Conchobair held the kingdom of Connacht in fee for a specified military service from Henry II, rather that Ruaidrí was the liege man of Henry committed to his service, 'paratus ad servitium suum'.

[16] Cf. Orpen, *Normans*, i. 265; Otway-Ruthven, *Med. Ire.* 49.
[17] But see also below, pp. 250–3.
[18] Text in *Anglo-Scottish relations*, ed. Stones, 1–5.

The service was not defined, although normally the phrase meant 'paratus cum equis et armis'.[19] Henry conceded to Ruaidrí 'that he shall be king under him'. Ruaidrí was 'to hold his land as fully and as peacefully as he held it before the lord king of England entered Ireland', with the addition, or novelty, that he was to pay a tribute to Henry of one hide from every ten animals rendered to Ruaidrí. Tribute was a consequence of political submission in pre-Norman Ireland, which was negotiable between the more powerful kings, and which did not necessarily give the superior any rights of disposition over the lands of his subordinates or their successors. The specification of tribute in the treaty highlights the Irish character of the link forged between the two kings. The treaty of Windsor referred to Ruaidrí Ua Conchobair as the liege man of Henry II, a traditional mode of expression within Anglo-Norman society of acceptance of the overlordship of the king, or of personal relations between rulers, but Ruaidrí did not thereafter hold the kingdom of Connacht by specified military tenure of Henry; nor were the terms of the treaty stated to be binding on the heirs of either Henry II or Ruaidrí Ua Conchobair.[20]

The treaty of Windsor drew a distinction between Ruaidrí's kingship of Connacht and a wider overlordship which was assigned beyond Connacht. Outside Connacht, with the exception of the areas reserved by Henry II, Ruaidrí was 'to have all the rest of the land and its inhabitants under him'. Ruaidrí's authority in that area was defined only in relation to Henry, and not its Irish inhabitants. Within that area Ruaidrí was to raise tribute on behalf of the king of England. There is a saving clause, however, that its inhabitants 'sua jura sibi

[19] Roger of Howden, *Gesta*, i. 138.

[20] Contrast the Treaty of Falaise. The fact that Irish kings did not succeed by primogeniture cannot be cited as a reason why the treaty of Windsor was not made binding on the successors of Henry II and Ruaidrí Ua Conchobair. In 1169 Ruaidrí gave 'a grant of ten cows every year from himself and from every king that should succeed him for ever to the chief scholar of Armagh in honour of Patrick to instruct the youths of Ireland and Scotland in literature': *AFM*. Cf. the charter of Diarmait Mac Murchada to All Hallows, Dublin, about 1162, which granted freedom 'a procuratione mea et expedicione mea et omnium in regimine Lageniae et Dublinie mihi succedencium': *Registrum prioratus omnium sanctorum*, 50; and the charter of Áed Ua Conchobair, king of Connacht, issued in 1224: 'heredes meos ad hoc obligo ut quicunque in perpetuum post me regnabunt et qui in regimine Connactie perpetuo mihi succedent sive sint filii mei sive cognati sive consanguinei, sive propinqui, sive extranei', G. H. Orpen, 'Some Irish Cistercian documents', *EHR* 23 (1913), 303–13 (at 304–5).

conservent'. In effect, this was an acknowledgement that payment of tribute to an overlord was negotiable in twelfth-century Ireland, and might fluctuate with the degree of intensity of the relationship between a superior king and his subordinates. Henry sought an annual tribute of one hide from every ten animals collected by Ruaidrí from the area under his wider overlordship.

Payment of tribute conceded to Henry a personal overlordship over Ruaidrí Ua Conchobair. Henry claimed no right to intervene personally either in Connacht or in the wider area of Ruaidrí's overlordship. The treaty of Windsor respected the integrity both of Ruaidrí's kingdom of Connacht and of the wider overlordship assigned to him. If any of the Irish within the area of overlordship assigned to Ruaidrí proved rebellious against him, or against the king of England, responsibility for taking redress or punitive action against them rested with Ruaidrí: 'eos justiciet'.

What retributive action for the withholding of tribute was envisaged by the drafters of the treaty in the phrase 'eos justiciet et amoveat'? Was it judicial action? The traditional view of the legislative functions of the Irish king, based almost exclusively on the eighth-century law tracts, has been that he played a very limited role in the enforcement of justice. There are few traces of royally administered justice in the Irish law tracts. These convey the impression that the declaration and recording of the law was vested in a privileged class of lawyers, who determined what constituted a crime and the appropriate legal remedy, the enforcement of which was left to the injured party and his kindred. The fact that the law tracts accorded equal status, or honour-price, to the king, the bishop, and the lawyer has led some historians to presume a threefold division of authority within pre-Norman Irish society.[21] As Ó Corráin has pointed out, however, the context in which the equality of the king, bishop, and judge was defined was a socio-legal and not a political one.[22] It cannot be presumed from an equality of status and honour-price that the three exercised equal political authority. In any event, the king referred to in the eighth-century law tracts was the petty king of a *tuath*, that is the

---

[21] Cf. Warren, 'Interpretation', 7.
[22] Ó Corráin, 'Nationality and kingship', 8–10.

lowest grade of king, who has to be distinguished from provincial kings and overkings in terms of his power, not only in the eighth century but even more so by the twelfth.

Although the king of the *tuath* appears to have played little part in the routine administration of the law, as depicted in the eighth-century law tracts, they allowed that he had powers to proclaim special ordinances at times of grave emergency, such as periods of plague, famine, or war, when the king could call a public assembly and declare a *rechtge*, or ordinance, which was binding on the *tuath*.[23]

The term *rechtge* was used occasionally of ecclesiastical regulations issued by individual churches, although these were more usually called *cána*.[24] The promulgation of ecclesiastical *cána* is recorded in the annals between 697 and 842, and overkings are associated with their enforcement within their overlordships. The declaration of such *cána* afforded kings opportunities to extend their powers to promulgate special ordinances. It may likewise be inferred that churches enlisted the support of overkings for their legislation because those kings exercised, or aspired to exercise, a similar role in the promulgation of secular legislation.

Although ecclesiastical *cána* are not recorded in the annals after 842, secular royal equivalents are noted in the Annals of Inisfallen as having been proclaimed by the Ua Briain overkings in the eleventh century. In 1040 Donnchad son of Brian Bóruma, king of Munster, proclaimed a 'cáin 7 rechtge' against theft, use of arms, and manual labour on Sundays.[25] The Church was not explicitly associated with Donnchad's ordinance, but its provisions are reminiscent, on the one hand, of the *Cáin Domnaig*, a ninth-century ecclesiastical ordinance on Sunday observance, and on the other hand, of the contemporary peace and truce of God movements fostered by ecclesiastics in France. Donnchad's ordinance of 1040 may be seen as a development from the earlier pattern of co-operation between overkings and churches in the promulgation of *cána*. In 1050 during a famine, when there was much suffering and disorder

[23] *Crith gablach*, ll. 507, 514. The king of a *tuath* had the right to appoint a judge within the *tuath* to deal with cases of public law: l. 498, cf. 36, 79.

[24] Ó Corráin, 'Nationality and kingship', 22–3; K. Hughes, 'The Church and the world in early Christian Ireland', *IHS* 13 (1962), 99–116.

[25] *Ann. Inisf.* 1040. 6.

and churches and secular buildings were being attacked, the annals recorded that the same Donnchad summoned an assembly of the kings and clerics of Munster at Killaloe and promulgated a *cáin mór* forbidding injustices.[26] In 1068 Donnchad's successor in the kingship of Munster, Toirdelbach Ua Briain, also proclaimed a 'cáin 7 rechtge', 'and no better law was enacted in Munster for a long time'.[27] These annalistic references reveal that by the eleventh century certainly the more powerful overkings proclaimed special ordinances, a function in which they appear to have been originally inspired and encouraged by ecclesiastics.[28] It is probable that kings also sought to extend their role in law enforcement by offering their protection to churches. In a charter of Diarmait Mac Murchada, king of Leinster, confirming a grant of one of his subordinate kings, Diarmait Ua Riain, king of Uí Dróna, to the monastery of Killenny about 1162–5, Mac Murchada claimed that he would punish anyone who violated the persons or property of the monastery by confiscating their goods, or if they had none by death:

Interdicimus ergo ne aliquis hominum de prefatis terris ausu temerario ab eisdem monachis et eorum in perpetuum successoribus nec passum pedum auferre nec violentiam monasterio si ibi fuit vel eius grangiis si habuit inferre aut ignem apponere sive aliquid ab eis furtim abstrahere presumat sed omnia in pace ecclesie integra et illibata dimittere. Quia siquis contra nos in Dei ecclesiam manum forefaciendo audacter porrexerit res suas si habuerit vitam si non irrevocabiliter perdet.[29]

The promulgation of special ordinances provides one instance of a judicial function which might be exercised by overkings beyond their patrimonial kingdoms. Another which may be identified from eleventh- and twelfth-century annalistic references was the exaction of compensation for injury on behalf of political clients. Irish law allowed for the right of a lord to compensation for injuries done to his clients.[30] Where an offence was committed against the client of a lord, the lord might intervene to levy the penalty. His encouragement to do

---

[26] *Ann. Inisf.* 1050. 2; *AFM*.   [27] *Ann. Inisf.* 1068. 4.
[28] Ó Corráin, 'Nationality and kingship', 21–4.
[29] Butler and Bernard, 'The charters of Duiske', 5–8; *Facs. nat. MSS Ire.* ii, pl. 62.
[30] *Críth gablach*, l. 85.

so was the proportion of the compensation, usually one-third of the amount, which he could retain for himself. This was termed the *forbach flatha* or 'lord's portion'.[31]

A decline in the importance of the kindred and a concomitant growth of lordship may also have contributed to an extension of the judicial functions of Irish kings. Just as *dominus* in feudal society might mean either 'lord' or 'king', so the Irish *flaith* was also used in the sense of 'lord', 'ruler', or 'king'. A king had the same potential to levy the lord's share. Political submission was modelled on the institution of clientship: when a subordinate king submitted to a superior he was deemed to enter a form of client relationship. The superior king, therefore, might try to levy the 'lord's portion' on behalf of those kings who had entered into a form of political clientship with him. Not only would this demonstrate to his client the efficacy of his overlordship, but it would also be to his material advantage, assuming he was able to exact a proportion of the compensation due to his subordinate. In a tract defining the relations between the overking of Locha Léin and the subordinate king of Ciarraige, it was envisaged that the king of Ciarraige would hand over to the king of Locha Léin a proportion of the fines which he himself had collected, as his lord's portion.[32] No amount is specified, but it is likely to have been one-third of the third already levied by the king of Ciarraige.[33] The possibility of exacting a lord's portion would also have contributed to the extension of interest in law enforcement by the overking beyond his patrimonial kingdom to the wider area over which he claimed hegemony.

The annals provide instances where in the twelfth century an overking intervened on behalf of a political subordinate to enforce payment of compensation for injury and to claim a proportion of the compensation. In 1092 Muirchertach Ua

[31] Binchy, 'Irish history and Irish law II', 23.

[32] Byrne, *Ir. kings*, 216–19, and the modifications suggested by Binchy, 'Irish history and Irish law', 22–5. Cf. 11th-century Wales, where kings were intruding themselves into the quarrels of their subjects, claiming that a third of the compensation for settling a feud belonged to them as of right: *Domesday Book*, i. 179b; Davies, *Conquest*, 65.

[33] The *Book of Rights*, ed. Dillon, 72–3, claimed that the Airgialla were entitled to a third of every levy from the king of Cenél nEógain, and a third of that third belonged to the line of Colla Mend. See also *trian tobaig* or 'levying third', ibid. 100–1. Cf. *Hy Many*, 62–6.

Briain, king of Munster and high-king of Ireland, installed his own nominee, Áed Ua Conchobair, in the provincial kingship of Connacht following the blinding of Ruaidrí na Saide Buide Ua Conchobair, king of Connacht, by the Uí Flaithbertaig. In the following year, when Muirchertach's protégé was slain by the Uí Flaithbertaig, Muirchertach exacted a fine of 50 cows in compensation for the killing.[34] In 1168 Ruaidrí Ua Conchobair mounted an expedition into Thomond to determine the regnal succession following the murder of Muirchertach Ua Briain, king of Thomond, his uterine half-brother, and at the same time exacted a fine of 720 cows from the men of Munster as compensation for the slaying of Muirchertach.[35] In these two instances the annals do not specify whether the overking received a proportion of the fines. But in 1168, when Ruaidrí Ua Conchobair is recorded to have levied a fine of 700 cows on the kingdom of Mide in compensation for the slaying of the king of Delbna, it is expressly stated that this was in addition to the compensation paid to the men of Delbna by the men of Mide.[36] The pretext for the campaign of Tigernán Ua Ruairc, king of Bréifne, against Diarmait Mac Murchada, king of Leinster, which led to the latter's exile in 1166, was the injury which Mac Murchada had inflicted upon Ua Ruairc in 1152 by abducting his wife. When Mac Murchada returned to Ireland and was obliged to submit to Ruaidrí Ua Conchobair as high-king in 1167, Ua Conchobair, as overlord of Tigernán Ua Ruairc, exacted a fine of 120 ounces of gold as compensation on behalf of Ua Ruairc from Mac Murchada.[37] In 1170, when Ruaidrí Ua Conchobair executed the hostages of Diarmait Mac Murchada, the Annals of Tigernach recorded 'for Ua Ruairc had sworn that Ruaidrí would not remain king of Ireland unless they were put to death'. Tigernán Ua Ruairc's acknowledgement of the high-kingship of Ruaidrí Ua Conchobair was conditional on Ruaidrí fulfilling his obligations as lord.

Closely allied to the exaction of compensatory fines was the

---

[34] *Ann. Inisf.* 1092. 3, 1093. 8.   [35] *AU, AFM* 1168.
[36] *Ann. Tig.*, *AFM* 1168. A distinction was drawn by the annalist between the payment of *éric* to the Delbna and *eineclann*, honour-price, to Ruaidrí Ua Conchobair and to the king of Airgialla, whose joint protection the king of Delbna had enjoyed.
[37] *Ann. Tig.* 1166, 1167; *AFM* 1167.

levying of tribute or tax. The interrelationship between law enforcement and taxation is reflected in the ecclesiastical *cána* of the eighth and ninth centuries, which served the twofold purpose of determining affiliation, or jurisdiction, and of collecting dues within that jurisdiction.[38] 'Cís 7 cáin', 'tax and ordinance', is a common doublet in twelfth-century sources. Some of the ordinances of an Irish king must have consisted of striking a tax rate. The ecclesiastical annalists provide little evidence of royal taxation unless it impinged directly on their own interests. In 986 Máel Sechnaill mac Domnaill, the overking of the Uí Neill dynastic federation, committed an outrage on the church of Armagh and, by way of compensation, conceded to the Armagh community 'a visitation of Mide, both Church and laity, as well as refection in every fortress or dwelling of his own'.[39] Máel Sechnaill appears to have granted to the church of Armagh the right to collect a tax which would normally have been due to him in Mide. In 1007 the same king made a donation to the church of Clonmacnoise and levied a hide from every *lis*, or enclosure, to pay for it.[40] This appears to be an instance of an extraordinary levy for a particular purpose.

A notable instance of an extraordinary tax is provided in 1166, when, as a prelude to his bid for the high-kingship, Ruaidrí Ua Conchobair convened an assembly at Athlone at which the kings of Mide, Bréifne, and the Ostmen of Dublin were present. The main issue was the negotiation of a transfer of allegiance by the Ostmen of Dublin from Diarmait Mac Murchada to Ruaidrí Ua Conchobair. It was decided at Athlone that Ruaidrí should levy a tax of 4,000 cows on the men of Ireland to pay as stipend, or *tuarastal*, to the Ostmen of Dublin. This was the price of their allegiance. The tax seems to have been raised speedily, for later in the same year the annals recorded that Ruaidrí journeyed to Dublin, where he received acknowledgement of his high-kingship and, in return, presented the Ostmen with their substantial endowment.[41] This extraordinary levy was raised by Ruaidrí for a purely political purpose, to ensure recognition of his high-kingship from the

---

[38] Ó Corráin, 'Nationality and kingship', 22.
[39] *AFM* 985 = 986, as cited by Ó Corráin, ibid.
[40] *Chron. Scot.* 1005 = 1007, as cited by Ó Corráin, ibid.
[41] *Ann. Tig.*, *AFM* 1166.

city of Dublin, which had become an essential prerequisite for any aspirant to that office. The expectation of the treaty of Windsor that Ruaidrí Ua Conchobair would be able both to collect tribute from the overlordship assigned to him and to take judicial action against recalcitrants was not unduly unrealistic.

Refusal by the Irish within Ruaidrí's wider overlordship to pay tribute was interpreted in the treaty of Windsor as a breach of fealty against Ruaidrí and Henry. Withholding of tribute was a typical act of defiance of overlordship in pre-Norman Ireland, which might be punished by the forcible seizure by the king or lord of the tribute due to him. A breach of fealty in feudal society resulted in sequestration, and possible confiscation, of the fief of land held by the vassal of the lord or king. The differing penalties reflect the predominant elements in the contractual nexus between lord and client in the two societies. Although the eighth-century Irish law tracts had depicted cattle as the usual fief advanced by a lord to a client, by the twelfth century the continued exercise of lordship was increasingly held to form part of the contractual nexus between an overking and his subordinate. A subordinate king who rejected the authority of an overking in twelfth-century Ireland might face removal from office and the installation of an alternative candidate. The deposition and exile of Diarmait Mac Murchada, and the installation in his place of his brother, Murchad, as king of Leinster by Ruaidrí Ua Conchobair in 1166 is only one of many instances.[42] The Annals of the Four Masters recorded that in 1169, when Diarmait Ua Máel Sechlainn, king of Mide (also styled 'king of the Foreigners of Dublin and of Uí Failge and Uí Fáeláin', which may indicate that he had been designated by Ruaidrí Ua Conchobair as governor of Dublin), was killed by Domnall Bregach Ua Máel Sechlainn, Ruaidrí Ua Conchobair hosted into Mide, expelled Domnall Bregach 'in revenge of that deed', and divided Mide into two parts, allocating the eastern half of Mide to Tigernán Ua Ruairc, king of Bréifne, and 'he kept the western half himself'. The distinction between being deposed from a kingship in pre-Norman Ireland, which is the mode of expression used by the Irish annalists, and which is reflected in the treaty of Windsor

[42] See above, p. 98, and below, p. 249.

in the phrase 'justiciet et amoveat', and being disseised of one's landed estate in feudal society may be more apparent than real. A concept of conditional tenure underlies both actions. A probably more important difference was that in Ireland overkings in the majority of instances did not have the means to implement an effective policy of forfeiture of lordship and land: witness the return from exile of Diarmait Mac Murchada, and his recovery of the kingship of Uí Chennselaig and of Leinster in 1167, which Ruaidrí Ua Conchobair proved unable to prevent. Permanent deposition of recalcitrants, and recurrent installation by the overking of his own appointee or arrogation of the kingdom of the deposed to his own use, might, in time, have led to the universal acknowledgement and acceptance of such actions as an automatic legal prerogative of an overking. An important limitation hindering such a development, however, was the inability of twelfth-century Irish overkings who attempted such depositions to set up structures of local government and administration which would enable them to effect permanent forfeitures.

The treaty of Windsor envisaged the removal of recalcitrant subordinate kings by Ruaidrí Ua Conchobair as a punitive action for defiance or breach of fealty. Henry II in turn granted to Ruaidrí 'that he should be king of Connacht under him as long as he serves him faithfully'. The implication was that Henry reserved to himself the right of installation of another candidate in the kingship of Connacht, and that Henry conceded this right to Ruaidrí in respect of subordinate kings within the area of overlordship assigned to Ruaidrí by the treaty of Windsor. The emphasis was on the right to remove a subordinate king from office and to install an alternative candidate, rather than on sequestration or confiscation of the lordship of a recalcitrant. This accurately reflected twelfth-century practice in Ireland, where the overking generally had to content himself with installing another candidate in the place of a defiant subordinate. But the remedy for defiance envisaged in the treaty of Windsor may also be said to be conservative, in so far as some overkings in twelfth-century Ireland had attempted and, in some cases, had succeeded in implementing more radical strategies, such as the permanent alienation and appropriation of a portion of the lordship of the disaffected subordinate. In 1165 Muirchertach Mac Lochlainn, king of Cenél nEógain and high-king of Ireland, following a military campaign against Eochaid mac Con Ulad Mac Duinn Sléibe, king of Ulaid, reappointed him as his client subject to specific conditions and obliged him to forfeit the district of Bairrche, which Muirchertach then granted to Donnchad Ua Cerbaill, overking of Airgialla.[43] Diarmait Mac Murchada as provincial king of Leinster appears to have been remarkably successful in permanently removing certain individuals and installing his own nominees. The Ua Gormáin dynasty, for example, appear to have been deprived by Diarmait of the kingship of Uí Bairrche in 1141 and expelled from Leinster, and to have taken refuge thereafter with the Ua Briain kings of Thomond.[44]

Clause 11 of the treaty of Windsor specified that Ruaidrí Ua Conchobair was to take hostages from all those committed to him by Henry II, and to give those hostages to Henry at the latter's will. No exact rendering of 'illos vel alios' is possible, but it presumably meant that from time to time Henry might nominate the hostages. Such a procedure would accord with an attested twelfth-century Irish practice. If an overking received the submission of a subordinate king, the superior might assign custody of a number of hostages to the subordinate as a public act of delegation of authority.[45] Alternatively, a subordinate king who acknowledged a superior might offer or be obliged to hand over hostages to his superior which he himself held, as an acknowledgement of his overlordship. Tigernán Ua Ruairc, king of Bréifne, handed over the hostages of Osraige and Uí Chennselaig to his overlord, Ruaidrí Ua Conchobair, after his campaign in Leinster against Diarmait Mac Murchada in 1166.[46]

Clause 13 of the treaty of Windsor specified that all those committed by Henry to the king of Connacht (taking *ipsi* to refer to the *omnibus* of clause 11 rather than to the *obsides*) 'shall do service to the lord king by making gifts to him each year of their hounds and birds'. This is an obscure clause.[47] The sense

---

[43] *AU* 1165.   [44] *NHI* ii. 27.

[45] Cf. *Ann. Inisf.* 997. 2, 998. 2, 1003. 4, 1071. 3, 1120. 4; *Ann. Tig.* 1063, 1167, 1169.

[46] *Ann. Tig.*; cf. *Ann. Inisf.* 1120. 4.

[47] It was left untranslated in Curtis and McDowell, *Ir. hist. docs.* 22–4.

appears to be that the Irish shall, as a matter of duty, make free-will offerings .of hounds and birds, not unlike the so-called *dona*, compulsory gifts, frequently demanded by Henry II. No figures are specified. There are numerous references in the pipe rolls to dues payable in hawks to Henry II: the county of Buckingham, for example, was saddled with an annual increment of four hawks.[48] Irish hawks were highly prized in England by the time of the treaty of Windsor, as evidenced by a reference to them in the *Dialogue of the Exchequer*, written in 1176.[49] Pipe roll entries testify to Henry II's passion for falconry and show that in England he arranged for large numbers of hawks and falcons to be delivered to him as 'gifts', and that he took a keen interest in their welfare.[50] In his *History and topography of Ireland*, Gerald of Wales noted that Ireland abounded in hawks, falcons, and sparrow-hawks; in the dedication of that work to Henry II, he stated that he could have sent the king falcons or hawks from Ireland, but had chosen instead to dedicate a more enduring work of literature to him.[51] In the *Expugnatio Hibernica*, Gerald stated that a suitable form of tribute from Ireland to Britain would be the 'birds which are so plentiful there'.[52] This may suggest familiarity on Gerald's part with this provision of the

---

[48] *Pipe roll 22 Henry II*, 16.

[49] *The course of the exchequer*, ed. C. Johnson (London, 1950), 121.

[50] Cf. *Pipe roll 22 Henry II*, 11, 16, 17, 35, 41, 62, 64, 69, 78, 79, 88, 93, 102, 117, 122, 167, and other pipe rolls s.n. *accipitres*, *aves*, *girfalcones*. Henry II was accompanied to Ireland in 1171–2 by William de Gerpunville, who is found acting as the king's falconer on the pipe rolls between 1179 and 1186: *Pipe roll 26 Henry II*, 148; *27 Henry II*, 160; *28 Henry II*, 115; *33 Henry II*, 131; see below, ch. 8 n. 48. There is no specific mention of Irish hawks on the pipe rolls of Henry II (only Norway and Iceland are specified as places of origin: *Pipe roll 22 Henry II*, 62, 64, 79, 88, 102, 107), but by the time of John the king was definitely receiving birds from Ireland: Rotulus misae 14 John, in *Documents illustrative of English history in the thirteenth and fourteenth centuries*, ed. H. Cole (London, 1844), 235, 245. For illustrations of John's concern for his birds, including detailed instructions to John fitz Hugh about the diet of his favourite falcon, Gibbun, see *Rot. litt. claus., 1204–24*, pp. xliii, 118, 192, 401, 407, 412. John fitz Hugh, who was a prominent official at John's court, was not expected to carry out the task of feeding Gibbun himself; that was left to an individual named Spark: Painter, *The reign of King John*, 81, 123, 144–5, 229, 269, 375. Cf. also Gerald of Wales's anecdote about Henry II pitting a Norwegian hawk against a falcon in the neighbourhood of Pembroke in 1171 while waiting to cross to Ireland, and being so impressed with the falcon's performance that thereafter about nesting time Henry regularly procured falcons from the area: Giraldus, *Expugnatio*, 90–1.

[51] J. J. O'Meara, 'Giraldus Cambrensis in Topographia Hibernie: text of the first recension', *RIA Proc.* 52 (1949), 113–78 (at 119, 123, 128).

[52] Giraldus, *Expugnatio*, 252–3.

treaty of Windsor. It is likely that Henry would have been interested to receive hawks from Ireland, and clause 13 may actually
have been an afterthought suggested by him.

The primary purpose of the treaty of Windsor was the
regularization of peaceful relations between Ruaidrí Ua
Conchobair and Henry II, and it has to be viewed in a
diplomatic and political rather than a legal or constitutional
context. That contemporaries viewed it in a diplomatic context
is borne out by the entry in the Annals of Tigernach, annals
which particularly favoured the Ua Conchobair royal dynasty
at this period, which recorded that 'Cadla Ua Dubthaig came
out of England from the son of the Empress, having with him
the peace of Ireland, and the kingship thereof, both Foreigner
and Gael, to Ruaidrí Ua Conchobair, and to every provincial
king his province from the king of Ireland and their tributes to
Ruaidrí'.[53] The annalist's description of the provincial kings
holding their provinces under Ruaidrí in this entry corre-
sponds closely to the terms of the treaty of Windsor. His use of
the term king of Ireland, implying that Ruaidrí was still high-
king, indicates his partisan stance and suppresses the fact that
Ruaidrí no longer exercised overlordship of Leinster and Mide
and the all-important city of Dublin. This entry presents the
treaty of Windsor as a significant gain for Ruaidrí.

The treaty of Windsor does not admit of a precise or definitive interpretation and this was almost certainly deliberate on
the part of the drafters. Clause 1 established Ruaidrí's submission. Clause 2 assumed that the treaty would not alter his
position apart from payment of tribute. Ruaidrí was to pay
tribute from Connacht and to produce tribute from the rest of
the Irish under his overlordship. Ruaidrí was to take hostages
as guarantors for payment. The Irish within the wider overlordship assigned to Ruaidrí were to make unspecified gifts to
Henry of hounds and birds, a clause perhaps inserted as a
symbol of Henry's ultimate overlordship. Ruaidrí could claim
that the relationship was a fairly light and loose one, acknow-

[53] *Ann. Tig.* 1175; Mac Niocaill, *The medieval Irish annals*, 27–8; K. Grabowski and
D. Dumville, *Chronicles and annals of medieval Ireland and Wales* (Woodbridge, 1984),
155–205. It is difficult to determine whether by foreigners in this entry the annalist
meant the Hiberno-Norse (of Limerick and Cork) or the Anglo-Normans, since,
although he sometimes referred to the Anglo-Normans as *Saxain*, he also used the term
Gaill quite indiscriminately after 1167 of both Hiberno-Norse and Anglo-Normans.

ledging Henry's superiority and paying tribute only. But Henry's lawyers had inserted words and phrases, such as 'paratus ad servitium sicut homo suus' and 'alia jura sua', which could be exploited if necessary. And the 'voluntas domini regis' of clauses 11 and 12 was a rather indiscreet intrusion of Henry's arbitrary authority.[54]

While the initiative for the negotiations almost certainly rests with Henry II, bearing in mind his regularization of relations with the Scottish king and the Welsh rulers in 1175 prior to the treaty of Windsor, what persuaded Ruaidrí Ua Conchobair without undue compulsion to negotiate with Henry? In the short term, the treaty of Windsor may be said to have brought a significant improvement in Ruaidrí's position. Following the return from exile of Diarmait Mac Murchada in 1167, Ruaidrí's overlordship had been rejected by the kingdoms of Leinster, Thomond, the eastern half of the kingdom of Mide, and Airgialla. After Mac Murchada's death in 1171, Ruaidrí had moved swiftly to take hostages from Domnall Mór Ua Briain, king of Thomond, and later in the same year Murchad Ua Cerbaill, overking of Airgialla, had hosted with Ruaidrí against the Anglo-Norman occupants of Dublin.[55] However, these gains were undermined by the expedition of Henry II to Ireland in 1171–2, for not only Domnall Mór Ua Briain, king of Thomond, and Murchad Ua Cerbaill, overking of Airgialla, made submission to Henry, but so also did the kings of Desmond, Bréifne, and Ulaid. Even if their submissions were not intended as an outright rejection of Ruaidrí's overlordship, it was certainly weakened by them.

By the treaty of Windsor, Ruaidrí Ua Conchobair ceded lordship of Leinster and Mide, and the Hiberno-Norse cities of Dublin and Waterford, to Henry II, but he had already lost control of all these areas to Diarmait Mac Murchada prior to Henry's intervention in Ireland in 1171. More significant were Ruaidrí's recoveries by the treaty of Windsor. The kings of Thomond, Desmond, Airgialla, Bréifne, and Ulaid had submitted to Henry in 1171–2; yet their kingdoms were assigned

---

[54] 'Ad voluntatem regis domini Angliae' translates as 'by Henry's arbitrary decision'. On the 'vis et voluntas' of Angevin kingship see Jolliffe, *Angevin kingship*, ch. 3.

[55] *Ann. Tig.*

without reservations by the treaty of Windsor to the overlordship of Ruaidrí Ua Conchobair. It may be inferred that Henry also relinquished the towns of Limerick and Cork, which during his expedition to Ireland in 1171–2 he had determined to retain as royal demesne, since these are not included in the lordship claimed by Henry in the treaty.[56]

In the overlordship assigned to Ruaidrí by the treaty of Windsor he was free to assert his authority. He might, in order to do so, seek assistance from the English king's constable. The mention of the constable and his household indicates that assistance was envisaged as military aid. Does this clause reflect the interest of Ruaidrí or of Henry II? Was this a ploy on the part of Henry to extend his influence beyond Leinster and Mide? Evidently Ruaidrí did not think so, for he was willing to avail himself of Anglo-Norman military aid: he campaigned with Anglo-Normans to take possession of Limerick at the expense of Domnall Mór Ua Briain shortly before or about the same time as the formal treaty documents were sealed and exchanged at Windsor. F. X. Martin has argued against any link between the Anglo-Norman expedition to Limerick and the treaty of Windsor: 'it was not due to any treaty obligations that the Anglo-Normans campaigned on the side of Ruaidrí against Domnall Ua Briain'.[57] It is more likely, however, that the Anglo-Norman expedition to Limerick was directly connected with the treaty of Windsor. Both events, on the evidence of the Annals of Tigernach, which virtually serves as the house chronicle of the Ua Conchobair kings of Connacht during this period, occurred very close in time. Gerald of Wales dated the taking of Limerick to a Tuesday about the calends of October.[58] The treaty of Windsor, according to Roger of Howden, was concluded on the octave of the feast of St Michael, that is 6 October, which in 1175 fell on a Monday.[59] If Gerald is correct in stating that the taking of Limerick occurred

---

[56] There is no evidence other than Gerald of Wales, *Expugnatio*, 94–5, for Henry II's retention of Cork and Limerick in 1171–2.

[57] *NHI* ii. 107, as against the two previous most detailed commentaries on the treaty of Windsor: O'Doherty, 'St Laurence O'Toole', *IER* 50 (1937), 621–5; 51 (1938), 131–46; R. Dudley Edwards, 'Anglo-Norman relations with Connacht, 1169–1224', *IHS* 1 (1938–9), 135–53.

[58] Giraldus, *Expugnatio*, 150–1.

[59] Roger of Howden, *Gesta*, i. 101; *Chronica*, ii. 83–4.

on a Tuesday it must have happened on either 30 September or 7 October, but in either case within a week of the ratification and exchange of the treaty documents.[60] It is inconceivable that the terms of the treaty would have been negotiated on 6 October by Ruaidrí's representatives without any prior reference back to him. It is likely that before his negotiators left for Windsor the outline, perhaps even the full text, of the treaty had been approved by him, and that all that remained to ratify the treaty was the formal exchange of Ruaidrí's and Henry's seals. The sequence of events immediately before and after the treaty of Windsor as recorded in the Annals of Tigernach is as follows:

A hosting by Ruaidrí Ua Conchobair into Thomond, and he banished Domnall Ua Briain into Ormond, and gave the kingship of Thomond to the son of Murchad [*sic*] Ua Briain,[61] to his own mother's son.

At the invitation of the king of Ireland, Ruaidrí Ua Conchobair, the Foreigners [Gaill] of Dublin, and Waterford, and Domnall Ua Gilla Pátraic, king of Osraige, came to Limerick without being perceived by the Dál Cais and plundered Limerick; and on this expedition the Connacht men burnt the greater part of Thomond.

Cadla Ua Dubthaig came out of England from the son of the Empress, having with him the peace of Ireland, and the kingship thereof, both Foreigner and Gael, to Ruaidrí Ua Conchobair, and to every provincial king his province from the king of Ireland and their tributes to Ruaidrí.

A great fleet led by the king of Ireland on Lough Derg, and he demolished the whole of Ormond, and brought from the Uí Briain seven hostages for their kingship and their land.

1176—Inis Cathaig was plundered by the English [Saxons] who dwelt in Limerick.

Domnall Ua Briain, king of Thomond, made peace with Ua Conchobair and gave him hostages.

Ruaidrí's deposition of Domnall Mór Ua Briain and the substitution of his own appointee, the son of Muirchertach Ua

---

[60] For the days of the week see C. R. Cheney (ed.), *Handbook of dates for students of English history* (2nd edn., London, 1970), 128–9. But cf. A. B. Scott's comment that 'a suspiciously large number of events are described as having happened *circa kalendas* of the month. Where Giraldus qualifies this by referring to a feast day the date sometimes turns out to be quite distant from the first day of the month': Giraldus, *Expugnatio*, p. xix.

[61] See n. 77 below.

Briain, may be compared with the clause of the treaty of Windsor which stipulated that Ruaidrí had the right to remove kings who were considered to be disloyal. The Anglo-Norman expedition to Limerick may be interpreted as putting Ruaidrí in possession of the city of Limerick, which Henry II had formally relinquished at Windsor.[62] The expedition occurred before the return of Cadla Ua Dubthaig from England at some unknown date after 6 October, but, since Gerald's 'about the calends of October' is not sufficiently precise, not necessarily before the formal conclusion of the treaty. There is no way of knowing what interval elapsed between the ratification of the treaty of Windsor on 6 October and Cadla's return. After Cadla's return, on the evidence of the Annals of Tigernach, Ruaidrí hosted once again into Thomond and took hostages 'for their kingship and their land' from the Uí Briain. Again, this can be related directly to a provision of the treaty of Windsor. An Anglo-Norman garrison remained in Limerick on the evidence of both the Annals of Tigernach and Gerald of Wales, but nevertheless Ruaidrí Ua Conchobair was unable to maintain his appointee in the kingship of Thomond and was obliged to accede to the reinstallation of Domnall Ua Briain early in 1176.

Gerald of Wales's account of 'the noble taking of Limerick' is markedly different in emphasis from that of the Annals of Tigernach, although it does not actually conflict with the annals. According to Gerald the expedition was occasioned by the fact that Domnall Mór Ua Briain went back on his oath of loyalty to Henry II. Gerald's relative, Raymond le Gros, therefore collected together a force of Anglo-Normans, who made a bold assault on the city of Limerick. Gerald made no mention of the participation of Domnall Mac Gilla Pátraic, king of Osraige. By contrast, the 'Song of Dermot' is in agreement with the Annals of Tigernach regarding the participation of Dom-

---

[62] Ruaidrí's father, Toirdelbach Ua Conchobair, had besieged Limerick from September 1124 to May 1125 in an attempt to take possession of the city: *Ann. Inisf.*, *AU*, *ALC*, *Misc. Ir. annals*, *AFM*. Toirdelbach Ua Briain, king of Thomond, had then attempted to take Limerick but was ousted by Cormac Mac Carthaig, king of Desmond, whom the Annals of Inisfallen described as king of Limerick in 1125. The descriptions of sieges of Dublin, Limerick, and Armagh in the pseudo-historical propaganda tracts *Cogadh Gaedhel re Gallaibh* and *Caithréim Cellacháin Chaisil* must reflect contemporary practices on the part of twelfth-century Irish kings.

nall Mac Gilla Pátraic, and further assigned him a vital role in escorting the Anglo-Normans safely to Limerick. The 'Song of Dermot' attributed the summoning of the force, which it stated was drawn from both Leinster and Mide, to Strongbow not Raymond le Gros.[63] The fact that it was drawn from Mide as well as Leinster suggests that Strongbow summoned the Anglo-Normans in his capacity as Henry II's agent in Ireland. This would accord with an interpretation of the Anglo-Norman expedition to Limerick as undertaken on behalf of Ruaidrí Ua Conchobair in accordance with the terms of the treaty of Windsor. According to Gerald, having taken considerable amounts of booty and gold, and having spent some time in provisioning the city, Raymond left a garrison in Limerick under the command of his cousin, Miles fitz David, and returned in triumph to Leinster. In the mean time, Hervey de Montmorency had sent messages to Henry II,

informing him that events had taken an ominous turn. He asserted morever, as a proven fact, that Raymond, acting against the king's honour and in contravention of his own pledge of loyalty, had planned that he and his relatives should now seize control, not only of Limerick, but of the whole of Ireland. And in order that the informer might bring this fiction to the king's ears at less risk to himself, and in a more credible guise, he alleged that, in order to accomplish his wishes, Raymond had formed bands of troops sworn to achieve this end, after the manner of Brabantine mercenaries. For Raymond had put the whole army under oath to produce all booty to be shared in common, to make a just division of spoils among themselves, and to set aside a portion for their leader.[64]

Hervey, who had negotiated on Strongbow's behalf with Henry in 1171, would have known that he would be highly sensitive to allegations that one of his subjects was seeking to carve out an independent kingdom in Ireland. Hervey was, in effect, accusing Raymond of usurping royal authority in Ireland, that is of raising an army and imposing on that army terms which only the king was entitled to do. He had mobilized sworn bands,

[63] *Song of Dermot*, ll. 3373–5.

[64] Giraldus, *Expugnatio*, 157–9. The Norman lords in South Wales were accustomed to claim a third of plunder, a prerogative taken over from the Welsh kings: J. G. Edwards, 'The Normans and the Welsh march', *Br. Acad. Proc.* 42 (1956), 155–77 (at 174).

that is, bands sworn to carry out his orders as their paymaster. He had made provision for a division of their gains, reserving for himself a share as their *princeps*. Possibly the reference to Brabançons implied that Raymond's troops were a peculiarly tough lot, since the Brabançons were singled out by contemporaries as brutal and licentious, but the main point was that Raymond was allegedly acting as an independent ruler (*princeps*), and so guilty of treason. The implication surely is that Raymond ought not to have 'seized control of Limerick'.

Henry's response was to send four envoys to Ireland, two of whom were to escort Raymond back to the king in England. While Raymond was waiting to depart, news arrived that Domnall Mór Ua Briain had besieged the Anglo-Norman garrison in Limerick, whose provisions had been almost entirely used up during the winter. According to Gerald, Strongbow would have led a force to relieve the Limerick garrison, but the Anglo-Normans were only willing to serve under Raymond, who, with the permission of the royal envoys, set out for the relief of Limerick, accompanied, as Gerald acknowledged on this occasion, by Domnall Mac Gilla Pátraic, king of Osraige, and 'Murchardus' of Uí Chennselaig. Raymond and his force entered the city and relieved the garrison on 6 April. He then engaged in separate talks with Ruaidrí Ua Conchobair, who came by boat down the river Shannon to meet him, and with Domnall Mór Ua Briain. Gerald does not explain why Ruaidrí Ua Conchobair should have been involved at this juncture, but if the treaty of Windsor ought to have given possession of the city of Limerick to Ruaidrí, he obviously would have been concerned about the possible restoration of Domnall Ua Briain in Limerick. According to Gerald, both Irish kings renewed their oaths of loyalty to Henry II and gave hostages to Raymond. Then Diarmait Mac Carthaig arrived to seek help from Raymond in regaining the kingship of Desmond, from which his son, Cormac Liathánach, had driven him. Raymond, 'who was never one to despise an opportunity for booty or a chance to win glory', made for Cork and was in the process of aiding Diarmait Mac Carthaig when news reached him of the death of Strongbow. Raymond returned to Limerick to inform the garrison there of Strongbow's death, and since 'he could not find anyone at all among the leaders willing to take command of the city' it was decided 'for the present' to abandon it. Raymond then voluntarily gave custody of the city to Domnall Mór Ua Briain 'tamquam baroni domini Anglorum regis'. The Anglo-Normans were still in sight of Limerick when it was set on fire by Domnall Mór Ua Briain. 'But when the king of England heard of this daring relief of Limerick he is said to have replied "the assault on Limerick was a bold enterprise, the relief of the city even more so, but only in abandoning the place did they show any wisdom".'[65] It is difficult to avoid the conclusion that the original purpose of the Anglo-Norman expedition to Limerick had been to give possession to Ruaidrí Ua Conchobair, and that Raymond had overstepped his commission. Gerald's account of the taking of Limerick was designed to redound to the credit of Raymond le Gros. It may be that Gerald suppressed knowledge of the treaty of Windsor precisely because the Anglo-Norman expedition to Limerick was so intimately connected with it and would have militated against his depiction of Raymond le Gros's enterprising role in Limerick.

F. X. Martin argued that 'the guiding influence in promoting the treaty came from Irish church leaders, and that their objects were not political but were church reform and peace, a continuation of the policy they had adopted with the first settlers and later with Henry II'.[66] But there is little to suggest that Church reform was a consideration in the negotiation of the treaty of Windsor. Martin attributed significance to the fact that Ruaidrí's negotiators were three ecclesiastics, the archbishop of Tuam, the abbot of Clonfert, and Master Laurence, his chancellor. But diplomatic missions frequently consisted largely or wholly of ecclesiastics: the Sicilian mission to Henry II in 1176 comprised three ecclesiastics and one layman, while Henry's mission to Flanders in the same year consisted of the archbishop of Canterbury and the bishop of Ely.[67] Since the treaty of Windsor was drafted in Latin, and since it is possible that letters of credence or procuration under the seal of Ruaidrí, which would also have had to be drafted in Latin,

---

[65] Giraldus, *Expugnatio*, 166–7.
[66] *NHI* ii. 107–8.
[67] Roger of Howden, *Chronica*, ii. 94–5; *Gesta*, i. 115–17. Diarmait Mac Murchada is known to have had an interpreter, who possibly was a layman: *Song of Dermot*, ll. 1–11.

accompanied his agents, who could have been more suitable negotiators on behalf of Ruaidrí? It was not merely their knowledge of Latin, but their wider education (often including law and Laurence's title *magister* indicates a university training), which led rulers to value ecclesiastics as diplomats, especially when the ecclesiastics had risen in the service of their rulers. The role of ecclesiastics, whether or not they were supporters of Church reform, in the negotiation of peace between rulers is well attested in pre-Norman twelfth-century Ireland.[68] Not a single provision in the treaty of Windsor related to the Church, not even a general statement that its rights ought to be protected. The detailed clauses of the treaty of Windsor suggest rather that Ruaidrí Ua Conchobair was closely involved, albeit by proxy, in its formulation, and that he stood to gain much from it. From Ruaidrí's standpoint a significant gain from the treaty of Windsor was almost certainly the right to request military assistance from his overlord, Henry II.

How long were the terms of the treaty of Windsor observed? While some historians have assumed that the treaty ceased to operate in 1177, when Henry II designated his son John king of Ireland and made speculative grants of Thomond and Desmond to Anglo-Norman feudatories,[69] others have argued that this merely modified but did not supersede the treaty of Windsor.[70] Certainly, a number of events occurred in 1176 which could be said to have placed the treaty in jeopardy. In burning the city of Limerick in sight of the departing Anglo-Norman garrison, Domnall Mór Ua Briain, who had sworn, according to Gerald of Wales, to keep it safely for the king of England and return it on demand, could be said to have chal-

---

[68] See above, pp. 208–10. Cadla Ua Dubthaig's commitment to reform is open to question. He was a grandson and great-grandson of earlier abbots or bishops of Tuam; despite his attendance at the third Lateran council in 1179, and the subsequent synod of Clonfert held by Laurence, archbishop of Dublin and papal legate, to implement the decrees of the Lateran council, Cadla was reported in 1201 by the papal legate, John de Monte Coelio, to have consecrated his own nephew as bishop 'absque titulo', so as to ensure the continuance of the succession in his family: Sheehy, *Pontificia Hib.* i, no. 53.

[69] Orpen, *Normans*, ii. 33–4; Lydon, *Lordship*, 49.

[70] O'Doherty, 'St Laurence O'Toole', *IER* 51 (1938), 136–8, followed by Edwards, 'Anglo-Norman relations with Connacht'; Otway-Ruthven, *Med. Ire.* 60–1; Warren, *Henry II*, 203; Frame, *Colonial Ire.* 16–17.

lenged the overlordship of both Ruaidrí Ua Conchobair and Henry II. A raid by the Anglo-Normans of Dublin after Strongbow's death in April 1176, which penetrated as far as Armagh, indicated that the Anglo-Normans were not confining their activities to the designated area of Angevin lordship. A subsequent raid into Mide by Máel Sechlainn Mac Lochlainn, king of Cenél nEógain, later in the same year, in which the Anglo-Norman castle of Slane was destroyed, and fortifications under construction at Kells, Galtrim, and Derrypatrick were forced to be abandoned, may have been undertaken in retaliation for the Anglo-Norman raid on Armagh.[71]

Any assessment of the duration of the treaty of Windsor must be closely linked to interpretation of the designation by Henry II of his son John as king of Ireland in 1177. Some historians have attributed Henry's action to disenchantment with the ineffectual lordship of Ruaidrí Ua Conchobair, and have seen this as the prime motivation for Henry's revision of the arrangements made in the treaty of Windsor for the Angevin lordship in Ireland.[72] The detailed provisions of the council of Oxford, 1177, at which John was designated king of Ireland, suggest, however, that it was the need to administer the vast lordship of Leinster during the minority following the death of Strongbow in April 1176 which was Henry's priority.

John's designation as king of Ireland need not necessarily have superseded the treaty of Windsor. Although Anglo-Norman feudatories from Ireland gave homage and swore fealty to John for their Irish lands in 1177, there is no evidence that Ruaidrí Ua Conchobair, or other Irish kings, were asked to recognize John as their lord.[73] This might be said to indicate that the treaty of Windsor had already been abandoned; but it could equally imply that Henry II was retaining his personal overlordship over Ruaidrí Ua Conchobair.

In support of the view that the treaty of Windsor had been abandoned by the time of, or at, the council of Oxford may be cited the speculative grants of Thomond and Desmond made respectively to Philip de Braose, and to Robert fitz Stephen and Miles de Cogan, by Henry II on the same occasion and the resumption of the cities of Limerick and Cork as royal

[71] *Ann. Tig.*   [72] See above, n. 69.
[73] Roger of Howden, *Gesta*, i. 161–5; *Chronica*, ii. 133–5.

demesne. These grants, in effect, removed Thomond and Desmond from the overlordship which had been assigned to Ruaidrí by the treaty of Windsor. But it is conceivable that Ruaidrí consented to this modification of the treaty of Windsor.[74] An important strategy of Ruaidrí's father, Toirdelbach Ua Conchobair, king of Connacht, had been to weaken the Ua Briain dynasty, who both threatened the security of Connacht's southern frontier and were Toirdelbach's most serious rivals in his bid for the high-kingship. In 1118, taking advantage of the illness of Muirchertach Ua Briain, king of Munster and high-king of Ireland, Toirdelbach had hosted into Munster and divided the province into a northern half (Tuadmumu, literally 'north Munster' = Thomond) and a southern half (Desmumu, literally 'south Munster' = Desmond), leaving the Ua Briain dynasty in possession of the northern half, and promoting the Mac Carthaig lineage of the Eóganachta dynasty, the chief political rivals of the Uí Briain, in the southern half.[75] Henry II's grants of Thomond and Desmond to Anglo-Norman feudatories in 1177 were made in terms of two spheres of political influence which had been imposed upon Munster in 1118 by Ruaidrí Ua Conchobair's father, Toirdelbach.

The treaty of Windsor had made provision that Ruaidrí Ua Conchobair might remove from office subordinate kings who proved unfaithful to him or to Henry II, and that he might invoke Henry's aid to do so. If Ruaidrí did indeed acquiesce in the granting of Desmond and Thomond to Robert fitz Stephen and Miles de Cogan and Philip de Braose, it is arguable that there may have been little difference for contemporaries between the imposition of Anglo-Norman feudatories and the replacement of a recalcitrant Irish king by an appointee of Ruaidrí Ua Conchobair. The installation of Anglo-Norman feudatories in Thomond and Desmond may well have had advantages for Ruaidrí. He had attempted to depose Diarmait Mac Murchada from the kingship of Leinster without permanent success. Not only had Diarmait regained his kingdom, but his chosen Anglo-Norman successor, Strongbow, had

---

[74] J. F. O'Doherty argued that the grants of Thomond and Desmond were 'necessary to safeguard the treaty position as a whole': 'St Laurence O'Toole', *IER* 51 (1938), 138.

[75] See Jefferies, 'Desmond'.

proved his staying-power. From Ruaidrí's standpoint, the granting of Thomond and Desmond to Anglo-Norman feudatories might effect a permanent deposition of Domnall Mór Ua Briain and Diarmait Mac Carthaig, which Ruaidrí had already attempted unsuccessfully in the case of Domnall Mór Ua Briain. That there was an attempt at the council of Oxford to justify the grants of Thomond and Desmond to Anglo-Norman feudatories as legally defensible is evidenced by the assertion of the court chronicler, Roger of Howden, that both the kings of Thomond and Desmond had broken fealty with Henry II. According to Roger, the grant of Thomond was occasioned by the fact that

Monoculus, who was king of Limerick and had done homage for it to the king of England, had been slain and one of his family, a powerful and active man, who invaded the kingdom of Limerick, gained possession of it, and ruled it with a strong hand, acknowledging no subjection to the king of England, and refusing to obey his officers, because of their faithless conduct and the evils they had inflicted on the people of Ireland without their deserving them.[76]

According to the Annals of Tigernach, Ruaidrí Ua Conchobair deposed Domnall Mór Ua Briain in 1175 'and gave the kingship of Thomond to the son of Murchad [*recte* Muirchertach] Ua Briain, his own mother's son'.[77] Ruaidrí's mother was Caillech Dé, daughter of Ua hEidin, king of Uí Fiachrach Aidne.[78] She also had issue by Toirdelbach Ua Briain, king of Thomond, father of Domnall Mór Ua Briain: the *Banshenchas* records a son, Muirchertach, by Caillech Dé and Toirdelbach Ua Briain.[79] Muirchertach would therefore have been a uterine

[76] Roger of Howden, *Gesta*, i. 173; *Chronica*, ii. 135–6.
[77] 'Slu la Ruaidhrí Ua C i Tuadhm cor' indarb Donall O Br a n-Urm 7 tuc rigi Tuadm do mc Mcaidh H Br, do mc a m fen.' Although the abbrevited form 'Mcaidh' would normally stand for Murchad, as Stokes expanded it in his translation, I have assumed that Muirchertach is intended, since Murchad is unattested in the Ua Briain genealogies, regnal lists of the kings of Dál Cais, or the *Banshenchas*, whereas Muirchertach son of Toirdelbach is named in *Ann. Tig.*, *Ann. Inisf.*, *AFM* 1168. *NHI* ii. 106, 109, 969, identifies Ruaidrí's nominee as Muirchertach Dall. This appears to depend on Martin, 'The first Normans', 67. The source cited there, however, is *Ann. Tig.* which does not specify Muirchertach Dall. Muirchertach Dall was a son of Domnall Mór Ua Briain: *Lr Muin.* 326, 342.
[78] Dobbs, 'The Ban-shenchus', *Rev. Celt.* 47 (1930), 234. *The O'Clery book of Genealogies*, ed. Pender, § 894, gives the daughter of Mac Diarmata, styled his *ben phosda*, as the mother of Ruaidrí. This is contradicted, however, by the *Banshenchas* and *AFM* s.a. 1168.   [79] Dobbs, 'The Ban-shenchus', *Rev. Celt.* 48 (1931), 191.

half-brother of Ruaidrí Ua Conchobair and half-brother of Domnall Mór Ua Briain.[80] On the death of Toirdelbach Ua Briain, king of Thomond, in 1167, Muirchertach, as a potential successor to the kingship, was slain by a rival dynast, Conchobar 'Slapar Salach' Ua Briain.[81] In 1176 the Annals of Tigernach recorded that 'Domnall Mór Ua Briain, king of Thomond, made peace with Ruaidrí Ua Conchobair'. Ruaidrí's nephew and appointee in the kingship of Thomond, therefore, had been ousted by Domnall Mór Ua Briain. The son of Muirchertach Ua Briain, whom Ruaidrí installed in the kingship of Thomond in 1175, may be identical with the Monoculus of Roger of Howden.[82] The term implies that he had lost an eye in an attempted blinding, an all too likely possibility.[83] If Ruaidrí's appointee for the kingship of Thomond in 1175 was the Monoculus of Roger of Howden's account, then, on the evidence of Roger of Howden, he had been slain and the grant of Thomond to Philip de Braose in 1177 may have been justified by the fact that Ruaidrí's appointee had been obliged to yield the kingship to Domnall Mór Ua Briain, whose burning of the city of Limerick in 1176 could certainly be construed as a breach of fealty.

It is more difficult, but not impossible, to reconcile the invasion of Ulaid by John de Courcy in February 1177 with the continued observance of the treaty of Windsor. Ulaid fell within the lordship assigned to Ruaidrí Ua Conchobair by the terms of the treaty. According to the 'Song of Dermot', Henry had made a speculative grant of Ulaid to John de Courcy during his expedition to Ireland in 1171–2.[84] There is, however, no independent evidence that John de Courcy had accom-

---

[80] Sadb, daughter of Donnchad Mac Gilla Pátraic, king of Osraige, was the mother of Domnall Mór Ua Briain: Dobbs, ibid. 233.

[81] *Ann. Inisf.* 1168. 1; *Ann. Tig.*, *AFM*.

[82] Gerald of Wales referred to Tigernán Ua Ruairc, king of Bréifne (d. 1171), as *monoculus*: Giraldus, *Expugnatio*, 90, 112, 114. Roger of Howden cannot have borrowed this term from Gerald, since Gerald did not write the *Expugnatio* until after 1183, whereas Roger was writing up the *Gesta* in diarial form at this period.

[83] In 1168 Domnall Mór Ua Briain blinded his own brother, Brian: *Ann. Inisf.* 1168. 6. In 1175 Diarmait, son of Tadc Ua Briain, and Mathgamain, son of Toirdelbach Ua Briain, were blinded by Domnall Mór Ua Briain: *Ann. Tig.* Ruaidrí's deposition of Domnall Mór Ua Briain and the installation of the son of Muirchertach Ua Briain occurred after these blindings: ibid.

[84] *Song of Dermot*, ll. 2300–34.

panied Henry to Ireland,[85] and such a grant seems inconsistent with Henry's immediate concerns and general policy towards the Irish kings from beyond Leinster and Mide in 1171–2. When, after Strongbow's death in April 1176, William fitz Audelin was sent as royal administrator to Ireland, John de Courcy was among his entourage. In February 1177 de Courcy marched from Dublin to Ulaid with a small band of Anglo-Norman soldiers, and some Irish, and took over the lordship of Ulaid.[86] Did Henry II authorize or condone John de Courcy's expedition into Ulaid in 1177? The evidence of the court chronicler, Roger of Howden, seems decisive that in marching to Ulaid in February 1177 John de Courcy acted 'contra prohibitionem Willelmi filii Aldelmi, qui ei praefuerat'.[87]

What was Ruaidrí Ua Conchobair's reaction, as the ostensible overlord of Ulaid, to de Courcy's action? Did Henry II initially contemplate that John de Courcy would be subject to Ruaidrí's overlordship? Unlike Strongbow, or Hugh de Lacy, John de Courcy held very little land in Henry's dominions and would therefore have constituted less of a threat to Henry. It is curious that the detailed provisions of the council of Oxford in May 1177, as reported by Roger of Howden, made no mention of Ulaid, or of John de Courcy. The Annals of Tigernach alone recorded that, although de Courcy initially captured the town of Downpatrick, he subsequently suffered a defeat at the hands of the Irish and was taken prisoner. The fact that this was recorded in the Annals of Tigernach, the house chronicle of the Connacht royal dynasty at this period, suggests that Ruaidrí Ua Conchobair had some knowledge of, and was interested in, that occurrence in Ulaid. It is possible that John de Courcy was still in captivity at the time of the council of Oxford in May 1177, that Henry II thought that he would be dealt with satisfactorily by the Irish, and that this explains the lack of any reference to Ulaid in the provisions made at Oxford for the administration of the Angevin lordship in Ireland.

[85] He is a notable absentee from the witness lists of charters granted by Henry while in Ireland: see below, ch. 8 n. 44.

[86] Giraldus, *Expugnatio*, 174–83.

[87] Roger of Howden, *Gesta*, i. 137, but omitted in *Chronica*, ii. 120. Cf. 'De Iohanne de Curci qui primus Ultoniam citra maioris auctoritatem invasit': Giraldus, *Expugnatio*, 16–17, also 176–7. *NHI* ii. 115 incorrectly has Hugh de Lacy rather than fitz Audelin as *custos* of Dublin in February 1177.

Certainly the speculative grants of Thomond and Desmond to Anglo-Norman feudatories, and John de Courcy's subsequent successful take-over of Ulaid in 1177, did not terminate relations between Henry II and Ruaidrí Ua Conchobair, for the two kings were still engaged in negotiations in 1180. Early in 1180 Laurence (Lorcán Ua Tuathail), archbishop of Dublin, and native papal legate in Ireland since his return from the third Lateran council of 1179, undertook an embassy to Henry on behalf of Ruaidrí.[88] The early thirteenth-century life of Laurence attributed his mission to a sudden and violent quarrel which had broken out between Henry and the king of Connacht.[89] Roger of Howden referred to Laurence's negotiations with Henry in 1180, recording that a son of the king of Connacht accompanied the archbishop as a pledge of Ruaidrí's good faith to pay tribute owing to Henry.[90] An entry on the pipe roll of 1181–2 confirms that the son of the king of Connacht was in England in that year.[91]

On his return from the Lateran council Laurence, in his capacity as native papal legate, had held a synod at Clonfert in

[88] Roger of Howden, s.a. 1179, recorded that an Irish deputation was received by Henry II, which complained of unjust and violent treatment at the hands of Henry's officials in Ireland, and that, as a result, Hugh de Lacy and William fitz Audelin were removed from office, notwithstanding that 'both men had enjoyed the king's trust for a long time: *Gesta*, i. 221; omitted in the *Chronica*. Whether Roger's account of an Irish mission to Henry in 1179 is accurate, and if so, whether Ruaidrí Ua Conchobair was involved, is unknown. Archbishop Laurence, Cadla Ua Dubthaig, archbishop of Tuam, Brictius, bishop of Limerick, and some other Irish bishops, travelled through England in 1179 on their way to the third Lateran council: Roger of Howden, *Gesta*, i. 221; *Chronica*, ii. 171; corroborated by pipe roll entries, where Cadla occurs as 'archbishop of Connacht': *Pipe roll 25 Henry II*, 35, 120, 124. It is possible that these could have made complaints about Henry's officials in Ireland. In 1181 Hugh de Lacy was recalled and replaced for a short period by John de Lacy, constable of Chester, and Richard of the Peak: *Gesta*, i. 270; *Chronica*, ii. 253–4. The possibility has been overlooked that Hugh de Lacy may have been recalled from Ireland in 1179, reinstated, and recalled again in 1181. Cf. *NHI* ix. 470.

[89] Plummer, 'Vie et miracles de S. Laurent', 152.

[90] *Gesta*, i. 270; *Chronica*, ii. 253. Inserted retrospectively into the year 1181, it stands after the narrative of events of January 1181, and is followed immediately by an account of the steps taken by Henry II to seize the temporalities of the see of Dublin once news had reached him of Laurence's death at Eu on 14 November 1180.

[91] *Pipe roll 28 Henry II*, 139, by writ of Ranulf de Glanville, who was overseeing Irish affairs. According to Laurence's *vita* he was accompanied by his nephew: Plummer, 'Vie et miracles de S. Laurent', 152. It is unlikely, although not impossible, that a son of the king of Connacht could have been a nephew of Laurence by some union of which there is no surviving record.

the autumn of 1179.[92] Laurence's contact with Ruaidrí around that time may be inferred from the translation of Ruaidrí's nephew Tommaltach Ua Conchobair, bishop of Elphin, to the see of Armagh early in 1180.[93] That translation implies that Ruaidrí still regarded himself as overlord of those parts of Ireland not under Angevin lordship; that he was, in effect, claiming a right of presentation as high-king to the see of Armagh.[94] It was shortly after the installation of Tommaltach as archbishop of Armagh that Laurence travelled to England to negotiate on behalf of Ruaidrí Ua Conchobair, accompanied by the latter's son. Discussions between Laurence and Henry took place, but they were inconclusive. Henry left for Normandy on 15 April, and Laurence, who was forbidden by Henry to return to Ireland before peace had been concluded, was obliged to remain in England. Late in October, or early November, Laurence crossed from Dover to Wissant near Boulogne. He was at Eu on 10 November, already suffering from a fever. On 11 November he sent a cleric, David, who was also the tutor of Ruaidrí Ua Conchobair's son, to Henry's court, where he handed over the youth as a hostage. On 13 November David returned to Laurence at Eu with the news that peace had been concluded with Henry. Laurence died in the monastery of Eu on 14 November 1180.[95]

Also in 1180 the Roman subdeacon, Alexis, was appointed papal legate for Scotland, Ireland, and the Isles.[96] The main purpose of Alexis's legation was to settle a disputed election to the see of St Andrews, but the inclusion of Ireland in his legation was more than a geographical formality.[97] That Alexis had

---

[92] *Ann. Clon.* 1170 (*recte* 1179). Cf. A. Gwynn, 'Tomaltach Ua Conchobair, coarb of Patrick (1181–1201)', *Seanchas Ardmhacha*, 8 (1975–7), 231–74 (at 238–9).

[93] Ibid.

[94] In a charter to the Augustinian priory of Ferns, granted between 1162 and 1166, Diarmait Mac Murchada, king of Leinster, claimed a right of assent to the election of candidates for the abbacy: Dugdale, *Monasticon Anglicanum*, vi. 2, 1141. In 1201 Pope Innocent III granted to the king of Connacht, probably at his request, the privilege that his assent should be sought in ecclesiastical elections, while at the same time warning the king that he must not abuse the privilege; he also wrote to the clergy of Connacht ordering them not to refuse a right of assent to the king: Sheehy, *Pontificia Hib.* i, nos. 47, 48.

[95] Plummer, 'Vie et miracles de S. Laurent', 152–3.

[96] M. T. Flanagan, 'Hiberno-papal relations', 61–3.

[97] From 1176 Ireland was joined to Scotland, the Isles, and the Isle of Man for the purpose of papal legatine missions: ibid. 59, 68 n. 17.

been briefed on Ireland is revealed in a judgement that he delivered in settlement of a dispute between the archbishop of York and the canons of Guisborough, in which he justified his authority to judge a case in England, although outside the area of his legation, because he was allowed jurisdiction there 'quamdiu moram ibi fecerimus pro pace reformanda inter illustrem regem Angliae et Ybernienses'.[98] The description of his role as mediator between the Irish and Henry II as 'pro pace reformanda' suggests that it may have been connected with the dispute between Henry and Ruaidrí Ua Conchobair, which Archbishop Laurence was attempting to resolve. The phrase 'pacem reformare' was used in the twelfth century to describe the restoration of the king's peace, particularly in the case of subjects who had broken fealty.[99] What it implies is that in 1180 the Irish, or some of the Irish, were considered to have broken faith with Henry II. Alexis was empowered to negotiate a restoration of relations. The involvement of the legate Alexis must have resulted from a petition made to the pope either by the Irish party, more particularly perhaps Archbishop Laurence, or by Henry II. In 1172 Pope Alexander III had exhorted the Irish kings to remain faithful to the oaths of loyalty which they had sworn to Henry, and the pope had empowered the Irish bishops to excommunicate those who violated their oaths. It could equally have been Henry who appealed to the pope for the application of this sanction.

The fact that Archbishop Laurence's burial at Eu was presided over by Alexis, who arrived there shortly after Laurence's death,[100] suggests that Alexis was involved in breaking the apparent impasse in negotiations between Laurence and Henry. The fate of Ruaidrí's son, who was given as a hostage to Henry, is unknown thereafter. The fact that Ruaidrí and Henry

---

[98] W. Holtzmann, *Papsturkunden in England*, i (Abhandlungen der Gesellschaft der Wissenschaften in Göttingen, phil.-hist. Klasse, 2nd ser., 25, 1930–1), 449–50.

[99] Magna Carta was a 'pacis reformatio', and Pope Innocent III was involved 'ad reformandam concordiam' during his negotiations between King John and the barons in 1215: *Selected letters of Pope Innocent III concerning England, 1198–1216*, ed. C. R. Cheney and W. H. Semple (London, 1953), nos. 75, 82. After a settlement had been reached, King John wrote to William, earl of Salisbury, that 'pax hoc modo reformata est inter nos et barones nostros': *Rot. litt. claus., 1204–24*, 215a. Cf. also Giraldus, *Expugnatio*, 34 l. 62, 50–1.

[100] Plummer, 'Vie et miracles de S. Laurent', 252.

were still negotiating tribute in 1180 suggests that the treaty of Windsor was in some respects still operable. It is possible that Henry had demanded very little of Ruaidrí in the period between 1175 and 1180 and that it was the installation of Tommaltach Ua Conchobair as archbishop of Armagh, with its obvious implication that Ruaidrí was claiming a right of presentation as high-king to the see of Armagh, which occasioned Henry's anger with Ruaidrí in 1180. On the other hand, Conchobar mac Meic Con Caille (*c.*1174–5) and Gilla in Choimded Ua Caráin (*c.*1175–80) had each been elected and consecrated archbishops of Armagh without any apparent reaction from Henry.[101]

Certainly, Ruaidrí Ua Conchobair was still anxious to negotiate with Henry II in 1180. The possibility has to be borne in mind that the quarrel between Ruaidrí and Henry in 1180 may have resulted from Ruaidrí's rather than Henry's dissatisfaction with the operation of the treaty of Windsor. No doubt Henry might have argued in 1180 that Ruaidrí had not fulfilled the role assigned to him in the treaty, but it might also be the case that Ruaidrí had sought military aid from Henry which was not forthcoming.

In August 1184, when John was sixteen, he was knighted by Henry II, and preparations were set in train for an expedition to Ireland by John to assume his Irish lordship in person. The timing of Henry's decision has been attributed by W. L. Warren to the abdication of Ruaidrí Ua Conchobair in favour of his son from the kingship of Connacht in 1183, and Ruaidrí's retirement into the monastery of Cong.[102] Robin Frame, by contrast, has stressed Henry's disquiet with the growing power of Hugh de Lacy.[103] A close reading of Gerald of Wales, including the order and chapter-headings of his narrative, suggests that in 1184 Henry was indeed preoccupied in the first instance with Hugh de Lacy's position in Ireland[104] rather than a change in the kingship of Connacht, although the two may have been linked. William of Newburgh recorded a rumour that Hugh de Lacy aspired to the kingship of Ireland, and had even made so

---

[101] *NHI* ix. 268.
[102] Warren, 'John in Ireland, 1185', 14.
[103] Frame, *Colonial Ire.* 20.
[104] Giraldus, *Expugnatio*, 16–19, 192–9, 226–9.

bold as to procure a crown for himself; Gerald of Wales
mentioned rumours of Hugh's disloyalty to Henry, and Roger
of Howden that Hugh had married a daughter of Ruaidrí Ua
Conchobair without Henry's permission.[105] There appear to
have been fears in England that Hugh de Lacy aspired to
succeed Ruaidrí as king of Connacht and overlord of the Irish
kings. It is probable that Ruaidrí for his part concluded a
marriage alliance with Hugh de Lacy in order to strengthen his
own position within Connacht, possibly to counter opposition
from some of his sons and to procure from Hugh de Lacy
military aid which was not forthcoming from Henry II;
although military aid may have been his prime motivation, it is
just conceivable that Ruaidrí may have contemplated offering
the succession to the kingship of Connacht to Hugh de Lacy.

Preliminary to John's expedition to Ireland, John Cumin,
archbishop of Dublin, Henry's appointee in succession to
Lorcán Ua Tuathail, was dispatched to take possession of his
new see, Hugh de Lacy was recalled, and Philip of Worcester
was appointed to take his place. One of Philip's 'very first
actions', according to Gerald of Wales, was to restore to the
royal demesne the lordship of Ua Cathasaig of Saithne which
Hugh de Lacy had appropriated, which adds weight to the
view that Hugh de Lacy's actions, not events in Connacht, were
Henry II's overriding concern.[106]

A primary purpose of curbing the activities of Hugh de Lacy
did not preclude John from establishing personal relations with
the Irish kings. It is possible that Henry intended that John
should assume direct lordship, not only over the Anglo-
Norman feudatories in Ireland, but also over the Irish. Whatever Henry's intentions may have been in that regard, they
were precluded by the disastrous failure of John's Irish expedition. Gerald of Wales stated that the kings of Limerick,
Connacht, and Cork, whom he described as 'the three
buttresses of Ireland at that time', had been prepared to proffer
submission to John, but when they received reports of unfavourable treatment from those Irish who had greeted John at
Waterford, they decided against this course of action. Accord-

---

[105] William of Newburgh, i. 239–40; Giraldus, *Expugnatio*, 190–3, 198–9; Roger of
Howden, *Gesta*, i. 270.
[106] Giraldus, *Expugnatio*, 198–9.

ing to Gerald, the Irish who had met John at Waterford, and formed such an unfavourable impression of him, removed themselves to the court of the king of Limerick.[107] If the Irish kings, as Gerald averred, 'made pacts with each other throughout the country, and those who had previously been enemies now became friends for the first time', then the treaty of Windsor may definitely be said to have been abandoned by Ruaidrí. The situation is complicated by the fact that in 1185 before John's arrival in Ireland[108] Ruaidrí Ua Conchobair re-emerged from the monastery of Cong to try to re-establish himself in the kingship of Connacht, concluded an alliance with his former enemy, Domnall Ua Briain, king of Thomond, and managed to secure a division of Connacht between himself and his son, Conchobar Máenmaige. Nothing further is known of relations between Henry II and Ruaidrí. If the treaty of Windsor, or a modified version of it, was still in observance in 1185, Ruaidrí may understandably have felt that the dispatch of John to Ireland marked Henry's abandonment of it. Whether John was to replace Henry or Ruaidrí as king designate of Ireland in 1185, either possibility had serious consequences for Ruaidrí.

In his attempt to establish himself as lord of the Anglo-Norman feudatories in Ireland, John was hardly more successful than in his dealings with the Irish kings. On the testimony of the Annals of Loch Cé, he faced opposition from Hugh de Lacy, who, as lord of Mide, was the most powerful of his vassals. John's expedition cannot be said to have seriously diminished de Lacy's standing. Of eighteen extant charters issued by John in Ireland in 1185 eight were witnessed by Hugh de Lacy, and in six of them he was styled 'constable'.[109] But John's expedition at least provides a clarification of John de Courcy's position in Ulaid. There can be no doubt that by 1185 de Courcy had acknowledged the lordship of John, for de Courcy witnessed at least two of John's charters granted while

---

[107] Ibid. 236–9.
[108] Following the sequence of *ALC*.
[109] Mac Niocaill, *Na Buirgéisí*, i. 77; *Chartul. St Mary's, Dublin*, i. 85, 87; Mac Niocaill, 'Charters of John', 285; *Ormond deeds, 1350–1413*, no. 426; *Black Book of Limerick*, ed. J. Mac Caffrey (Dublin, 1907), 103; *Cal. charter rolls*, i. 251; *Cal. pat. rolls, 1334–8*, 402; Dugdale, *Monasticon Anglicanum*, vi. 2, 1136. Since four of the six charters in which Hugh was styled constable relate to Dublin, the probability is that his constableship was associated with that city.

in Ireland.[110] The area of direct Angevin lordship had thereby been extended to include Ulaid, which had been within the jurisdiction assigned to Ruaidrí Ua Conchobair by the treaty of Windsor. This in turn made the subjection of Airgialla, which lay between Anglo-Norman Mide and Ulaid, to Angevin lordship inevitable, although grants to Anglo-Norman feudatories were not made in Airgialla until after Henry II's death in 1189.[111] While John's grant of a portion of the kingdom of Thomond jointly to Ranulf de Glanville and Theobald Walter in 1185,[112] strictly speaking, did not constitute a new grant, since in 1177 Thomond had been granted by Henry II to Philip de Braose, who, however, had failed in his attempt to take possession of it, the absorption of Ulaid into the area of direct Angevin lordship further reduced the area which had been assigned to the overlordship of Ruaidrí Ua Conchobair by the treaty of Windsor.

Historians, depending solely on Gerald of Wales's *Expugnatio*, and ignoring contradictory evidence from his *De rebus a se gestis*, have assumed that de Courcy was appointed justiciar by John before he left Ireland in 1185 and that he held that office until about 1192, when William Petit is found acting as John's agent in Ireland.[113] Gerald recounted that

Our most excellent prince (*summus princeps*) then decided to prove the worth of men who were veterans and had long experience in the conquest of that island, and entrusted the overall administration to John de Courcy. Under his rule the kingdom immediately began to enjoy a greater measure of tranquillity due to his outstanding courage and experience as a soldier. For he immediately made a vigorous thrust in the most remote parts of the country, the regions of Cork and Connacht, and did not allow the garrison to become indolent through inactivity.[114]

[110] *Ormond deeds, 1350–1413*, no. 426; Dugdale, *Monasticon Anglicanum*, vi, 2. 1136.

[111] *Ormond deeds, 1172–1350*, no. 863. Murchad Ua Cerbaill, king of Airgialla, died in 1189: *AFM*.

[112] *Ormond deeds, 1350–1413*, no. 426.

[113] *NHI* ix. 469–70, and the previous lists of chief governors of Ireland cited there.

[114] Giraldus, *Expugnatio*, 240–1. The first preface of the *Expugnatio* was dedicated to Richard, 'illustrious count of Poitou'. It is presumed to date from 1189, after the death of Henry II and before the coronation of Richard. The narrative towards the end of the second *distinctio* is sketchy. Gerald himself acknowledged in his second preface the inequality of the earlier and later parts of the *distinctio*: ibid., pp. xxxi–xxxii. He stated that he was leaving the narrative of John's deeds after 1185 'and those of his followers' to

The passage occurs towards the end of the second book and follows a description of John's expedition to Ireland and the reasons for the Anglo-Norman lack of success in conquering Ireland up to the time when Gerald was writing. To this point Gerald had referred to John as 'filius regis', whereas de Courcy is stated to have been appointed justiciar by the 'summus princeps'. De Courcy is known to have been appointed justiciar by Richard I in 1194, when John's lands were sequestrated temporarily by Richard during the rebellion of John against his brother.[115] 'Summus princeps' would be a more apposite designation of Richard, in his capacity as head of the Angevin dominions, than John in 1185, especially following immediately as it does upon Gerald's criticisms of John, 'filius regis'. Furthermore, Gerald stated that, after his appointment, de Courcy undertook expeditions into Cork and Connacht. This sequence of campaigns accords with de Courcy's justiciarship under Richard I. In 1195 the Annals of Loch Cé recorded a campaign by John de Courcy into Leinster and Munster followed by an expedition into Connacht. By contrast, there is no record in the annals between 1185 and 1192 of de Courcy campaigning first in Cork and then in Connacht. In his *De rebus a se gestis* Gerald recounted that, when John left Ireland in 1185, Bertram de Verdon, 'senescallus Hiberniae', remained behind, as did Gerald himself.[116] Since there cannot have been both a seneschal and a justiciar of Ireland simultaneously, this is conclusive evidence that John de Courcy was not appointed justiciar by John prior to his departure in 1185.

In 1188 John de Courcy led a force of Anglo-Normans into Connacht, which Orpen may well have been correct in thinking was connected with an attempt to restore Ruaidrí Ua Conchobair to the full kingship of Connacht and to oust his

---

other writers: ibid. 18–19, 234–6. There are no signs of the second *distinctio* having been changed despite its very fragmentary nature, and despite Gerald's usual propensity for altering his writings.

[115] *Reg. St Thomas, Dublin*, 383; *Chartul. St Mary's, Dublin*, i. 125, ii. 4, 12, 21; *Hist. and mun. doc. Ire.* 56; E. St J. Brooks, 'A charter of John de Courcy to the abbey of Navan', *RSAI Jn.* 63 (1933), 38–45. The Navan charter is stated to have been granted 'de communi consilio domini regis in Hybernia'. The dating clause 'fifth Henry' refers to the inspeximus of Henry IV and was not, as Brooks thought, part of de Courcy's text referring to Henry II.

[116] *Gir. Camb. op.* i. 65. For the title *senescallus* see below, pp. 289–91, 303.

son, Conchobar Máenmaige.[117] It has been assumed that de Courcy was acting in Connacht in 1188 as justiciar appointed by John. It is more likely that he and his men were hired as mercenaries by a faction within the Ua Conchobair royal dynasty, the choice of de Courcy being determined by the recent death of Hugh de Lacy.[118] De Courcy's expedition to Connacht in 1188 cannot be viewed, therefore, as an episode in relations between the king of Connacht and the Angevin lord of Ireland.

Reviewing Henry II's relations with Ruaidrí Ua Conchobair, king of Connacht, there is no reason to dispute J. F. O'Doherty's assessment that 'Henry sincerely hoped and intended that the treaty of Windsor would work', as against J. F. Lydon's view that 'as an attempt to delimit a frontier in Ireland the treaty of Windsor was bound to be a failure, even if Henry II had been genuine in his attempts, and sufficiently interested, to uphold it—a matter of considerable doubt'.[119] Henry's dealings with the Irish kings, which reveal a sympathetic understanding of Irish practices, are less surprising when it is borne in mind that his relationship as duke of Normandy with the king of France, or as king of England with the rulers of Wales and Scotland, was characterized by varieties and degrees of subjection. In his relations with the Welsh and Scottish rulers Henry was content with an insubstantial interpretation of the seigneurial link. This was true also of the initiation of relations with the Irish kings in 1171–2 and in the treaty of Windsor. The future development of those relations depended

---

[117] *AU, ALC, AFM* 1188; Orpen, *Normans*, ii. 115–17, 179–81. In ch. 35, Gerald of Wales recorded separately from his subsequent account of John de Courcy's campaigns as justiciar into Munster and Connacht that 'thirteen noble knights were killed while returning from Connacht under John de Courcy': Giraldus, *Expugnatio*, 234, 242. This referred to the 1188 expedition to Connacht.

[118] In 1177 Murchad son of Ruaidrí Ua Conchobair had brought Miles de Cogan into Connacht 'for evil against his father': *Ann. Tig., AU, ALC, AFM*; cf. Giraldus, *Expugnatio*, 182–3. While Gerald's narrative may be said to suggest that de Cogan's incursion into Connacht preceded the council of Oxford in May 1177, the Annals of Tigernach indicate that it post-dated Hugh de Lacy's appointment at Oxford as *custos* of Dublin. In 1189 Conchobar Máenmaige was described by *AFM* as 'king of Connacht, both English and Irish'. Orpen, *Normans*, ii. 182, was almost certainly correct in assuming that there were Anglo-Norman mercenaries employed, and perhaps even settled, in Connacht, by members of the Ua Conchobair family before any formal grant in Connacht was made by the Angevin overlord.

[119] O'Doherty, 'St Laurence O'Toole', *IER* 51 (1938), 131; J. F. Lydon, 'The problem of the frontier in medieval Ireland', *Topic*, 13 (1967), 5–22.

on the degree of political authority and force which each party might invest in the relationship. Ruaidrí Ua Conchobair failed to exercise effectively the overlordship assigned to him by the treaty of Windsor. His failure may be contrasted with the success of the Welsh rulers, Rhys ap Gruffydd of Deheubarth and Dafydd ap Owain of Gwynedd, who managed to exercise and intensify their control over the overlordships of North and South Wales assigned to them by Henry II in 1177.[120]

Why did Ruaidrí Ua Conchobair not derive a like advantage from the lordship deputed to him by Henry II? It could be argued that Henry had made it possible for Ruaidrí to exercise a more effective overlordship of a more limited area of Ireland by taking over the lordships of Leinster and Mide. Ruaidrí is invariably depicted as an ineffectual high-king, who was short-sighted in his response to Anglo-Norman intervention in Ireland. There is a marked contrast between the perception of Ruaidrí's reign and that of his father, Toirdelbach. No detailed analyses of the careers of these two kings, or of internal politics, or the nature of control which they exercised in twelfth-century Connacht have been undertaken. Toirdelbach's high standing derives in large part from the identification of a series of defensive structures which he built around Connacht and his strategic diversion of the river Suck.[121] Ruaidrí's expulsion of Diarmait Mac Murchada, had it not resulted in Anglo-Norman intervention in Ireland, would undoubtedly be used by Irish historians as an illustration of his power and resources. His high-kingship certainly had an auspicious beginning, with his negotiation of the transfer of allegiance of the city of Dublin, the celebration of the feast of Tailtiu in 1166, his presiding over the synod of Athboy in 1167, and his endowment in 1169 of a lectureship at Armagh for the education of Irish and Scottish students. Ruaidrí's negotiation of the treaty of Windsor in 1175[122] and the installation of his nephew Tommaltach in the

[120] For an assessment of Rhys's career see Davies, *Conquest*, 217–27.
[121] Ó Corráin, *Ireland before the Normans*, 150–62; *NHI* ii. 33–4; J. Ryan, *Toirdelbach O Conchobair* (Dublin, 1966). Jefferies, 'Desmond', 81–99, argues persuasively for the collapse of Toirdelbach Ua Conchobair's high-kingship in 1133.
[122] Cf. 'Ruaidrí Ua Conchobair, a weak ruler, was high-king in name, unchallenged largely in default of a strong opponent': *NHI* ii. 91; contrast on the treaty of Windsor: 'Ruaidrí thus emerges unexpectedly as a man of sophisticated judgement and diplomatic foresight, qualities notably absent hitherto in his career': ibid. 107.

see of Armagh in 1180 were also not inconsiderable achievements. It is unfortunate that the Annals of Tigernach, the
house chronicle of the Ua Conchobair family, terminate at
1177, that the (Connacht) Annals of Boyle are not more
detailed, and that the Annals of Connacht do not begin until
1224. A more informed assessment of Ruaidrí Ua Conchobair
and his immediate successors, and in particular their exploitation of Anglo-Norman mercenaries within Connacht, must
await more detailed investigation of twelfth-century Connacht,
but Anglo-Norman intervention in Ireland should not be
allowed to colour unduly the interpretation of Ruaidrí's reign.

Some general remarks may, however, be ventured. The
methods by which twelfth-century Irish kings sought to extend
their authority may have been too ambitious for the resources
at their disposal. The Capetian kings of France had recognized
the limitations of their resources and relied upon a policy of
'concentric concentration' of lordships by their major vassals,
actively fostering the bond between lord and vassal at all levels
of society and then, as supreme lords, invoking the strength of
that same bond over the greatest lordships in their kingdom.
By contrast, twelfth-century Irish high-kings and provincial
kings sought to dismantle the lordships of their political rivals,
to abolish mediate lordships and forge direct links with the
clients of their subordinates.[123] This made the exercise of lordship more unwieldy. By encouraging the insubordination of
their political rivals' clients, overkings may also have unwittingly engendered disrespect for the bond between lord and
client, which ultimately worked to their disadvantage. Anglo-
Norman intervention in Ireland occurred at a time when the
dismantling of rival lordships was being actively pursued by
the most powerful Irish kings, but before those kings had had
the opportunity to replace effectively with their own authority

[123] Many instances could be given. In 1113 Domnall Mac Lochlainn, king of Cenél
nEógain, dismantled the overlordship of the kings of Ulaid east of the Bann and
arrogated to himself direct lordship of Uí Echach and Dál nAraide: *AFM*. The mesne
kingship of Brega in eastern Mide was destroyed by the Clann Colmáin overkings of
Mide, who in turn suffered the arrogation of lordship of portions of the overkingdom of
Mide by Toirdelbach Ua Conchobair and Ruaidrí Ua Conchobair as high-kings; that
Ruaidrí acted as surety for the king of Delbna against the king of Mide is but one illustration of his attempts to diminish the lordship of the kings of Mide: see above, p. 240.
In 1161 Ruaidrí Ua Conchobair attempted to detach Uí Failge and Uí Fáeláin from the
provincial kingship of Leinster: *Ann. Tig.*

the lordships which they had sought to eliminate. The provincial kingdom of Leinster had received less attention from the twelfth-century contenders for the high-kingship than either Mide or Munster. Diarmait Mac Murchada, in particular, had enjoyed a long reign (1126/a. 1132–1166) and a relatively free hand to consolidate a strong lordship. It was to prevent the permanent destruction of his considerable achievements by Ruaidrí Ua Conchobair that Diarmait sought Anglo-Norman help in 1166. The 'Song of Dermot' placed great emphasis on loyalty and disloyalty to Diarmait Mac Murchada by a number of his vassals.[124] This may reflect the social ethos of the Anglo-Norman author, but it may also be that it was a genuine concern of Diarmait himself, and more broadly reflects twelfth-century Irish preoccupations. It is noteworthy that, although the twelfth-century annals record numerous revolts by political subordinates against their superiors, there is also an increasing concern on the part of the annalists to explain those revolts as due to transgressions or inadequacies on the part of the over-king.

Whatever causes for the failure of Ruaidrí Ua Conchobair's kingship may be attributed to the pre-Norman Irish polity, part of the responsibility for the collapse of the arrangements of the treaty of Windsor must also rest with Henry II, who failed to contain his Anglo-Norman vassals within the delimited area of Angevin lordship, as the activities of Raymond le Gros and John de Courcy so graphically illustrate. Henry, not unnaturally, concentrated his efforts on intensifying Angevin lordship in his Continental dominions. The Capetian kings of France were pursuing an identical policy in the same geographical area and, as overlords of the count of Anjou, duke of Normandy, and duke of Aquitaine, they had the legal advantage. The strength of the Capetian position on the Continent was not apparent during the reign of Henry II and did not manifest itself as a real threat until the forfeiture effected by King Philip Augustus of John's Continental dominions in 1204. Even if the loss of Normandy, Anjou, and Aquitaine after 1204 caused King John to devote more attention to his Irish lordship, by 1204 the results of a half-century of inadequate

[124] *Song of Dermot*, ll. 134–212, 560–99, 837–44, 935–40, 960–3.

Angevin lordship in Ireland were already becoming too difficult to redress.

Henry II's acceptance of the submissions of the Irish kings in 1171–2 in the context of their own political institutions, which also characterized the treaty of Windsor, laid the basis for relations between the English Crown and Irish rulers which subsequent kings of England made no significant attempts to modify until the policy of surrender and regrant. The strategy, that a single Irish king would exercise a mediate lordship under the king of England in the areas over which Henry II had not asserted a direct lordship in 1171–2, did not endure, both because of the failure of Ruaidrí Ua Conchobair to exercise such a lordship effectively and to pass it on to his successors, and because of Henry's failure to confine his Anglo-Norman vassals to the delimited Angevin lordship. However, Henry's general policy, which envisaged a division of Ireland into two different spheres of lordship under the common overlordship of Henry and his successors, survived, with the modification that English overlordship of the Irish kings thereafter was asserted on an individual basis, rather than through one mediate Irish king, as Henry had attempted with Ruaidrí Ua Conchobair and the treaty of Windsor. The written indentures of submission from individual Gaelic lords which survive from the fourteenth century onwards, and which provided for a simple act of fealty to the English king as overlord, an undertaking to abide by the king's peace, and, if practicable, an agreement to render some modest form of tribute, are the lineal descendants of the acts of submission of the Irish kings to Henry II in 1171–2.[125] They are testimony to the fact that the Irish kings did not enter into a hereditary tenurial relationship with Henry, and that this was not claimed by succeeding English kings.

---

[125] Cf. the texts of submissions of the Irish kings to Richard II in 1395 in Curtis, *Rich. II in Ire.*; D. Johnston, 'Richard II and the submissions of Gaelic Ireland', *IHS* 22 (1980), 1–21.

The Lordship of Ireland within the Angevin Dominions

IN 1172 Henry II left Ireland, having asserted lordship over Leinster and Mide and reserved the cities of Dublin, Waterford, Wexford, Cork, and Limerick as royal demesne. A portion of Ireland was now claimed to be subject to the lordship of the head of the Angevin dominions. What did Henry envisage would be the relationship between his new Irish lordship and his other dominions during his lifetime and after? This question is tied up with the wider issue of the origins and nature of the Angevin dominions and of Henry's intentions for their disposition after his death.

The origins of the lands which formed the Angevin dominions of Henry II was the marriage of 1128 between Matilda, daughter and sole heir of Henry I, king of England and duke of Normandy, and Geoffrey, eldest son of Count Fulk V of Anjou. It has been argued by C. W. Hollister and T. K. Keefe that the assemblage of territories which resulted from this marriage alliance was neither planned nor envisaged by Henry I, that Henry arranged the marriage for immediate tactical reasons with no long-term strategy in mind.[1] While Hollister and Keefe's arguments in respect of Henry I's immediate intentions in negotiating the marriage between Matilda and Geoffrey in 1128 are convincing, their view that Count Fulk V or his son, Geoffrey, likewise did not entertain the notion of an Angevin empire, may be questioned. According to Hollister and Keefe, Count Geoffrey willed an eventual partition of the lands which he held at the time of his death in 1151, with Matilda's inheritance of England and Normandy going to his eldest son, Henry, the future Henry II, while his own inheritance, the counties of Anjou, Maine, and Touraine, were to go

---

[1] Hollister and Keefe, 'The making of the Angevin empire'; T. K. Keefe, 'Geoffrey Plantagenet's will and the Angevin succession', *Albion*, 6 (1974), 266–74.

to his second son, Geoffrey, after Henry became king of England. Henry, however, did not honour the terms of his father Count Geoffrey's will in his subsequent refusal to share the inheritance with his brother Geoffrey, after his accession as king of England in 1154. 'The Angevin empire had its genesis in Henry's actions and policies during the years between 1152 and 1156.'[2] The factor which determined that Henry II did not comply with his father's will for the separation of the Angevin lands from Normandy and England was, according to Hollister and Keefe, Henry II's acquisition of Aquitaine in 1152 by his marriage to Eleanor.

As Bachrach has pointed out, discussion of the origins of the Angevin empire cannot be limited to the intentions of Henry I or Henry II. Also to be taken into consideration are the views of the counts of Anjou, particularly Count Fulk V, who agreed to the marriage settlement of 1128.[3] The counts of Anjou were certainly no strangers to the notion of expanding their possessions through marriage. The idea of uniting Normandy, and possibly even England, to Anjou by marriage would not have seemed fanciful to Count Fulk, who had secured the final union of the county of Maine to Anjou by his first marriage and won himself a kingly crown by his second marriage to the daughter of the king of Jerusalem. The power and consequence of the counts of Anjou, such as it was in the twelfth century, had been built largely on the consequences of fortunate marriages. Coupled with this was a long tradition of unity of inheritance, preserved against the claims of younger brothers, which had not only maintained the integrity of Anjou but also made possible its expansion. More specifically, W. L. Warren, followed by J. Le Patourel, has raised serious doubts about Hollister and Keefe's presentation of Count Geoffrey's will, the sole evidence for which is William of Newburgh, writing in the last decade of the twelfth century. According to Le Patourel, 'Geoffrey left his lands, authority and claims, so far as they were his to leave, intact to his eldest son, Henry. He provided three important castles in Anjou for his second son, under his elder brother's suzerainty, enough, and just enough to keep him in

---

[2] Hollister and Keefe, 'The making of the Angevin empire', 21.
[3] B. S. Bachrach, 'The idea of the Angevin empire', *Albion*, 10 (1978), 293–9.

the style to which he had been accustomed.'[4] This was in accordance with a practice which in the house of Anjou went back almost to the ninth century.

The origins of the assemblage of territories of which Henry II was lord have a bearing on Henry's plans for their disposition after his death. If their agglomeration was an accident not envisaged by either Henry I or the counts of Anjou, this would lead credence to the notion that it was simply a transitory phenomenon. It is ironic that Henry II, who is considered to have overturned his father's wishes in respect of a separation of the Angevin lands from Normandy and England, should then be considered subsequently to have planned a similar partition himself. In the view of Holt and Warren, Henry did not envisage that the territories over which he ruled would continue as a unit beyond his lifetime; he planned a partition between his sons, with England, Normandy, and Anjou going to his eldest son, Henry, who was crowned king of England in 1170, Aquitaine to his son Richard, who was installed as duke in 1172. Brittany to the third son, Geoffrey, and Ireland to the fourth son, John, who was designated king of Ireland in 1177.[5] According to Holt, this was in accordance with the 'ordinary rules of feudal descent which distinguished between inherited and acquired lands'. Le Patourel has argued cogently, however, that there is a case to be made for regarding the Angevin territories as an integral political unit, that certainly more than 'rules of inheritance were involved, and that the rulers concerned took every opportunity to add to their possessions, to hold on to what they had, and to pass it all on, substantially intact, to their successors'.[6] Henry II's plans for the disposition of his territories in Le Patourel's view were very much in the Angevin tradition: Henry did not envisage a partition in the Carolingian manner, but assumed an overriding superiority of lordship in the various dominions would go to his eldest son.

---

[4] Warren, *Henry II*, 45–6, 64; J. Le Patourel, 'Angevin successions and the Angevin empire', in *Feudal empires: Norman and Plantagenet* (London, 1984), art. 9, pp. 1–17 (at p. 10). Hollister and Keefe's arguments have been accepted by J. C. Holt, 'The end of the Anglo-Norman realm', *Br. Acad. Proc.* 61 (1975), 223–65 (at 240), and J. Gillingham, *The Angevin empire* (London, 1984), 32.

[5] Warren, *Henry II*, 108–9, 206, 229–30; Holt, 'The end . . .', 240–1.

[6] Le Patourel, 'Angevin successions', 2. Cf. also his 'The Plantagenet dominions', *History*, 50 (1965), 289–308.

These arguments, which have been endorsed by John Gillingham,[7] have a bearing on the interpretation of the relationship between the lordship of Ireland and the Angevin dominions after 1172.

There is no expression of Henry II's will relating to the succession that can be attributed directly to Henry himself. Henry's idea of the succession has generally been deduced from the positions which he gave to his sons during his lifetime, and from the events of his later years, when the succession clearly was very much in the minds of contemporaries. There can be no doubt that Henry intended his sons to have rule over the lands he assigned to them during his lifetime. The question is, in what sense? Despite their various ceremonies of installation, Henry gave no authority to his sons in Normandy, Anjou, Aquitaine, or Brittany which was independent of him during his lifetime. This is evidenced by the terms of the treaty between Henry and his sons which brought the rebellion of 1173–4 to an end: his sons were to return to a feudal as well as a familial relationship with their father; all barons who had taken part in the rebellion were to return to his allegiance; all castles were to be restored to him. In support of the view that Henry envisaged an overriding superiority for his eldest son as head of the Angevin dominions after his death is the fact that in 1173, and again in 1183, he went to some lengths to make Richard, as duke of Aquitaine, perform an act of homage to the young King Henry.[8]

In regard to Henry II's plans for that part of Ireland over which he claimed lordship after his expedition of 1171–2, there is little conclusive evidence. Henry issued a number of charters during his stay in Ireland in 1171–2, and thereafter, but although he used a multiplicity of titles to indicate the variety of lordships which he exercised elsewhere, he did not assume any title to indicate his lordship in Ireland between 1172 and his designation of his son John as king of Ireland in 1177. Warren has interpreted this as an early indication that Henry did not envisage his lordship in Ireland being linked permanently to the other Angevin dominions.[9] In 1177, when Henry desig-

---

[7] Gillingham, *The Angevin empire*, 31.   [8] Ibid.
[9] W. L. Warren, 'The Normans', in P. Loughrey (ed.), *The peoples of Ireland* (Belfast, 1988), 85–97 (at 92–3).

nated John as king of Ireland, his intention, according to Roger of Howden, was that John should be crowned as such; to that end Henry petitioned Pope Alexander III for a crown for John. In the contemporaneous *Gesta* entry under 1177 there is no indication of Alexander's response, but in a later passage in the same work relating to events of 1185 Roger stated that Henry II had asked many things of Alexander III's successor, Pope Lucius III (1181–5), including a crown for John, but that the pope 'fortiter resistebat', and that when Henry received news of the death of the uncooperative Lucius and the election of Urban III (1185–7) he renewed his request and a crown was brought to England by papal legates.[10] The implication of this passage is that neither Alexander III nor his immediate successor, Lucius III, was prepared to give Henry a crown for Ireland. However, in the *Chronica*, an abridged version of the *Gesta* written up some time after 1192, it is stated that John was declared king in Ireland in 1177 'concessione et confirmatione Alexandri summi pontificis', although this is implicitly contradicted by the subsequent inclusion in the *Chronica* under 1185 of the entry from the *Gesta* about the uncooperativeness of Lucius III and the compliance of Urban III.[11] The earlier and more detailed account of the *Gesta*, which implied an unfavourable response from Alexander III, would appear to be more accurate than the abridged version of the *Chronica*. Neither Pope Alexander III nor Lucius III seems to have been willing to grant Henry a crown for John.

Henry II's decision to petition the papacy in 1177 for a crown for John as king of Ireland must have been occasioned by the notion that the pope had sovereignty over islands, a claim which derived from the so-called Donation of Constantine and was embodied in the papal bull *Laudabiliter*. It is difficult to discern what Henry thought of *Laudabiliter* when it was produced about 1155–6, or whether it entered into his preparations for his expedition to Ireland in 1171–2. There is no evidence that Henry exploited the text of *Laudabiliter* during his expedition to Ireland in 1171–2, although, given that his relations with the papacy could not have been on a worse footing after the recent murder of Thomas Becket, this is

[10] Roger of Howden, *Gesta*, i. 161, 339.
[11] Roger of Howden, *Chronica*, ii. 133, contradicted 306–7.

perhaps not surprising. Henry's subsequent decision to involve the papacy in sanctioning John's assumption of the kingship of Ireland in 1177 may have resulted from the favourable reception which he had received from the Irish episcopate during his expedition in 1171–2. The Irish bishops appear to have taken the initiative in suggesting that letters be sent to Pope Alexander III, informing him of the English king's intervention in Ireland and the possibilities it might afford for the furtherance of reform of the Irish Church. Henry may have taken his cue from them in realizing the propaganda value of papal support for Angevin lordship in Ireland. According to Gerald of Wales, following the synod of Cashel in 1172, Henry sent messengers to the papal curia with letters from the Irish bishops outlining Irish abuses of canon law, and obtained, in return, a confirmation from Pope Alexander III of *Laudabiliter*.[12] Three authentic letters from Pope Alexander III, addressed respectively to the Irish bishops, to Henry II, and to the Irish kings, support Gerald's account of the synod of Cashel.[13] However, the text of a letter to Henry, which Gerald cited as Pope Alexander III's confirmation of *Laudabiliter*, is indubitably a forgery. Gerald asserted that *Laudabiliter* and the text of the alleged privilege of Alexander III, both of which he included in his *Expugnatio Hibernica*, were proclaimed at a synod at Waterford by William fitz Audelin and Nicholas, prior of Wallingford.[14] Gerald's account of this event occurs in his narrative after Strongbow's return from Normandy to Ireland in 1173 and before the taking of Limerick in 1175. William fitz Audelin arrived in Ireland before Strongbow's departure for Normandy in 1173. He is not otherwise attested in Ireland after Strongbow's return in the autumn of 1173 and before the Anglo-Norman expedition to Limerick in 1175, although it is conceivable that he may have been in Ireland during that period to administer the royal demesne of Waterford, or to negotiate the treaty of Windsor. If Gerald's account of the proclamation of *Laudabiliter* by William fitz Audelin at Waterford between 1173 and 1175 is trustworthy, this suggests that Henry II already at that time may have been contemplating an appeal to the papacy for a

---

[12] Giraldus, *Expugnatio*, 142–7.
[13] Sheehy, *Pontificia Hib.* i, nos. 5–7.
[14] Giraldus, *Expugnatio*, 142–3.

crown for Ireland. It might serve to explain why he himself did not assume a title to indicate his lordship in Ireland between 1172 and 1177.

The fact that Henry II wished his son John to assume the title king of Ireland in 1177 has been interpreted as further evidence that Henry envisaged the separation of Ireland from the rest of the Angevin dominions; it was only the genealogical accident that John, lord of Ireland, became king of England in 1199 which ensured that Ireland remained linked to the English crown.[15] This is open to question. The permanent separation of the lordship of Ireland from the rest of the Angevin dominions would surely have created the very situation which Henry had worked to avoid in Ireland in 1171–2, namely that those Anglo-Normans who had acquired lands there, and who also held lands in England, Normandy, and elsewhere, might have been faced with a conflict of lordship, or, worse still, a lack of effective lordship in Ireland, given that the high-king, Ruaidrí Ua Conchobair, had failed signally to assert control over Strongbow after Diarmait Mac Murchada's death in 1171. When Henry II designated John as king of Ireland in 1177 he was already an important landholder, who had been assigned a castle and lordship in each part of the young King Henry's inheritance. The earldom of Cornwall had been set aside for him, and he had been betrothed to Isabella, daughter and heiress of the earl of Gloucester.[16] It is more likely that Henry II envisaged that John, even as a crowned king of Ireland, would be under the superior lordship of the head of the Angevin dominions. This is strongly implied by Roger of Howden, who recorded that it was Henry's expressed intention at the council of Oxford that Ireland should be subjected to him and to his son John, 'ad subjiciendam eam [Ireland] sibi et Johanni filio suo, cui eam concesserat', that is, John was not to be independent of his father.[17] The young Henry was crowned king of England in 1170, and yet remained subject to his father King Henry's lordship until his death in 1183. Of course John was still a child in 1177, but Henry may have intended that during his lifetime Ireland was to be subjected to John as its king

[15] Warren, *Henry II*, 206.
[16] W. L. Warren, *King John* (2nd edn., London, 1978), 30.
[17] Roger of Howden, *Gesta*, i. 161.

(over Irish and settlers alike) while John was to be subjected to him. Although Henry was prepared to partition his dominions among his sons, there is little doubt that he himself maintained an overriding superiority during his lifetime. He may have envisaged that reservation being passed on to, and exercised by, his eldest son after his death, that John, even as a crowned 'king of Ireland', would remain subordinate to the head of the Angevin dominions. In the event, this is what happened after Henry II's death in 1189.

That Henry exercised an overriding lordship over John after his personal assumption of the lordship of Ireland in 1185 is suggested by the fact that it was Henry who, on his death-bed in 1189, gave Isabella, heiress of Leinster, to William Marshal in marriage.[18] Admittedly she was also heiress of Strigoil, but this surely highlights the difficulties which would have been created by the separation of the Angevin lordship in Ireland from the rest of the Angevin dominions. It could be argued that Henry's continued exercise of an overriding lordship in Ireland after John's assumption of the lordship of Ireland in 1185 was a result of the failure of John's expedition, rather than the continuance of a policy for the lordship of Ireland which Henry had intended previously. While in Ireland in 1185, and thereafter between 1185 and his father's death in 1189, John gave grants of land in the royal demesnes of Waterford and Dublin without explicit reference to his father. In confirming his father's charter to the city of Dublin, he described it as 'civitatem meam', and the citizens were to hold 'de me et heredibus meis'.[19] His charter granting to Theobald Walter and Ranulf de Glanville five and a half cantreds of land in the kingdom of Limerick reserved 'crosses and donations of bishoprics and abbeys and dignities which belong to the royal crown which I have retained to myself'.[20] A charter of confirmation to William son of Maurice fitz Gerald in 1185 excepted 'placitis et querelis que ad coronam regiam pertinent que ad opus meum retinui'.[21] In these charters John claimed that the rights of the Crown were his rights. On the other hand,

---

[18] *Histoire de Guillaume le Maréchal*, ll. 8303.
[19] Mac Niocaill, *Na Buirgéisí*, i. 77.
[20] *Ormond deeds, 1350–1413*, no. 426.
[21] *Gormanston reg.* 145, 193.

John's grant of the lordship of Arklow to Theobald between 1185 and 1189 is stated to have been given 'de voluntate et assensu domini regis Henrici patris mei'.[22] This suggests that John acknowledged the superior lordship of his father.

Henry's request to the pope for a crown for John in 1177 may have been designed to facilitate John's assertion of lordship over the Irish kings rather than the Anglo-Normans. In 1171–2 the Irish kings had submitted readily to Henry, 'son of the Empress', as a superior king.[23] It may be because the crown was intended primarily to advance John's lordship over the Irish kings that Henry did not proceed with plans for John's coronation after his return from Ireland in 1185, even though papal legates eventually arrived in England on 24 December 1186 with a crown.[24] The major hindrance to John's lordship over the Anglo-Norman settlers in Ireland had been removed shortly after John's return to England with the death of Hugh de Lacy in 1186.[25] Although lordship did not have the same aura of authority as kingship, John's physical power over the Anglo-Norman settlers would not have been strengthened materially as a crowned king of Ireland.

Whatever Henry II's intentions in respect of his lordship of Ireland may have been between 1172 and 1189, there is no doubt that after Richard I's accession as king of England in 1189 he exercised an overriding lordship over John as lord of Ireland. In view of the fact that in 1189 Richard created John count of Mortain, and that John also was married to the heiress of the earldom of Gloucester and given the English shires of Nottingham, Derby, Devon, Cornwall, Somerset, and Dorset to hold independently of the royal administration, this is hardly surprising.[26] Before his departure on crusade in 1190, King Richard secured from Pope Clement III that William de Longchamp, bishop of Ely, would act as papal legate in England, in Wales, 'et in illis partibus Hibernie in quibus nobilis vir Johannes comes Moritoniensis frater ipsius regis iurisdictionem habet et

---

[22] *Ormond deeds, 1170–1350*, no. 17 = NLI, D. 19.

[23] *Ann. Inisf.* 1171. 5. Cf. *NHI* ii. 42.

[24] Roger of Howden, *Gesta*, ii. 3–4; *Chronica*, ii. 317; Gervase of Canterbury, i. 346; Ralph of Diss, ii. 47.

[25] William of Newburgh averred that Henry II rejoiced when he received news of Hugh de Lacy's death: William of Newburgh, i. 240.

[26] Warren, *King John*, 39–40.

dominium'.[27] The dating clauses of a number of John's Irish charters according to Richard's regnal year indicate that he acknowledged Richard's superior lordship in Ireland, even before his rebellion against Richard in 1194.[28] Following John's rebellion against Richard in April 1194, his lordship of Ireland was sequestrated along with his other lands within the Angevin dominions. Richard removed John's agent in Ireland, Peter Pippard, and appointed John de Courcy and Walter de Lacy in his stead. Marleburgh's chronicle recounted that in 1194 'Walter de Lacy received the lordship of Mide and Peter Pippard, justiciar, with his men was taken prisoner'.[29] The Annals of Loch Cé in 1195 recorded

A hosting by John de Courcy and the son of Hugh de Lacy to assume power over the Foreigners of Leinster and Munster.

A great gathering of the men of Connacht by Cathal Crobderg Ua Conchobair, king of Connacht, to Athlone, where there were twelve hundred men or more and John de Courcy and the son of Hugh de Lacy and the nobles of the Foreigners came to meet him when they made their peace.[30]

As the entry in Marleburgh's chronicle implies, it was during Richard I's personal exercise of the lordship of Ireland that Walter de Lacy gained seisin of the lordship of Mide. When Hugh de Lacy died in 1186, his son Walter was a minor. That Walter had come of age by 1190 is evidenced by the fact that administration of the demesne estates of the Lacy honor of Weobley ceased to be accounted for by the sheriff of Herefordshire in that year.[31] However, Walter does not appear to have gained possession of the lordship of Mide until Richard's assumption of the lordship of Ireland in 1194. There is evidence that John had taken the lordship of Mide into his own hands. On 13 May 1192, John granted a charter to the Augustinian monastery of Kells in Meath which confirmed 'omnes terras suas redditus et possessiones quas habent de dono Hugonis de

---

[27] Sheehy, *Pontificia Hib.* i, no. 22; Ralph of Diss, ii. 83.
[28] Mac Niocaill, *Na Buirgéisí*, i. 81, ii. 326, *Notitiae*, 38–9, and 'Charters of John', nos. 9, 10, 11; *Ormond deeds, 1170–1350*, nos. 13, 863; Oxford, Bodleian Library, Rawl. B. 499, fo. 3ᵛ.
[29] TCD MS E. 3. 20, 135. Cf. Mac Niocaill, *The medieval Irish annals*, 39, 41.
[30] Cf. *AFM* 1195.
[31] W. E. Wightman, *The Lacy family in England and Normandy, 1066–1194* (Oxford, 1966), 16, 201.

Lacy', and went on to grant 'de proprio dono meo villam de Dormach', that is Durrow, which Hugh de Lacy had retained in demesne, and where he had been killed in 1186 while overseeing the building of a castle there.[32] According to Roger of Howden, when Henry II learnt of the death of Hugh de Lacy in 1186 he determined that John should cross over to Ireland again 'ad saisandam terram et castella Hugonis in manu sua'. It was news of the death of Henry's son Geoffrey in Paris which occasioned that the king 'revocavit Johannem filium suum qui adhuc exspectabat ventum itineri suo prosperum ad transfretandum in Hiberniam'.[33] Although John did not personally return to Ireland in 1186 to seize Hugh de Lacy's estates, it is probable that agents acting on his or his father's behalf did so. In 1194 King Richard issued a charter of confirmation for the lordship of Mide to Walter de Lacy.[34] On 5 July 1194 Walter de Lacy 'dominus Midie' granted a charter in favour of the burgesses of Drogheda, which significantly was dated 'anno regni regis Anglie Ricardi quinto, die martis proxima post festum apostolorum Petri et Pauli'.[35] The recovery of Hugh de Lacy's remains from the Irish and the solemn burial of his body at Bective Abbey and his head in St Thomas's Abbey, Dublin, in 1195 may also be linked to Walter's assumption of the lordship of Mide about that time.[36] It is apparent from the *Histoire de Guillaume le Maréchal* that John had also attempted to retain the lordship of Leinster for his own use at the expense of William Marshal, and that it was only through the agency of King Richard that the Marshal gained full seisin in Leinster.[37] It is possible that John may have been demanding fines for seisin from both William Marshal and Walter de Lacy which both men had refused to pay. Certainly, after John's accession as king, William Marshal and Walter de Lacy are found acting in concert to protect their rights as tenants-in-chief in Ireland.[38]

[32] Mac Niocaill, *Notitiae*, 38–9; *Cal. pat. rolls, 1388–1392*, 300.

[33] Roger of Howden, *Gesta*, i. 350; omitted in *Chronica*, ii. 309.

[34] *Gormanston reg.* 6, 177–8. John subsequently granted Walter a charter for Mide which stated 'sciatis me *reddidisse* et concessisse et hac presenti carta mea confirmasse Waltero de Lacy et heredibus suis pro homagio et servicio suo totam terram Midie cum pertinenciis suis sicuti Hugo de Lacy pater ejus tenuit eam anno et die quo obiit': ibid. 6–7, 178.

[35] Mac Niocaill, *Na Buirgéisí*, i. 172–3.　　[36] *Chartul. St Mary's, Dublin*, ii. 307.

[37] *Histoire de Guillaume le Maréchal*, ll. 9581–618.

[38] Orpen, *Normans*, ii. 209–18; Jolliffe, *Angevin kingship*, 121–6.

The Angevin lordship in Ireland was permanently linked to the English Crown by the accession of John, lord of Ireland, as king of England in 1199. Although this has been interpreted as due to the fact that Henry II's youngest son, John, became king of England, a circumstance unforeseen by Henry, the evidence suggests that Henry intended that John as king of Ireland would be subject to the overriding lordship of the head of the Angevin dominions. That the lordship of Ireland remained under the king of England after 1199 was, therefore, no accident, but in accord with Henry II's intentions.

Henry's intentions regarding the disposition of the Angevin dominions have been assessed not only in terms of his plans for its inheritance by his sons after his death, but also in respect of his administrative provisions for the different lands which he ruled during his lifetime. While Le Patourel interpreted the administrative evidence as indicating that the Angevin dominions constituted 'an effective unity',[39] Holt reached a contrary conclusion. According to Holt, although the Angevin kings encouraged the development of strong centralized systems of government within certain provinces of their dominions, especially in Normandy and England, they did not seek to impose a similar centralization on their dominions as a whole; the number of what might be described as imperial edicts was very small. 'Improvisation rather than premeditated design' characterized their administration, 'for none of the Plantagenets intended their dominions to continue as a single estate'.[40]

Since Henry reserved the towns of Dublin, Waterford, and Wexford, with their surrounding districts, as royal demesne in 1172, he was obliged to contemplate some administrative arrangements for those towns, if for no other area. Whatever scheme he may have had in mind, he had little time to implement it, as he left Ireland earlier than he had anticipated: messengers came to inform him that two papal legates awaited his arrival in Normandy to attempt a settlement of the breach between Henry and the pope following the murder of Thomas Becket. In addition, rumours had been reaching him that the young King Henry intended to revolt in Normandy and had

---

[39] Le Patourel, 'The Plantagenet dominions', 307.
[40] Holt, 'The end . . .', 240.

secured support from magnates in both England and France.[41]
Accordingly, Henry set sail at the earliest opportunity, and
provision for the administration of his new Irish acquisitions
must have had to be decided upon hastily. That he left Ireland
in a state which he regarded as less than ideal is evidenced by a
remark which he is alleged to have made to the legates when
negotiations were proving difficult: he threatened to return to
Ireland, 'ubi multi mihi incumbunt'.[42] Roger of Howden
stated that Henry had intended to secure the submission of the
king of Connacht, 'qui ad eum venire nolebat'.[43]

A list of the most important of his subjects who had accompanied Henry II to Ireland may be constructed from the
witness lists of the extant texts of charters issued by Henry
while in Ireland,[44] and partially confirmed and supplemented
by information provided by Roger of Howden,[45] Gerald of
Wales,[46] and the 'Song of Dermot'.[47] Henry's entourage was
composed of a mixture of regular members of his household
and feudal magnates. William fitz Audelin, Ranulf de Glanville,

---

[41] Giraldus, *Expugnatio*, 104–5; *Song of Dermot*, ll. 2699–706, 2761–6; Ralph of Diss,
i. 350.

[42] *Materials for the history of Thomas Becket*, vii, ed. J. C. Robertson and J. B. Sheppard
(Rolls series, London, 1885), 514.

[43] Roger of Howden, *Gesta*, i. 29, omitted in *Chronica*, ii. 33–4. Cf. Ralph of Diss,
i. 348.

[44] Charter in favour of Aelelmus brother of Hamund (?Mac Turcaill) witnessed by
William de Braose, Reginald de Curtenai, Hugh de Lacy, Hugh de Gundeville,
William de Stuteville: *Chartul. St Mary's, Dublin*, i. 140–1; charter for the city of Dublin
witnessed by William de Braose, Reginald de Curtenai, Hugh de Gundeville, William
fitz Audelin, Ranulf de Glanville, Hugh de Cressy, Reginald de Pavilli: *Mac Niocaill,
Na Buirgéisí*, i. 75–6; charter for Hugh de Lacy witnessed by Earl Richard fitz Gilbert,
William de Braose, William d'Aubigny, Reginald de Curtenai, Hugh de Gundeville,
William fitz Audelin, *dapifer*, Hugh de Cressy, William de Stuteville, Ralph de Hay,
Reginald de Pavilli, Ralph de Verdun, William de Gerpunville, Robert de Ruilli:
Orpen, *Normans*, i. 285–6; charter for All Hallows, Dublin, witnessed by 'R. Comite
Destr' [?R. comite de Strigoil]', Hugh de Lacy, Ralph de Verdun, Robert Poer,
William 'cancellario meo'; *Cal. charter rolls, 1257–1300*, 342–3; *Registrum prioratus
omnium sanctorum*, 20.

[45] William fitz Audelin, Robert fitz Bernard, Hugh de Lacy: *Gesta*, i. 25, 30;
Chronica, ii. 29–30, 34.

[46] Robert fitz Bernard, William fitz Audelin, Philip de Hastings, Philip de Braose,
Humphrey de Bohun, Hugh de Gundeville: Giraldus, *Expugnatio*, 94–5, 104–6.

[47] William fitz Audelin, Humphrey de Bohun, Hugh de Lacy, Robert fitz Bernard,
Bertram de Verdon: *Song of Dermot*, ll. 2601–8. It is Ralph de Verdun, however, who
occurs as a witness to Henry II's charter to All Hallows, Dublin, and to Hugh de Lacy.
Ralph de Verdun was acting as castellan of Tillières in 1180: *Magni rotuli scaccarii
Normanniae*, i. 84.

Reginald de Pavilli, Reginald de Curtenai, and Hugh de Cressy, as members of Henry's *familia*, had been continuously in the company of the king for at least four months before they journeyed with him to Ireland.[48] By contrast, Hugh de Lacy,[49] Humphrey de Bohun,[50] and William de Braose[51] may be classed as feudal magnates who were called upon specifically to accompany him to Ireland.

Of these latter, Hugh de Lacy was given a considerable stake in Ireland when Henry made him a grant of the kingdom of Mide. Hugh de Lacy was an important tenant-in-chief of the Crown, but not a regular member of Henry's *familia*. Henry's appointment of Hugh de Lacy as keeper of the city of Dublin before his departure in 1172 was atypical, in that he normally employed members of his *familia* for such tasks. By virtue of his office as keeper of Dublin, Hugh de Lacy has been placed at the head of the list of chief governors of Ireland appointed by English kings.[52] There would appear to be little justification either for attributing to him so exalted a position, or for singling him out in preference to the custodians whom Henry appointed for Waterford and Wexford at the same time. There is no evidence that Hugh de Lacy's commission in 1172 extended beyond the city of Dublin. The charter by which Henry granted de Lacy the kingdom of Mide referred to him as bailiff of Dublin, and made him an additional grant of the fees around Dublin for the duration of his tenure of the office, 'et de incremento illi dono omnia feoda que prebuit vel que prebebit circa Duveliniam dum ballivus meus est ad faciendum mihi servicium apud civitatem meam Duveliniae.'[53] The charter, dated at Wexford, suggests the hasty arrangements which Henry had to make before his departure. Roger of Howden

---

[48] Eyton, *Itinerary*, 154–65. Robert fitz Bernard, Robert Poer, Hugh de Gundeville, William de Stuteville, William de Gerpunville, and Philip de Hastings were also regular members of the king's household. For William de Gerpunville, the king's falconer, see above, ch. 7 n. 50.

[49] Lord of the honour of Weobley in Herefordshire: Wightman, *The Lacy family*.

[50] Lord of the honour of Trowbridge in Wiltshire. In 1166 Humphrey de Bohun answered for 30½ knights' fees *de veteri* and for 9½ *de novo*: Sanders, *English baronies*, 91.

[51] Lord of the honour of Bramber in Sussex and of the Welsh marcher lordships of Radnor, Builth, Brecon, and Abergavenny: ibid. 21, 108.

[52] Most recently in *NHI* ix. 470; E. B. Fryde *et al.* (edd.), *Handbook of British chronology* (3rd edn., 1986), 161.

[53] Orpen, *Normans*, i. 285–6.

and Gerald of Wales agree that Hugh was given custody of the city of Dublin.[54] The 'Song of Dermot' stated the same thing:

> Dyvelin[e] li rei Henri
> a Huge baillad de Laci.[55]

A *custos* was a keeper and, in the official sense, ordinarily meant an officer who had to account for all the items of revenue; he was distinguished from a farmer, who contracted to produce a fixed amount. A bailiff was a local official with both judicial and financial responsibilities who, like a *custos*, held office entirely at the king's pleasure.[56] A bailiff might account for revenue by a fixed farm. He might or might not also be castellan of the castle in his bailiwick. Henry II, as part of his reconstruction of local government, had organized Normandy into bailiwicks before 1172. It looks as if Henry was treating Hugh de Lacy in Dublin much as he did his bailiff at Verneuil, which, like Dublin, was a newly created administrative unit, that is as an omnicompetent official responsible for finance, justice, and military security in the city of Dublin and its surrounding area.[57] Although Gerald of Wales claimed that Robert fitz Stephen and Maurice fitz Gerald were appointed custodians of Dublin in conjunction with Hugh de Lacy, this is unlikely.[58] According to the 'Song of Dermot', Robert fitz Stephen, Meilir fitz Henry, and Miles fitz David 'all stayed with Hugh by King Henry's command'.[59] These almost certainly formed part of the garrison over which Hugh de Lacy had control, which, if Gerald may be relied upon, amounted to forty knights. None of them could be described as the king's men. They had all come to Ireland as adventurers before

---

[54] Giraldus, *Expugnatio*, 104–5; Roger of Howden, *Gesta*, i. 30; *Chronica*, ii. 34, adds 'et constituit justitiarium Hiberniae'. There is no other evidence to support this addition. The contemporary account of the *Gesta* is to be preferred: cf. above, p. 277. Richardson and Sayles, *Admin. Ire.* 8, 73, doubted whether there was any authority for Roger of Howden's revision.

[55] *Song of Dermot*, ll. 2653–4.

[56] Cf. Henry II's charter to Robert fitz Stephen and Miles de Cogan which gave them 'custodiam civitatis meae de Cork cum cantredo quod erat Hostmanorum ejusdem civitatis quod retineo in manu . . . habenda et tenenda ea simul quamdiu mihi placuerit et bene mihi servient': J. Ware, *De Hibernia et antiquitatibus eius* (London, 1654), 237–9; Lyttleton, *Henry the Second*, vi. 406–7.

[57] Powicke, *Loss of Normandy*, 52–4.

[58] Giraldus, *Expugnatio*, 104–5.

[59] *Song of Dermot*, ll. 2717–22.

Henry's arrival, but were now to receive payment from the king, or his agent, as part of the Dublin garrison.

According to Roger of Howden, Robert fitz Bernard, a member of Henry's *familia*, was given custody of both Waterford and Wexford.[60] The 'Song of Dermot' also mentions Robert in connection with Waterford.[61] Gerald of Wales stated that Robert shared responsibility for Waterford with Humphrey de Bohun and Hugh de Gundeville, while Wexford was assigned to William fitz Audelin, Philip de Hastings, and Philip de Braose.[62] Waterford, therefore, was assigned to two regular members of the king's *familia*, Robert fitz Bernard[63] and Hugh de Gundeville,[64] and one tenant-in-chief, Humphrey de Bohun.[65] Wexford was assigned to two members of Henry's *familia*, William fitz Audelin and Philip de Hastings, while Philip de Braose was a younger brother of William de Braose, who accompanied Henry to Ireland.[66] With the exception of Robert fitz Bernard, and possibly Humphrey de Bohun and William fitz Audelin, none remained long in Ireland,[67] and their attempts at setting up an administration must have been negligible.

The custodies of Dublin, Waterford, and Wexford reveal little of Henry II's plans for the future administration of his Irish lordship. They indicate no more than that Henry

[60] Roger of Howden, *Gesta*, i. 30; *Chronica*, ii. 34.
[61] *Song of Dermot*, ll. 2715–16.
[62] Giraldus, *Expugnatio*, 104–5.
[63] He is mentioned on the pipe roll of 1165 and on all those between 1168 and 1186. See also Giraldus, *Expugnatio*, 318 n. 193.
[64] See Giraldus, *Expugnatio*, 318 n. 194.   [65] See above, n. 50.
[66] *Cal. doc. Ire., 1171–1251*, no. 147, where William III de Braose is styled nephew of Philip de Braose. In 1177 Henry made Philip de Braose a speculative grant of the kingdom of Limerick, of which, however Philip failed to gain possession: Giraldus, *Expugnatio*, 178–9, 184–7. He probably went to Ireland in the train of his brother William in 1171–2, and by taking royal service in Wexford in 1172 hoped for preferment.
[67] Hugh de Gundeville had left Ireland by December 1172 when he witnessed a charter of Henry II granted at the Christmas court at Caen, and by 1173 was acting as sheriff of Hampshire: Eyton, *Itinerary*, 177 n. 2, 185. Hugh de Lacy was at Canterbury on 29 December 1172, where, according to Gerald of Wales, he reproved Archbishop Richard for boastful language: *Gir. Camb. op.* vii. 69. Philip de Hastings was acting as overseer for repairs to the castle of Norwich between September 1172 and September 1173: *Pipe roll 19 Henry II*, 117. According to the 'Song of Dermot', l. 2919, Robert fitz Bernard was summoned from Ireland to fight for Henry in 1173. He was at the battle of Fornham, October 1173: *Jordan Fantosme's chronicle*, ed. R. C. Johnston (Oxford, 1981), l. 1051, cf. l. 1544. Humphrey de Bohun left Ireland at the latest by September 1173, when he fought for Henry against the king of the Scots: Eyton, *Itinerary*, 177.

intended to exploit those three towns as royal demesne. They do not provide evidence that Henry had decided to set up a regional administration for his Irish lordship. If any one of the custodians appointed for Dublin, Waterford, and Wexford in 1172 was more important than another, it was more likely to have been William fitz Audelin than Hugh de Lacy. From 1173 onwards, and possibly as early as Henry's expedition to Ireland, fitz Audelin was referred to as 'dapifer domini regis'. Jolliffe interpreted his stewardship as relating specifically to Ireland, arguing that William was created a *dapifer* of Henry's Irish lordship in much the same way as there was a steward of Normandy, Brittany, or of an honour such as Lancaster.[68] The earliest reference to William as *dapifer* in an official document would appear to be in the witness list of the charter granted by Henry II at Wexford to Hugh de Lacy shortly before the king's departure. The textual tradition of the witness list is not absolutely reliable. The text of the charter survives in the Gormanston register, but the witness list is supplied from another manuscript[69] and may include additional names and titles which could belong to a later charter granted to Hugh de Lacy by Henry II.[70] In the charter granted by Henry to All Hallows, Dublin, which was supposedly given at Dublin,[71] William fitz Audelin occurs as a witness without the title of *dapifer*. On the other hand, in support of the accuracy of the witness list of Henry's charter in favour of Hugh de Lacy is the fact that Roger of Howden described William fitz Audelin as *dapifer* in the passage where he stated that William fitz Audelin, Robert fitz Bernard, and 'quosdam alios de familia sua' were awaiting Henry when he disembarked at Waterford in 1171, the king

[68] Jolliffe, *Angevin kingship*, 213, 217 n.

[69] See *Gormanston reg.* 6, 177. J. H. Round, *Commune of London* (London, 1899), 152, followed by Orpen, *Normans*, i. 285–6, printed the list of witnesses from BL MS Hargrave 313, fo. 44d. A similar list is contained in the Black Book of Christ Church, Dublin; H. J. Lawlor, 'A calendar of the Liber Niger and Liber Albus of Christ Church, Dublin', *RIA Proc.* 27 (1908), 1–93 (at 65, no. 121). I have not been able to check whether this is independent of Hargrave 313.

[70] Henry's charter at Wexford granted Mide to Hugh de Lacy for the service of 50 knights, but if Roger of Howden may be relied upon this was increased to 100 knights at the council of Oxford in 1177 and might have occasioned a new charter: Roger of Howden, *Gesta*, i. 163; *Chronica*, ii. 134. Richard I confirmed Mide to Walter de Lacy for the service of 50 knights; *Gormanston reg.* 6, 177–8.

[71] The chancery enrolment has 'apud Dublin', but the cartulary copy does not: see above, n. 44.

having sent them on ahead of him to Ireland.[72] In the letter of credence issued by Henry to cover William fitz Audelin's mission to Ireland in 1173 he is styled *dapifer*.[73] However, the entries relating to him on the pipe roll of 1172–3, including details of the preparations for his mission to Ireland, make no reference to his stewardship;[74] he is first named as steward on the pipe roll of 1174–5.[75] Whether fitz Audelin was appointed *dapifer* by Henry in 1171–2, or on the occasion of his mission to Ireland in 1173, either date could be said to support Jolliffe's view that William fitz Audelin was appointed steward in respect of Ireland. This would imply that from an early stage Henry contemplated the setting up of a provincial administration in Ireland. Jolliffe traced the origins of the justiciarship of Ireland back to the stewardship of William fitz Audelin, the link being that the terms *dapifer* and *senescallus* were synonymous, that seneschal and justiciar were interchangeable, the former being the preferred usage of the Angevin Continental dominions, the latter of England, and that the seneschalsies of Normandy and Anjou were true justiciarships, combining the functions of administration and justice. The difficulty is that Henry II gave or used 'household' titles for some of his 'provincial' offices, as, for example, the seneschal of Normandy. Jolliffe based his assumption about fitz Audelin's stewardship of Ireland on the fact that there were already stewards appointed both for the king's household and for the other regions by 1171–2. It is not impossible, however, that Henry could have had several stewards attached to his household at any given time. The *Constitutio domus regis*, an account of the household compiled probably for King Stephen's benefit shortly after his accession, listed the holders of the six principal offices of the household as a chancellor, *dapiferi*, a *pincerna*, a master chamberlain, constables, and a master marshal.[76] The chamberlainship was allowed to lapse in 1158 and the constableships

[72] Roger of Howden, *Gesta*, i. 25; *Chronica*, ii. 29–30.

[73] *Recueil des actes de Henri II*, ed. Delisle and Berger, i. 458–9, where Orpen's remarks in *Normans*, i. 313–15, on the date of this text have been ignored and it is incorrectly assigned to July 1171.

[74] *Pipe roll 19 Henry II*, 145, 172.

[75] *Pipe roll 22 Henry II*, 190, 191, 213.

[76] See G. H. White, 'The household of the Norman kings', in *R Hist. Soc. Trans.*, 4th ser., 30 (1948), 127–56.

in 1163. By 1172 the most important member of the household was the *dapifer*, who might also be styled *senescallus*.[77] The function of Henry II's stewards remains largely a matter of conjecture, since their activities, as Jolliffe remarked, rarely impinged on the pipe rolls. There is a distinction to be drawn between the working household and those honorific ministries which in England descended more or less of right in some of the great English families. Whatever the nature of fitz Audelin's stewardship, whether it was conceived as an office of the household or of a provincial Irish administration, it was certainly not honorific, for fitz Audelin was a regular member of the king's *familia* employed on a wide variety of administrative duties.[78] The fact that in 1165 and 1166 fitz Audelin occurs as 'marescallus regis' might suggest that his stewardship also was held as a household office.[79] On the other hand, that fitz Audelin was employed on two important missions to Ireland in 1173 and 1176–7 and, until the assumption by John of the lordship of Ireland in 1185, was sometimes present in England when Irish matters were dealt with, might be said to indicate that his stewardship did indeed relate to Ireland. It is significant that fitz Audelin was the sole witness to a writ given at Winchester about the time of the treaty of Windsor, October 1175, in the name of Henry II, granting the burgesses of Chester licence to buy and sell in Dublin.[80] This suggests that fitz Audelin was overseeing Irish affairs in England.

The occurrence of Hervey de Montmorency as 'marshal of Ireland' might be said to support the view that from the outset Henry II envisaged a provincial administration in Ireland. In two charters, one in favour of Dunbrody Abbey and another to Osbert fitz Robert, Hervey styled himself 'marescallus domini regis de Hibernia'.[81] Whether this office was bestowed on him

---

[77] William fitz Audelin, William de Curcy, Alured de Saint Martin, and Gilbert Malet are all styled seneschals in the witness list of the treaty of Falaise: *Recueil des actes de Henri II*, ed. Delisle and Berger, ii. 23.

[78] In December 1170 fitz Audelin was named as one of the guardians of the young King Henry: *Materials for the history of Thomas Becket*, ed. Robertson and Sheppard, i. 108–9.

[79] T. Madox, *Formulare Anglicanum* (London, 1702), xix, = September 1165, sitting at the exchequer in Westminster; *Red Book of the Exchequer*, i. 208, = feudal inquest of 1166.

[80] Round, *Feudal England*, 353; *HMC rep. 8*, part 1, sect 2, 356a. Cf. Eyton, *Itinerary*, 196.   [81] *Chartul. St Mary's, Dublin*, ii. 152; Halstead, *Succinct genealogies*, 446.

during Henry's expedition to Ireland, and for how long he may have held it, are unknown.[82] One of the chief duties of the marshal was the payment of troops. That Hervey did exercise such a function may be inferred from Gerald of Wales, who made the accusation against Hervey of having squandered the wages of the troops.[83] Gerald, however, described Hervey as constable of Strongbow's troops, rather than as the holder of a royal office.[84] A possible further indication that a separate administration was intended by Henry II for Ireland in 1172 is the occurrence of William, 'cancellario meo', as a witness to Henry's charter granted at Dublin in 1171–2 to the monastery of All Hallows.[85] This individual does not occur elsewhere as a signatory of any of Henry's charters, whether they related to Ireland, England, or Henry's Continental dominions. Orthodox opinion holds that Henry 'had only one chancery' operating for 'all of his various dominions', that there were no regional or provincial chancellors.[86] It is conceivable that the witness list is defective and that William was a local ecclesiastical chancellor and not a royal chancellor, although the fact that there are two different and apparently independent sources for the text of the charter, namely a chancery enrolment and a cartulary copy, argues against it. About 1161 a Guillermus Martini and Germanus, 'scriptoribus meis', witnessed a charter of Henry II following immediately upon Geoffrey Ridel, chancellor. A William, styled *capellanus*, witnessed another charter of Henry, dated by Delisle to about 1172–3 or 1175, at Rouen, where he again followed immediately upon G. (Geoffrey Ridel), chancellor.[87] It is possible that it was this William who was styled 'chancellor' for the duration of Henry's sojourn in Ireland. As W. L. Warren has

[82] Hervey de Montmorency, without title, was the final witness, suggesting his relative unimportance, to Henry II's charter granted at Oxford, 1177, to Miles de Cogan and Robert fitz Stephen: see above, n. 56. After the council at Oxford, 1177, Robert Poer, styled 'marshal', was sent to Ireland. It is uncertain whether Poer was accorded this title in respect of a household office or a regional Angevin administration in Ireland: see below, n. 115.

[83] Giraldus, *Expugnatio*, 134–7.

[84] That Hervey de Montmorency was employed by Henry II in Ireland is evidenced by the provision of a ship to transport him and 300 seams of wheat to Ireland after the council of Oxford in 1177: *Pipe roll 23 Henry II*, 17.

[85] See above, n. 44.

[86] C. H. Haskins, *Norman institutions* (Cambridge, 1918), 191.

[87] *Recueil des actes de Henri II*, ed. Delisle and Berger, i. 334, ii. 33.

pointed out, in 1173, according to Ralph of Diss, Ralph de Warnerville was appointed 'chancellor of England' and Walter of Coutances 'vice chancellor *in curia regis*'.[88]

William fitz Audelin's letter of credence for his Irish mission in 1173, which was occasioned by the summoning of Hugh de Lacy, Strongbow, and other feudatories from Ireland for military service in Normandy, was addressed to the archbishops, bishops, kings, earls, barons, and all *fideles* in Ireland.[89] There was no mention of justices, bailiffs, custodians, or other ministers. The terms suggest that fitz Audelin was given a general authority, a viceregal commission, until such time as Henry could give his personal attention to Ireland: 'ego vero quam cito potero vacabo magnis negotiis meis Hibernie.' Fitz Audelin remained in Ireland from about March/April 1173 until August 1173. Little is known of his activities during that period apart from an inquisition—the exercise of a judicial function—undertaken 'ex precepto domini Henrici regis' into the lands held by St Mary's Abbey, Dublin, before the advent of the Anglo-Normans in Ireland.[90]

From the evidence it is impossible to gauge whether Henry II intended to make William fitz Audelin *dapifer* of a regional administration in Ireland. It may be that Henry did so initially, but subsequently found that he was unable to back fitz Audelin with the necessary troops, castellans, and subordinate officers, so that he then treated fitz Audelin's stewardship as a household office. A strictly royal administration in Ireland would have entailed the appointment of a viceroy, styled seneschal or justiciar, with a subordinate network of castellans (who could be called constables of their castles), bailiffs, and justices, all being distinctively Henry's men, normally seconded from his household and holding office during his pleasure. Henry may have thought during his time in Ireland that such an organization could be initiated in his new Irish lordship. In practice, he does not seem to have been able to spare the men, money, and effort required, and had to recognize the actual balance of power between the Anglo-Norman

[88] Warren, *Henry II*, 308.   [89] *Recueil*, i. 458–9.
[90] *Chartul. St Mary's, Dublin*, i. 138. The lands named in this inquisition were confirmed by Henry II in a charter given at Feckenham about the time of the treaty of Windsor, October 1175: ibid. 79–80.

settlers and his officials, seeking to maintain his formal claims by treating Strongbow and Hugh de Lacy, and others in possession, as, in part, royal agents and officers.

Following Strongbow's service to Henry II in Normandy in 1173 he returned to Ireland as Henry's agent, replacing William fitz Audelin.[91] Strongbow's appointment in 1173 in succession to William fitz Audelin suggests the weakness of Henry's position in Ireland. Of Strongbow's sixteen extant Irish charters, five were issued on behalf of the king.[92] In two of these, Strongbow described his royal office as 'vices regis Anglie in Hibernia agens'. Otherwise, they are characterized by such expressions as 'ex parte domini regis Anglie'. The charters issued by Strongbow on behalf of Henry II all related to the city of Dublin or its surrounding area. As in the case of Hugh de Lacy's custodianship of Dublin, Strongbow was probably assigned some fees within the royal demesne in 'payment' of his services. This is suggested by grants which he made in his own name within the city to St Mary's Abbey, Dublin, and to Vivien Cursun, and his foundation of a hospital of St John of Jerusalem at Kilmainham.[93] Strongbow's charters issued on behalf of the king to Hamund Mac Turcaill and Thomas, abbot of Glendalough, were witnessed by Nicholas, cleric, of whom in the Glendalough charter it is stated 'qui hanc cartam sigillavit'. Since Nicholas witnessed four charters granted by Strongbow on his own behalf,[94] he was almost certainly Strongbow's personal scribe. This suggests that, as Henry's agent in Ireland, Strongbow was obliged to rely on the resources of his own household.

Raymond le Gros is found acting alongside Strongbow in the period 1173–6 with the title of constable. Although Gerald implied that he did so as a royal agent, the weight of evidence

---

[91] According to Roger of Howden, 'rex Angliae fecerat justitiam Hiberniae': *Gesta*, i. 125; *Chronica*, ii. 100.

[92] Glendalough: *Chart. privil. immun.* 1; *Crede mihi*, 46–7; Aldred Gulafre: ibid. 47; Hamund Mac Turcaill: Sheehy, 'The registrum novum', 254; Savaric Sellarius: *Reg. St Thomas, Dublin*, 369; Walter de Ridelsford: Brooks, 'The de Ridelesfords', *RSAI Jn.* 81 (1951), 118.

[93] *Chartul. St Mary's, Dublin*, i. 78–9, 83–4, 258; Gwynn and Hadcock, *Med. relig. houses*, 334.

[94] Charters in favour of the Hospitallers, Maurice fitz Gerald, and St Mary's Abbey, Dublin: *Calendar of ancient deeds and muniments*, 11–12; *Gormanston reg.* 145, 193; *Chartul. St Mary's, Dublin*, i. 79.

suggests that he did so as constable of Strongbow's *familia*.[95] Given that Strongbow was acting as Henry's agent in Ireland between 1173 and 1176, the distinction is a fine one. Certainly, Gerald of Wales cannot be relied upon to have made it; in fact, he almost certainly would have obscured it. The term constable was used in a number of senses. A constable might be a member of the king's household. According to the *Constitutio domus regis* there were four such constables, who had charge of the knights of the household; but these offices were abolished in 1163 and their functions assigned to the marshal. The term constable was also used for the castellan of a royal castle who had command of a garrison. More commonly, the term was applied to almost any person in a position to command men; it was used for a ship's captain, or for an officer in command of a company of soldiers in the field. From Gerald's account it is apparent that there was rivalry between Hervey de Montmorency and Raymond le Gros over the command of Strongbow's troops. It was Hervey who complained to the king of Raymond's conduct during the Anglo-Norman taking of Limerick in 1175–6.[96] Hervey's complaints related specifically to Raymond's military conduct, and would have been made most appropriately by Hervey de Montmorency in his capacity as marshal of the king in Ireland, although that Hervey held such an office, characteristically, is nowhere revealed by Gerald of Wales. If the Anglo-Norman expedition to Limerick in 1175 had been instigated by Strongbow as Henry's agent in compliance with the treaty of Windsor,[97] it is plain that by 1176 Raymond had overstepped his brief and was engaged in freelance activities.

Early in 1176 Henry II dispatched four members of his household to Ireland to investigate Hervey de Montmorency's complaints against Raymond,[98] namely Robert Poer,[99] Adam de Gernemes,[100] William de Bendinges,[101] and Osbert de

---

[95] See above, ch. 5 n. 81.
[96] Giraldus, *Expugnatio*, 134–5, 138–9, 158–9; see above, pp. 251–3.
[97] See above, pp. 248–50.   [98] Giraldus, *Expugnatio*, 160–1, 166–7.
[99] He had been in Ireland with Henry in 1171–2; see above, n. 44.
[100] At Michaelmas 1169, Adam de Gernemes served as one of the ten barons of the exchequer: Eyton, *Itinerary*, 130. In 1173–4 he was among those who conducted an assize on the king's demesne: *Pipe roll 20 Henry II*, 45.
[101] Eyton, *Itinerary*, 227–8, 231, 236 n., 241, 245.

Herlotera.[102] Two were to remain in Ireland and two were to escort Raymond le Gros to England. William de Bendinges and Adam de Gernemes had both served Henry in legal capacities: they were suitable 'investigators'. Robert Poer had accompanied Henry to Ireland in 1171–2.[103] Hardly had this royal investigatory team arrived in Ireland when, following the sudden death of Strongbow in April 1176, Henry's representatives were obliged to revise their arrangements. According to Gerald, Raymond was left in Ireland as *procurator*, while Henry's agents, 'as soon as they had a favourable westerly wind, went to the king, informing him of the changed situation arising out of the earl's death. When the king learned of this he immediately sent William fitz Audelin to Ireland.'[104] The purpose of his mission, according to Roger of Howden, was to seize all the castles which had been held by Strongbow.[105]

Gerald of Wales recounted that fitz Audelin was accompanied by ten knights 'de privata familia', that is, of the king's household,[106] to which were added John de Courcy with a further ten, as well as Robert fitz Stephen and Miles de Cogan with twenty. In 1172 Henry II had sought to detach fitz Stephen and de Cogan from Strongbow and engage them in the furtherance of the royal interest in Ireland.[107] The attachment of John de Courcy, who was not a member of Henry's *familia*, to William fitz Audelin's mission may perhaps be connected with the recent death of William de Courcy, steward of Normandy. That John de Courcy was a relative of the de Courcy lords of Stogursey in Somerset is certain, although the exact relationship is unknown.[108] William III de Courcy, lord

---

[102] The name Osbert de Herlotera is unique to Giraldus and otherwise unattested. A *magister* Osbert de Butterly occurs as a witness to charters relating to Mide between 1177 and 1212: *Chartul. St Mary's*, Dublin, i. 103, 105, 156, 157, 173, 232; ii. 25; *Reg. St Thomas, Dublin*, 36, 265; *Ir. cartul. Llanthony*, 18, 49, 51, 76, 92, 108–9.

[103] When, after the council of Oxford, 1177, Robert Poer was sent again to Ireland he was styled 'marescallus': Roger of Howden, *Gesta*, i. 161; *Chronica*, ii. 134. Henry may have intended that Robert should assume military leadership of the Anglo-Norman garrisons in Ireland in 1176. Gerald of Wales later accused Robert of abandoning the castle of Leighlin: Giraldus, *Expugnatio*, 190–1.

[104] Giraldus, *Expugnatio*, 166–73.

[105] Roger of Howden, *Gesta*, i. 125; *Chronica*, ii. 100.

[106] Not 'from his own private retinue' as translated in Giraldus, *Expugnatio*, 169. For 'de privata familia' as the king's household see Roger of Howden, *Gesta*, i. 160, 207.

[107] See above, p. 152.

[108] He was probably illegitimate. De Courcy's foundation of Black Abbey, or St

of Stogursey, had died in 1171. His son, William, was a minor, who did not succeed his father until 1189. Between 1171 and 1189 the lordship of Stogursey was administered by the Crown.[109] In 1177 William de Courcy, steward of Normandy, died.[110] John de Courcy may also have been related to this William de Courcy; he may have had some expectation of enjoying the wardship of either or both estates. He may, for instance, have felt that he should have been allowed to act as custodian of the young William, lord of Stogursey. St Anselm, in his treatment of the service of God in terms of service to a secular ruler, had written that some men fought in their lord's service to fulfil their duty; those already held lands and were secularly established and rooted. Others served for wages; others still in the hope of winning back a lost patrimony.[111] John de Courcy may have gone to Ireland with William fitz Audelin in 1177 for the latter reason.

There survives the text of a grant of land to St Thomas's Abbey, Dublin, made by fitz Audelin on behalf of Henry II.[112] Significantly, both in the cartulary of St Thomas's Abbey and on the chancery enrolment, fitz Audelin's grant of 1177 is preceded by a copy of Henry's letter of credence issued to him in 1173. This suggests that the letter of credence was considered the guarantee that the king would honour the grant made by fitz Audelin in 1177. Possibly the letter covered both missions, or indeed all fitz Audelin's actions in Ireland between 1173 and John's assumption of the lordship of Ireland in 1185. This might be said to support Jolliffe's view that William fitz Audelin was appointed *dapifer* in respect of Ireland, although it has to be said that fitz Audelin is not described as seneschal of Ireland in any royal document.

William fitz Audelin remained in Ireland from about March/April 1176 until about May 1177, during which time

Andrew in Ards, Co. Down, was founded as a cell of Stogursey in Somerset: Gwynn and Hadcock, *Med. relig. houses*, 108. A number of de Courcy's feudatories, such as Poer and fitz Urze, bear names linked with Somerset: *Stogursey charters*, p. xx.

[109] Sanders, *English baronies*, 143.

[110] Roger of Howden, *Gesta*, i. 125; *Chronica*, ii. 100.

[111] M. Chibnall, 'Mercenaries and the *familia regis* under Henry I', *History*, 22 (1977), 15–23 (at 15).

[112] The charter was given 'in presencia Viviani cardinalis et Laurentii archiepiscopi Dublinensis et plurimorum episcoporum Hiberniae': *Cal. chart. rolls, 1257–1300*, 386–7; Oxford, Bodl. Rawl. B. 499, fo. 1ʳ⁻ᵛ.

Gerald of Wales would have us believe that 'he never ceased inflicting injustices on Raymond, Meilir, the Fitz Maurices, and fitz Stephen'. Specifically Gerald accused fitz Audelin of taking the castle of Wicklow from the sons of Maurice fitz Gerald, depriving Raymond le Gros of lands which he held in the vale of Dublin and adjacent to Wexford, and depriving fitz Stephen of a cantred in Uí Fáeláin.[113] The hostility between the adventurer-settlers and William fitz Audelin, as the king's agent, emerges very clearly from Gerald's account.

Although Gerald avers that fitz Audelin was recalled to England in May 1177 because of incompetence in Ireland, it may rather have been tensions between him and the adventurer-settlers, as described by Gerald, and the delicate balance of power between the two groups which occasioned Henry's major conference on his lordship of Ireland held at Oxford in May 1177. The outcome was the designation of John as king of Ireland. Lists of the chief governors of Ireland give Hugh de Lacy in succession to William fitz Audelin in 1177 following the council of Oxford. This is solely in reliance on Gerald of Wales, who described de Lacy as 'procurator generalis' and headed the chapter in which he did so 'fitz Audelin recalled and Hugh de Lacy appointed in his place'.[114] Gerald's account conflicts with the court chronicler, Roger of Howden. According to Roger, at the council of Oxford John was designated king of Ireland; William fitz Audelin, the king's steward, was given custody of all the lands of Strongbow, including the town of Wexford; sent to Ireland with him were Hugh de Lacy, to whom the king gave custody of the city of Dublin with its appurtenances, and Robert Poer, styled 'marshal',[115] to whom custody of the city of Waterford with its adjacent province was given; 'et multos cum eis misit tam milites quam servientes de regno Angliae.'[116] The occurrence of Robert Poer with the title of

---

[113] Giraldus, *Expugnatio*, 170–3.   [114] Ibid. 182–3.

[115] Roger of Howden, *Gesta*, i. 161, and *Chronica*, ii. 134, is the only source in which Robert Poer is so styled. He is mentioned without title on all pipe rolls between 1177 and 1186: see above, n. 63.

[116] Roger of Howden, *Gesta*, i. 161–5; *Chronica*, ii. 133–6. In 1177 the Annals of Tigernach recorded 'the arrival in Ireland of three fleets of Englishmen, to wit the fleet of Hugh de Lacy, the fleet of William fitz Audelin, and the fleet of Philip de Braose; Hugo's to Dublin, William's to Wexford, Philip's to Waterford'. Although Hugh de Lacy here precedes William fitz Audelin no special significance can be attached to this

marshal may indicate that Henry was making another attempt to set up a regional administration in Ireland. Roger of Howden's depiction of William fitz Audelin's and Hugh de Lacy's relative importance is supported by Henry's charters granted at Oxford 1177 about the time of the council, where William fitz Audelin preceded Hugh de Lacy in the witness lists.[117] Significantly, Gerald of Wales suppressed any knowledge of William fitz Audelin's reappointment in 1177; by his account, Robert Poer was to act as *custos* of both Waterford and Wexford. Although Hugh de Lacy attested Irish charters as 'constable' in the period between 1177 and his death in 1186,[118] he is not mentioned in any other capacity, nor are there any extant charters issued by him on behalf of Henry II in Ireland. Given that five Irish charters issued by Strongbow on behalf of the king survive from the short period 1173–6,[119] this would appear to be due to more than the vagaries of chance survival. Gerald's presentation of Hugh de Lacy's appointment in 1177 appears to have been wishful thinking on his part. In his view the settlers rather than royal bureaucrats knew best how to manage affairs in Ireland, and Henry II would have been better advised to appoint Hugh de Lacy as his chief agent rather than William fitz Audelin. Gerald's *Expugnatio* is sometimes interpreted as a family history. But it was more than that. It was also an account of the achievements of all the adventurer-settlers, made despite the hindrances of royal agents in Ireland: hence the inclusion of Hugh de Lacy and John de Courcy, although not Geraldines, among his heroes.

The chapter in Gerald's narrative following on 'fitz Audelin recalled and Hugh de Lacy appointed in his place' was titled 'Ireland pacified under Hugh de Lacy', and was intended to reinforce the impression that Hugh de Lacy was acting as Henry's principal agent in Ireland. Hugh de Lacy is said to have made an excellent job of fortifying not only Mide but also Leinster with castles. His building of castles in Leinster would have been undertaken on behalf of the king, whose responsibility the lordship of Leinster was for the duration of the

order, since Hugh de Lacy would have been of most interest to the Connacht annalist. Philip de Braose's destination was Limerick not Waterford.

[117] *Cal. chart. rolls, 1257–1300*, 387; see above, n. 56.
[118] See above, ch. 7 n. 109.   [119] See above, n. 92.

minority. Among the castles which Hugh de Lacy is said to have built was that of Leighlin 'situated beyond Uí Dróna', 'the castle from which Robert Poer, to whose keeping the king had entrusted it, had previously decamped'.[120] Gerald went on to describe how Hugh de Lacy's activities in Ireland occasioned the suspicions of the king and a summons to England. The impression is given that Hugh had been building castles in Leinster on his own initiative prior to his summons to England. Yet some doubt must attach to this, in view of the fact that in a subsequent chapter it emerges that the royal agents, John, constable of Chester, and Richard of the Peak, who arrived in Ireland in 1181 to summon de Lacy to England to answer for his conduct in person to the king, joined with de Lacy in building castles in Leinster prior to de Lacy's departure: 'for hitherto very many castles had been built in Meath, but few in Leinster'.[121] It may rather be that it was at the instigation of Henry's agents that castles were constructed in Leinster in 1181. The fact that Henry's agents drew on assistance from Hugh de Lacy before his departure suggests the paucity of the king's resources in Ireland. According to Roger of Howden, John, constable of Chester, and Richard of the Peak were sent to Ireland 'ad custodiendum civitatem Dublinae quam Hugo de Laci custodierat', which implies that Hugh de Lacy held no higher office in 1181 than *custos* of Dublin.[122]

Following his visit to Henry II, de Lacy was reinstated as *custos* of Dublin; there is no evidence to suggest that after 1181 he exercised any wider authority. By 1184, de Lacy had rearoused Henry's suspicions, and the king determined to transfer the lordship of Ireland in person to his son John. In preparation he dispatched John Cumin, archbishop of Dublin, and Philip of Worcester to Ireland. Philip of Worcester is said to have restored to the royal demesne of Dublin the revenues of Saithne, which Hugh de Lacy had appropriated, suggesting

---

[120] Giraldus, *Expugnatio*, 190–1. Gerald's hostility to Robert Poer may derive from friction between his relative Raymond le Gros, who held Uí Dróna, and Robert Poer as castellan of Leighlin.

[121] Giraldus, *Expugnatio*, 194–5.

[122] Roger of Howden, *Gesta*, i. 270; *Chronica*, ii. 253. Mentioned by Roger of Howden but, significantly, not by Gerald of Wales was the fact that it was Hugh de Lacy's marriage to the daughter of Ruaidrí Ua Conchobair which occasioned Henry's suspicion.

again that de Lacy's commission did not extend beyond Dublin.[123] During John's visit Hugh de Lacy witnessed a number of John's charters as constable (of Dublin Castle ?).[124] It would appear that John found it impossible to dislodge de Lacy from the castle of Dublin; the title of constable does not necessarily imply that de Lacy was still custodian of the royal demesne of Dublin. The fact that the Irish annals accorded Hugh such a prominent role, and stated that he was 'king in Ireland, when the son of the king of the Saxons came', has served to reinforce the impression put forward by Gerald of Wales that Hugh de Lacy had acted as Henry's chief agent in Ireland. In fact, apart from Gerald of Wales's account, there is no independent evidence that he did so.

If it was William fitz Audelin who returned to Ireland in 1177 as Henry's principal agent, how long did he remain there? His presence in England is unattested from 1177 until December 1181, when he witnessed a charter of Henry II in favour of the monastery of Godstow.[125] It is possible that he was recalled to England in 1179 along with Hugh de Lacy,[126] and he may have returned again to Ireland. After 1181 fitz Audelin appears to have had no further contact with Ireland. That he still enjoyed the king's favour is evidenced by entries on the pipe rolls between 1183 and 1188 which show him holding escheated lands in Hampshire at the pleasure of the king.[127] In these entries he is not styled *dapifer*. In 1189 he occurs without title overseeing the honour of Carlisle, which was in the hands of the king.[128] Some time between 1181 and 1189 William fitz Audelin without title witnessed a charter of Henry II dated at Anjou.[129] This could be said to support the view that his stewardship had been held in respect of Ireland and ceased with John's assumption of the lordship of Ireland in 1185, when Bertram de Verdon witnessed charters of John as *senescallus*.[130] On the other hand, on 17 March 1186 William fitz Audelin made a grant to the Hospitallers in which he styled himself 'domini

---

[123] Giraldus, *Expugnatio*, 198–9.   [124] See above, ch. 7 n. 109.
[125] Eyton, *Itinerary*, 245.   [126] See above, ch. 7 n. 88.
[127] *Pipe roll 30 Henry II*, 81; *31 Henry II*, 208; *32 Henry II*, 170; *33 Henry II*, 196; *34 Henry II*, 173.
[128] *Pipe roll 34 Henry II*, 8.
[129] *Recueil des actes de Henri II*, ed. Delisle and Berger, ii. 368.
[130] See below, p. 303.

regis dapifer', which suggests that he, at any rate, still regarded himself as a steward of the king.[131]

Whatever Henry's intentions for the administration of his Irish lordship may have been in 1171–2, in practice he had neither the time, resources, nor control over the early settlers to implement them. Having overcome the challenge of Strong-bow 'iam pene regnantem' in Ireland by his personal interven-tion there in 1171–2, he subsequently faced similar challenges from Raymond le Gros and Hugh de Lacy, each of whom, according to rumours, aspired to the kingdom of Ireland, as well as from John de Courcy. John's expedition of 1185 failed in its main purpose of bringing Hugh de Lacy to heel. It was only de Lacy's death in 1186 which freed Henry II from the immediate threat.[132] Although Henry had retained the city of Limerick and a surrounding cantred as royal demesne when he made a speculative grant of Thomond to Philip de Braose in 1177, he did not pursue his claims in that city after Philip tried and failed, later in the same year, to make his grant operative. John failed signally to take possession of Limerick in 1185. It was not until after the death of Domnall Mór Ua Briain in 1194 that Henry's original reservation of Limerick as royal demesne could be made good, and this was due more to the enterprise of Anglo-Norman settlers in the region than to any initiative by John.[133] In 1177 Henry had also retained the city of Cork and a cantred as royal demesne, appointing Robert fitz Stephen and Miles de Cogan as *custodes*.[134] Miles de Cogan was killed about 1182–3, which meant that responsibility not just for the admin-istration of the city but also for his portion of the kingdom of Cork devolved on Henry. Henry's response to Miles de Cogan's death, according to Gerald of Wales, was to send Richard de Cogan 'to take his brother's place'; Raymond le Gros is said by Gerald to have 'succeeded as heir to his uncle

---

[131] *The cartulary of the knights of St John of Jerusalem in England: secunda camera: Essex*, ed. M. Gervers (British Academy: Records of social and economic history, NS 6; Oxford, 1982), 59.

[132] See n. 25 above.

[133] John issued a charter in favour of the church of St Mary, Limerick, at Ardfinan in 1185: *Black Book of Limerick*, 103. In 1197 John issued a charter confirming to the citizens of Limerick the fee farm of the city as it had been determined by Hamo de Valognes: Mac Niocaill, *Na Buirgéisí*, i. 236–7; see also C. A. Empey, 'The settlement of the kingdom of Limerick', in Lydon, *Eng. and Ire.* 1–25.

[134] See above, n. 56.

fitz Stephen'.[135] Whether or not Gerald's account of the devolution of the kingdom of Cork can be relied upon in detail, it is plain that Henry II's control of the royal demesnes of Limerick and Cork was negligible before 1185 and was not materially strengthened by John's expedition.

Henry may have intended that John's assumption in person of the Angevin lordship of Ireland in 1185 should occasion the establishment of a regional administration for the Angevin lordship of Ireland. As W. L. Warren has highlighted, John was accompanied to Ireland by trusted members of his father's *familia*.[136] Charters granted by John in Ireland in 1185 were witnessed by Bertram de Verdon, styled seneschal, and William de Wenneval, styled *dapifer*.[137] According to Gerald of Wales, when John returned to England in 1185 Bertram de Verdon remained in Ireland as 'senescallus Hiberniae'.[138] This suggests that Bertram de Verdon was intended to head a regional administration in Ireland, while William de Wenneval was *dapifer* of John's household. If this was Henry's plan it proved abortive. Bertram de Verdon, without title, witnessed a charter of John issued as lord of Ireland between 1185 and 1189.[139] Upon the accession of Richard I he appears to have joined his household, witnessing charters of Richard between December 1189 and January 1190, accompanying him to the Holy Land, and dying there in 1192.[140]

Henry's administrative arrangements for his Irish lordship suggest that his control of it remained severely restricted. The appointment of Strongbow between 1173 and 1176, and the several reinstatements of Hugh de Lacy as *custos* or constable of Dublin, highlight the weakness of royal authority in Ireland. Henry's employment of major landholders in such capacities was not usual. Gerald of Wales, in detailing the reasons for the failure of John's expedition to Ireland in 1185, described John's

---

[135] Giraldus, *Expugnatio*, 186–9. A detailed examination of the subinfeudation of the kingdom of Cork and the devolution of the fees of Miles de Cogan and Robert fitz Stephen is being undertaken by K. W. Nicholls.

[136] Warren, 'John in Ireland'.

[137] *Ormond deeds, 1172–1350*, no. 7, and *1350–1413*, no. 426; Mac Niocaill, *Na Buirgéisí*, 77; *Chartul. St Mary's, Dublin*, i. 84–7; *Gormanston reg.* 145, 193; *HMC rep.* 77, part 1 (1925), 30–1; Mac Niocaill, 'Charters of John', 285; *Cal. pat. rolls, 1334–38*, 402.

[138] *Gir. Camb. op.* i. 65.

[139] *Ormond deeds, 1172–1350*, no. 863.

[140] *DNB* xx. 217. His career is summarized by Warren, *Henry II*, 310.

associates as men of the same type as William fitz Audelin.[141] The comparison was apt, for fitz Audelin, like those who accompanied John to Ireland, was a trusted member of Henry's *familia*. That fitz Audelin was the main butt of Gerald's criticisms of royal agents in Ireland supports the view that he was, in fact, the king's principal agent there until 1181. Gerald brings out very clearly the antipathy between Henry's royal agents in Ireland and the adventurer-settlers and their anti-bureaucratic sentiments. These would have known the conditions of Stephen's reign when royal administration was weak, when both Stephen and the empress had been forced to accept earls as civil and military governors of their counties, instead of being able to nominate their own officials. In England Henry II had very effectively put an end to that state of affairs. By 1171 the king controlled a highly efficient administration. Peter of Blois referred to royal officials covering the land like a plague of locusts.[142] From Gerald of Wales one gets the impression that such anti-bureaucratic sentiments had been translated to Ireland, that the earliest Anglo-Norman settlers there were seeking to recreate the conditions which had obtained before Henry's accession, to establish in Ireland an 'old world' to redress the 'new world' in England and Normandy. The different balance of power in Ireland, where Henry's resources were severely limited, which gave the settlers the advantage, appears to have sharpened the ideological conflict between the representatives of Angevin rule and its critics and opponents.

Whether or not Henry II had a 'premeditated design' for the administration of his Irish lordship in 1171–2, it was 'improvisation' which subsequently characterized it. That improvisation, however, was apparently not because Henry envisaged the Angevin lordship in Ireland as eventually being separated from the rest of his dominions, but because of a lack of time, men, resources, and control over the adventurer-settlers in Ireland.

[141] Giraldus, *Expugnatio*, 238–9.
[142] *Petri Blesensis opera omnia*, ed. J. A. Giles, i (Oxford, 1846), 298.

APPENDIX I

Charter of John, count of Eu, in favour of Ralph Picot, dated 'at Winchester in the year in which a conquest of Ireland was discussed'

BL Harl. charter 83 C. 25
15.5×12 cm
Remnants of red equestrian seal on double tag
Calendared in *Index to the charters and rolls in the British Museum* ii (London, 1912), 419.

Iohannes comes Augensis[1] omnibus baronibus suis atque omnibus hominibus Francis et Anglis salutem. Notum facio vobis omnibus me concessisse Radulfo Picot[2] et suis heredibus feodum suum quod de me tenet tenendum et habendum de me et de meis heredibus libere et quiete per servicium trium militum mihi et meis heredibus reddendum. Hoc vero idem feci concessisse comitissam uxorem meam.[3] Pro hac vero concessione donavit mihi Radulfus predictus xl marcas et comitissa duas untiae auri. Hec autem concessio facta est apud Wincestriam eo anno quo verbum factum est de Hibernia conquirenda. Hanc vero cartulam magister Mobertus[4] fecit anno[a] liiii ab incarnato Domino.[5] Testibus his, Roberto de Sancto Petro,[6] Rainaldo de Sancto Leodegario,[7] Henrico de Novo Mercato,[8] Hugone Rossello, Bartholomeo de Rothomago, Simone monacho, Elwardo, Ivone de grandi curia, Willelmo de Carlentona, Hugone filio Nigelli et pluribus aliis,[b] Petro de Ceresbroc,[9] Ricardo Costentin,[10] Salom. presbitero.

---

[a] The scribe left a space as if unsure how to write the full date in Roman numerals.
[b] The scribe filled the space to the end of this line with an undulating line as if he did not intend to write any more names, but then added three others.

---

1. John, count of Eu, and lord of Hastings in direct descent from the first feoffee of William the Conqueror, succeeded his father, Henry, in 1140. In 1166 he answered for 62½ knights' fees enfeoffed *de veteri*: *Red Book of the Exchequer*, i. 202. He died in 1170.
2. Ralph Picot witnessed three charters of King Stephen in favour of the

archbishop of Canterbury. He was constable of Theobald, archbishop of Canterbury, and sheriff of Kent in 1153 and 1155–6: *Reg. regum Anglo-Normannorum*, ii, nos. 142, 145, 151, 163. Cf. Eyton, *Itinerary*, 19.

3. John, count of Eu, married Adelise, daughter of William d'Aubigny, earl of Arundel, from whom he held 11 knights' fees in Kent *in maritagio*: *Red Book of the Exchequer*, i. 398. In 1166 Alan Pirot (*recte* Picot) was listed as holding 6 of those fees: ibid.

4. Mobertus is styled chaplain of John, count of Eu, in a charter to Hilary, bishop of Chichester, 18 December 1148: see below, n. 5(*a*).

5. The dating of this charter by reference to a specific event and by the year of incarnation is unusual in an English context. It was more common in French charters, where the style was set by the Capetian chancery. The dating clause of this charter may be compared with others granted by John, count of Eu, of which the following is a selection:

   (*a*) 18 December 1148, charter of John, count of Eu, in favour of Hilary, bishop of Chichester, 'at London in St Paul's 18 calends December on the day of the translation of St Ercenwald, confessor, in the same church': *Cal. chart. rolls, 1327–1341*, 440–1; *The chartulary of the high church of Chichester*, ed. W. D. Peckham (Sussex Record Society, 46; [Lewes], 1942–3), no. 299; Dugdale, *Monasticon Anglicanum*, vi. 1171.

   (*b*) 1151, charter of John, count of Eu, confirming the church of St Mary, Hastings, to the monastery of St Michael of Le Tréport, 'actum est hoc anno ab incarnatione domini MCLI': *Documents preserved in France*, no. 234.

   (*c*) 30 July 1153, charter of John, count of Eu, granting ecclesiastics freedom to buy and sell at Eu without payment of dues, 'this gift for which his daughter, Matilda, pleaded is given at the burial of his sister, Matilda, on the third before the calends of August in the church at Eu': *Documents preserved in France*, no. 235.

   (*d*) 26 August 1154, charter of John, count of Eu, in favour of Roger de Mowbray, 'anno ab incarnatione domini MCLIIII vii kalendas Septembris rege Francorum Ludovico, duce Normannorum Henrico': *Charters of the honour of Mowbray, 1107–1191*, ed. D. E. Greenaway (British Academy: Records of Social and Economic History, NS 1; London, 1972), no. 19.

   (*e*) 1170, charter of John, count of Eu, confirming the gift of his father, Henry, to the priory of St Martin du Bosc, 'acta sunt hec incarnationis dominice anno MCLXX coram his testibus': *Documents preserved in France*, no. 400.

The charter dated at Winchester in the year in which a conquest of Ireland was discussed appears less unusual by comparison with the dating clauses of other charters granted by John, count of Eu. The date by year of incarnation raises a difficulty: it should be 1155 not 1154, but it is obvious that the scribe had difficulty with this method of dating. Not only did he fail to write the Roman numerals MC, leaving a space for them to be added later, but the phrase *ab incarnato* would normally read *ab incarnatione*. He also ran into difficulties with the list of witnesses, which he amended after he had finished writing the charter. The charter of John, count of Eu, in favour of Roger de Mowbray, dated 26 August 1154 'rege Francorum Ludovico, duce Normannorum Henrico', confirms the impression that the scribe has misdated the charter to Ralph Picot by one year.

6. Robertus de Sancto Petro witnessed the charter of John, count of Eu, to Roger of Mowbray: see above, n. 5(d).

7. I have not traced another reference to Rainaldus, but in 1166 Thomas de Sancto Leodegario held 4 knights' fees of John, count of Eu: *Red Book of the Exchequer*, i. 202.

8. Henry of Newmarket witnessed three charters of King Stephen between 1140 and 1154: *Reg. regum Anglo-Normannorum*, ii, nos. 38, 139, 655.

9. In 1166 Petrus de Caesaris Burgo held three knights' fees of John, count of Eu, in Kent: *Red Book of the Exchequer*, i. 398.

10. In 1166 Richard de Costentin held half a knight's fee of John, count of Eu, in Kent: ibid. 399.

APPENDIX 2

Irish kings who submitted to Henry II
in 1171–1172

DIARMAIT MAC CARTHAIG, KING OF DESMOND

Ann. Inisf. 1171. 5
Ann. Tig. 1171
Misc. Ir. annals, 1172. 3 *(recte* 1171)
AU 1171 (= submission of Munster)
Giraldus, *Expugnatio*, 92–3 (rex Corcagiensis Dermitius)
Roger of Howden, *Gesta*, i. 25 (rex Corcensis)
Roger of Howden, *Chronica*, ii. 30 (rex Corcensis)
Ralph of Diss, i. 348 (regulus de Chorc)
Gervase of Canterbury, i. 235 (rex Corcensis)

DOMNALL MÓR UA BRIAIN, KING OF THOMOND

Ann. Inisf. 1171. 5
Misc. Ir. annals, 1172. 3 *(recte* 1171)
Ann. Tig. 1171 (= submission of Leth Moga)
AU 1171 (= submission of Munster)
Giraldus, *Expugnatio*, 92–3 (Duvenaldus rex Limericensis)
Roger of Howden, *Gesta*, i. 25 (rex de Limeric)
Roger of Howden, *Chronica*, ii. 30 (rex de Limerich)
Ralph of Diss, i. 348 (regulus de Limelic)
Gervase of Canterbury, i. 235 (rex Limeric')

DONNCHAD UA MATHGAMNA, KING OF UÍ ECHACH

Misc. Ir. annals, 1172. 3 *(recte* 1171). The entry 1172. 2 gives his pedigree as
Donnchad son of Cian son of Donnchad Donn son of Cú Mara son of Brodcú
son of Mathgamain son of Cian Máel Muad
Ann. Tig. 1171 (= submission of Leth Moga)
AU 1171 (= submission of Munster)

RAGNALL, KING OF WATERFORD

Roger of Howden, *Gesta*, i. 25
Roger of Howden, *Chronica*, ii. 30

MÁEL SECHLAINN UA FÁELÁIN, KING OF DÉISE

Giraldus, *Expugnatio*, 94–5 (Machsachelino Ophelano)
Ann. Tig. 1171 (= submission of Leth Moga)
AU 1171 (= submission of Munster)

DOMNALL MAC GILLA PÁTRAIC, KING OF OSRAIGE

Giraldus, *Expugnatio*, 94–5 (Duvenaldo Ossiriensi)
Roger of Howden, *Gesta*, i. 25 (rex de Oxeria)
Roger of Howden, *Chronica*, ii. 30 (rex de Oxeria)
Gervase of Canterbury, i. 235 (rex Osseria)
Ann. Tig. 1171 (= submission of Leth Moga)
AU 1171 (= submission of Leinster)

FÁELÁN MAC FÁELÁIN, KING OF UÍ FÁELÁIN

Giraldus, *Expugnatio*, 94–5 (Machelanus Ophelan)
AU 1171 (= submission of Leinster)
Ann. Tig. 1171 (= submission of Leth Moga)

DOMNALL CAEMÁNACH MAC MURCHADA

Misc. Ir. annals, 1172. 4 (= submission of the men of Leinster and of Domnall Caemánach; the entry of 1172. 2 lists him as ruler over the men of Leinster)
AU 1171 (= submission of Leinster)
Ann. Tig. 1171 (= submission of Leth Moga)

MAC DALBAIG UA DOMNAILL, KING OF UÍ FELMEDA

Giraldus, *Expugnatio*, 94–5 (Machtalewi)
AU 1171 (= submission of Leinster)
Ann. Tig. 1171 (= submission of Leth Moga)

UA TUATHAIL, KING OF UÍ MUIREDAIG

Giraldus, *Expugnatio*, 94–5 (Othuetheli)
AU 1171 (= submission of Leinster)
Ann. Tig. 1171 (= submission of Leth Moga)

MAC GILLA MO CHOLMÓC, KING OF UÍ DUNCHADA

Giraldus, *Expugnatio*, 94–5 (Gillemeholmoch)

UA CATHASAIG, KING OF SAITHNE

Giraldus, *Expugnatio*, 94–5 (Ocathesi)

MURCHAD UA CERBAILL, KING OF AIRGIALLA

Misc. Ir. annals, 1172. 5
Giraldus, *Expugnatio*, 94–5 (Ocaruel Urieliensis)
AU 1171 (= submission of Airgialla)
Ann. Tig. 1171 (= submission of Airgialla)

TIGERNÁN UA RUAIRC, KING OF BRÉIFNE

Misc. Ir. annals, 1172. 5
Giraldus, *Expugnatio*, 95 (Ororicius Medensis)
?Ralph of Diss, i. 348 (regulus ille que dicebatur monoculus). Cf. Giraldus,
Expugnatio, 113
AU 1171 (= submission of Bréifne)
Ann. Tig. 1171 (= submission of Bréifne)

DONN SLÉBE MAC DUINN SLÉIBE, KING OF ULAID

Misc. Ir. annals, 1172. 5
AU 1171 (= submission of Ulaid)
Ann. Tig. 1171 (= submission of Ulaid)
Giraldus, *Expugnatio*, 97, stated that the kings of Ulster did not submit to
Henry II. Giraldus used the term Ulster to refer to the ancient provincial
kingdom, which in pseudo-historical tradition was believed to have embraced
the whole of the north of Ireland. In the twelfth century the kingdom of Ulaid

was confined to the area east of the river Bann, and the king of this reduced area, Mac Duinn Sléibe, did submit to Henry II, as the Irish annals prove. Allowing that Gerald used the term Ulster to refer to the whole of the north of Ireland, his statement has substance in so far as neither the king of Cenél nEógain nor the king of Cenél Conaill, who were more powerful than the king of Ulaid, submitted to Henry II

?UA MÁEL SECHLAINN, KING OF MIDE

AU 1171 (= submission of Mide)
Ann. Tig. 1171 (= submission of Mide)
Roger of Howden, *Gesta*, i. 25 (rex de Mida)
Roger of Howden, *Chronica*, ii. 30 (rex de Mida)
Gervase of Canterbury, i. 235 (rex de Mida)

Since Gerald of Wales referred to Tigernán Ua Ruairc, king of Bréifne, as king of Mide, it is possible that Roger of Howden and Gervase of Canterbury were also using the term king of Mide to refer to Tigernán Ua Ruairc, whose submission they did not otherwise record. The Irish annals recorded the submissions both of the men of Mide and of Bréifne, but this does not prove that a member of the Mide royal dynasty of Ua Máel Sechlainn submitted on behalf of the men of Mide. There was a disputed succession in Mide in 1171–2 between Domnall Bregach Ua Máel Sechlainn, who was recognized as king of East Mide, and his brother Art, who was installed in West Mide. In fact, Tigernán Ua Ruairc exercised a considerable degree of control over eastern Mide, which explains why some of the Anglo-Norman chroniclers referred to him as king of Mide

RUAIDRÍ UA CONCHOBAIR, KING OF CONNACHT, AND HIGH-KING OF IRELAND

Giraldus, *Expugnatio*, 97, stated that Ruaidrí Ua Conchobair made submission to emissaries of Henry II at the banks of the river Shannon in 1172. He is the only authority for this submission, which is denied explicitly by:
Roger of Howden, *Gesta*, i. 25
Roger of Howden, *Chronica*, ii. 30
Ralph of Diss, i. 348
Gervase of Canterbury, i. 235
The Irish annals make no mention of it

APPENDIX 3

The treaty of Windsor, 1175

Roger of Howden, *Gesta*, i. 102–3; cf. *Chronica*, ii. 84–5.

1. Hic est finis et concordia quae facta fuit apud Windeshoveres in octavis Sancti Michaelis, anno ab Incarnatione Domini MᵒcᵒLXXᵒVᵒ, inter dominum regem Angliae Henricum, filium Matillis [*sic*] imperatricis, et Rodericum regem Connactensem, per Chatholicum archiepiscopum Tuamensem, et Cantordem abbatem Sancti Brandani, et Magistrum Laurentium cancellarium regis Connactensis. Scilicet quod Henricus rex Angliae concessit praedicto Roderico, ligio homini suo, regi Connactae, quamdiu ei fideliter serviet, quod sit rex sub eo, paratus ad servitium suum sicut homo suus;

2. et quod terram suam teneat ita bene et in pace, sicut tenuit antequam dominus rex Angliae intraret Hiberniam, reddendo ei tributum;

3. et totam aliam terram et habitatores terrae habeat sub se et justiciet, ut tributum regi Angliae integre persolvant, et per manum ejus et sua jura sibi conservent.

4. Et illi qui modo tenent, teneant in pace, quamdiu permanserint in fidelitate regis Angliae, et ei fideliter et integre persolverint tributum et alia jura sua quae ei debent, per manum regis Connactae; salvo in omnibus jure et honore domini regis Angliae et suo.

5. Et si qui ex eis regi Angliae et ei rebelles fuerint, et tributum et alia jura regis Angliae per manum suam solvere noluerint, et a fidelitate regis Angliae recesserint, ipse eos justiciet et amoveat.

6. Et si eos per se justiciare non poterit, constabularius regis Angliae et familia sua de terra illa juvabunt eum ad hoc faciendum, cum ab ipso fuerint requisiti, et ipsi viderint quod necesse fuerit.

7. Et propter hunc finem reddet praedictus rex Connactae domino regi Angliae tributum singulis annis; scilicet de singulis decem animalibus unum corium placabile mercatoribus, tam de tota terra sua quam de alia.

8. Excepto quod de terris illis, quas dominus rex Angliae retinuit in dominio suo, et in dominio baronum suorum, nihil se intromittet; scilicet Duvelina cum pertinentiis suis; et Mida cum omnibus pertinentiis suis, sicut unquam Murchat Va Mailethlachlin eam melius

et plenius tenuit aut aliqui qui de eo eam tenuerunt; et excepta Wesefordia cum omnibus pertinentiis suis, scilicet cum tota Lagenia; et excepta Vaterfordia cum tota terra illa quae est a Vaterfordia usque ad Duncarvan; ita quod Duncarvan sit cum omnibus pertinentiis suis infra terram illam.

9. Et si Hybernenses qui aufugerunt redire voluerint ad terram baronum regis Angliae, redeant in pace, reddendo tributum praedictum sicut alii reddunt, vel faciendo antiqua servitia quae facere solebant pro terris suis. Et hoc sit in arbitrio et voluntate dominorum suorum.

10. Et si aliqui redire noluerint, et domini eorum requisierint regem Connactae, ipse cogat eos redire ad terram suam, ut ibi remaneant et pacem habeant.

11. Et rex Connactae accipiat obsides ab omnibus quos ei commisit dominus rex Angliae ad voluntatem domini regis et suam.

12. Et ipse dabit obsides ad voluntatem domini regis Angliae, illos vel alios;

13. et ipsi servient domino regi de canibus suis et avibus, singulis annis de praesentiis suis.

14. Et nullum omnino de quacunque terra domini regis sit retinebunt, contra voluntatem domini regis et mandatum domini regis.

Testibus his: Ricardo episcopo Wintoniensi, Gaufrido episcopo Eliensi, Laurentio Duvelinensi archiepiscopo, Gaufrido et Nicholao et Rogero, capellanis regis, Villelmo comite de Exessae et Ricardo de Luci, Gaufrido de Pertico, Reginaldo de Curteneia.

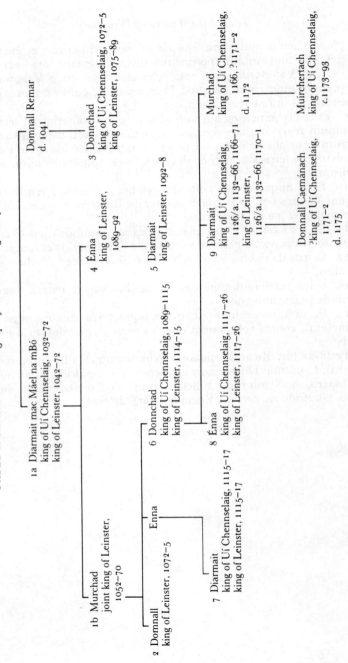

TABLE I: *Succession to the Kingships of Uí Chennselaig and of Leinster*

Domnall Remar
d. 1041

1a Diarmait mac Máel na mBó
king of Uí Chennselaig, 1032–72
king of Leinster, 1042–72

3 Donnchad
king of Uí Chennselaig, 1072–5
king of Leinster, 1075–89

1b Murchad
joint king of Leinster,
1052–70

4 Énna
king of Leinster,
1089–92

5 Diarmait
king of Leinster, 1092–8

2 Domnall
king of Leinster, 1072–5

Enna

6 Donnchad
king of Uí Chennselaig, 1089–1115
king of Leinster, 1114–15

7 Diarmait
king of Uí Chennselaig, 1115–17
king of Leinster, 1115–17

8 Énna
king of Uí Chennselaig, 1117–26
king of Leinster, 1117–26

9 Diarmait
king of Uí Chennselaig,
1126/a. 1132–66, 1166–71
king of Leinster,
1126/a. 1132–66, 1170–1

Murchad
king of Uí Chennselaig,
1166, ?1171–2
d. 1172

Domnall Caemánach
?king of Uí Chennselaig,
1171–2
d. 1175

Muirchertach
king of Uí Chennselaig,
c.1173–93

TABLE 2: *Immediate Family of Diarmait Mac Murchada*

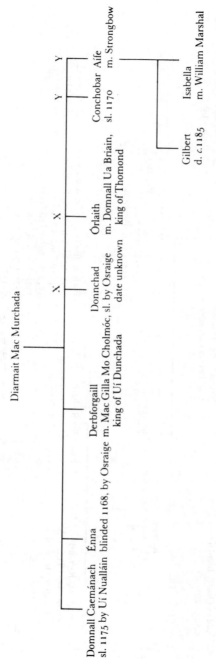

X by Sadb, daughter of Cerball Mac Fáeláin, king of Uí Fáeláin.
Y by Mór, daughter of Muirchertach Ua Tuathail, king of Uí Muiredaig.

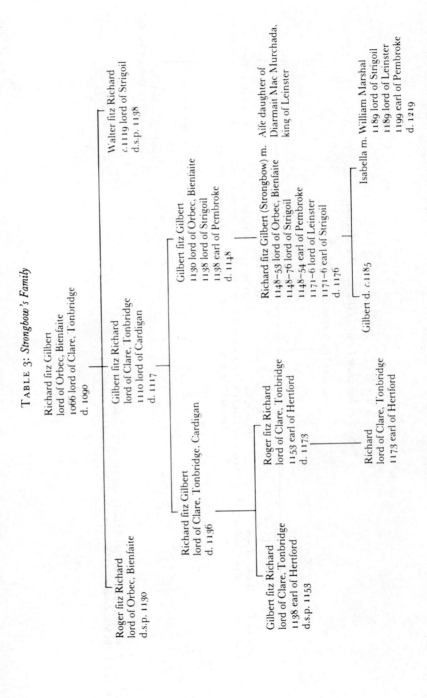

TABLE 3: *Strongbow's Family*

Richard fitz Gilbert
lord of Orbec, Bienfaite
1066 lord of Clare, Tonbridge
d. 1090

├─ Roger fitz Richard
│ lord of Orbec, Bienfaite
│ d.s.p. 1130
│
├─ Gilbert fitz Richard
│ lord of Clare, Tonbridge
│ 1110 lord of Cardigan
│ d. 1117
│ │
│ ├─ Richard fitz Gilbert
│ │ lord of Clare, Tonbridge. Cardigan
│ │ d. 1136
│ │ │
│ │ ├─ Gilbert fitz Richard
│ │ │ lord of Clare, Tonbridge
│ │ │ 1138 earl of Hertford
│ │ │ d.s.p. 1153
│ │ │
│ │ └─ Roger fitz Richard
│ │   lord of Clare, Tonbridge
│ │   1153 earl of Hertford
│ │   d. 1173
│ │   │
│ │   └─ Richard
│ │   lord of Clare, Tonbridge
│ │   1173 earl of Hertford
│ │
│ └─ Gilbert fitz Gilbert
│   1130 lord of Orbec, Bienfaite
│   1138 lord of Strigoil
│   1138 earl of Pembroke
│   d. 1148
│   │
│   └─ Richard fitz Gilbert (Strongbow) m. Aífe daughter of
│   1148–53 lord of Orbec, Bienfaite   Diarmait Mac Murchada.
│   1148–76 lord of Strigoil   king of Leinster
│   1148–54 earl of Pembroke
│   1171–6 lord of Leinster
│   1171–6 earl of Strigoil
│   d. 1176
│   │
│   ├─ Isabella m. William Marshal
│   │   1189 lord of Strigoil
│   │   1189 lord of Leinster
│   │   1199 earl of Pembroke
│   │   d. 1219
│   │
│   └─ Gilbert d. *c.*1185
│
└─ Walter fitz Richard
   *c.*1119 lord of Strigoil
   d.s.p. 1138

BIBLIOGRAPHY

A. MANUSCRIPTS

Dublin, NLI MS 1.
London, BL Harleian charter 83. C. 25.
London, PRO, E 159/82/m. 62.
Oxford, Bodleian Library, Rawl. B. 499.

B. PRINTED PRIMARY SOURCES

AELFRIC, *Life of Swithun*, trans. D. Whitelock (London, 1955).
Aisling Meic Conglinne, ed. K. Meyer (London, 1892).
Ancient laws and institutes of Ireland (6 vols., Dublin, 1865–1901).
ANDERSON, A. O., and ANDERSON, M. O., *The chronicle of Melrose* (London, 1936).
Annála Connacht, ed. A. Martin Freeman (Dublin, 1944).
Annála ríoghachta Éireann: Annals of the kingdom of Ireland by the Four Masters, ed. J. O'Donovan (7 vols., Dublin, 1851, repr. 1854).
Annales Cambriae, ed. J. Williams (Rolls series, London, 1860).
Annales monastici, ed. H. R. Luard (5 vols., Rolls series, London, 1864–9).
[Annals of Boyle], 'The Annals in Cotton MS Titus A xxv', ed. A. M. Freeman, *Rev. Celtique*, 41 (1924), 301–30; 42 (1925), 283–305; 43 (1926), 358–84; 44 (1927), 336–61.
Annals of Clonmacnoise, ed. D. Murphy (Dublin, 1896).
Annals of Inisfallen, ed. S. Mac Airt (Dublin, 1951).
Annals of Inisfallen reproduced in facsimile, ed. R. I. Best and E. Mac Neill (Dublin, 1933).
Annals of Loch Cé, ed. W. M. Hennessy (2 vols., Rolls series, London, 1871).
'The Annals of Tigernach', ed. W. Stokes, *Rev. Celt.* 16 (1895), 374–419; 17 (1896), 6–33, 119–263, 337–420; 18 (1897), 9–59, 150–97, 267–303.
Annals of Ulster, ed. W. M. Hennessy and B. MacCarthy (4 vols., Dublin, 1887–1901).
Annals of Ulster (to AD 1131), ed. S. Mac Airt and G. Mac Niocaill (Dublin, 1983).
Audacht Morainn, ed. F. Kelly (Dublin, 1976).

BARTRUM, C. C. (ed.), *Early Welsh genealogical tracts* (Cardiff, 1966).
—— *Welsh genealogies, A.D. 300–1400* (8 vols., Aberystwyth, 1983).
BEDE, *Ecclesiastical history*, ed. B. Colgrave and R. A. B. Mynors (Oxford, 1969).
BERNARD OF CLAIRVAUX, *St Bernard of Clairvaux's life of St Malachy of Armagh*, ed. H. J. Lawlor (London, 1920).
—— *Sancti Bernardi opera*, ed. J. Leclercq and H. M. Rochais (8 vols. in 9, Rome, 1957–77).
BIELER, L. (ed.), *The Irish penitentials* (Scriptores Latini Hiberniae, 7; Dublin, 1975).
—— *The Patrician texts in the Book of Armagh* (Scriptores Latini Hiberniae, 10; Dublin, 1979).
Betha Colmáin maic Luacháin, ed. K. Meyer (Dublin, 1911).
Black Book of Limerick, ed. J. Mac Caffrey (Dublin, 1907).
The Book of Leinster, ed. R. Atkinson (Dublin, 1880).
The Book of Leinster, ed. R. I. Best, O. Bergin, M. A. O'Brien, and A. O'Sullivan (6 vols., Dublin, 1954–83).
The Book of Obits and martyrology of the cathedral church of the Holy Trinity, ed. J. H. Todd (Dublin, 1844).
Branwen verch LLyr, ed. D. S. Thomas (Dublin, 1961).
Brenhinedd y Saesson, ed. T. Jones (Cardiff, 1971).
BROOKS, E. St J., 'A charter of John de Courcy to the abbey of Navan', *RSAI Jn.* 63 (1933), 38–45.
—— *Irish cartularies of Llanthony prima and secunda* (IMC, Dublin, 1953).
—— *Knights' fees in counties Wexford, Carlow and Kilkenny* (IMC, Dublin, 1950).
—— 'An unpublished charter of Raymond le Gros', *RSAI Jn.* 69 (1939), 167–9.
—— 'Unpublished charters relating to Ireland, 1177–82, from the archives of the city of Exeter', *RIA Proc.* 43 C (1935–7), 313–66.
Brut y Tywysogyon or the Chronicle of the princes: Peniarth MS. 20 version, ed. T. Jones (Board of Celtic Studies, University of Wales History and Law series, 11; Cardiff, 1952).
Brut y Tywysogyon or the Chronicle of the princes: Red Book of Hergest version, ed. T. Jones (Board of Celtic Studies, University of Wales History and Law series, 16; Cardiff, 1955).
BUTLER, C. M., and BERNARD, J. H., 'The charters of the Cistercian abbey of Duiske in the county of Kilkenny', *RIA Proc.* 35 C (1918), 1–188.
Caithréim Cellacháin Caisil, ed. A. Bugge (Christiania, 1905).
Calendar of ancient deeds and muniments preserved in the Pembroke Estate Office, Dublin (Dublin, 1891).

Calendar of Archbishop Alen's Register, c.1172–1534, ed. C. MacNeill (Dublin, 1950).

Calendar of charter rolls (6 vols., London, 1903–27).

Calendar of documents relating to Ireland, ed. H. S. Sweetman (5 vols., London, 1875–6).

Calendar of the Gormanston register, ed. J. Mills and M. J. McEnery (RSAI, Dublin, 1916).

Calendar of Ormond deeds, ed. E. Curtis (6 vols., Dublin, 1932–43).

Calendar of patent rolls, 1232–47 (etc.) (London, 1906–71).

A calendar of the public records relating to Pembrokeshire, ed. H. Owen (3 vols., London, 1911–18).

Canterbury professions, ed. M. Richter (Canterbury and York Society, 67; Torquay, 1973).

Cartae antiquae rolls, 1–10 (Pipe Roll Society, NS 17; London, 1939); *11–20* (NS 71; 1957).

Cartulaires de Saint Ymer-en-Auge et de Bricquebec, ed. C. Bréard (Société de l'Histoire de Normandie, 71; Rouen, 1908).

Cartularium S. Johannis Baptistae de Carmarthen, ed. T. Phillips (Cheltenham, 1865).

The cartulary of the knights of St John of Jerusalem in England: secunda camera: Essex, ed. M. Gervers (British Academy: Records of social and economic history, NS 6; Oxford, 1982).

Chartae, privilegia et immunitates (Irish Record Commission, Dublin, 1829–30).

Charters of the honour of Mowbray, 1107–1191, ed. D. E. Greenaway (British Academy: Records of Social and Economic history, NS 1; London, 1972).

Chartularies of St Mary's Abbey, Dublin, ed. J. T. Gilbert (2 vols., Rolls series, London, 1884–6).

The chartulary of the high church of Chichester, ed. W. D. Peckham (Sussex Record Society, 46; [Lewes], 1942–3).

Chronica regum Manniae et insularum, ed. G. Broderick (Belfast, 1979).

The Chronicle of Battle Abbey, ed. E. Searle (Oxford, 1980).

Chronicles of the reigns of Stephen, Henry II and Richard I, ed. R. Howlett (4 vols., Rolls series, London, 1885–90).

Chronicon Scotorum, ed. W. M. Hennessy (Rolls series, London, 1866).

Cogadh Gaedhel re Gallaibh, ed. J. H. Todd (Rolls series, London, 1867).

Corpus iuris Hibernici, ed. D. A. Binchy (6 vols., Dublin, 1978).

Councils and synods with other documents relating to the English Church, ed. D. Whitelock, M. Brett, and C. N. L. Brooke (Oxford, 1981).

The course of the exchequer, ed. C. Johnson (London, 1950).

Crede mihi, ed. J. T. Gilbert (Dublin, 1897).

Crith gablach, ed. D. A. Binchy (Dublin, 1941).

CURTIS, E., 'Two unpublished charters of John de Courcy, *princeps Ulidiae*', *Belfast Nat. Hist. Soc. Proc.*, session 1928–9 (1930), 2–9.

—— and McDOWELL, R. B. (ed.), *Irish historical documents, 1172–1922* (London, 1943).

DAVIES, J. C. (ed.), *Episcopal acts relating to Welsh dioceses, 1066–1272* (2 vols., Historical Society of the Church in Wales, 1, 1946; 3–4, 1948).

DELISLE, L., and BERGER, E. (ed.), *Recueil des actes de Henri II* (4 vols., Paris, 1909–27).

DILLON, M., *The cycles of the kings* (London, 1946).

DOBBS, M. C., 'The Ban-Shenchus', *Rev. Celt.* 47 (1930), 282–339; 48 (1931), 163–234; 49 (1932), 437–89.

Documents illustrative of English history in the thirteenth and fourteenth centuries, ed. H. Cole (London, 1844).

Documents preserved in France, ed. J. H. Round (London, 1899).

Domesday Book (4 vols., London, 1783–1816).

DUGDALE, W., *Monasticon Anglicanum*, ed. J. Caley, H. Ellis, and B. Bandinel (6 vols. in 8, London, 1817–30; reprint, 6 vols., 1846).

EADMER, *Historia novorum*, ed. M. Rule (Rolls series, London, 1884).

—— *The life of St Anselm, archbishop of Canterbury by Eadmer*, ed. R. W. Southern (Oxford, 1962).

Earldom of Gloucester charters, ed. R. B. Patterson (London, 1973).

Facsimiles of national manuscripts of Ireland, ed. J. T. Gilbert (4 vols., Dublin, 1874–84).

FANTOSME, JORDAN, *Jordan Fantosme's chronicle*, ed. R. C. Johnston (Oxford, 1981).

Fled Bricrend, ed. G. Henderson (Ir. Texts Soc. 2; Dublin, 1899).

FLORENCE OF WORCESTER, *Chronicon ex chronicis*, ed. B. Thorpe (2 vols., London, 1848–9).

FRASER, J., et al., *Irish texts*, 2 vols. (London, 1931).

GEOFFREY OF MONMOUTH, *Historia regum Britanniae*, ed. A. Griscom (London, 1929).

GERALD OF WALES, *Expugnatio Hibernia: the conquest of Ireland*, ed. A. B. Scott and F. X. Martin (Dublin, 1978).

—— *Giraldi Cambrensis opera*, ed. J. S. Brewer, J. F. Dimock, and G. F. Warner (8 vols., Rolls series, London, 1861–91).

—— *Topography of Ireland*, trans. J. J. O'Meara (Dundalk, 1951).

GERVASE OF CANTERBURY, *Historical works*, ed. W. Stubbs (2 vols., Rolls series, London, 1879–80).

Gesta Stephani, ed. K. R. Potter (Oxford, 1976).

[Glanvill], *The treatise on the laws and customs of the realm of England commonly called Glanvill*, ed. G. D. G. Hall (London, 1965).

The great roll of the pipe for the first year of the reign of King Richard the First, 1188–1189, ed. J. Hunter (London, 1844).

The Great Rolls of the Pipe for the Second, Third and Fourth Years of the Reign of King Henry the Second, 1155–1158, ed. J. Hunter (London, Record Commission, 1844).

The Great rolls of the Pipe for the Reign of Henry the Second, 5th to 34th years (30 vols., London, Pipe Roll Society, 1884–1925).

GWYNN, A., 'Some unpublished texts from the Black Book of Christ Church, Dublin', *Anal. Hib.* 16 (1946), 281–337.

HADDAN, A. W., and STUBBS, W. (edd.), *Councils and ecclesiastical documents relating to Great Britain and Ireland* (3 vols., Oxford, 1869–78).

Histoire de Guillaume le Maréchal, ed. P. Meyer (3 vols., Paris, 1891–1901).

Historia et cartularium monasterii sancti Petri Gloucestriae, ed. W. H. Hart (3 vols., Rolls series, London, 1863–7).

Historia Gruffud vab Kenan, ed. D. Simon Evans (Cardiff, 1977).

Historic and municipal documents of Ireland, 1172–1320, ed. J. T. Gilbert (Rolls series, London, 1870).

The history of Gruffydd ap Cynan, ed. A. Jones (Manchester, 1910).

HOLTZMANN, W., *Papsturkunden in England* (Abhandlungen der Gesellschaft der Wissenschaften in Göttingen, phil.-hist. Klasse, 2nd ser. 25, 1930–1; 3rd ser. 14, 15, 33, 1933–52).

HUGH THE CHANTOR, *The history of the church of York, 1066–1127,* ed. C. Johnson (London, 1961).

JOHN OF SALISBURY, *Historia pontificalis,* ed. M. Chibnall (London, 1956).

—— *The letters of John of Salisbury,* ed. W. J. Millor and H. E. Butler (London, 1955).

—— *Metalogicon,* ed. C. C. J. Webb (Oxford, 1929).

JOHN OF WORCESTER, *The chronicle of John of Worcester, 1118–1140,* ed. J. R. H. Weaver (Anecdota Oxoniensia, Oxford, 1908).

KNOTT, E., 'Filidh Éireann go haointeach: Ó Ceallaigh's Christmas feast to the poets of Ireland, A.D. 1351', *Ériu,* 5 (1911), 50–69.

LANFRANC, *The letters of Lanfranc, archbishop of Canterbury,* ed. H. Clover and M. Gibson (Oxford, 1979).

LAWLOR, H. J., 'A calendar of the Liber Niger and Liber Albus of Christ Church, Dublin', *RIA Proc.* 27 (1908), 1–93.

—— 'A fresh authority for the Synod of Kells', *RIA Proc.* 36 (1922), 16–22.

LAWRIE, A. C., *Early Scottish charters* (Glasgow, 1905).

An leabhar Muimhneach maraon le suim aguisíní, ed. Tadhg Ó Donnchadha (Dublin, Irish Manuscripts Commission, 1940).

Lebor na Cert: the Book of Rights, ed. M. Dillon (Ir. Texts Soc. 46; Dublin, 1962).

LECLERCQ, J., 'Deux épitres de Saint Bernard et de son secrétaire', in J. Leclercq (ed.), *Recueil d'études sur Saint Bernard et ses écrits*, ii (Rome, 1966), 313–18.

LEES, B. A. (ed.), *Records of the Templars in England in the twelfth century: the inquest of 1185* (London, 1935).

Liber Eliensis, ed. E. O. Blake (Camden Society, 92; London, 1962).

Liber Luciani de laude Cestrie, ed. M. V. Taylor (Lancashire and Cheshire Record Society, 54; Manchester, 1912).

LIEBERMANN, F., *Die Gesetze der Angelsachsen* (3 vols., Halle 1903–16).

Litterae Cantuarienses, ed. J. B. Sheppard (3 vols., Rolls series, London, 1887–9).

The Mabinogion, trans. G. Jones and T. Jones (London, 1974).

MACERLEAN, J., 'The synod of Ráith Bresail: boundaries of the dioceses of Ireland', *Archiv. Hib.* 3 (1914), 1–33.

MAC NIOCAILL, G., 'The charters of John, lord of Ireland, to the see of Dublin', *Reportorium Novum*, 3 (1963–4), 282–306.

—— *Na Buirgéisi, XII–XV aois* (2 vols., Dublin, 1964).

—— *Notitiae as Leabhar Cheanannais, 1033–1161* (Dublin, 1961).

Magni rotuli scaccarii Normanniae, ed. T. Stapleton (2 vols., London, 1840–4).

MAP, WALTER, *De nugis curialium*, ed. M. R. James (Oxford, 1914).

MEERSEMAN, G. G., 'Two unknown confraternity letters of St Bernard', in *Cîteaux in de Nederlanden*, vi (1955), 173–8.

Memorials of St Dunstan, ed. W. Stubbs (Roll series, London, 1874).

The metrical Dindshenchas, ed. E. Gwynn (5 vols., RIA, Todd lecture series 8–12, Dublin, 1903–35).

MEYER, K. (ed.), *The instructions of King Cormac mac Airt* (RIA, Todd Lecture series, 15; Dublin, 1909).

Miscellaneous Irish annals (A.D. 1114–1437), ed. S. Ó hInnse (Dublin, 1947).

Móirtimchell Éirenn uile dorigne Muirchertach mac Néill, ed. E. Hogan (Dublin, 1901).

O'BRIEN, M. A., *Corpus genealogiarum Hiberniae* (Dublin, 1962).

O'DALY, M., 'A poem on the Airgialla', *Ériu*, 16 (1952), 179–88.

O'DONOGHUE, T., 'Advice to a prince', *Ériu*, 9 (1921), 43–54.

O'DONOVAN, J., 'The circuit of Ireland by Muircheartach mac Neill, prince of Aileach', in *Tracts relating to Ireland* (Dublin, 1841), i. 24–68.

Ó DUBHAGÁIN, S., and Ó hUIDRÍN, G., *Topographical poems*, ed. J. O'Donovan (Dublin, 1862).

—— *Topographical poems*, ed. J. Carney (Dublin, 1943).

O'MEARA, J. J., 'Giraldus Cambrensis in Topographia Hibernie: text of the first recension', *RIA Proc.* 52 (1949), 113–78.

ORDERIC VITALIS, *Historia ecclesiastica*, ed. M. Chibnall (6 vols., Oxford, 1969–80).

ORPEN, G. H., 'Some Irish Cistercian documents', *EHR* 23 (1913), 303–13.

PATRICK, bishop of Dublin, *The writings of Bishop Patrick, 1074–84*, ed. A. Gwynn (Scriptores Latini Hiberniae, 1; Dublin, 1955).

PENDER, S. (ed.), *The O'Clery book of genealogies, Anal. Hib.* 18 (1951).

Petri Blesensis opera omnia, ed. J. A. Giles (4 vols., Oxford, 1846–7).

Pipe roll 31 Henry I, ed. J. Hunter (London, Record Commission, 1833; facsimile reprint, 1929).

PLUMMER, C. (ed.), *Two Saxon chronicles parallel* (Oxford, 1892).

—— 'Vie et miracles de St Laurent, archevêque de Dublin', *Anal. Bolland.* 33 (1914), 121–85.

The poems of Blathmac son of Cú Brettan, ed. J. Carney (Ir. Texts Soc. 47; Dublin, 1964).

RAINE, J. (ed.), *Historians of the church of York* (3 vols., Rolls series, London, 1879–94).

RALPH OF DISS, *Opera historica*, ed. W. Stubbs (2 vols., Rolls series, London, 1876).

Red Book of the Exchequer, ed. H. Hall (3 vols., Rolls series, London, 1897).

Red Book of the earls of Kildare, ed. G. Mac Niocaill (IMC, Dublin, 1964).

Red Book of Ormond, ed. Newport B. White (IMC, Dublin, 1932).

Regesta regum Anglo-Normannorum, 1066–1154 (4 vols., Oxford, 1913–69).

Regesta regum Scottorum, ed. G. W. S. Barrow (2 vols., Edinburgh, 1960–71).

Register of the abbey of St Thomas the Martyr, Dublin (Rolls series, London, 1889).

Registrum de Kilmainham, 1326–50, ed. C. McNeill (Dublin, Irish Manuscripts Commission, 1932).

Registrum prioratus omnium sanctorum iuxta Dublin, ed. R. Butler (Dublin, 1845).

Regularis concordia, ed. T. Symons (London, 1953).

ROBERTSON, A. J. (ed.), *The laws of the kings of England from Edmund to Henry I* (Cambridge, 1925).

ROBERTSON, J. C. (ed.), *Materials for the history of Thomas Becket, archbishop of Canterbury* (7 vols., Rolls series, London, 1875–85).

ROGER OF HOWDEN, *Chronica*, ed. W. Stubbs (4 vols., Rolls series, London, 1868–71).

ROGER OF HOWDEN, *Gesta regis Henrici secundi Benedicti abbatis*, ed. W. Stubbs (2 vols., Rolls series, London, 1867).

Rotuli de dominabus et pueris et puellis de xii comitatibus (PRS 25; London, 1913).

The rule of Tallaght, ed. E. Gwynn (Dublin, 1927).

SAWYER, P. H., *Anglo-Saxon charters: an annotated list and bibliography* (London, 1968).

SHEEHY, M. P., *Pontificia Hibernica: medieval papal chancery documents concerning Ireland, 640–1261* (2 vols., Dublin, 1962–5).

—— 'The registrum novum: a manuscript of Holy Trinity Cathedral: the medieval charters', *Reportorium Novum*, 3 (1963–4), 249–81.

Sir Christopher Hatton's book of seals, ed. L. C. Loyd and D. M. Stenton (Northamptonshire Record Society, 15; Oxford, 1942–50).

SOMERVILLE, R. (ed.), *Scotia pontificia* (Oxford, 1982).

The song of Dermot and the earl, ed. G. H. Orpen (London, 1892).

STENTON, F. M. (ed.), *Facsimiles of early charters from Northamptonshire collections* (Northamptonshire Record Society, 4; [Northampton], 1929).

Stogursey charters, ed. T. D. Tremlett and N. Blakiston (Somerset Record Society, 61; London, 1946).

Stoke by Clare cartulary, ed. C. Harper-Bill and R. Mortimer (3 vols., Suffolk Record Society: Suffolk charters, 4–6; Ipswich, 1982–4).

STONES, E. L. G. (ed.), *Anglo-Scottish relations, 1174–1328: some selected documents* (London, 1965).

SUGER, *Vie de Louis VI le Gros*, ed. H. Waquet (Paris, 1964).

SYMEON OF DURHAM, *Historical works*, ed. T. Arnold (2 vols., Rolls series, London, 1882–5).

THURNEYSEN, R., 'Aus dem irischen Recht I: das Unfrei-Lehen', *ZCP* 14 (1923), 335–94; 'Aus dem irischen Recht II', 15 (1924), 238–60.

The tribes and customs of Hy-Many, ed. J. O'Donovan (Dublin, 1843).

Vita Edwardi, ed. F. Barlow (London, 1962).

Vita Wulfstani, ed. R. R. Darlington (Camden Society, 40; London, 1928).

WILLIAM OF JUMIÈGES, *Gesta Normannorum ducum*, ed. J. Marx (Rouen, 1914).

WILLIAM OF MALMESBURY, *Gesta pontificum*, ed. N. E. S. A. Hamilton (Rolls series, London, 1870).

—— *Gesta regum*, ed. W. Stubbs (2 vols., Rolls series, London, 1887–9).

—— *Historia novella*, ed. K. R. Potter (London, 1955).

WILLIAM OF POITIERS, *Gesta Guillelmi ducis Normannorum et regis Anglorum*, ed. R. Foreville (Paris, 1952).

The Worcester cartulary, ed. R. R. Darlington (Pipe Roll Society, NS 38; London, 1962–3).

C. SECONDARY WORKS

ALTSCHUL, M., *A baronial family in medieval England: the Clares, 1217–1314* (Baltimore, 1965).

Ancient Irish histories of Spencer, Campion, Hanmer and Marleburgh, ed. J. Ware (2 vols., Dublin, 1809).

ANDERSON, A. O., 'Anglo-Scottish relations from Constantine II to William', *Scot. Hist. Rev.* 42 (1963), 1–20.

BACHRACH, B. S., 'The idea of the Angevin empire', *Albion*, 10 (1978), 293–9.

BAKER, D., 'Legend and reality: the case of Waldef of Melrose', *Studies in Church History*, 12 (1975), 59–82.

—— '*Viri religiosi* and the York election dispute', *Studies in Church History*, 7 (1971), 87–100.

BARLOW, F., *Edward the Confessor* (London, 1970).

—— *The English Church, 1000–1066* (London, 1963, 2nd edn., 1979).

—— *The English Church, 1066–1154* (London, 1979).

—— *The feudal kingdom of England, 1014–1216* (London, 1955).

—— *William Rufus* (London, 1983).

BARROW, G. W. S., 'The Anglo-Scottish border', *Northern History*, 1 (1966), 21–42.

—— 'King David I and the honour of Lancaster', *EHR* 70 (1955), 85–9.

BARTLETT, R., *Gerald of Wales, 1146–1223* (Oxford, 1982).

BAUER, C., BOEHM, L., and MÜLLER, M. (edd.), *Speculum historiale: Geschichte im Spiegel von Geschichtsschreibung und Geschichtsdeutung* (Freiburg, 1965).

BENVENISTE, E., *Indo-European language and society* (London, 1973).

BETHELL, D., 'English monks and Irish reform in the eleventh and twelfth centuries', *Hist. Studies*, 8 (1971), 111–35.

BINCHY, D. A., 'Aimser Chue', in *Féil-sgríbhinn Eóin Mhic Néill*, 18–22.

—— *Celtic and Anglo-Saxon kingship* (Oxford, 1970).

—— 'Distraint in Irish law', *Celtica*, 10 (1973), 22–71.

—— 'The fair of Tailtiu and the feast of Tara', *Ériu*, 18 (1958), 113–38.

—— 'Irish history and Irish law II', *Studia Hib.* 16 (1976), 7–45.

BINCHY, D. A., 'The linguistic and historical value of the Irish law tracts', *Brit. Acad. Proc.* 29 (1943), 195–228.

BLOCH, M., *Feudal society* (2nd edn., London, 1962).

BOSSY, J., and JUPP, P. (edd.), *Essays presented to Michael Roberts* (Belfast, 1976).

BRETT, M., *The English Church under Henry I* (Oxford, 1975).

—— 'John of Worcester and his contemporaries', in R. H. C. Davis *et al.* (edd.), *The writing of history in the Middle Ages* (Oxford, 1981), 101–26.

BRODERICK, G., 'Irish and Welsh strands in the genealogy of Godred Crovan', *Journal of the Manx Museum*, 8 (1980), 32–8.

BROOKE, C., 'The archbishops of St David's, Llandaff and Caerleon-on-Usk', in N. K. Chadwick (ed.), *Studies in the early British Church* (Cambridge, 1958), 201–42.

BROOKE, Z. N., *The English Church and the papacy* (London, 1931).

BROOKS, E. St J., 'The de Ridelesfords', *RSAI Jn.* 81 (1951), 115–38; 82 (1952), 45–51.

—— 'The family of de Marisco', *RSAI Jn.* 41 (1931), 22–35.

BROWN, R. A., 'A list of castles, 1154–1216', *EHR* 74 (1959), 249–80.

—— 'Royal castle-building in England, 1154–1216', *EHR* 70 (1955), 353–98.

BULLOUGH, D. A., and STOREY, R. L. (edd.), *The study of medieval records: essays in honour of Kathleen Major* (London, 1971).

BYRNE, F. J., *Irish kings and high-kings* (London, 1973).

CAMPBELL, J., 'Some twelfth-century views of the Anglo-Saxon past', *Peritia*, 3 (1984), 131–50.

—— (ed.), *The Anglo-Saxons* (London, 1982).

CHAPLAIS, P., 'English diplomatic records to the end of Edward's reign', in D. A. Bullough and R. L. Storey (edd.), *The study of medieval records: essays in honour of Kathleen Major* (London, 1971).

CHARLES, B. G., *Old Norse relations with Wales* (Cardiff, 1934).

CHARLES-EDWARDS, T. M., 'The date of the four branches of the Mabinogi', *Cymmrod. Soc. Trans.*, session 1970, part ii, 263–98.

—— 'Kinship, status and the origins of the hide', *Past and Present*, 65 (1972), 3–33.

—— 'The social context of Irish *peregrinatio*', *Celtica*, 11 (1976), 43–59.

CHENEY, M., 'Some observations on a papal privilege of 1120 for the archbishop of York', *Jn. Ecc. Hist.* 31 (1980), 429–39.

CHRIMES, S. B., *King Edward I's policy for Wales* (Cardiff, 1969).

COCKAYNE, G. E., *The complete peerage of England, Scotland, Ireland,*

Great Britain and the United Kingdom (8 vols., Exeter, 1887–98, ed. Vicary Gibbs and others; 13 vols., London, 1910–40).

Contributions to a dictionary of the Irish language, 22 fascicules (Royal Irish Academy, Dublin, 1913–76) [fascicules 1–4 titled *Dictionary of the Irish language*].

CORNER, D., 'The *Gesta regis Henrici secundi* and *Chronica* of Roger, parson of Howden', *Bulletin of the Institute of Historical Research*, 56 (1983), 126–44.

COSGROVE, A. (ed.), *Marriage in Ireland* (Dublin, 1985).

CROUCH, D., 'Oddities in the early history of the Marcher lordship of Gower, 1107–1166', *Bulletin of the Board of Celtic Studies*, 31 (1984), 133–42.

CURTIS, E., 'The Fitz Rerys, Welsh lords of Cloghran, Co. Dublin', *Louth Arch. Soc. Jn.* 5 (1921), 13–17.

—— *A history of medieval Ireland* (2nd edn., London, 1938).

—— 'Murchertach O'Brien, high-king of Ireland, and his Norman son-in-law, Arnulf de Montgomery, *circa* 1100', *RSAI Jn.* 51 (1921), 116–24.

DAVIES, R. R., *Conquest, coexistence and change: Wales, 1063–1415* (Oxford, 1987).

—— 'King Henry I and Wales', in H. Mayr-Harting and R. I. Moore (edd.), *Studies in medieval history presented to R. H. C. Davis* (Oxford, 1985), 132–47.

DAVIES, W., *Wales in the early Middle Ages* (Leicester, 1982).

DAVIS, R. H. C., *King Stephen, 1135–1154* (London, 1967).

—— *The Normans and their myth* (London, 1976).

—— *et al.* (edd.), *The writing of history in the Middle Ages* (Oxford, 1981).

DOLLEY, M., *Anglo-Norman Ireland* (Dublin, 1972).

DOUGLAS, D. C., *William the Conqueror* (London, 1964).

EDWARDS, J. G., 'The Normans and the Welsh march', *Br. Acad. Proc.* 42 (1956), 155–77.

EDWARDS, R. DUDLEY, 'Anglo-Norman relations with Connacht, 1169–1224', *IHS* 1 (1938–9), 135–53.

ELLIS, A. S., 'On the landholders of Gloucestershire named in Domesday book', *Transactions of the Bristol and Gloucestershire Archaeological Society*, 4 (1879–80), 86–198.

EMPEY, C. A., 'The settlement of the kingdom of Limerick', in Lydon, *Eng. and Ire.* 1–25.

EYTON, R. W., *Court, household and itinerary of King Henry II* (London, 1878).

FARRER, W., *Honors and knights' fees* (3 vols., London, 1923–5).

Féil-sgríbhinn Eóin Mhic Néill: Essays and studies presented to Professor Eoin

MacNeill on the occasion of his seventieth birthday, ed. John Ryan (Dublin, 1940).

FENTON, R., *A historical tour through Pembrokeshire* (London, 1811; repr. Brecon, 1903).

FLANAGAN, M. T., 'Henry II and the kingdom of Uí Fáeláin', in J. Bradley (ed.), *Settlement and society in medieval Ireland: studies presented to F. X. Martin, O.S.A.* (Kilkenny, 1988), 312–24.

—— 'Hiberno-papal relations in the late twelfth century', *Archiv. Hib.* 34 (1976–7), 55–70.

—— 'Mac Dalbaig, a Leinster chieftain', *RSAI Jn.* 111 (1981), 5–13.

—— 'Strongbow, Henry II and Anglo-Norman intervention in Ireland', in J. Gillingham and J. C. Holt (edd.), *War and government in the Middle Ages: essays in honour of J. O. Prestwich* (Woodbridge, 1984), 62–77.

FOWLER, G. H., 'The Drayton charters', *Bedfordshire Historical Record Society*, 11 (1927).

FRAME, R., *Colonial Ireland, 1169–1369* (Dublin, 1981).

—— 'The justiciar and the murder of the MacMurroughs in 1282', *IHS* 18 (1972), 223–30.

FREEMAN, E. A., *The history of the Norman conquest of England* (6 vols., Oxford, 1867–79).

—— *The reign of William Rufus* (2 vols., Oxford, 1882).

GANSHOF, F. L., *Feudalism* (2nd edn., London, 1964).

GERRIETS, M., 'Economy and society: clientship according to the Irish laws', *Cambridge Medieval Celtic Studies*, 6 (1983), 43–61.

'The organization of exchange in early Christian Ireland', *Journal of Economic History*, 41 (1981), 171–8.

GIBSON, M., *Lanfranc of Bec* (Oxford, 1978).

GILBERT, J. T., *A history of the city of Dublin* (3 vols., Dublin, 1854–9).

GILLINGHAM, J., *The Angevin empire* (London, 1984).

GLEBER, H., *Papst Eugen III* (Jena, 1936).

GRABOWSKI, K., and DUMVILLE, D., *Chronicles and annals of medieval Ireland and Wales* (Woodbridge, 1984).

GRANSDEN, A., *Historical writing in England, c.550–1307* (London, 1974).

GRIERSON, P., 'Election and inheritance in early Germanic kingship', *Cambridge Hist. Jn.* 7 (1941), 1–22.

GRIFFITHS, R., 'The cartulary and muniments of the Fort family of Llanstephan', *Bulletin of the Board of Celtic Studies*, 24 (1970–2), 311–84.

GWYNN, A., 'Brian in Armagh, 1005', *Seanchas Ardmhacha*, 9 (1978–9), 35–50.

—— 'The centenary of the Synod of Kells', *IER*, 5th ser., 77 (1952), 161–76; 78 (1952), 250–64.

—— 'The diocese of Limerick in the twelfth century', *N Munster Antiq. Jn.* 5 (1946–7), 35–48.

—— 'The first bishops of Dublin', *Reportorium Novum*, 1 (1955), 1–26.

—— 'The first synod of Cashel', *IER*, 5th ser., 66 (1945), 81–92; 67 (1946), 109–22.

—— 'Ireland and Rome in the eleventh century', *IER* 57 (1941), 213–32.

—— 'Lanfranc and the Irish Church', *IER*, 5th ser., 57 (1941), 381–500; 58 (1941), 1–15.

—— 'Medieval Bristol and Dublin', *IHS* 5 (1947), 275–86.

—— 'The origins of St Mary's Abbey, Dublin', *RSAI Jn.* 79 (1949), 110–25.

—— 'The origins of the diocese of Waterford', *IER*, 5th ser., 59 (1942), 289–96.

—— 'The origins of the see of Dublin', *IER* 57 (1941), 40–55, 97–112.

—— 'Papal legates in Ireland during the twelfth century', *IER* 58 (1944), 361–70.

—— 'Pope Gregory VII and the Irish Church', *IER* 63 (1941), 97–109.

—— 'St Anselm and the Irish Church', *IER*, 5th ser., 59 (1942), 1–14.

—— 'St Malachy of Armagh', *IER*, 5th ser., 70 (1948), 961–78; 71 (1949), 134–48, 317–31.

—— 'Tomaltach Ua Conchobair, coarb of Patrick (1181–1201)', *Seanchas Ardmhacha*, 8 (1975–7), 231–74.

—— *The twelfth-century reform* (Dublin, 1968).

—— 'Were the "Annals of Inisfallen" written at Killaloe?', *N Munster Antiq. Jn.* 8 (1958–61), 20–33.

—— and GLEESON, D., *A history of the diocese of Killaloe* (Dublin, 1962).

—— and HADCOCK, R. N., *Medieval religious houses: Ireland* (London, 1970).

HALSTEAD, R., *Succinct genealogies of the noble and ancient houses of Alno or de Alneto, etc.* (London, 1685).

HANNAY, R. K., 'The date of the *filia specialis* bull', *Scot. Hist. Rev.* 23 (1926), 171–7.

HASKINS, C. H., *Norman institutions* (Cambridge, 1918).

HESLIN, A., 'The coronation of the young king in 1170', *Studies in Church History*, 2 (1965), 165–78.

HILL, D., *Atlas of Anglo-Saxon England* (Oxford, 1981).

HOCKEY, F., 'The house of Redvers and its monastic foundations', *Anglo-Norman Studies*, 5 (1982), 146–52.

HOGAN, E., *Onomasticon Goedelicum* (Dublin, 1910).

HOGAN, J., 'The Ua Briain kingship in Tlach Óc', in *Féil-sgríbhinn Eóin Mhic Néill*, 406–44.

HOLLISTER, C. W., 'Normandy, France and the Anglo-Norman *regnum*', *Speculum*, 51 (1976), 202–42.

—— and KEEFE, T. K., 'The making of the Angevin empire', *Journal of British Studies*, 12 (1973), 1–25.

HOLT, J. C., 'The end of the Anglo-Norman realm', *Br. Acad. Proc.* 61 (1975), 223–65.

—— 'Politics and property in early medieval England', *Past and Present*, 57 (1972), 1–52.

HUDSON, B., 'The family of Harold Godwinson and the Irish sea province', *RSAI Jn.* 109 (1979), 92–100.

JEFFERIES, H. A., 'Desmond: the early years, and the career of Cormac Mac Carthy', *Cork Hist. Soc. Jn.* 81 (1983), 81–284.

JOHN, E., *Land tenure in early England* (Leicester, 1960).

—— *Orbis Britanniae* (Leicester, 1966).

JOHNSEN, A. O., 'Nicholaus Brekespear and the Norwegian church province, 1153', *The Norseman*, 11 (1953), 244–51.

JOHNSTON, D., 'Richard II and the submissions of Gaelic Ireland', *IHS* 22 (1980), 1–21.

JOLLIFFE, J. E. A., *Angevin kingship* (2nd edn., London, 1963).

KANTOROWICZ, E. H., *Laudes regiae* (Berkeley, 1946).

KEATING, G., *Foras feasa ar Éirinn*, ed. D. Comyn and P. S. Dineen (4 vols., Ir. Texts Soc. 4, 8, 9, 15; Dublin, 1902–14).

KEEFE, T. K., 'Geoffrey Plantagenet's will and the Angevin succession', *Albion*, 6 (1974), 266–74.

KENNEY, J. F., *The sources for the early history of Ireland* (New York, 1929).

KING, D. J. CATHCART, *Castellarium Anglicanum* (2 vols., London, 1983).

KNOWLES, D., 'The case of Saint William of York', *Cambridge Hist. Jn.* 5 (1935), 162–77, 212–14.

KÖRNER, S., *The battle of Hastings, England, and Europe, 1035–1066* (Lund, 1964).

LAWRENCE, C. H. (ed.), *The English Church and the papacy in the Middle Ages* (London, 1965).

LECLERCQ, J. (ed.), *Recueil d'études sur Saint Bernard et ses écrits* (3 vols., Rome, 1962–9).

LE PATOUREL, J., *Feudal empires: Norman and Plantagenet* (London, 1984).

—— *The Norman empire* (Oxford, 1976).

—— 'The Plantagenet dominions', *History*, 50 (1965), 289–308.

LEECH, R. H., 'Cogadh Gaedhel re Gallaibh and the annals of Inis-fallen', *N Munster Antiq. Jn.* 11 (1968), 13–21.

LEMARIGNIER, J. F., *Recherches sur l'hommage en marche et les frontières féodales* (Lille, 1945).

LEYSER, K., 'Frederick Barbarossa, Henry II and the hand of St James', *EHR* 96 (1975), 481–506.

—— *Rule and conflict in an early medieval society: Ottonian Saxony* (London, 1979).

LLOYD, J. E., *A history of Carmarthenshire* (Cardiff, 1935).

—— *A history of Wales from the earliest times to the conquest* (2 vols., London, 1911).

LOYD, L. C., *The origins of some Anglo-Norman families* (Harleian Society, 103; Leeds, 1951).

LOYN, H. R., 'The imperial style of the tenth-century Anglo-Saxon kings', *History*, 40 (1955), 111–15.

—— 'Wales and England in the tenth century: the context of the Athelstan charters', *Welsh History Review*, 10 (1981), 283–301.

LYDON, J. (ed.), *England and Ireland in the later Middle Ages* (Dublin, 1981).

—— *The lordship of Ireland in the middle ages* (Dublin, 1972).

—— 'The problem of the frontier in medieval Ireland', *Topic*, 13 (1967), 5–22.

LYTTELTON, G., *History of the life of King Henry II* (3rd edn., 6 vols., London, 1769–73).

MAC CANA, P., *Branwen daughter of Llyr: a study of the Irish affinities and of the composition of the second branch of the Mabinogion* (Cardiff, 1958).

—— 'The influence of the Vikings on Celtic literature', in B. Ó Cuív (ed.), *The impact of the Scandinavian invasions on the Celtic-speaking peoples, c.800–1100 A.D.* (Dublin, 1975), 78–118.

MAC CURTAIN, M., and Ó CORRÁIN, D. (edd.), *Women in Irish society: the historical dimension* (Dublin, 1978).

MACNEILL, E., *Celtic Ireland* (Dublin, 1921).

—— *Phases of Irish history* (Dublin, 1919).

MAC NIOCAILL, G., 'The "heir designate" in early medieval Ireland', *Ir. Jurist*, NS 3 (1968), 326–9.

—— *The medieval Irish annals* (Dublin, 1975).

MARTIN, F. X., 'The first Normans in Munster', *Cork Hist. Soc. Jn.* 76 (1971), 48–71.

—— and BYRNE, F. J. (edd.), *The scholar revolutionary* (Shannon, 1973).

MARTIN, J., 'John of Salisbury as a classical scholar', in M. Wilks (ed.), *The world of John of Salisbury* (Studies in Church History: subsidia, 3; Oxford, 1984), 179–201.

MASON, J. F. A., 'Roger de Montgomery and his sons (1067–1102)', *R. Hist. Soc. Trans.*, 5th ser., 13 (1963), 1–28.

MAUSS, M., *The gift: forms and function of exchange in archaic societies* (London, 1969).

MAYR-HARTING, H., and MOORE, R. I. (edd.), *Studies in medieval history presented to R. H. C. Davis* (Oxford, 1985).

MOISL, H., 'The Bernician royal dynasty and the Irish in the seventh century', *Peritia*, 2 (1983), 103–26.

MURRAY, H., 'Documentary evidence for domestic buildings in Ireland, *c.*400–1200 in the light of archaeology', *Medieval Archaeology*, 23 (1979), 81–97.

NELSON, J., 'Inauguration rituals', in P. H. Sawyer and I. N. Wood (edd.), *Early medieval kingship* (Leeds, 1977), 50–71.

NELSON, L., *The Normans in South Wales, 1070–1171* (Austin, 1966).

A new history of Ireland (Oxford, 1976–).

NÍ BHROLCHÁIN, M., 'The manuscript tradition of the Banshenchas', *Ériu*, 33 (1981), 109–35.

NICHOLL, D., *Thurstan, archbishop of York (1114–1140)* (London, 1964).

NICHOLLS, K. W., 'The Kavanaghs, 1400–1700', *Ir. Geneal.* 5, no. 4 (1977), 435–47; no. 5 (1978), 573–80; no. 6 (1979), 730–4; 6, no. 2 (1981), 189–203.

—— 'The land of the Leinstermen', *Peritia*, 3 (1984), 535–58.

NORGATE, K., *England under the Angevin kings* (2 vols., London, 1887).

Ó BUACHALLA, L., 'Contributions towards the political history of Munster, 450–800 A.D.', *Cork Hist. Soc. Jn.* 56 (1951), 87–90; 57 (1952), 67–86; 59 (1954), 111–26; 61 (1956), 89–102.

Ó CONBHUÍ, C., 'The lands of St Mary's Abbey, Dublin', *RIA Proc.* 62 (1962), 21–84.

Ó CÓRRÁIN, D., 'Aspects of early Irish history', in B. G. Scott (ed.), *Perspectives in Irish archaeology* (Belfast, 1974), 64–75.

—— 'Caithréim Chellacháin Chaisil: history or propaganda', *Ériu*, 25 (1974), 1–69.

—— 'The career of Diarmait mac Máel na mBó, king of Leinster', *Old Wexford Soc. Jn.* 3 (1971), 27–35; 4 (1972–3), 17–24.

—— 'The education of Diarmait Mac Murchada', *Ériu*, 28 (1977), 71–81.

—— 'High-kings, Vikings and other kings', *IHS* 21 (1979), 283–323.

—— *Ireland before the Normans* (Dublin, 1972).

—— 'Irish regnal succession: a reappraisal', *Studia Hib.* 11 (1971), 7–39.

—— 'Marriage in early Ireland', in A. Cosgrove (ed.), *Marriage in Ireland* (Dublin, 1985), 5–24.

—— 'Nationality and kingship in pre-Norman Ireland', *Hist. Studies* 11 (1978), 1–35.

—— 'Onomata', *Ériu*, 30 (1979), 165–80.

—— 'The Uí Chennselaig kingship of Leinster, 1072–1126', *Old Wexford Soc. Jn.* 5 (1974–5), 26–31; 6 (1976–7), 45–53; 7 (1978–9), 46–9.

—— 'Women in early Irish society', in M. Mac Curtain and D. Ó Corráin (edd.), *Women in Irish society: the historical dimension* (Dublin, 1978), 1–13.

Ó Cuív, B. (ed.), *The impact of the Scandinavian invasions on the Celtic-speaking peoples, c.800–1100 A.D.* (Dublin, 1975).

O'Doherty, J. F., 'The Anglo-Norman invasion, 1167–71', *IHS* 1 (1938–9), 154–7.

—— *Laurentius von Dublin und das irische Normannentum* (Doc. diss., Munich, 1933).

—— 'Rome and the Anglo-Norman invasion of Ireland', *IER*, 5th ser., 42 (1933), 131–45.

—— 'St Laurence O'Toole and the Anglo-Norman invasion', *IER* 50 (1937), 449–77, 600–25; 51 (1938), 131–46.

Ó Fiaich, T., 'The church of Armagh under lay control', *Seanchas Ardmhacha*, 5 (1969), 75–127.

O'Rahilly, C., *Ireland and Wales: their historical and literary relations* (London, 1924).

O'Rahilly, T. F., *Early Irish history and mythology* (Dublin, 1946).

Ó Riain, P., 'Battle site and territorial extent in early Ireland', *ZCP* 33 (1974), 67–80.

—— 'Boundary association in early Irish society', *Studia Celtica*, 16 (1972), 12–29.

Orpen, G. H., *Ireland under the Normans, 1169–1333* (4 vols., Oxford, 1911–20).

Otway-Ruthven, A. J., *A history of medieval Ireland* (London, 1968).

Owen, G., *The description of Pembrokeshire*, ed. H. Owen (3 vols., London, 1892–1906).

Owen, H., *Old Pembroke families* (London, 1902).

Painter, S., *The reign of King John* (Baltimore, 1949).

—— *William Marshal* (Baltimore, 1933).

Parsons, D. (ed.), *Tenth-century studies* (London, 1975).

Patterson, N. T., 'Material and symbolic exchange in early Irish clientship', *Proceedings of the Harvard Celtic Colloquium*, 1 (1981), 53–61.

Patterson, R. B., 'William of Malmesbury's Robert of Gloucester: a re-evaluation of the *Historia novella*', *AHR* 70 (July 1965), 983–97.

POLLOCK, F., and MAITLAND, F. W., *The history of English law before the time of Edward I* (2nd edn., 2 vols., Cambridge, 1898, repr. 1968).

POOLE, A. L., *From Domesday Book to Magna Carta, 1087–1216* (2nd edn., Oxford, 1955).

POWER, R., 'Magnus Barelegs' expeditions to the West', *Scot. Hist. Rev.* 65 (1986), 107–32.

POWICKE, F. M., *The loss of Normandy* (2nd edn., London, 1961).

PRESTWICH, J. O., 'The military household of the Norman kings', *EHR* 96 (1981), 1–35.

—— 'War and finance in the Anglo-Norman state', *R. Hist. Soc. Trans.*, 5th ser., 6 (1964), 19–43.

REES, W., *An historical atlas of Wales from early to modern times* (2nd edn., London, 1959).

RICHARDSON, H. G., *The English Jewry under the Angevin kings* (London, 1960).

—— 'Some Norman monastic foundations in Ireland', in J. A. Watt, J. B. Morrall, and F. X. Martin (edd.), *Medieval studies presented to Aubrey Gwynn, S.J.* (Dublin, 1961), 29–43.

—— and SAYLES, G. O., *The administration of Ireland, 1172–1377* (Dublin, Irish Manuscripts Commission, 1963).

RICHTER, M., 'Canterbury's primacy in Wales and the first stage of Bishop Bernard's opposition', *Jn. Ecc. Hist.* 22 (1971), 177–89.

—— 'The first century of Anglo-Irish relations', *History*, 59 (1974), 195–210.

—— 'The political and institutional background to national consciousness in medieval Wales', *Hist. Studies*, 11 (1978), 37–55.

—— 'Professions of obedience and the metropolitan claims of St David's', *National Library of Wales Journal*, 15 (1967–8), 197–214.

ROBINSON, J. A., *The times of St Dunstan* (Oxford, 1923).

RODERICK, A. J., 'The feudal relations between the English Crown and the Welsh princes', *History*, 37 (1952), 201–12.

ROSS, A., *Pagan Celtic Britain: studies in iconography and tradition* (London, 1967).

ROUND, J. H., *Commune of London* (London, 1899).

—— 'The countess of Ireland', *The Genealogist*, NS 18 (1901), 166–7.

—— *Feudal England* (London, 1909; new edn., 1964).

—— *Studies in the Red Book of the Exchequer* (London, 1898).

ROWLANDS, I. W., 'The making of the March: aspects of the Norman settlement in Dyfed', in *Proceedings of the Battle Conference on Anglo-Norman studies*, 3, 1980, ed. R. A. Brown (Woodbridge, 1981), 142–57, 221–5.

RYAN, J., 'The ancestry of St Laurence O'Toole', *Reportorium Novum*, 1 (1955), 64–75.

—— 'The O'Briens in Munster after Clontarf', *N Munster Antiq. Jn.* 2 (1941), 141–52.

—— *Toirdelbach O Conchobair (1088–1156), king of Connacht, king of Ireland 'co fresabra'* (Dublin, 1966).

RYNNE, E. (ed.), *North Munster studies* (Limerick, 1967).

SALTMAN, A., *Theobald, archbishop of Canterbury* (London, 1956).

SANDERS, I. J., *English baronies: a study of their origins and descent, 1086–1327* (London, 1960).

SAWYER, P. H., 'Charters of the reform movement: the Worcester archive', in D. Parsons (ed.), *Tenth-century studies* (London, 1975).

—— and WOOD, I. N. (edd.), *Early medieval kingship* (Leeds, 1977).

SCOTT, B. G. (ed.), *Studies on early Ireland: essays in honour of M. V. Duignan* [Belfast, 1982].

SHEEHAN, M., *The will in medieval England* (Toronto, 1963).

SHEEHY, M. P., *When the Normans came to Ireland* (Dublin, 1975).

SMYTH, A. P., *Celtic Leinster* (Dublin, 1982).

—— *Scandinavian kings in the British Isles, 850–880* (Oxford, 1977).

—— *Scandinavian York and Dublin: the history of two related Viking kingdoms* (2 vols., Dublin, 1975–9).

SMYTH, JOHN, of Nibley, *The lives of the Berkeleys*, ed. J. Maclean (3 vols., Gloucester, 1883).

SOUTHERN, R. W, 'The Canterbury forgeries', *EHR* 53 (1958), 193–226.

—— *St Anselm and his biographer* (Cambridge, 1963).

STAFFORD, P., 'The king's wife in Wessex', *Past and Present*, 91 (1981), 3–27.

TAYLOR, A. J., 'Usk castle and the pipe roll of 1185', *Archaeologia Cambrensis*, 99 (1947), 249–55.

THURNEYSEN, R., 'Colmán mac Lénnéni and Senchán Torpéist', *ZCP* 19 (1932), 193–209.

—— *Die irische Helden- und Königsage bis zum siebzehnten Jahrhundert* (Halle, 1921).

—— *et al.*, *Studies in early Irish law* (Dublin, 1936).

ULLMANN, W., 'On the influence of Geoffrey of Monmouth in English history', in C. Bauer, L. Boehm, and M. Müller (edd.), *Speculum historiale* (Freiburg, 1965), 257–76.

USSHER, JAMES, *The whole works of the most Reverend James Ussher, D.D.*, ed. C. R. Elrington (17 vols., Dublin, 1847–64).

WAGNER, A. R., 'A seal of Strongbow in the Huntingdon Library', *Antiquaries Journal*, 21 (1941), 128–32.

WAGNER, H., 'Der königliche Palast in keltischer Tradition', *ZCP* 33 (1974), 6–14.

—— 'Near Eastern and African connections with the Celtic world', in

R. O. O'Driscoll (ed.), *The Celtic consciousness* (Mountrath, 1982), 51–67.

WAGNER, H., 'Zur Bezeichnung des Kranichs im Keltischen', *ZCP* 29 (1962–4), 301–4.

WAKEMAN, T., 'On the town, castle, and priory of Usk', *Journal of the British Archaeological Association*, 10 (1885), 257–65.

WALLACE, P. F., 'The archaeology of Viking Dublin', in H. B. Clarke and A. Simms (edd.), *The comparative history of urban origins in non-Roman Europe* (2 vols., BAR international series, 255; Oxford, 1985).

—— 'The origins of Dublin', in B. G. Scott (ed.), *Studies on early Ireland: essays in honour of M. V. Duignan* [Belfast, 1982], 129–43.

WALSH, P., 'An Leabhar Muimhneach', *IHS* 3 (1942), 135–43.

—— 'Leinster states and kings in Christian times', *IER* 53 (1939), 47–61.

WARD, J. C., 'Fashions in monastic endowment: the foundations of the Clare family', *Jn. Ecc. Hist.* 32 (1981), 427–51.

WARE, J., *De Hibernia et antiquitatibus ejus* (London, 1654).

WARREN, W. L., 'John in Ireland, 1185', in J. Bossy and P. Jupp (edd.), *Essays presented to Michael Roberts* (Belfast, 1976), 11–23.

—— *Henry II* (London, 1973).

—— 'The interpretation of twelfth-century Irish history', *Hist. Studies*, 7 (1969), 1–19.

—— *King John* (2nd edn., London, 1978).

WATKINS, C., 'The etymology of Irish *duán*', *Celtica*, 11 (1976), 270–7.

WATT, J. A., *The Church and the two nations in medieval Ireland* (Cambridge, 1970).

—— *The Church in medieval Ireland* (Dublin, 1972).

—— MORRALL, J. B., and MARTIN, F. X. (edd.), *Medieval studies presented to Aubrey Gwynn, S.J.* (Dublin, 1961).

WHITE, G. H., 'The household of the Norman kings', *R Hist. Soc. Trans.*, 4th ser., 30 (1948), 127–56.

WIGHTMAN, W. E., *The Lacy family in England and Normandy, 1066–1194* (Oxford, 1966).

—— 'The palatine earldom of William fitz Osbern in Gloucestershire and Worcestershire (1066–1071)', *EHR* 77 (1962), 6–17.

WILKS, M. (ed.), *The world of John of Salisbury* (Studies in Church History: subsidia, 3, 1984).

WILLIAMS, A., 'Land and power in the eleventh century: the estates of Harold Godwinson', *Proceedings of the Battle Conference on Anglo-Norman studies*, ed. R. A. Brown, 3 (1980), 171–87.

—— 'Some notes and considerations on problems connected with the English royal succession, 860–1066', in R. A. Brown (ed.), *Proceedings of the Battle Conference on Anglo-Norman Studies, 1978* (Ipswich, 1979), 144–67, 225–33.

WOOD, I. N., 'Kings, kingdoms and consent', in P. H. Sawyer and I. N. Wood (edd.), *Early medieval kingship* (Leeds, 1977), 6–29.

WROTTESLEY, G., *The Giffards from the Conquest to the present time* (William Salt Archaeological Society, NS 5; London, 1902).

INDEX

The following abbreviations are used:

abp	archbishop
bld	blinded
bp	bishop
dau.	daughter
kg	king
s.	son

Adrian IV, pope (1154–9) 7, 38, 51, 53, 54, 103 n.
see also Laudabiliter
Aelelmus, brother of Hamund 285 n.
Aelfgar, earl of East Anglia 61
Afflighem, monastery of 40
Affreca, dau. of Godred, kg of Man 128
Aghade, co. Carlow, convent of 102, 125 n.
Airgialla:
  king of 189, 195
  queen of 94
Aisling meic Conglinne 192, 205
Aldfrith, kg of Northumbria (685–704) 57
Alen, John, abp of Dublin (1529–34) 102 n.
Alestan of Buscombe 113 n.
Alexander II, pope (1061–73) 14, 19 n., 41
Alexander III, pope (1139–81) 102 n., 208, 209, 216, 224, 262, 277, 278
Alexis, papal legate 261–2
All Hallows priory, Dublin 75 n., 235 n., 285 n., 289, 292
Anastasius IV, pope (1153–4) 38
Angevin lordship of Ireland 131, 272–304
  party (1135–54), 38, 53, 69–76
Angle, Pembrokeshire 160
de Angulo, Gilbert 160 n.
——, Jocelin 160 n.
——, William 160
Anjou, 212, 214, 215, 271, 273, 274, 275, 276, 290
Annals of Inisfallen 174, 175, 176, 177, 178, 179, 181, 194, 199, 200, 237

Annals of Loch Cé 265, 267, 282
Annals of Tigernach 175, 233, 240, 246, 248, 249, 250, 257, 258, 259, 270
Annals of Ulster 180
Anselm, St, abp of Canterbury (1093–1109) 19–25, 28, 43, 44, 51 n., 52, 63 n., 68, 102 n., 297
Aquitaine 56, 76, 214, 271, 275, 276
Arklow, co. Wicklow 132, 133, 281
Armagh 255
  church of 241, 269
  comarba of 17,
  see of 31, 32, 33, 36
Arthur of Bardsey, 65
Athboy, synod of (1167) 269
Athelstan, kg of England (924–39) 42, 43
Athlone, co. Westmeath 241, 282
d'Aubigny, William 285 n.
Augustine, abp of Canterbury (597–604) 13, 15, 41

Bachrach, B. S. 274
Bairrche, co. Down 244
Baitinglass, co. Wicklow, abbey of 102 n.
Bangor (Wales), see of 34, 64, 65
Banshenchas 91, 257
Barlow, F. 55, 172
Barrow, G. W. S. 219
de Barry family 148
——, Philip 149, 152
——, Robert 148, 152
——, William 148
Backet, Thomas, abp of Canterbury (1162–70) 40 n., 65, 169, 229, 277, 284
Bective, co. Meath, monastery of 283

Bede, the Venerable, *Ecclesiastical history* 14, 15, 41, 44
de Bendinges, William 295, 296
de Bermingham, Robert 161
Bernard of Clairvaux, St 71, 72, 73, 74, 102 n., 103, 209 n.
Bernard, bp of St Davids (1115–48) 34, 35, 38, 54–5, 70, 71, 139, 142, 147, 148
Bethell, Denis 8, 36, 55
Biddlesden, Bucks., abbey of 158
Bigod, Roger, earl of Norfolk (d. 1306) 110
Binchy, D. A. 85, 174, 175
Bleddyn ap Cynfyn, kg of Powys (d. 1075) 66
Bloet family 156, 159
——, Ralph I 157
——, Ralph II 129
——, Walter 157
de Bohun, Humphrey, 285 n., 286, 288
de Boisrohard, Gilbert 157, 159
——, Robert 158
Book of Ballymote 108
Book of Leinster 57, 88, 106, 108, 109, 225
Book of Rights 94, 185–7, 189, 190, 191, 192, 200, 205
Bourne, Lincs., honour of 113 n., 160 n.
Bran mac Máel Mórda, kg of Leinster (1016–18) 56
Brandub mac Echach, kg of Leinster (d. 605/8) 105, 108
Branwen, dau. of Llyr 204–5
de Braose, Philip 255, 256, 258, 266, 288, 298 n., 302
——, William 285 n., 288
Braunton, Devon 146 n.
Breakspear, Nicholas *see* Adrian IV, pope (1154–9)
Brega 270 n.
Bréifne, kingdom of 100
Brian, s. of Count Odo of Brittany 60
Brian Bóruma, kg of Munster (d. 1014) 10, 48 n., 176, 177, 178, 179, 181, 182, 191, 204
Brictius, bp of Limerick (1167/78–c.1186–9) 260 n.
Bristol 58, 68, 69, 70, 75, 76, 114, 117, 127, 168
Brittany 212, 275, 276, 289
Brycheiniog 140
Byland, North Yorks., abbey of 73

Byrne, F. J. 81

Cadwaladr (d. 1172), s. of Gruffydd ap Cynan, kg of Gwynedd (d. 1137) 65
Cadwaladr, s. of Owain, kg of Gwynedd (d. 1170) 163
Cadwgan ap Bleddyn, kg of Powys (1111–16) 65, 66, 194
Caerleon Castle 157 n.
Cáin Daerraith 188
Cáin Saerraith 185, 188
Cairpre, co. Kildare 160, 225 n.
Caithréim Cellacháin Chaisil 189, 192, 196
Callistus II, pope (1119–24) 26, 28, 44, 113 n.
Cambro-Normans 137, 149, 156, 161, 162
de Camville, William 147 n.
Canterbury, see of 7–9, 12–33, 37, 40, 41, 42–3, 46–7, 50, 51 n., 54, 65, 70–1
Canterbury, Christ Church 19, 24, 25, 27 n., 30, 51 n., 156, 169, 170
Cantordis, abbot of Clonfert 230, 253, 312
Cantref Bychan 139, 143, 144, 162
Cantref Mawr 67, 139, 143, 144
Cardigan, castle of 140, 144, 145, 146
Carew, Pembrokeshire 138, 146, 147
de Carew, Odo 146 n.
Carmarthen 139, 140, 141, 143, 147, 148
priory of St John 147
Cashel 200
council of (1171–2) 102 n., 104 n., 278
kingship of 89, 187, 191, 195, 196, 200
see of 26 n., 31, 32, 33, 36
synod of (1101) 21, 102 n.
Cathal mac Finguine, kg of Cashel (721–42) 192, 205
Céle Dabhaill, abbot of Bangor (d. 929) 11
Cellach, s. of Áed, abp of Armagh (1105–29) 21, 23, 30
Cemais 139, 145, 146, 147, 152
Cenél Connaill, kg of 311
Cenél nEógain, kg of 229, 311
Ceredigion 139, 140, 141, 144, 145, 147, 152, 162, 194
Chaumont, siege of (1168) 162, 163, 164
Chepstow 113 n., 114, 118, 129, 157 n.
de Chesney, Robert, bp of Lincoln (1148–68) 32
Chester 68, 75, 144, 168, 291

Chesterford, Essex 124, 126
Christina, wife of Owain, kg of Gwynedd
    (1137–70) 65
Chronicon Scotorum 175
Cilgerran 144, 146
Citeaux 73
de Clahull, Hugh 160
——, John 157, 159
Clairvaux 36, 73, 74
Clane, synod of (1162) 103
Clann Cholmáin lineage 225, 270 n.
de Clare family 145, 161 n., 162
——, Aline, dau. of Richard fitz Gilbert
    (Strongbow) 153
——, Baldwin fitz Gilbert 113 n., 140
——, Basilia, sister of Richard fitz
    Gilbert (Strongbow) 155
——, Gilbert fitz Gilbert, earl of
    Pembroke (d. 1148) 113, 135, 141–2,
    149, 316
——, Gilbert fitz Richard, lord of Clare
    (d. 1117) 112, 113, 139, 316
——, Gilbert (d. *c.*1185), s. of Richard
    fitz Gilbert (Strongbow) 111, 123,
    124, 125, 130 n., 315, 316
——, Isabella, mother of Richard fitz
    Gilbert (Strongbow) 130 n.
——, Isabella, dau. of Richard fitz
    Gilbert (Strongbow) 111, 115,
    116 n., 123, 124, 130, 131, 133 n.,
    134, 135 n., 280, 315, 316
——, Richard fitz Gilbert (d. 1090) 112,
    115, 315
——, Richard fitz Gilbert, lord of Clare
    (d. 1136) 140, 316
——, Richard fitz Gilbert (Strongbow)
    80–1, 82, 87, 90–2, 95, 97, 98, 99,
    100, 104–5, 108, 109, 110, 111, 112,
    114–33, 134, 135, 136, 137, 142, 143,
    149–61, 167–70, 222, 223, 225, 251,
    252, 255, 256, 259, 278, 279, 285 n.,
    293, 294–5, 296, 298, 299, 302, 303,
    315, 316
    styled 'earl of Strigoil' 122, 123, 126
——, Roger fitz Richard, lord of Orbec
    and Bienfaite (d. 1130) 112, 113, 316
——Roger, fitz Richard, earl of Hertford
    (d. 1173) 115, 143, 144, 316
——, Walter fitz Richard, lord of Strigoil
    (d. 1138) 112, 113, 117, 126 n., 139,
    157, 316
Clement III, pope (1187–91) 281
clientship 182–8

Clifford family 140, 145, 162
——, Walter 143
Clonfert, synod of (1179) 254 n., 260
Clonmacnoise, co. Offaly 93, 241
Clontarf, battle of (1014) 10, 75
Cnut, kg of England (1016–35) 10, 11, 46
Cogadh Gaedhel re Gallaibh 89, 94, 178,
    179, 191, 192
de Cogan, Miles 152, 153–5, 255, 256,
    268 n., 287 n., 292 n., 296, 302
——, Richard 154–5, 302
Cong, co. Mayo, monastery of 263, 265
Conmaicne 191
Connacht 232, 266, 267
    kingdom of 99, 234, 235, 243, 246, 263
Corco Laigde 205
Cork, city 63 n., 248, 255, 273, 302
    kingdom of 151, 152, 154, 266, 267,
    303
    see also Desmond
Cornwall, earldom of 279
de Courcy, John 128, 258–60, 265–8,
    271, 282, 296–7, 299, 302
de Courcy, William III, lord of Stogur-
    sey 296
de Courcy, William IV, lord of Stogur-
    sey, 297
de Courcy, William, steward of
    Normandy, 291 n., 296–7
Coutances, Walter of 293
de Cressy, Hugh 285 n., 286
Cumin, John, abp of Dublin (1181–
    1212) 133, 134, 264, 300
Cursun, Vivien 154, 294
de Curtenai, Reginald 285 n., 286, 313
Curtis, Edmund 81, 100, 172
Cynan (d. 1071), s. of Iago, kg of
    Gwynedd (d. 1039) 61

Dafydd ap Owain, kg of Gwynedd
    (1175–95) 65, 218
Dál Cais dynasty 89, 170, 176, 177, 178,
    179, 191
Danish attack on England 59–61
Daugleddau, cantred of 139, 149
    church of 141
David I, kg of Scotland (1124–53) 29, 35,
    37, 50, 70, 71
David, earl of Huntingdon (d. 1219) 201
David 'the Irishman', bp of Bangor
    (1120–?1139) 34, 64
Deheubarth, kingdom of 139, 140
Déise (Munster) 170, 200

Delbna (Mide) 240, 270 n.
Delvin, co. Westmeath, motte of 229
derbfine 81–6
Derrypatrick, co. Meath 255
Desmond 200, 207
   grant of 254, 255, 256, 257, 260
   see also Cork, kingdom of
Dialogue of the Exchequer 245
Diarmait mac Máel na mBó, kg of
   Leinster (1047–72) 58, 59, 75, 88,
   94, 106, 108, 314
Dindshenchas 203
Domnall, s. of Amalgaid, *comarba* of
   Armagh (d. 1105) 21
Donnchad (s. of Brian Bóruma), kg of
   Munster (1014–63) 56, 174, 175,
   177, 179, 194, 237–8
Donnchad, s. of Domnall Remar, kg of
   Leinster (d. 1089) 62
Donnchad mac Gilla Pátraic, kg of
   Osraige (1003–39) and Leinster
   (1033–9) 106
Donngus, bp of Dublin (1085–95) 19, 20,
   21
Downpatrick, co. Down 259
Drogheda, co. Louth 283
Dublin, city 9–10, 12, 21, 30, 44–5, 58,
   64, 67, 68, 69, 70, 75, 88, 99, 101,
   106, 107, 110, 117, 119, 120, 127,
   168, 169, 196, 200, 222, 223, 241–2,
   246, 247, 259, 269, 285 n., 291, 312
   Anglo-Norman garrison of 151, 153,
   155, 249, 255, 288
   Christmas feast at (1171) 172, 173,
   201–3, 206–7
   custody of 286–7, 289, 294, 300–1
   fleet of 57, 61, 66, 67, 76, 144
   provincial synod of (1186) 104 n.
   royal demesne of 132 n., 154, 223, 230,
   273, 280, 284, 294, 300–1
   see of 8–9, 20, 21, 26, 29, 30–1
   siege of 97, 100, 168, 225 n.
Dudo of St Quentin, chronicler 47–8
Duffry, co. Wexford 158
Dunán, bp of Dublin (*c.* 1028–74) 9, 12–
   13, 15, 16, 17, 18 n.
Dunbrody Abbey, co. Wexford 154, 291
Durrow, co. Laois 283

Eadmer, chronicler 20, 25, 29, 43–4, 46–
   7
Ealdred, abp of York (1061–9) and bp of
   Worcester (1046–62) 16, 58 n.

Ealgyth, dau. of Aelfgar, earl of Mercia
   59 n.
easter house (*tech cásca*) 203
Edgar, kg of England (d. 975) 42, 44–7
Edgar, kg of the Scots (d. 1107) 219
Edred, kg of England (d. 955) 43
Edward 'the Confessor', kg of England
   (d. 1066) 58, 61
Edwy, kg of England (d. 959) 42
Eleanor of Aquitaine, wife of Henry II,
   kg of England 274
Ellesmere 218
Emly, monastery of 176
Emlyn 139, 144, 146, 149, 162
Eóganachta dynasty 87, 89
Erenagh, co. Down, monastery of 74
Eu, John, count of 40, 305–7
Eu, William of, lord of Strigoil 113, 117,
   126 n., 157, 158
Eugenius III, pope (1145–53) 36, 38, 71,
   72
Eustace, s. of Stephen, kg of England 50,
   213
Exeter 59, 60, 69

Fachtna, lector of Clonmacnoise 11
Falaise, treaty of (1174) 201, 220, 234,
   235 n., 291 n.
Ferann na gCenél, co. Wexford 161
Ferns, co. Wexford 80, 167
   Augustinian priory of 261 n.
Fitz Audelin, William 135 n., 208, 231–2,
   233, 259, 260 n., 278, 285, 288, 289–
   91, 293, 294, 296, 297, 299, 301, 304
Fitz Bernard, Robert 285 n., 286 n., 288,
   289
Fitz David, Miles 160, 251, 287
Fitz Dermot, family 223
   see also Mac Gilla Mo Cholmóc
Fitz Elidor, Robert, lord of Stackpole
   154 n.
Fitz Gerald, David, bp of St Davids
   (1148–76) 32, 38, 148
——, Maurice 99, 100, 140, 141, 147–8,
   151, 153, 287, 294 n., 298
——William 140, 141, 146, 147, 148, 150,
   155, 162
Fitz Godebert, Richard 149
Fitz Harding, Nicholas 117
——, Robert 76, 116, 117
Fitz Hay, William 141, 148
Fitz Henry, Henry 139, 142, 148
——, Meilir 142, 148, 160, 287, 298

Fitz Herbert, William, abp of York (1143–7) 72
Fitz Martin family 146
——, Robert, lord of Cemais 140
Fitz Maurice, William 132 n., 153, 280, 298
——, Nesta 153
Fitz Osbern, William, earl of Hereford 113 n.
Fitz Rery family 223
Fitz Richard, Robert 161
Fitz Robert, Osbert 291
Fitz Stephen, Robert 99, 100 n., 110, 118, 142, 144, 145–6, 147, 149–50, 151–3, 154, 171, 255, 256, 287, 292 n., 296, 298, 302–3
Fitz William, Alard 131
Fitz Wizo, Walter 141
le Fleming, Thomas 161
Fornham, battle of 288 n.
Fotharta, co. Carlow 155
Foucarmont, abbey of 158
Frame, Robin 263
Frederick I Barbarossa, kg of Germany (1152–90) and emperor (1155–90) 215–16
Fulk V, count of Anjou 273, 274
Furness, Lancs., abbey of 73, 74

Gailenga, co. Meath 90 n., 225 n.
Galtrim, co. Meath, motte of 255
Geoffrey, brother of Henry II, kg of England 53, 274
Geoffrey, s. of Henry II, kg of England 275, 283
Geoffrey, count of Anjou 50, 69, 73, 213, 273, 274
Geoffrey of Monmouth, chronicler 49
Gerald of Wales 41 n., 48–9, 55, 95, 99–100, 101, 103, 116, 117, 119, 121, 123, 145–6, 150–5, 157 n., 170, 171, 172, 199–201, 202, 206–7, 208, 210, 223, 226, 229, 232–4, 245, 248, 250, 252, 254, 263–4, 265, 266–7, 278, 285, 287, 288, 292, 295, 296, 298, 299, 300, 301, 303, 311
Gerald of Windsor, castellan of Pembroke 66, 137, 138, 140, 141
Geraldines 151, 155
de Gernemes, Adam 295, 296
de Gerpunville, William 245 n., 285 n., 286 n.

Gervase of Canterbury, chronicler 168–70, 171, 172, 233, 311
Giffard, honour of 116, 121, 135, 158 n.
——, Peter 156, 161
——, Rohesia 135
——, Walter, Earl 115
Gilla Espaic (Gilbert), bp of Limerick (d. 1145) 21, 22, 202
Gilla Pátraic, bp of Dublin (1074–84) 8–9, 13, 14–19, 41, 46
Gillingham, John 276
Giraldus Cambrensis *see* Gerald of Wales
Gisors (Eure) 122, 214
Glanvill, *Laws and customs of England* 211, 221
de Glanville, Ranulf, 132, 133, 260 n., 266, 280, 285
Glastonbury, 46
Glendalough, co. Wicklow, abbey of 101
   see of 26, 30, 31
Gloucester 69
Godred II, kg of Man (d. 1187), 103, 128
Godstow, oxon., monastery of 301
Godwin, earl of Wessex (d. 1053) 57–8
Godwinson, Leofwine 58
Gofraid, kg of Dublin (d. 1075) 14, 17, 18 n., 102 n., 179
Gofraid Méránach, kg of Man (d. 1095) 63, 64
Gormflaith, wife of Brian Bóruma, kg of Munster (d. 1014) 93, 94
Gregory I, pope (590–604) 13, 41
Gregory VII, pope (1073–85) 13, 17, 18
Gréne (Gregorius), bp of Dublin (1152–61) 30, 31, 46
Gruffydd ap Cynan, kg of Gwynedd (d. 1137) 34, 61, 64, 65
Gruffydd ap Llewelyn, kg of Gwynedd (d. 1063) 59 n., 61, 66
Gruffydd ap Rhys, kg of Cantref Mawr (Deheubarth, d. 1137) 67, 140
Gulafre, Aldred 294 n.
de Gundeville, Hugh 285 n., 286 n., 288
Gwenllian, wife of Gruffydd ap Rhys, kg of Cantref Mawr (Deheubarth) 140
Gwladus, wife of Owain Gwynedd (d. 1170), dau. of Llywarch ap Trahaearn 65
Gwynn, Aubrey 9, 10–12, 14, 16, 21
Gwynedd 140
Gytha, wife of Godwin, earl of Wessex 59–60

Hanes Gruffydd ap Cynan 62
Harold, kg of England (1066) 58–9, 60
Hastings, battle of (1066) 58–60
de Hastings, Philip 285 n., 286 n., 288
hawks as tribute 245–6
de Hay, Ralph 285 n.
Henry I, kg of England (1100–35) 22, 25, 27, 29, 41 n., 50, 67–9, 138–40, 142, 147 n., 148, 213, 219, 273, 274, 275
Henry II, kg of England (1154–89) 7–8, 38–41, 51–4, 69, 133, 134, 136, 146 n., 147 n., 148–55, 157 n., 168–74, 212, 214–17, 254, 259, 273, 274–81, 283, 284–91
  styled 'fitz Empress' 174, 201, 246, 249, 281, 312
  and Diarmait Mac Murchada 7, 56, 76, 79, 150
  and Ruaidri Ua Conchobair 227, 229–72
  and Scottish rulers 217, 218–20, 268
  and Strongbow 111, 114–23, 126, 128–31, 142, 149
  and Welsh rulers 142–4, 161–4, 217–18, 268
  Irish kings' submissions to 170–1, 172–4, 199–203, 205–11, 228, 308–11
Henry (d. 1183), s. of Henry II, kg of England 122, 144, 168 n., 171, 206, 219, 234, 275, 276, 279, 284, 291 n.
Henry of Sully, abbot of Fécamp 72
de Hereford, Adam 97 n., 161
de Herlotera, Osbert 296
Histoire de Guillaume le Maréchal 131, 134, 283
Hollister, C. W. 273–4
Holt, J. C. 275, 284
Holy Trinity, Dublin, church of 9, 12
homage 195, 211–15, 220–4, 232–5
Honorius II, pope (1124–30) 34
Hywel ap Edwin, kg of Deheubarth (d. 1044) 66
Hwyel (d. 1170), s. of Owain Gwynedd, kg of Gwynedd (1137–70) 65

Iago ap Idwal, kg of Gwynedd (d. 1039) 61
Ickleton, Cambs., nunnery of 124, 126
illegitimacy 101–5
Innocent II, pope (1130–43) 32, 36
Innocent III, pope (1198–1216) 216, 261 n.

Iorwerth ap Owain (Gwynllwg) 157 n.
Iorwerth Goch, s. of Maredudd ap Bleddyn, kg of Powys (d. 1132) 163
Isabella, dau. of Robert, earl of Gloucester 279
Ivry, treaty of (1177) 215

John, kg of England (1199–1216) 135, 216
  as lord of Ireland 102 n., 131, 133–4, 254, 255, 263–7, 268, 275, 277–84, 291, 298, 300–1, 302, 303
John of Hexham, chronicler 36
John of Salisbury, chronicler 36–7, 51–2, 53
John, cardinal priest of St Stephen *in monte coelio*, papal legate 254 n.
Jolliffe, J. E. A. 289, 290, 297

Keefe, T. K. 273–4
Kells, co. Meath, church of 90 n.
  Augustinian monastery of 282
  synod of (1152) 8, 37, 38, 40–1, 50, 51, 53, 55
Kidwelly, castle of 143
  lordship of 140
Kilcavan, co. Wexford 101
Kilculiheen, co. Kilkenny, nunnery of 125 n.
Kildare, 132 n.
  abbess of 37
  church of, 101
Kilkenny 157 n.
Killaloe, co. Clare 176, 238
Killenny Abbey, co. Kilkenny 97, 238
Kilmainham, co. Dublin, preceptory of Knights' Hospitallers 154, 160, 194
Kincora (co. Clare) 177, 178, 181, 194

de Lacy, Hugh (d. 1186) 122, 160 n., 161 n., 203 n., 223, 224, 226, 232, 233, 259, 260 n., 263–4, 265, 268, 281, 283, 285 n., 286–7, 288 n., 293, 294, 298–301, 302, 303
——, John, constable of Chester 260 n., 263, 300
——, Walter 282, 283, 289 n.
Lanfranc, abp of Canterbury (1070–89) 9, 13–16, 17–19, 20, 23, 24–5, 28, 41–2, 43, 46, 51 n., 52, 102 n.

Lateran councils 32, 71, 216, 254n., 260
Laudabiliter 7–8, 52, 53–4, 277–8
Laurence, abp of Canterbury (604–19)
15, 44
Laurence, chancellor of Ruaidrí Ua
Conchobair, kg of Connacht 230,
253, 312
Leabhar Muimhneach 178
Leighlin, co. Carlow, castle of 296n., 300
Leinster, 118, 121, 152, 155, 170, 200,
201, 207, 227, 246, 248, 251
kingship/lordship of 10, 79–81, 82, 84,
88, 90–1, 97–8, 105, 107–8, 110–11,
121, 127, 131, 133–4, 167–8, 170,
196, 222, 243, 247, 269, 271, 273,
283, 299
constable of 155, 158, 159
marshal of 159
seneschal of 159
Leofric, earl of Mercia 61
Le Patourel, John 274, 275, 284
Limerick, city 255, 258, 302
Anglo-Norman campaign in 1175:
248, 250–3, 278, 295
Anglo-Norman garrison of 249, 250,
251, 252
royal demesne of 248, 255, 303
see of 23, 31, 32, 33
de Limesi, Ralph 113n.
Lismore, church of 176, 196
diocese of 26
Llandaff, church of 33, 113n.
Llandovery 140, 143, 144
Llanfrynach (Cemais), church of 146
Llansteffan, castle of 141, 143
lordship of 147, 148
Lloyd, Sir John 162, 164
de Longchamps, William, bp of Ely,
papal legate 281
Louis VI, kg of France (1108–1137) 49,
213
Louis VII, kg of France (1137–80) 53,
163, 213, 214, 215
Lucius II, pope (1144–5) 73
Lucius III, pope (1181–5) 277
Lydon, J. F. 268

Mabinogion 204
Mac Carthaig family 170, 176, 256
——, Cormac, kg of Desmond (d. 1138)
196, 250n.
——, Cormac Liathánach, kg of
Desmond (1175–6) 252

——, Diarmait, kg of Desmond (1143–
85) 170–1, 174, 190n., 196, 199–200,
207, 208, 221, 226, 227, 233, 247,
252, 257, 308
——, Orlaith, sister of Diarmait Mac
Carthaig, kg of Desmond (d. 1185)
226n.
Mac Con Caille, Conchobar, abp of
Armagh (*c.*1174–5) 263
Mac Dalbaig, kg of Uí Felmeda *see* Ua
Domnaill, Mac Dalbaig, kg of Uí
Felmeda
Mac Duinn Sléibe, Donn Slébe, kg of
Ulaid (1171–2) 227, 228, 246, 310
——, Eochaid, kg of Ulaid (1158–66) 92,
244
——, Ruaidrí, kg of Ulaid (1172–1201)
229
Mac Fáeláin, Domnall, kg of Uí Fáeláin
(d. 1141) 107
——, Faelán, kg of Uí Fáeláin (d. 1203)
222, 309
——, Sadb, dau. of Cerball, kg of Uí
Fáeláin (d. 1127) 96, 101, 315
Mac Gilla Mo Cholmóc, Domnall, kg of
Uí Dunchada 101n., 223, 311, 315
Mac Gilla Pátraic, kg of Osraige (1053)
94
——, Conchobar mac Cerbaill, joint kg
of Osraige (1123–*c.*1126) 97n.
——, Domnall, kg of Osraige (1072) 179
——, Domnall, kg of Osraige (1165–76)
96, 98, 99, 101, 190n., 200, 207, 208,
222, 249, 250–1, 252, 309
——, Sadb, dau. of Donnchad, kg of
Osraige, wife of Domnall Mór Ua
Briain 258
Mac Lochlainn, Finnguala, dau. of Niall
Mac Lochlainn, kg of Cenél
nEógain (1170–6) 103
——, Máel Sechlainn, kg of Cenél
nEógain (1177–85) 255
——, Muirchertach, kg of Cenél
nEógain (1136–66) 79, 88n., 92, 95,
192, 244
——, Niall, s. of Domnall, kg of Cenél
nEógain (1083–1121) 88n.
Mac Murchada, Aife, dau. of Diarmait,
kg of Leinster (d. 1171) 80, 91, 92,
95, 97, 99, 100, 102n., 103–5, 111,
112, 118, 123, 124–30, 133–4, 315,
316
——, Art (d. 1282) 110

Mac Murchada, Conchobar, s. of
Diarmait, kg of Leinster (d. 1171)
87 n., 96–7, 103, 104, 167, 315
——, Derbforgaill, dau. of Diarmait, kg
of Leinster (d. 1171) 96, 101 n., 315
——, Diarmait, s. of Énna, kg of Leinster
(1092–8) 63 n.
——, Diarmait, s. of Énna, kg of Leinster
(1115–17) 63 n., 107
——, Diarmait, kg of Leinster (d. 1171)
57, 58, 75–6, 79, 80, 84, 88, 91–2,
94–105, 108–11, 125 n., 134, 137,
145, 146, 151, 152, 153, 159, 162,
164, 167, 168, 169, 170, 174 n., 224–
5, 226, 235 n., 238, 240, 242, 243,
244, 253 n., 261 n., 279, 314, 315, 316
and Henry II 7, 8, 56, 76, 79, 150, 171
and Ruaidrí Ua Conchobair 167, 240,
242–3, 247, 256, 269, 271
and Strongbow 80–2, 87–8, 90–1, 95,
98–100, 104–5, 112, 116–17, 118,
122, 127–8, 135–6, 167, 169, 222
——, Domnall Cáemánach, s. of Diarmait, kg of Leinster (d. 1171) 96, 97,
101, 104, 309, 314, 315
son of 103 n., 157 n.
——, Donnchad, s. of Diarmait, kg of
Leinster (d. 1171) 96, 315
——, Donnchad, s. of Murchad, kg of Uí
Chennselaig and Leinster (d. 1115)
107, 314
——, Énna, s. of Diarmait, kg of Leinster
(d. 1171) 87 n., 96, 98, 101, 314, 315
——, Énna, s. of Donnchad, kg of Uí
Chennselaig and Leinster (d. 1126)
30, 107, 108, 196, 314
——, Máel Sechlainn, s. of Diarmait, son
of Murchad styled *tigerna* of Uí
Chennselaig 108
——, Muirchertach, s. of Murchad,
brother of Diarmait, kg of Leinster
(d. 1171) 97, 314
——, Muirchertach (d. 1282) 110
——, Murchad, brother of Diarmait, kg
of Leinster (d. 1171) 97–8, 104, 109,
226 n., 242, 314
——, Orlaith, dau. of Diarmait, kg of
Leinster (d. 1171) 96, 98, 226 n., 315
MacNeill, Eoin 81–4, 86, 87, 172
Mac Turcaill, Hamund 154, 233 n., 294
Mac Turcaill, Ragnall 65 n.
Madoc (d. 1088), s. of Bleddyn ap
Cynfyn, kg of Powys (1063–75) 66

Máel Brigte mac Tornáin, *comarba* of
Armagh (883–927) 43
Maelgwn, s. of Owain, kg of Gwynedd
(1137–70) 65
Maelienydd 218
Máel Mórda mac Murchada, kg of Lein-
ster (1003–14) 181, 182
Máel Sechnaill mac Domnaill, kg of
Tara (975/6–1022) 241
Magnus III Bareleg, kg of Norway
(1093–1103) 48–9 n., 67
Magnus, s. of Harold III Hardráda, kg
of Norway (1047–66) 61
Maine, county of 212, 214, 273, 274
Malachy (Máel Máedoc Ua Morgair),
St, bp of Down (1124–48), abp of
Armagh (1132–6) 32, 35–6, 37, 50,
55, 70, 71–2, 74, 102 n., 209 n.
Malcolm IV, kg of the Scots (1153–65)
143, 219, 220
Manorbier, Pembrokeshire 138
Marleburgh's chronicle 282
Marmion, Geoffrey 147 n.
——, Robert 147 n.
——, Roger 147 n.
marriage in pre-Norman Ireland 91–105
Marshal, Walter 160 n.
——, William, lord of Leinster (1189–
1219), earl of Pembroke (1199–
1219) 109 n., 115 n., 116 n., 124,
126 n., 130, 131, 132 n., 133–5, 280,
283, 315, 316
Martin, F. X. 248, 253
Maskerell, William 152
Matilda, wife of Henry I, kg of England
35 n.
Matilda, empress (d. 1167) 50, 53, 69, 71,
213, 273, 304
Matilda, sister of Edgar, kg of the Scots
(1097–1107) 29
Matilda, dau. of kg Henry II 114 n., 117
Matilda, dau. of Waltheof, earl of
Northampton and Huntingdon 29
Meath *see* Mide
Mellifont abbey, co. Louth 92
Meurig (Mauritius), bp of Bangor (1139/
40–1161) 34, 64
Mide 100, 167, 225, 227, 229, 230, 240,
241, 246, 247, 251, 255, 271, 273,
299
kingship/lordship of 89, 224, 225, 269,
273, 282, 283, 286
East, kingship of 95, 224, 225, 247

de Montfort, Hugh 115 n.
——, Robert 114, 130
de Montgomery, Arnulf, lord of Pembroke 22, 67–8, 137, 138
——, Hugh, earl of Shrewsbury (d. 1098) 67
——, Robert, earl of Shrewsbury (deprived 1102) 67, 138
——, Roger, earl of Shrewsbury (d. 1094) 137
de Montmorency, Hervey de 99, 118, 119–20, 130, 150, 153, 155, 156, 159, 170, 251, 291–2, 295
Mór, wife of Conchobar Ua Máel Sechlainn, kg of Mide (c. 1039–49) 93
Morgan ap Owain, lord of Caerleon (Gwynllwg, d. 1158) 157 n.
Muirchertach mac Néill, kg of Cenél nEógain (938–43) 191, 192
Murchad, s. of Brian Bóruma, kg of Munster (d. 1014) 181
Murchad, s. of Diarmait mac Máel na mBó, joint kg of Leinster (1052–70) 58, 62 n., 86, 88, 106, 196
'Murchardus' of Uí Chennselaig 252
Murdac, Henry, abp of York (1147–53) 72

Narberth, lordship of (Pembrokeshire) 139, 148
Navan, St Mary's abbey 267 n.
Neath, West Glamorgan, abbey of 73
Nelson, Lynn H. 145, 149
Nesta, dau. of Rhys ap Tewdwr, kg of Deheubarth (1078–93) 66, 139, 141 n.
Newry abbey, co. Down 88 n.
Nicholas, cleric, charter witness 294
Nicholas, prior of Wallingford 278
Nicholas, prior of Worcester 46–7
Norgate, Kate 122
Normandy 114, 271, 275, 276, 278, 279, 284, 289, 290, 293, 294, 304
and Capetian kings 212–15
Northampton, assize of (1176) 210
Not, William 154 n.

Ó Corráin, Donnchadh 83, 84, 85, 86, 236
Oda, abp of Canterbury (d. 958) 43
Odo, bp of Bayeux 60, 61
O'Doherty, J. F. 7, 55, 268

oenach 187 n., 193, 269
Olaf Cuaran, kg of Dublin (d. 980) 12 n.
Orbec and Bienfaite, lordship of 112, 113, 114, 116, 121, 130, 135
Orderic Vitalis, chronicler 58, 60, 67 n.
Orpen, G. H. 1, 7, 82, 83, 172, 267
Osraige, raid on (1169) 99, 152
Otir, s. of Otir 65 n.
Otto I, kg of Germany (936–73) and emperor (962–73) 43
Otway-Ruthven, A. J. 2, 172
Owain Gwynedd, kg of Gwynedd (1137–70) 34, 64, 142, 143–4, 161, 163, 164
Owain, s. of Cadwgan ap Bleddyn, kg of Powys (1111–16) 65, 66
Owain Cyfeiliog, kg of Southern Powys (1160–95) 163
Owain ap Madog, s. of Madog ap Maredudd, kg of Powys (1116–32) 163
Oxford, council of (1177) 131, 255, 257, 259, 268 n., 279, 289 n., 292 n., 296 n., 298, 299

Paparo, Cardinal John 36, 40, 51, 102
patricius, bp of Limerick (? 1140–49) 31–2
de Pavilli, Reginald 285 n., 286
Pebidiog, cantred of 139, 148
Pembroke, castle of 135 n., 137, 138, 171
earldom of 113, 116, 123, 126, 135, 149
lordship of 115, 121, 127, 128, 137, 138, 139, 141, 148, 149, 150, 160, 161, 164
sheriff of 115 n.
Peter of Blois 304
Petit, William 266
Philip Augustus, kg of France (1180–1223) 215, 232, 271
Philip of Worcester 223, 264, 300
Pichán mac Máelfind, kg of Uí Echach 205
Picot, Ralph 305, 307
Pippard, Peter 282
Poer, Robert 285 n., 286 n., 292 n., 295, 296, 298, 299
Poole, A. L. 172
de Prendergast, Maurice 149, 160

Quarr (Isle of Wight), abbey of 73
de Quency, Robert 158–9
——, Saher 159

Raglan 157 n.
Ragnailt, dau. of Amlaib (d. 1034), s. of
    Sitric, kg of Dublin (d. 1042) 62
Ragnall, kg of Waterford 223, 309
Ráith Bressail, synod of (1111) 25–6, 29,
    30, 32, 50
Ralph d'Escures, abp of Canterbury
    (1114–22) 15 n., 25–8, 29, 31, 34, 44,
    46
Ralph of Diss, chronicler 36, 171, 172,
    209, 211, 233, 293
Raymond 'le Gros' fitz William 100, 118,
    119, 150, 152, 155, 156, 271, 294–6,
    298, 302
    and Limerick campaign 250–3
    regnal succession 80–91
Regularis concordia 42
Rheims, council of (1049) 16
Rheims, council of (1148) 36
Rhiryd ap Bleddyn (d. 1088), s. of
    Bleddyn ap Cynfyn, kg of Powys
    (1063–75) 66
Rhodri, s. of Owain, kg of Gwynedd
    (1137–70) 65
Rhos, cantred of 138, 140, 141, 149
Rhys ap Gruffydd, kg of Deheubarth
    (1165–97) 142–5, 146, 161, 162, 163,
    164, 194, 218, 269
Rhys ap Tewdwr, kg of Deheubarth
    (c. 1078–93) 63, 66–7, 141 n.
Richard I, kg of England (1189–99) 135,
    216, 220, 232, 275, 276, 303
    and Ireland, 131, 133, 134, 267, 281–3,
    289 n.
Richard II, duke of Normandy (995–
    1026) 47
Richard of the Peak 260 n., 300
de Ridelsford, Walter 132 n., 160, 294 n.
ridomna 86–7, 96 n., 97
Robert, earl of Gloucester 69–70, 73, 74,
    163
Robert of Torigny, chronicler 36–7, 39,
    40, 53, 119–20, 130, 171, 172, 206,
    220
Roger, earl of Hereford (deprived 1075)
    113 n.
Roger, earl of Hereford (d. 1155) 163
Roger of Howden, chronicler 36, 169,
    171, 172, 173, 201, 202–3, 206–7,
    208, 209, 211, 222, 224, 229, 230,
    233, 248, 257–8, 259, 260, 264, 277,
    279, 283, 285, 286, 288, 289, 296,
    298, 299, 300, 311

Rome 9, 11, 12, 27, 32, 36, 56
Rouen 22
de Ruilli, Robert 285 n.

St Andrew in Ards, co. Down, priory of
    297 n.
St Andrews, see of 35, 37, 261
St Davids, see of 33, 34–5, 38, 41, 139
    archdeacon of 141
    stewardship of 139
de Saint Martin, Alured 291 n.
St Mary's abbey, Dublin 14 n., 19 n., 74,
    154
St Mary de Hogges, abbey, Dublin
    125 n.
Saint-Saëns (Seine Maritime) 130
    convent of 130 n.
St Thomas's abbey, Dublin 283, 297
Saithne, co. Dublin 222, 223, 264, 300
Savignac houses 72–4
Scotland 18 n., 29, 36
Sellarius, Savaric 294 n.
Síl nOnchon (Uí Chennselaig) 86, 87
Sitric, kg of Dublin (989–1036) 9, 11–12
Slane, co. Meath, castle of 255
Slebech, Knights' Hospitallers 146
'Song of Dermot' 94, 95, 98, 149, 154,
    167, 171, 225, 229, 251, 258, 271,
    285, 287, 288
Stephen, kg of England (1135–54) 36, 38,
    50, 53, 69, 70, 71, 72, 73, 74–5, 113,
    114–15, 140, 163, 213, 290, 304, 305
Stephen, constable of Cardigan 140, 142
Stigand, abp of Canterbury (1052–70)
    15–16, 17
stipend 177
    see also tuarastal
Stogursey, lordship of 296, 297
Strata Florida, Dyfed, monastery of 145,
    146
Strigoil, castle of *see* Chepstow
    countess of 124
    earl of 122, 123, 126
    lordship of 112, 113, 117, 124, 127,
    139, 157, 158
Strongbow *see* de Clare, Richard fitz Gil-
    bert
de Stuteville, William 285 n., 286 n.
Suir, river 200, 207
Swein Estrithson, kg of Denmark (1047–
    74) 59, 60
Swords, co. Dublin 62

tanaise 86–7
de Tancarville, William 202
Tara, kingship of 193
   queen of 94
Tenby, castle of 143
Theobald of Bec, abp of Canterbury
   (1138–61) 31, 32–4, 35, 38, 40n.,
   50–1, 65, 142, 306
Thomas, abbot of Glendalough 122n.,
   294
Thomas of Bayeux, abp of York (1070–
   1100) 13, 18n.
Thomas II, abp of York (1108–14) 24
Thomond 249, 250
   grant of 254, 255–8, 260, 266, 280, 302
Thurles, battle of (1174) 229
Thurstan, abp of York (1119–40) 26, 27,
   28, 50, 71
tribute, payment of 190, 200, 226, 235–6,
   245, 249, 260, 263, 312
Trim, co. Meath, castle of 229
tuarastal 59, 180–2, 187–8, 192, 197, 241
   see also stipend
Tulach Óc, kingship of 90n.
Tullach Chiaráin (Tullaherin, co. Kil-
   kenny) 132n.
Tullach Ua Felmeda (Tullow, co.
   Carlow) 132, 133
Tulketh, Lancs., monastery of 73
Turcail mac Eola 66

Ua hAingliu, Samuel, bp of Dublin
   (1096–1121) 20, 21, 22–3
Ua hAinmere, Máel Ísu (Malchus), bp
   of Waterford (1096–1135) 20, 21, 23,
   26n., 63n.
Ua Briain, Brian (bld 1168) brother of
   Domnall Mór, kg of Thomond (d.
   1194) 258n.
——, Cennétig, kg of Tulach Óc (d.
   1084) 90n.
——, Conchobar, kg of Tulach Óc (d.
   1078) 90n.
——, Conchobar, *leth-rí* of Thomond
   (1118–42) 196
——, Conchobar Slapar Salach (d. 1168)
   258
——, Diarmait, s. of Tadc (bld 1175)
   258n.
——, Diarmait, s. of Toirdelbach, kg of
   Munster (d. 1086) 20, 63, 64
——, Domnall, s. of Toirdelbach, kg of
   Munster (d. 1086) 88n.

——, Domnall Mór, kg of Munster
   (1168–94) 157n., 174, 199–200, 207,
   208, 226–7, 229, 233, 247, 248–9,
   250, 252, 253, 254, 257–8, 302, 308,
   315
   submits to Henry II, 174, 199–200,
   207, 208, 226–7, 233, 247
——, Mathgamain, s. of Toirdelbach
   (bld) 258n.
——, Mór, dau. of Toirdelbach, kg of
   Munster (d. 1086) 92n.
——, Mór (d. 1137), dau. of Muirchertach, kg of Munster (d. 1119) 94
——, Muirchertach, kg of Munster
   (1086–1119) 19, 20–1, 62, 63n., 64,
   67–8, 75, 88n., 102n., 170, 191,
   194n., 240, 256
——, Muirchertach, kg of Thomond
   (1167–8) 240, 249, 258
   s. of Muirchertach 257, 258
——, Tadc, s. of Toirdelbach, kg of
   Munster (1063–86) 88n.
——, Toirdelbach, kg of Munster (1063–
   83), high-kg (1072–86) 12n., 17, 18,
   19n., 20, 21, 58, 62, 63n., 64, 88n.,
   92, 93, 102n.
——, Toirdelbach, kg of Thomond
   (1118–67) 196, 250n., 257, 258
Ua Cáellaide, Murchad, son of 103n.
Ua Caráin, Gilla in Choimded, abp of
   Armagh (*c.*1175–80) 263
Ua Cathasaig, kg of Saithne 221, 223,
   311
——, Imar, lord of Saithne 223
Ua Cellaig, Flannacán, kg of Brega 11
Ua Cerbaill, Donnchad, kg of Airgialla
   (d. 1168) 88n., 90n., 102n., 191, 244
——, Murchad, kg of Airgialla (d. 1189)
   88n., 229, 266n.
   submits to Henry II 227, 228, 247, 311
Ua Conchobair, Aed, kg of Connacht
   (1046–67) 175, 177
——, Áed, s. of Cathal (d. 1093) 240
——, Áed, kg of Connacht (d. 1224)
   235n.
——, Cathal Crobderg, kg of Connacht
   (1189–1224) 282
——, Conchobar (d. 1144), s. of Toirdel-
   bach, kg of Connacht (d. 1156) 95,
   107
——, Conchobar Máenmaige, kg of
   Connacht (1183–9) 229, 265, 267,
   268

Ua Conchobair, Murchad (bld 1177), s.
of Ruaidrí, kg of Connacht (d. 1198)
268 n.
——, Ruaidrí na Saide Buide, kg of
Connacht (1087–92, d. 1118) 240
——, Ruaidrí, kg of Connacht (d. 1198)
98, 99, 110, 190 n., 191, 229, 240,
265, 267, 268
and high-kingship 79, 167, 190 n., 193,
226, 227, 228, 240, 241
and Diarmait Mac Murchada 79, 95,
96–7, 98, 99, 103, 105, 109 n., 167,
240, 260–2
and Strongbow 111, 119, 167, 168
and Henry II 229–36, 242–63, 266,
268, 311, 312–13
dau. marries Hugh de Lacy, 264, 300 n.
——, Toirdelbach, kg of Connacht (d.
1156) 30, 75, 79, 90 n., 91, 92 n., 94,
107, 193, 196, 224, 250 n., 256, 269,
270 n.
——, Tommaltach, abp of Armagh
(1180–4) 261, 263, 270
Ua Conchobair, Conchobar, kg of Uí
Failge (1071–1115) 107
——, Mór, dau. of Congalach Ua
Conchobair, kg of Uí Failge (d.
1051) 94
Ua Domnaill, Mac Dalbaig, kg of Uí
Felmeda 222, 309
Ua Dublaích, Cú Caille, kg of Fir
Tulach 93
Ua Dubthaig, Cadla, abp of Tuam
(c. 1167–1201) 230, 246, 249, 250,
253, 254 n., 260 n., 312
Ua hEidin, kg of Uí Fiachrach Aidne,
Caillech Dé, dau. of 257
Ua hÉnna, Domnall, bp of Killaloe (d.
1098) 19, 20
Ua Fáeláin, Máel Sechlainn, kg of Déise
200, 207, 208, 309
Ua Flaithbertaig family 191 n., 240
Ua Focarta, kg of Éle, Gormflaith, dau.
of, wife of Toirdelbach Ua Briain,
kg of Munster (d. 1086) 92, 93
Ua Gormáin family of Uí Bairrche (co.
Laois) 244
Ua Máel Doraid, Máel Runaid, kg of
Cenél Connaill (d. 1027) 11, 177
——, Flaithbertach, kg of Cenél Connaill
(d. 1197) 229
Ua Máel Sechlainn, kg of Mide (in 1166)
224 n.

——, kg of Mide (in 1174) 229
——, Art, kg of Mide (1173–84) 225, 311
——, Conchobar, kg of Mide (1030–72)
93, 94
Mór, wife of 93
son of 179
——, Derbforgaill, dau. of Murchad, kg
of Mide (d. 1153) 92, 94, 95, 240
——, Diarmait, kg of Mide (1155–69)
242
——, Domnall Bregach, kg of Mide
(1169–73) 225, 242, 311
——, Máel Sechlainn, kg of Mide (1152–
5) 94, 95
——, Murchad, kg of Mide (d. 1153) 92,
95, 226, 312
Ua Mathgamna, Donnchad, kg of Uí
Echach 308
Ua Morgair, Máel Máedoc see Malachy,
St
Ua Néill, Áed, kg of Cenél nEógain
(1167–77) 229
Ua Nualláin family of Fotharta (co.
Carlow) 315
Ua Ragallaig family of Tír Briúin 225 n.
——, Gofraid, kg of Gailenga (d. 1161)
90 n.
Ua Riain, Diarmait, kg of Uí Dróna (d.
1171) 258
Ua Ruairc, Áed, s. of Gilla Braite, kg of
Bréifne (1172–6) 94, 229
——, Art, kg of Bréifne and Connacht
(1030–46) 196
——, Donnchad (d. 1039), s. of Art kg of
Bréfne and Connacht (1030–46) 196
——, Donnchad, kg of Bréifne (d. 1084)
90
——, Tigernán, kg of Bréifne (d. 1172)
90 n., 92, 94–5, 103 n., 191 n., 224,
225, 227, 240, 241, 244, 258 n.
submits to Henry II 247, 310, 311
Ua Tuathail, kg of Uí Muiredaig 310
Ua Tuathail, Lorcán (Laurence), abp of
Dublin (1162–80) 101, 103, 104,
260, 261, 262, 264, 313
——, Mór, dau. of Muirchertach, kg of
Uí Muiredaig 96, 101, 102, 103, 315
——, Muirchertach, kg of Uí Muiredaig
(d. 1164) 96, 101, 315
Uí Bairrche, (co. Wexford) 156 n., 159
Uí Bairrche, (co. Laois) 244
Uí Chennselaig 79, 96, 98, 99, 101, 107,
127, 152, 159

dynasty 10, 84, 85–6, 87, 88, 97, 105, 106
kingship 90, 105, 108, 109, 110, 167, 243
Uí Dega (co. Kilkenny) 155
Uí Dróna (co. Carlow) 155, 156, 299
Uí Dunlainge dynasty, 10, 105, 106
Uí Echach (co. Cork) 192, 205
Uí Fáeláin (north co. Kildare) 132 n., 151, 153, 270 n., 298
Uí Failge 270 n.
Uí Felmeda, co. Wexford 157
Uí Felmeda (co. Carlow) 160
Uí Meith (co. Louth) 88
Uí Muiredaig 160, 161
Uí Néill dynasty 178
Ulaid 265, 266, 310–11
Ulster *see* Ulaid
Urban II, pope (1088–99) 44
Urban III, pope (1185–7) 277
Urban, bp of Llandaff (1107–1133/4) 23
Usk, castle of 129, 140, 157 n.
lordship of 139
nunnery of 125 n.

de Valognes Hamo 302 n.
de Verdon, Bertram 267, 285 n., 301, 303
de Verdon, Ralph 285 n.
Verneuil (Eure) 287
Vivian, Cardinal, papal legate 103

Waldef, prior of Kirkham 71–2
Walden, Essex, abbey of 156 Wales:
relations with English kings 29, 49–50, 142–4, 161–4, 217–18, 268
South, adventurers from 98, 137–45, 164, 251 n.
Walchelin, bp of Winchester 20
Walter, Theobald 131, 132, 133, 266, 280, 281
de Warnerville Ralph 293
Warren, W. L. 39, 162, 163, 172, 173, 263, 274, 275, 276, 292, 303
Waterford, city 20, 21, 57, 58, 63, 64, 67, 68, 75, 100, 118, 119, 120 n., 122, 127, 151, 168, 170, 174, 199, 200, 202, 207, 247, 264, 265
Anglo-Norman garrison of 157 n., 249
custody of 159, 286, 288, 289, 298, 299

royal demesne of 132 n., 223, 273, 280, 284, 313
see of 23, 26, 29
synod of 278
Watt, J. A. 54, 55
de Wenneval, William 303
Weston, Herts. 113, 118, 124, 129, 142 n.
Wexford 57, 58, 62, 75, 96, 99, 110, 122, 127, 131 n., 132 n., 133 n., 150, 152, 153, 154, 155, 168, 171, 200, 286, 312
custody of 286, 288–9, 298, 299
royal demesne 122, 132 n., 151, 153, 171 n., 222, 223–4, 273, 284
Wicklow, 132 n.
castle of 122, 132 n., 153, 298
William I, kg of Scotland (1165–1214) 201, 220, 230, 234
William I, 'the Conqueror', kg of England (1066–87) 13, 24, 48, 49, 59, 60, 61, 112, 113 n., 115, 210, 305
William II, kg of England (1087–1100) 28, 44, 48–9, 67, 137, 138
William II, kg of Sicily 231
William, brother of Henry II, kg of England 213, 40 n.
William, s. of Henry I, kg of England 213
William Clito, pretender to Normandy 213
William of Aumale, earl of York 72
William of Malmesbury, chronicler 68, 69, 70, 74
William of Newburgh, chronicler 97 n., 118, 119, 123, 171, 172, 208, 219, 263, 274
William of Poitiers, chronicler 48, 59
William, chancellor 285 n.
Winchester, council of (1155) 7, 38–40, 51–2, 54, 305
Windsor, treaty of (1175) 123 n., 226 n., 227, 229–72, 278, 291, 293 n., 295, 312–13
Worcester 15, 16, 17, 44–7, 58 n., 141
Wulfstan, St, bp of Worcester (1062–95) 15, 16, 17, 46

York, see of 12, 13–14, 19 n., 24–9, 35, 37, 51 n.

ISBN 0–19–	Author	Title
8143567	ALFÖLDI A.	The Conversion of Constantine and Pagan Rome
6286409	ANDERSON George K.	The Literature of the Anglo-Saxons
8228813	BARTLETT & MacKAY	Medieval Frontier Societies
8111010	BETHURUM Dorothy	Homilies of Wulfstan
8114222	BROOKS Kenneth R.	Andreas and the Fates of the Apostles
8203543	BULL Marcus	Knightly Piety & Lay Response to the First Crusade
8216785	BUTLER Alfred J.	Arab Conquest of Egypt
8148348	CAMPBELL J.B.	The Emperor and the Roman Army 31 BC to 235 AD
826643X	CHADWICK Henry	Priscillian of Avila
826447X	CHADWICK Henry	Boethius
8219393	COWDREY H.E.J.	The Age of Abbot Desiderius
8148992	DAVIES M.	Sophocles: Trachiniae
825301X	DOWNER L.	Leges Henrici Primi
8154372	FAULKNER R.O.	The Ancient Egyptian Pyramid Texts
8221541	FLANAGAN Marie Therese	Irish Society, Anglo-Norman Settlers, Angevin Kingship
8143109	FRAENKEL Edward	Horace
8201540	GOLDBERG P.J.P.	Women, Work and Life Cycle in a Medieval Economy
8140215	GOTTSCHALK H.B.	Heraclides of Pontus
8266162	HANSON R.P.C.	Saint Patrick
8224354	HARRISS G.L.	King, Parliament and Public Finance in Medieval England to 1369
8581114	HEATH Sir Thomas	Aristarchus of Samos
8140444	HOLLIS A.S.	Callimachus: Hecale
8212968	HOLLISTER C. Warren	Anglo-Saxon Military Institutions
8223129	HURNARD Naomi	The King's Pardon for Homicide – before AD 1307
8140401	HUTCHINSON G.O.	Hellenistic Poetry
8142560	JONES A.H.M.	The Greek City
8218354	JONES Michael	Ducal Brittany 1364–1399
8271484	KNOX & PELCZYNSKI	Hegel's Political Writings
8225253	LE PATOUREL John	The Norman Empire
8212720	LENNARD Reginald	Rural England 1086–1135
8212321	LEVISON W.	England and the Continent in the 8th century
8148224	LIEBESCHUETZ J.H.W.G.	Continuity and Change in Roman Religion
8141378	LOBEL Edgar & PAGE Sir Denys	Poetarum Lesbiorum Fragmenta
8241445	LUKASIEWICZ, Jan	Aristotle's Syllogistic
8152442	MAAS P. & TRYPANIS C.A .	Sancti Romani Melodi Cantica
8148178	MATTHEWS John	Western Aristocracies and Imperial Court AD 364–425
8223447	McFARLANE K.B.	Lancastrian Kings and Lollard Knights
8226578	McFARLANE K.B.	The Nobility of Later Medieval England
8148100	MEIGGS Russell	Roman Ostia
8148402	MEIGGS Russell	Trees and Timber in the Ancient Mediterranean World
8142641	MILLER J. Innes	The Spice Trade of the Roman Empire
8147813	MOORHEAD John	Theoderic in Italy
8264259	MOORMAN John	A History of the Franciscan Order
8116020	OWEN A.L.	The Famous Druids
8131445	PALMER, L.R.	The Interpretation of Mycenaean Greek Texts
8143427	PFEIFFER R.	History of Classical Scholarship (vol 1)
8111649	PHEIFER J.D.	Old English Glosses in the Epinal-Erfurt Glossary
8142277	PICKARD–CAMBRIDGE A.W.	Dithyramb Tragedy and Comedy
8269765	PLATER & WHITE	Grammar of the Vulgate
8213891	PLUMMER Charles	Lives of Irish Saints (2 vols)
820695X	POWICKE Michael	Military Obligation in Medieval England
8269684	POWICKE Sir Maurice	Stephen Langton
821460X	POWICKE Sir Maurice	The Christian Life in the Middle Ages
8225369	PRAWER Joshua	Crusader Institutions
8225571	PRAWER Joshua	The History of The Jews in the Latin Kingdom of Jerusalem
8143249	RABY F.J.E.	A History of Christian Latin Poetry
8143257	RABY F.J.E.	A History of Secular Latin Poetry in the Middle Ages (2 vols)
8214316	RASHDALL & POWICKE	The Universities of Europe in the Middle Ages (3 vols)
8148380	RICKMAN Geoffrey	The Corn Supply of Ancient Rome
8141076	ROSS Sir David	Aristotle: Metaphysics (2 vols)
8141092	ROSS Sir David	Aristotle: Physics
8264178	RUNCIMAN Sir Steven	The Eastern Schism
814833X	SALMON J.B.	Wealthy Corinth
8171587	SALZMAN L.F.	Building in England Down to 1540
8218362	SAYERS Jane E.	Papal Judges Delegate in the Province of Canterbury 1198–1254
8221657	SCHEIN Sylvia	Fideles Crucis

8148135	SHERWIN WHITE A.N.	The Roman Citizenship
8113927	SISAM, Kenneth	Studies in the History of Old English Literature
8642040	SOUTER Alexander	A Glossary of Later Latin to 600 AD
8222254	SOUTHERN R.W.	Eadmer: Life of St. Anselm
8251408	SQUIBB G.	The High Court of Chivalry
8212011	STEVENSON & WHITELOCK	Asser's Life of King Alfred
8212011	SWEET Henry	A Second Anglo-Saxon Reader—Archaic and Dialectical
8148259	SYME Sir Ronald	History in Ovid
8143273	SYME Sir Ronald	Tacitus (2 vols)
8200951	THOMPSON Sally	Women Religious
8201745	WALKER Simon	The Lancastrian Affinity 1361–1399
8161115	WELLESZ Egon	A History of Byzantine Music and Hymnography
8140185	WEST M.L.	Greek Metre
8141696	WEST M.L.	Hesiod: Theogony
8148542	WEST M.L.	The Orphic Poems
8140053	WEST M.L.	Hesiod: Works & Days
8152663	WEST M.L.	Iambi et Elegi Graeci
822799X	WHITBY M. & M.	The History of Theophylact Simocatta
8206186	WILLIAMSON, E.W.	Letters of Osbert of Clare
8114877	WOOLF Rosemary	The English Religious Lyric in the Middle Ages
8119224	WRIGHT Joseph	Grammar of the Gothic Language